Tell us what you think about SHONEN JUMP manga!

Our survey is now available online.
Go to: www.SHONENJUMP.com/mangasurvey

Help us make our product offering better!

D0124988

P9·Oem·499

ICHIGO   MUSICAL VERSION

JUST IMAGINE RUKIA AS HERSELF IN THE COMIC.

久保帯人

Bleach is now a musical. I know it sounds weird, but I saw it and it was really cool. There was Ichigo, looking better than he does in the comic, and Rukia, looking exactly like she does in the comic, singing and dancing and fighting. I want people who aren't into musicals to check it out. I'm convinced it will change their minds.
Why am I being so serious?
—Tite Kubo

BLEACH is author Tite Kubo's second title. Kubo made his debut with *ZOMBIEPOWDER.*, a four-volume series for *WEEKLY SHONEN JUMP.* To date, *BLEACH* has been translated into numerous languages and has also inspired an animated TV series that began airing in the U.S. in 2006. Beginning its serialization in 2001, *BLEACH* is still a mainstay in the pages of *WEEKLY SHONEN JUMP.* In 2005, *BLEACH* was awarded the prestigious Shogakukan Manga Award in the *shonen* (boys) category.

BLEACH
Vol. 20: End of Hypnosis
The SHONEN JUMP Manga Edition

STORY AND ART BY
TITE KUBO

English Adaptation/Lance Caselman
Translation/Joe Yamazaki
Touch-Up Art & Lettering/Mark McMurray
Design/Sean Lee
Editors/Yuki Takagaki & Pancha Diaz

Editor in Chief, Books/Alvin Lu
Editor in Chief, Magazines/Marc Weidenbaum
VP of Publishing Licensing/Rika Inouye
VP of Sales/Gonzalo Ferreyra
Sr. VP of Marketing/Liza Coppola
Publisher/Hyoe Narita

Printed in the U.S.A.

Published by VIZ Media, LLC
P.O. Box 77010
San Francisco, CA 94107

SHONEN JUMP Manga Edition
10 9 8 7 6 5 4 3 2 1
First printing, August 2007

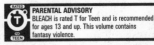

PARENTAL ADVISORY
BLEACH is rated T for Teen and is recommended for ages 13 and up. This volume contains fantasy violence.

Those who do not know what love is
Liken it to beauty

Those who claim to know what love is
Liken it to ugliness

BLEACH20 end of hypnosis

STARS AND

Gin Ichimaru

Rangiku Matsumoto

Ichigo Kurosaki

plot

Having achieved Bankai, Ichigo rescues Rukia in the nick of time and defeats the fearsome Byakuya Kuchiki!

Meanwhile, Soul Reaper Tôshiro Hitsugaya discovers the corpses of the Council of 46 and hurries to get to Momo before the murderer does! And as Rukia and Renji race for safety, they find themselves facing a foe far worse than those they have fled...

BLEACH ALL

Sajin Komamura

Sôsuke Aizen

Kaname Tôsen

STORIES

BLEACH20

end of hypnosis

Contents

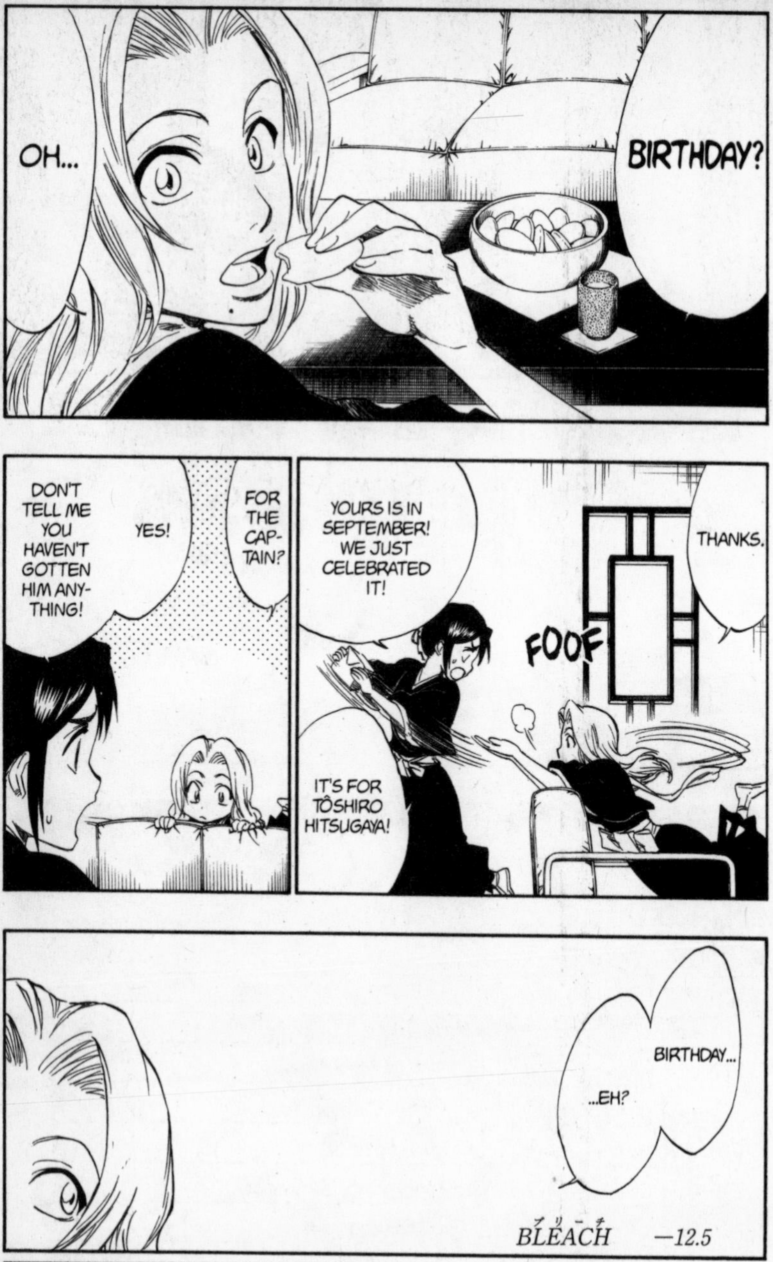
BIRTHDAY?
OH...
THANKS.
YOURS IS IN SEPTEMBER! WE JUST CELEBRATED IT!
FOOF
IT'S FOR TÔSHIRO HITSUGAYA!
FOR THE CAP-TAIN?
YES!
DON'T TELL ME YOU HAVEN'T GOTTEN HIM ANY-THING!
BIRTHDAY...
...EH?
ブリーチ
BLEACH —12.5

BLOOMING UNDER A COLD MOON

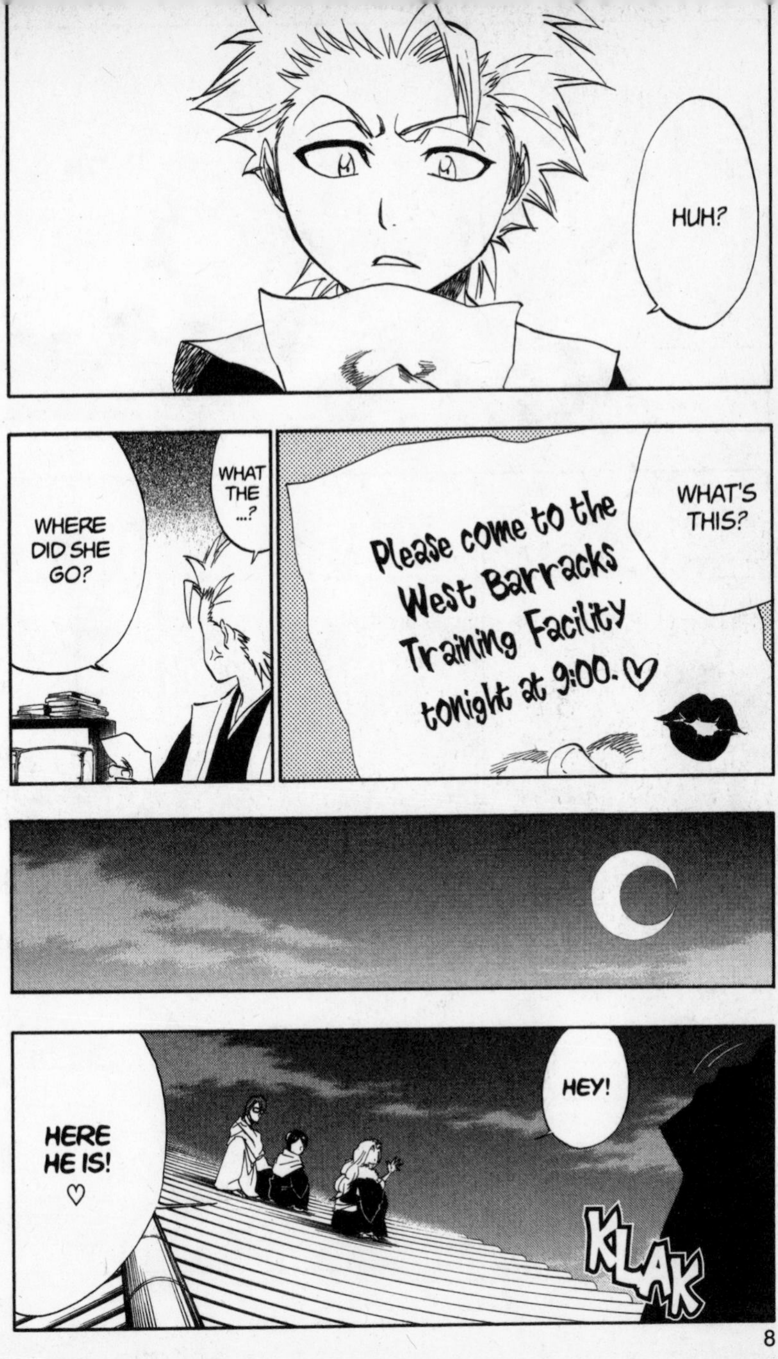
HUH?
WHAT'S THIS?
Please come to the West Barracks Training Facility tonight at 9:00.♡
WHAT THE ...?
WHERE DID SHE GO?
HEY!
KLAK
HERE HE IS! ♡

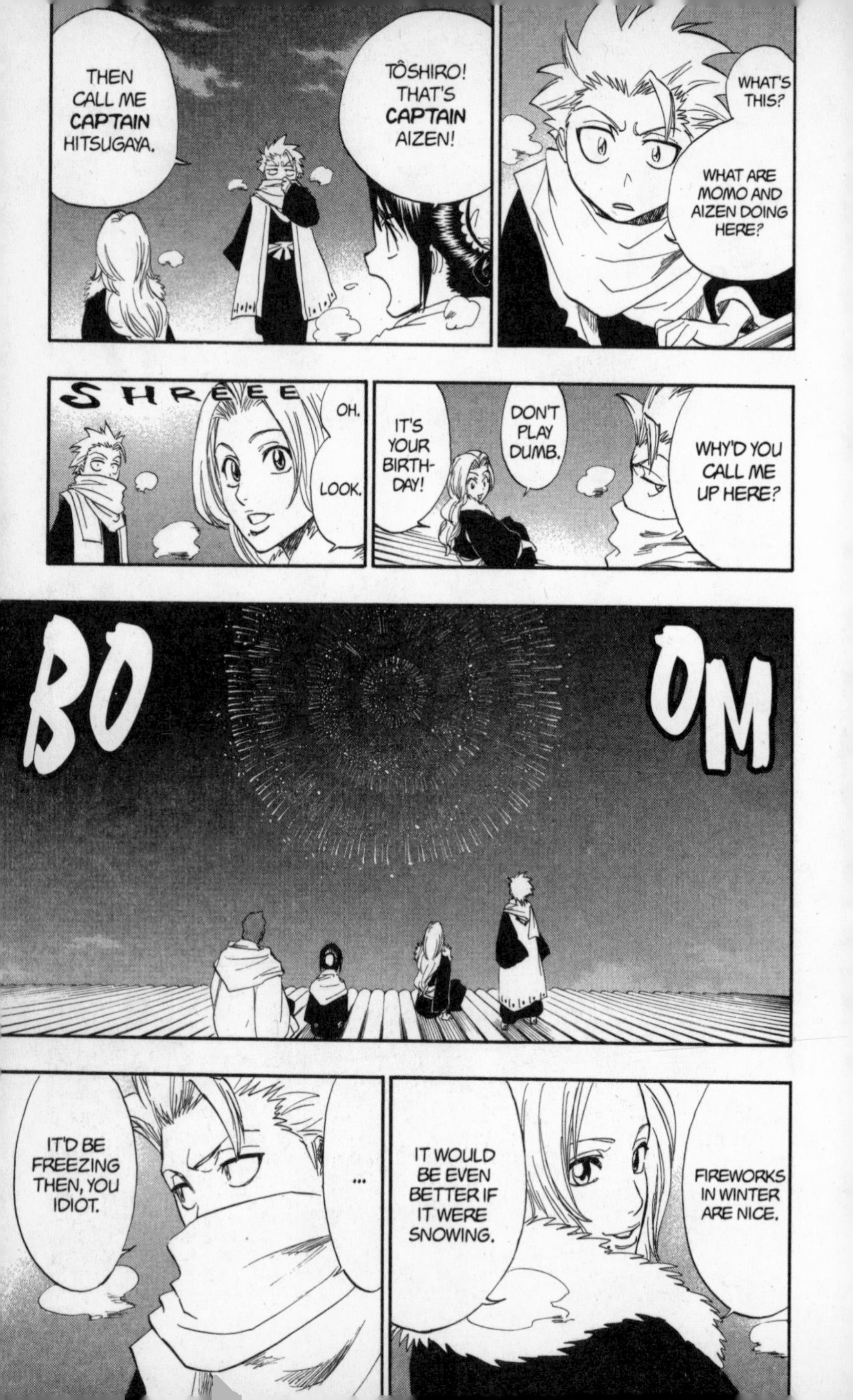
WHAT'S THIS?
WHAT ARE MOMO AND AIZEN DOING HERE?
TÔSHIRO! THAT'S CAPTAIN AIZEN!
THEN CALL ME CAPTAIN HITSUGAYA.
WHY'D YOU CALL ME UP HERE?
DON'T PLAY DUMB.
IT'S YOUR BIRTH-DAY!
SHREEE
OH.
LOOK.
BO OM
FIREWORKS IN WINTER ARE NICE.
IT WOULD BE EVEN BETTER IF IT WERE SNOWING.
...
IT'D BE FREEZING THEN, YOU IDIOT.

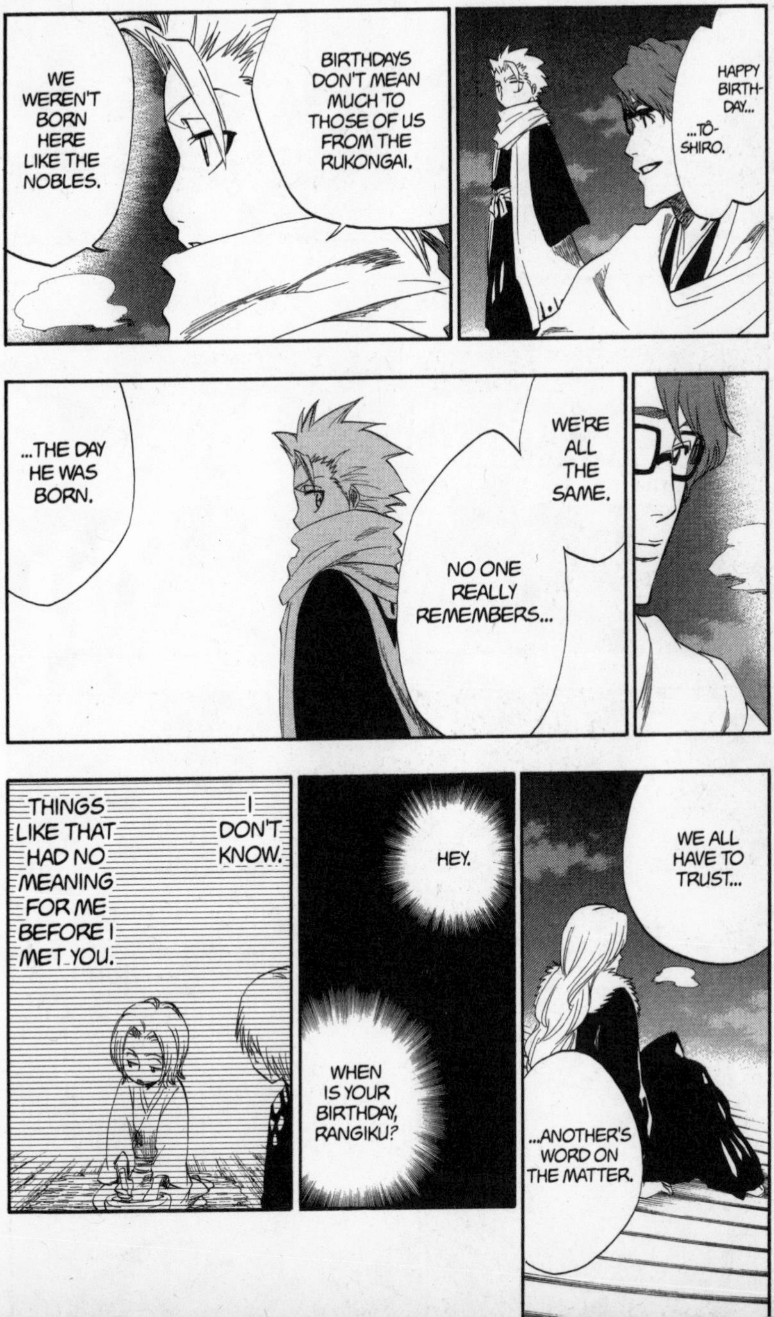
HAPPY BIRTHDAY...
...TÔSHIRO.
BIRTHDAYS DON'T MEAN MUCH TO THOSE OF US FROM THE RUKONGAI.
WE WEREN'T BORN HERE LIKE THE NOBLES.
WE'RE ALL THE SAME.
NO ONE REALLY REMEMBERS...
...THE DAY HE WAS BORN.
WE ALL HAVE TO TRUST...
...ANOTHER'S WORD ON THE MATTER.
HEY.
WHEN IS YOUR BIRTHDAY, RANGIKU?
I DON'T KNOW.
THINGS LIKE THAT HAD NO MEANING FOR ME BEFORE I MET YOU.

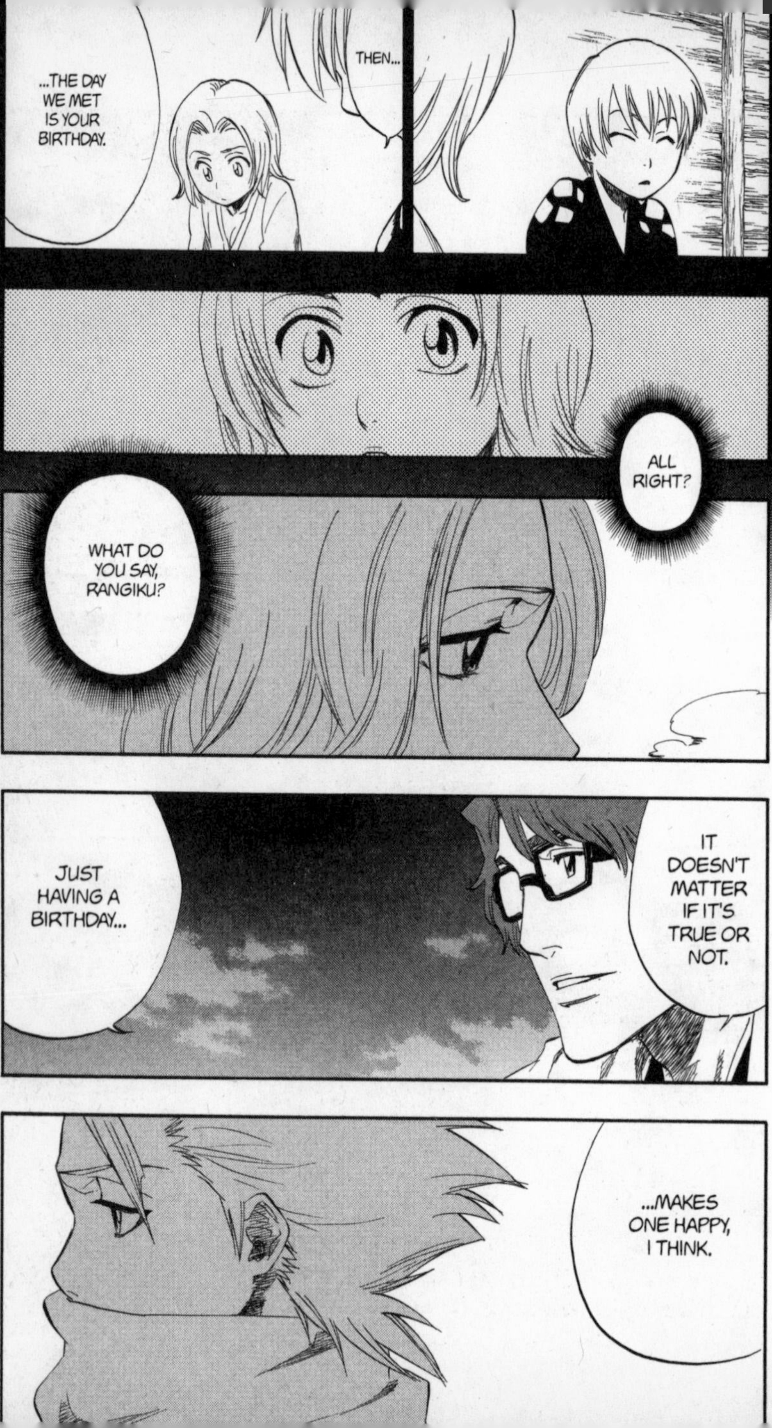
THEN...
...THE DAY WE MET IS YOUR BIRTHDAY.
ALL RIGHT?
WHAT DO YOU SAY, RANGIKU?
IT DOESN'T MATTER IF IT'S TRUE OR NOT.
JUST HAVING A BIRTHDAY...
...MAKES ONE HAPPY, I THINK.

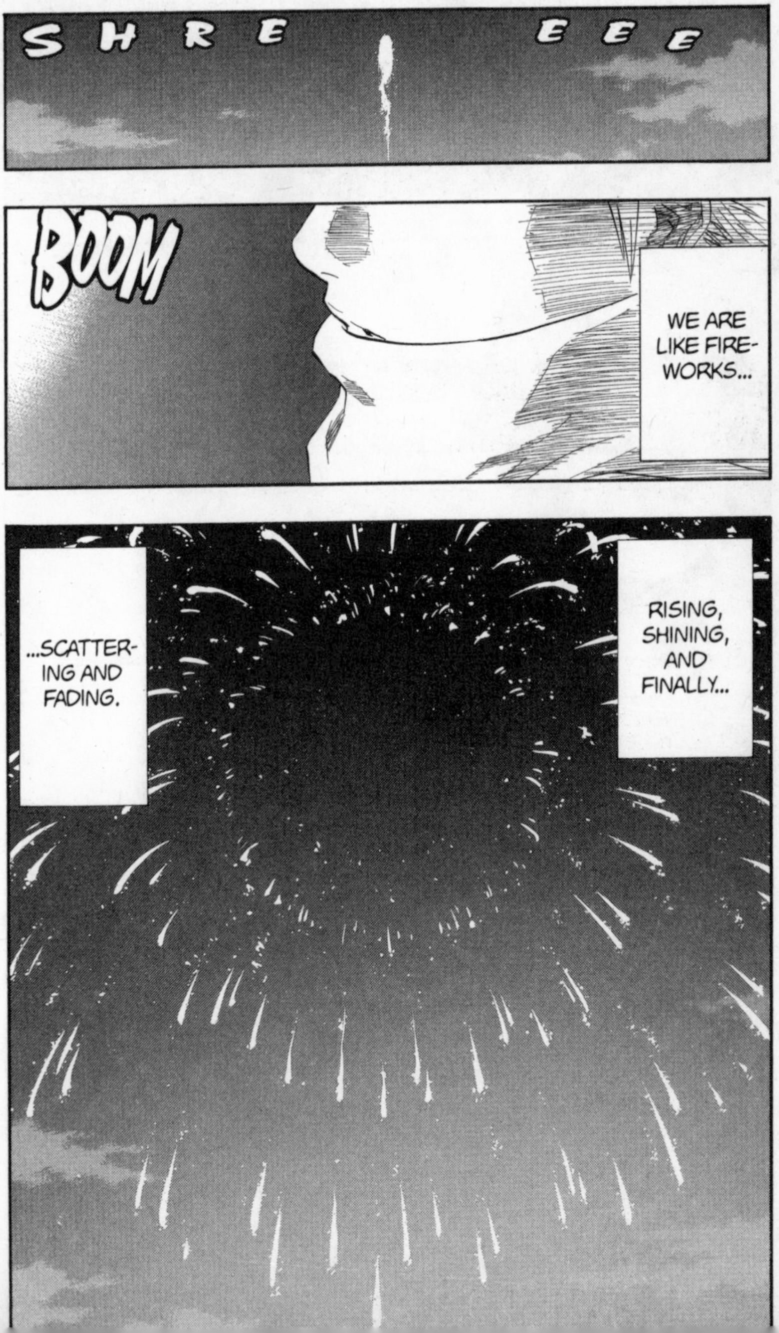
SHREEEE
WE ARE LIKE FIRE-WORKS...
BOOM
RISING, SHINING, AND FINALLY...
...SCATTER-ING AND FADING.

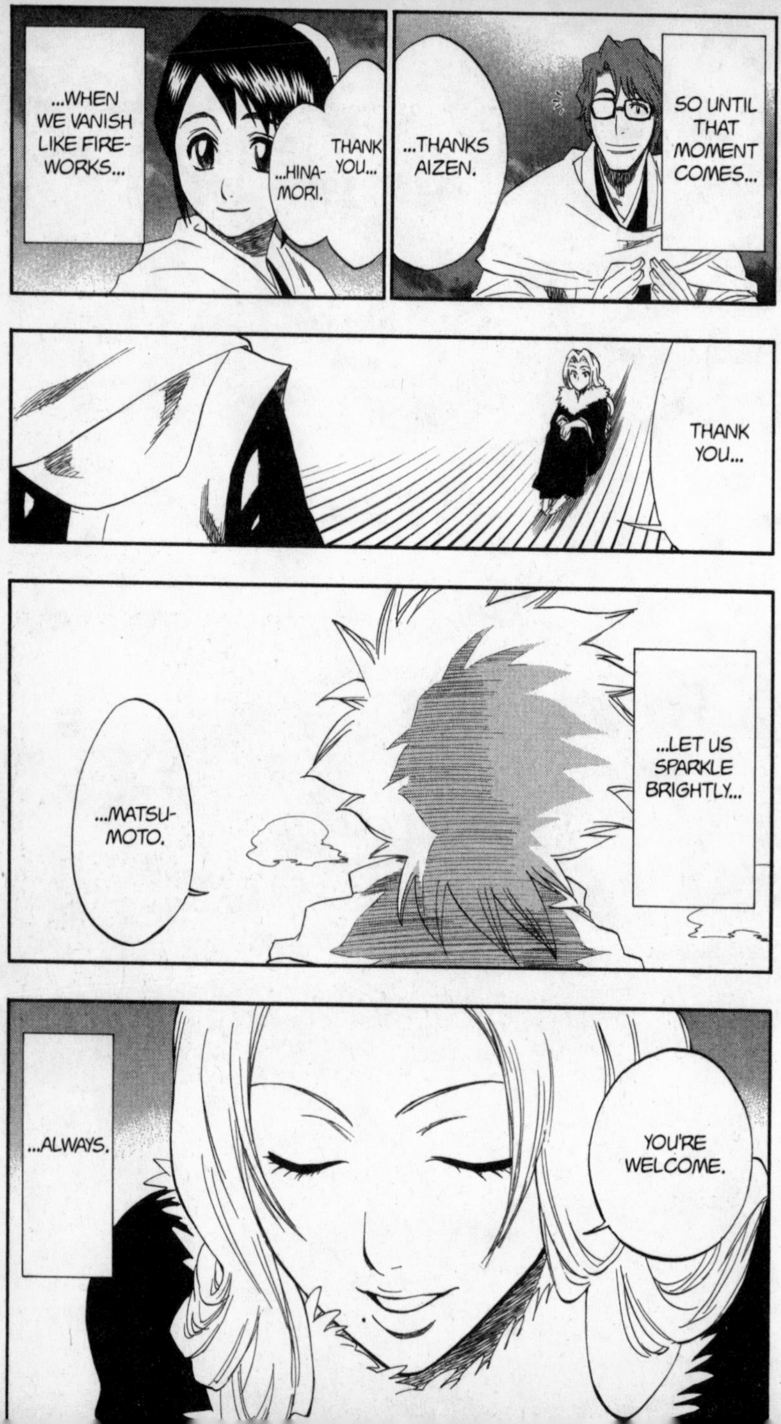
SO UNTIL THAT MOMENT COMES...
...THANKS AIZEN.
THANK YOU... ...HINAMORI.
...WHEN WE VANISH LIKE FIREWORKS...
THANK YOU...
...LET US SPARKLE BRIGHTLY...
...MATSUMOTO.
YOU'RE WELCOME.
...ALWAYS.

BLEACH
ブリーチ

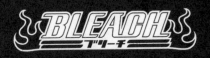

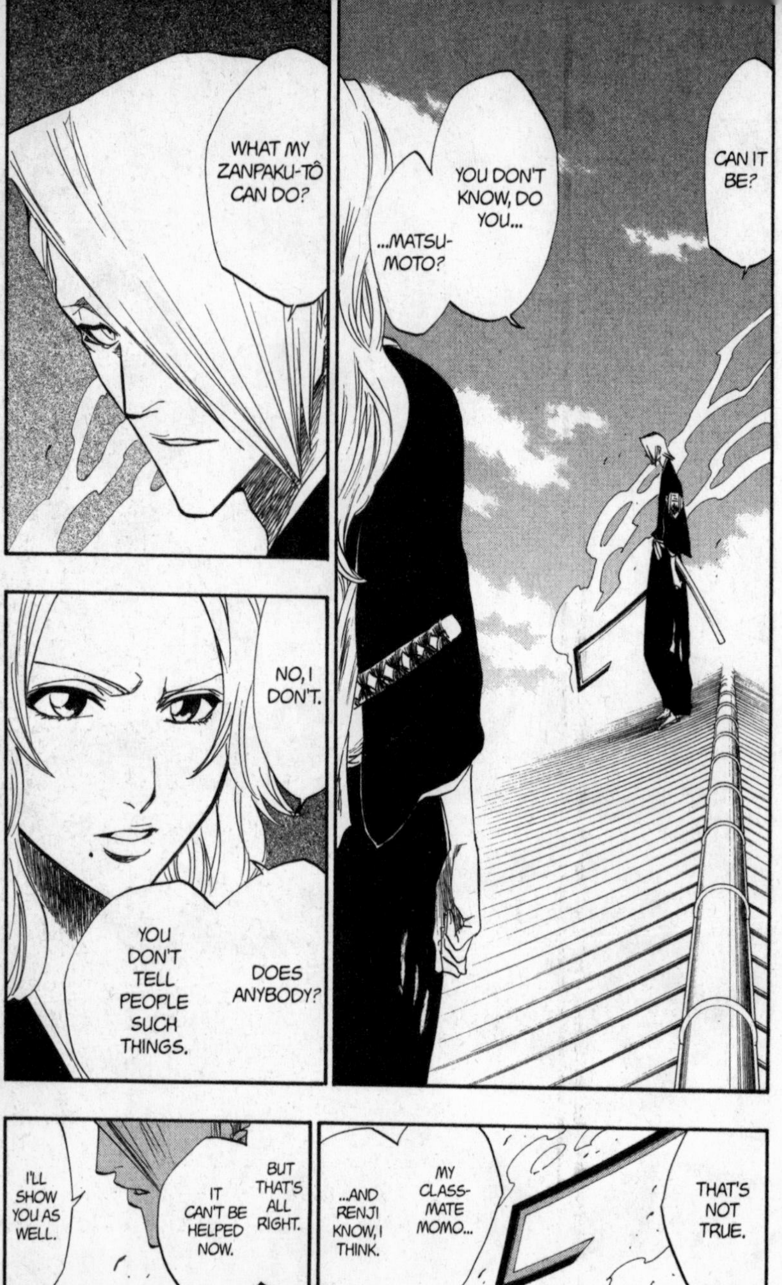
CAN IT BE?
YOU DON'T KNOW, DO YOU...
...MATSU-MOTO?
WHAT MY ZANPAKU-TÔ CAN DO?
NO, I DON'T.
DOES ANYBODY?
YOU DON'T TELL PEOPLE SUCH THINGS.
THAT'S NOT TRUE.
MY CLASS-MATE MOMO...
...AND RENJI KNOW, I THINK.
BUT THAT'S ALL RIGHT.
IT CAN'T BE HELPED NOW.
I'LL SHOW YOU AS WELL.

169. end of hypnosis

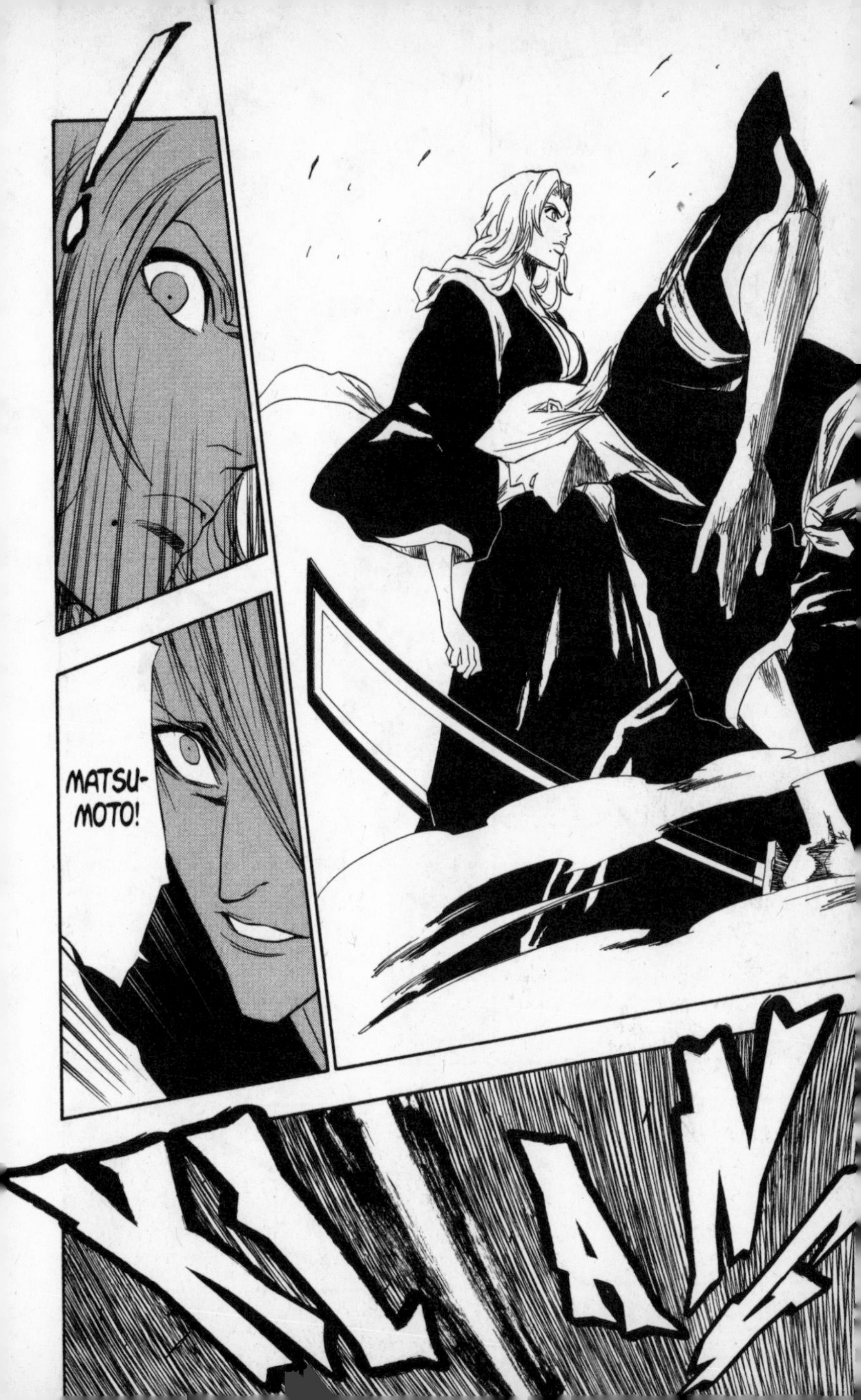
MATSU-MOTO!

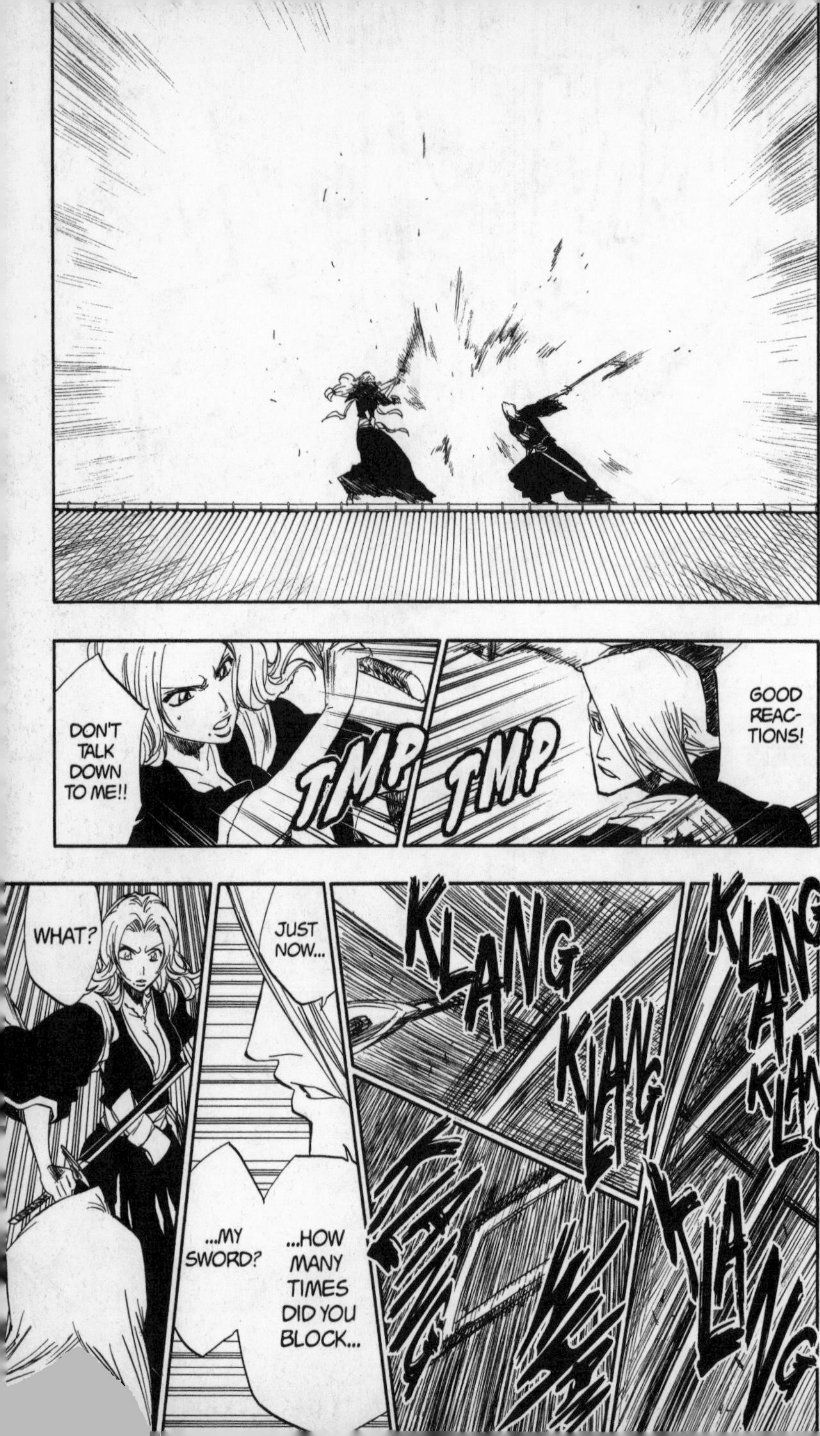
GOOD REACTIONS!
TMP
TMP
DON'T TALK DOWN TO ME!!
KLANG
KLANG
KLANG
KLANG
KLANG
KLANG
KLANG
KLANG
JUST NOW...
...HOW MANY TIMES DID YOU BLOCK...
...MY SWORD?
WHAT?

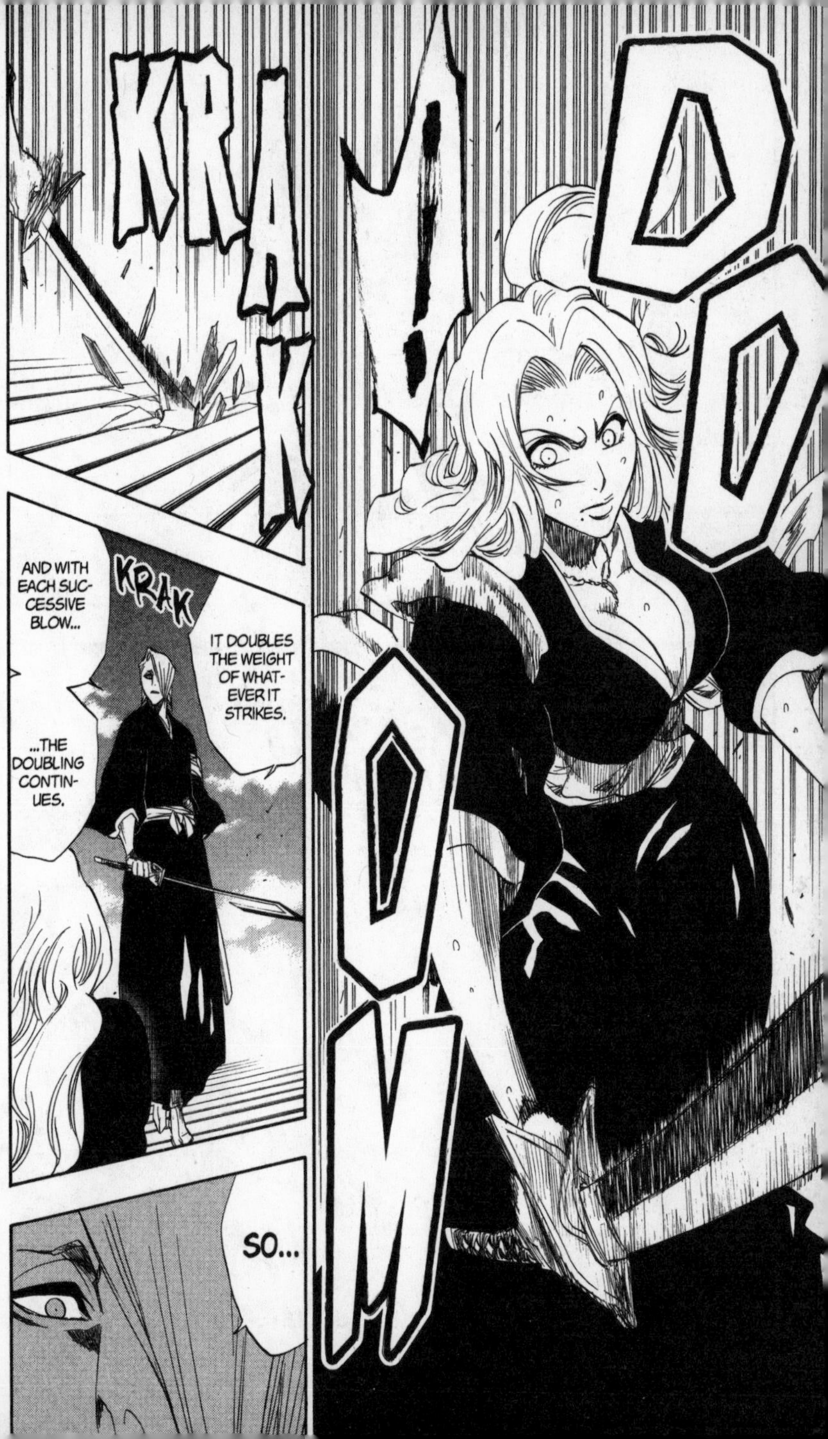
DOOM
KRAK
KRAK
IT DOUBLES THE WEIGHT OF WHATEVER IT STRIKES.
AND WITH EACH SUCCESSIVE BLOW...
...THE DOUBLING CONTINUES.
SO...

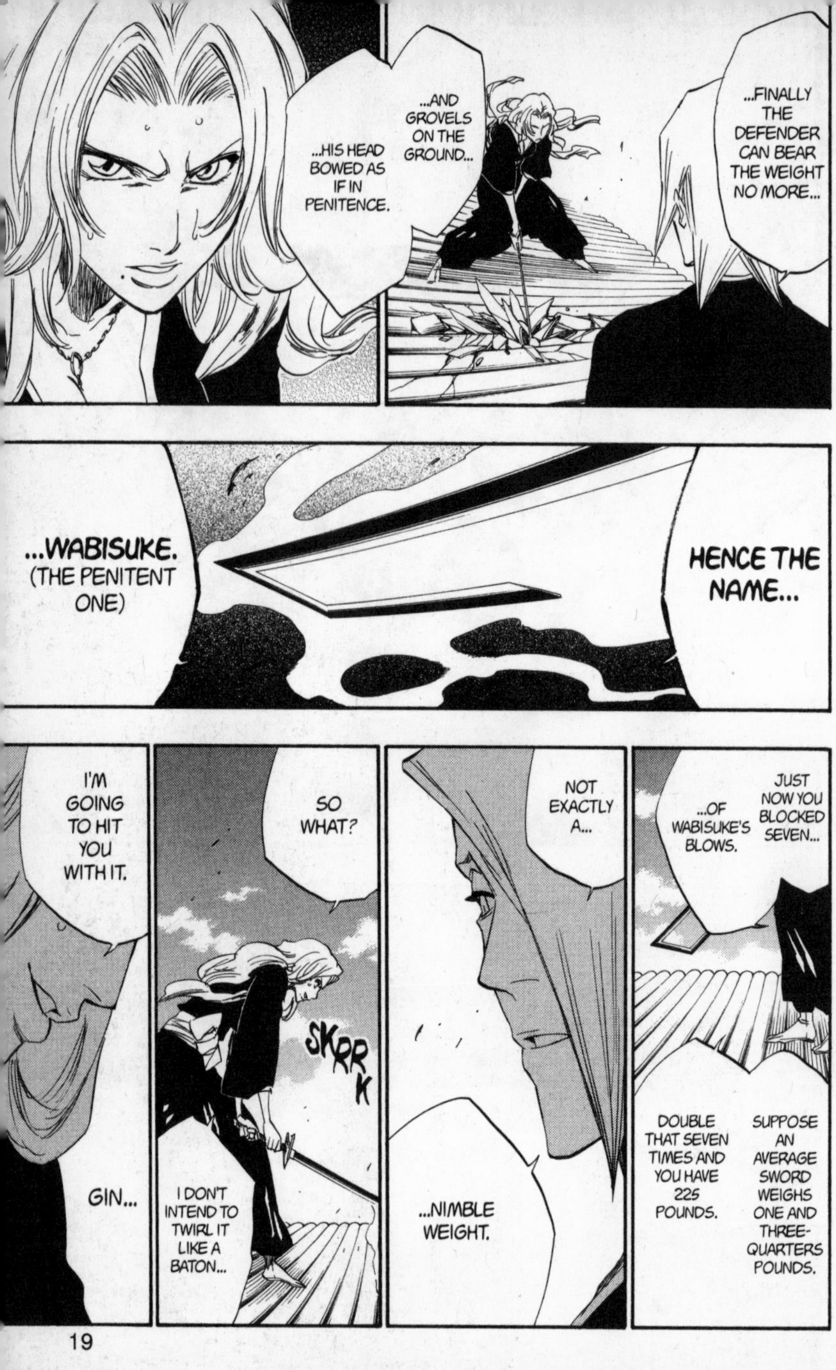
...FINALLY THE DEFENDER CAN BEAR THE WEIGHT NO MORE...
...AND GROVELS ON THE GROUND...
...HIS HEAD BOWED AS IF IN PENITENCE.
HENCE THE NAME...
...WABISUKE. (THE PENITENT ONE)
JUST NOW YOU BLOCKED SEVEN...
...OF WABISUKE'S BLOWS.
SUPPOSE AN AVERAGE SWORD WEIGHS ONE AND THREE-QUARTERS POUNDS.
DOUBLE THAT SEVEN TIMES AND YOU HAVE 225 POUNDS.
NOT EXACTLY A...
...NIMBLE WEIGHT.
SO WHAT?
SKRRK
I DON'T INTEND TO TWIRL IT LIKE A BATON...
I'M GOING TO HIT YOU WITH IT.
GIN...

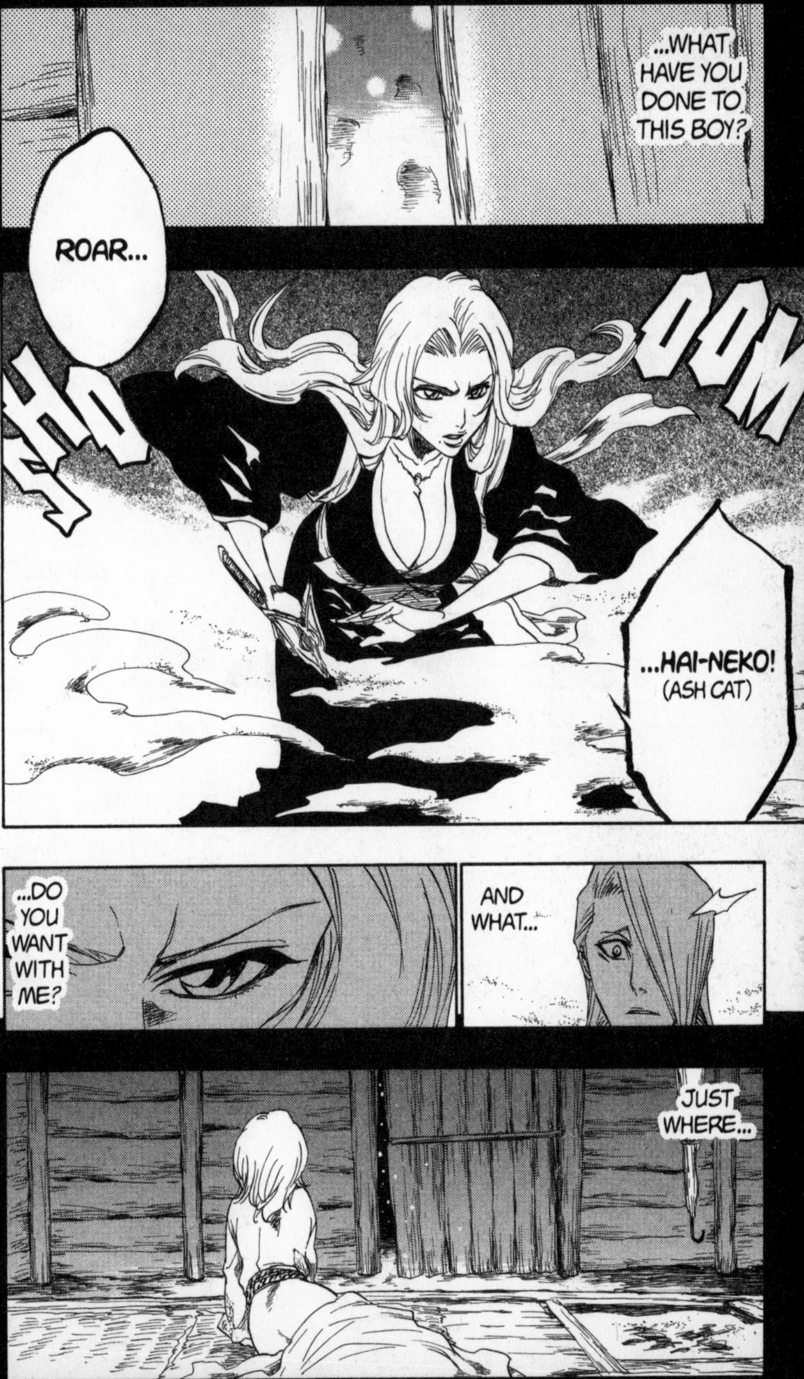

...WHAT HAVE YOU DONE TO THIS BOY?
ROAR...
...HAI-NEKO!
(ASH CAT)
AND WHAT...
...DO YOU WANT WITH ME?
JUST WHERE...

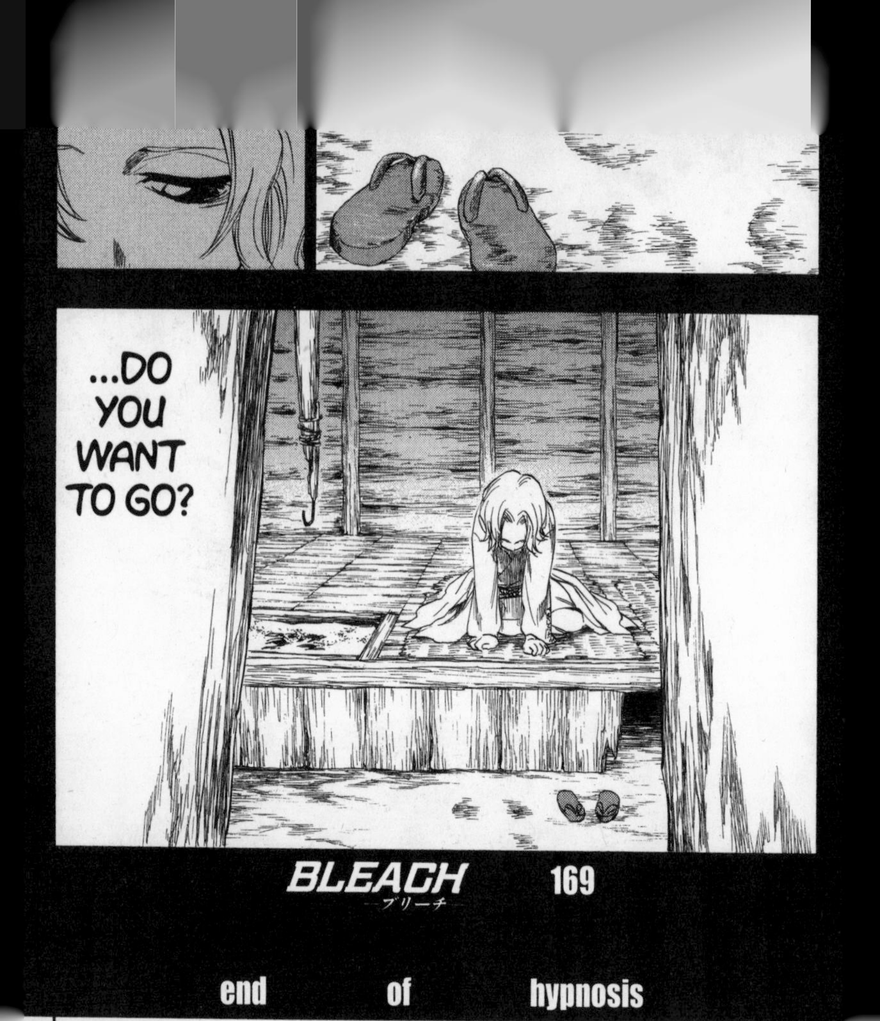
...DO YOU WANT TO GO?

BLEACH 169

ブリーチ

end of hypnosis

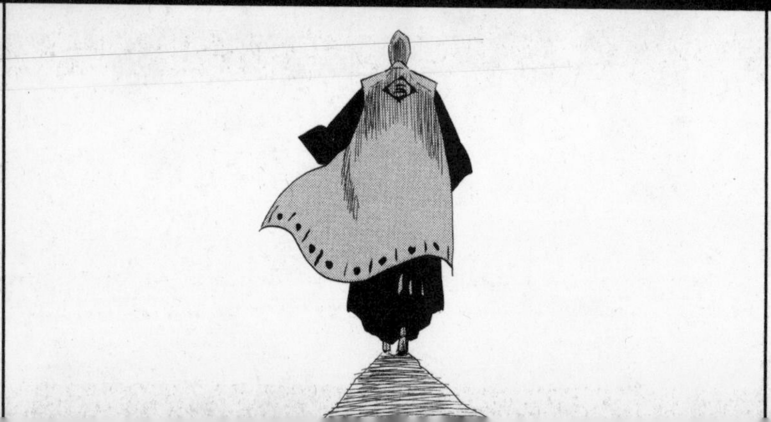

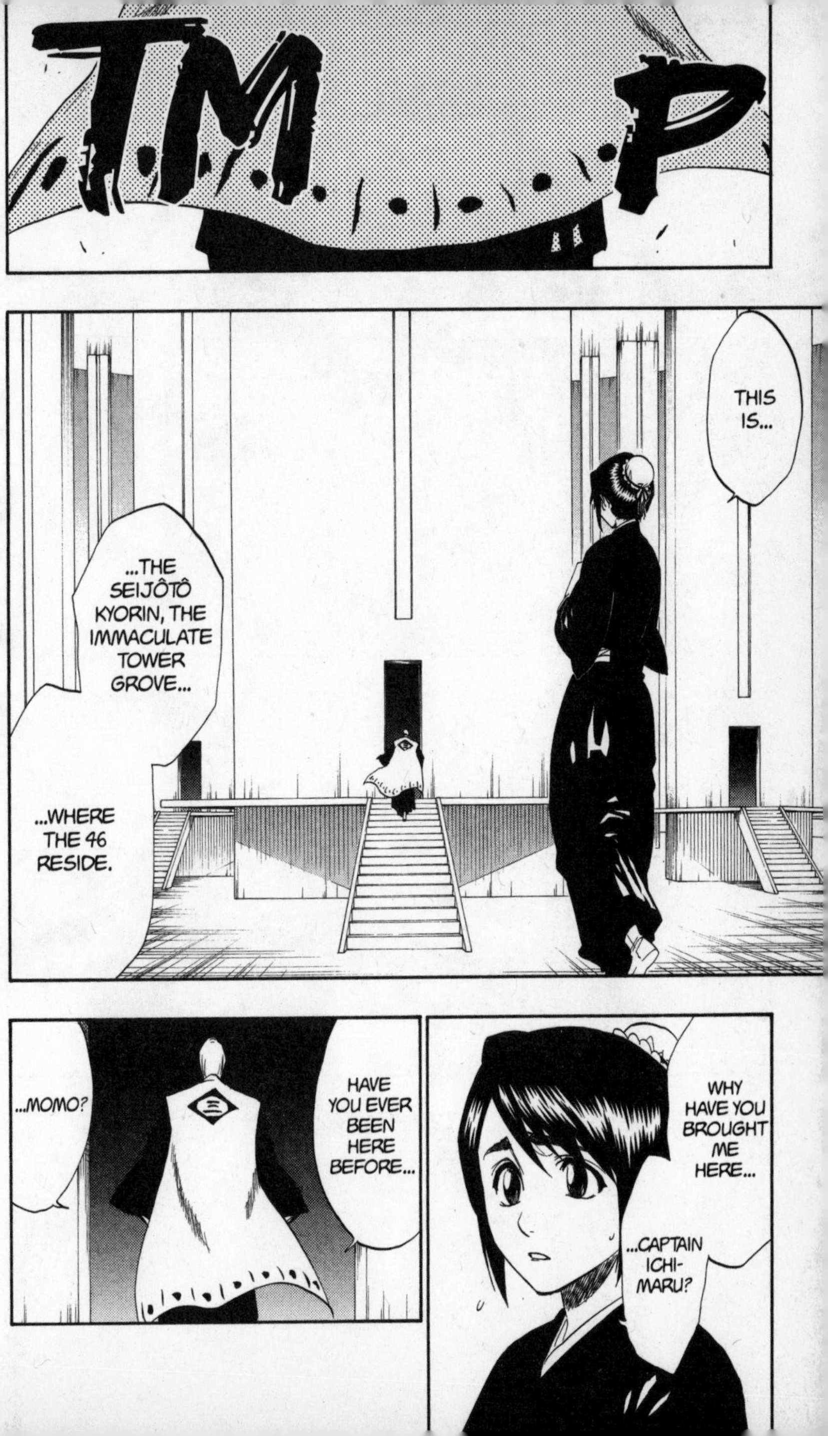
T.M....P
THIS IS...
...THE SEIJÔTÔ KYORIN, THE IMMACULATE TOWER GROVE...
...WHERE THE 46 RESIDE.
WHY HAVE YOU BROUGHT ME HERE...
...CAPTAIN ICHI-MARU?
HAVE YOU EVER BEEN HERE BEFORE...
...MOMO?

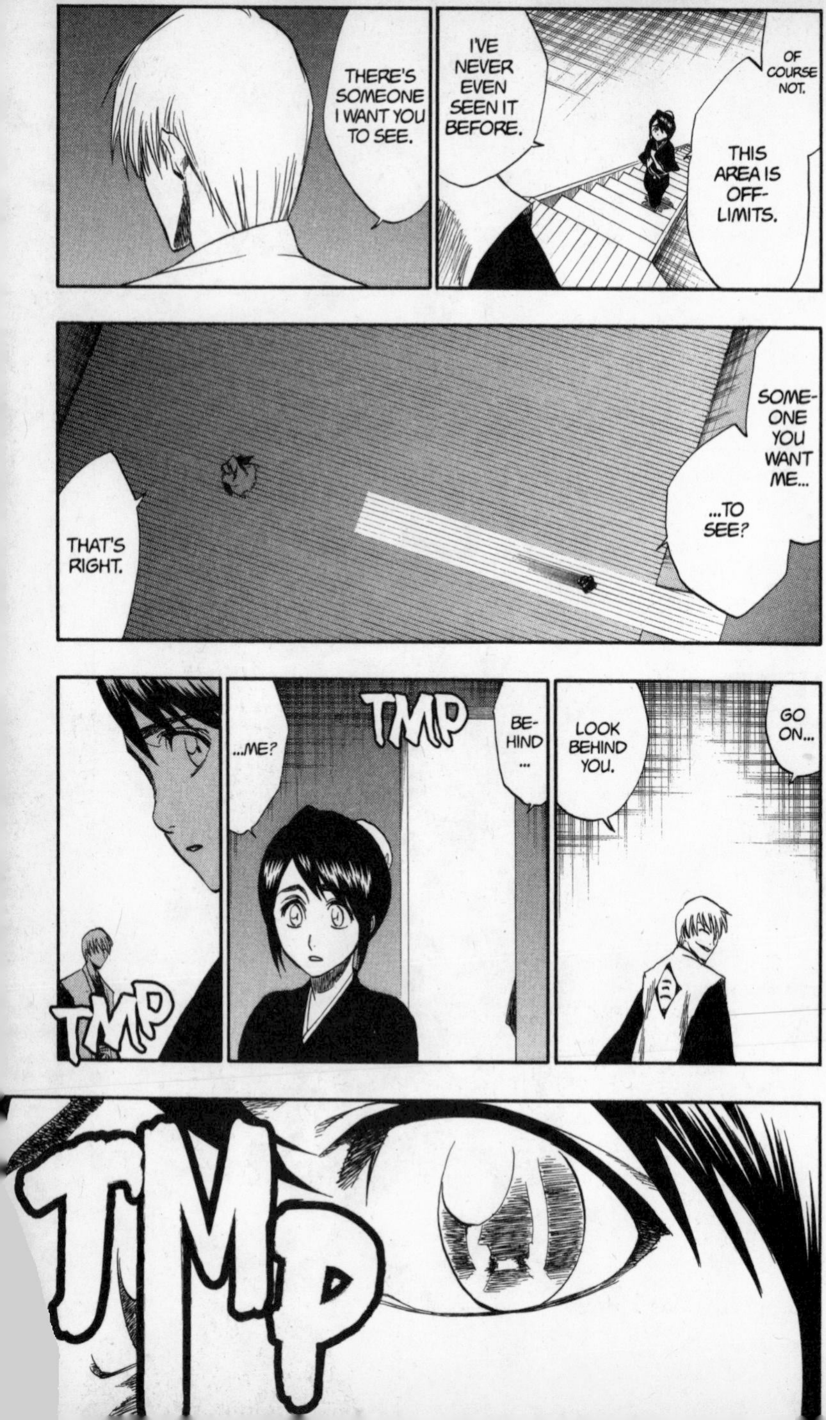

I'VE NEVER EVEN SEEN IT BEFORE.
OF COURSE NOT.
THIS AREA IS OFF-LIMITS.
THERE'S SOMEONE I WANT YOU TO SEE.
SOME-ONE YOU WANT ME...
...TO SEE?
THAT'S RIGHT.
GO ON...
LOOK BEHIND YOU.
BE-HIND ...
TMP
...ME?
TMP
TMP

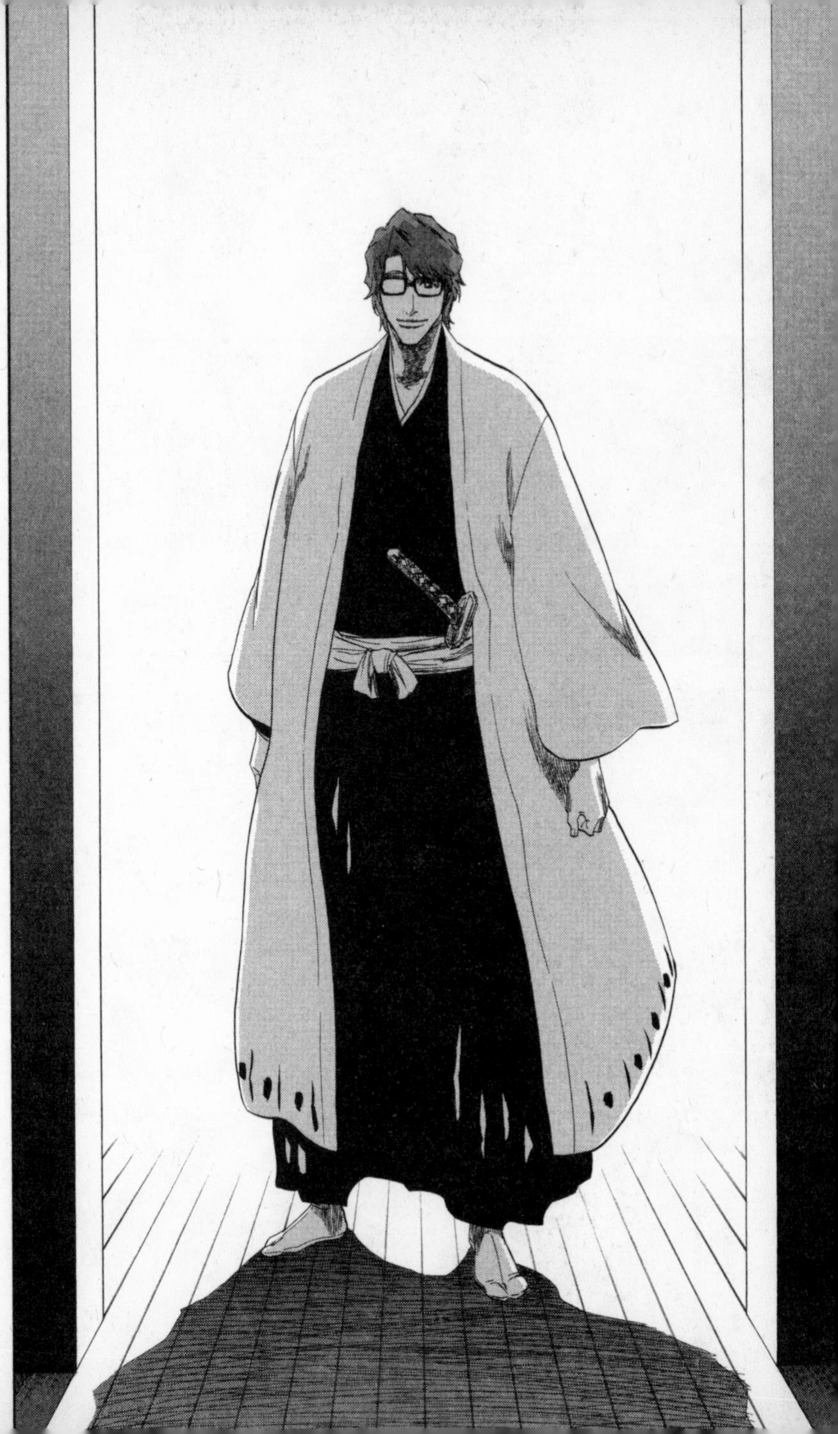

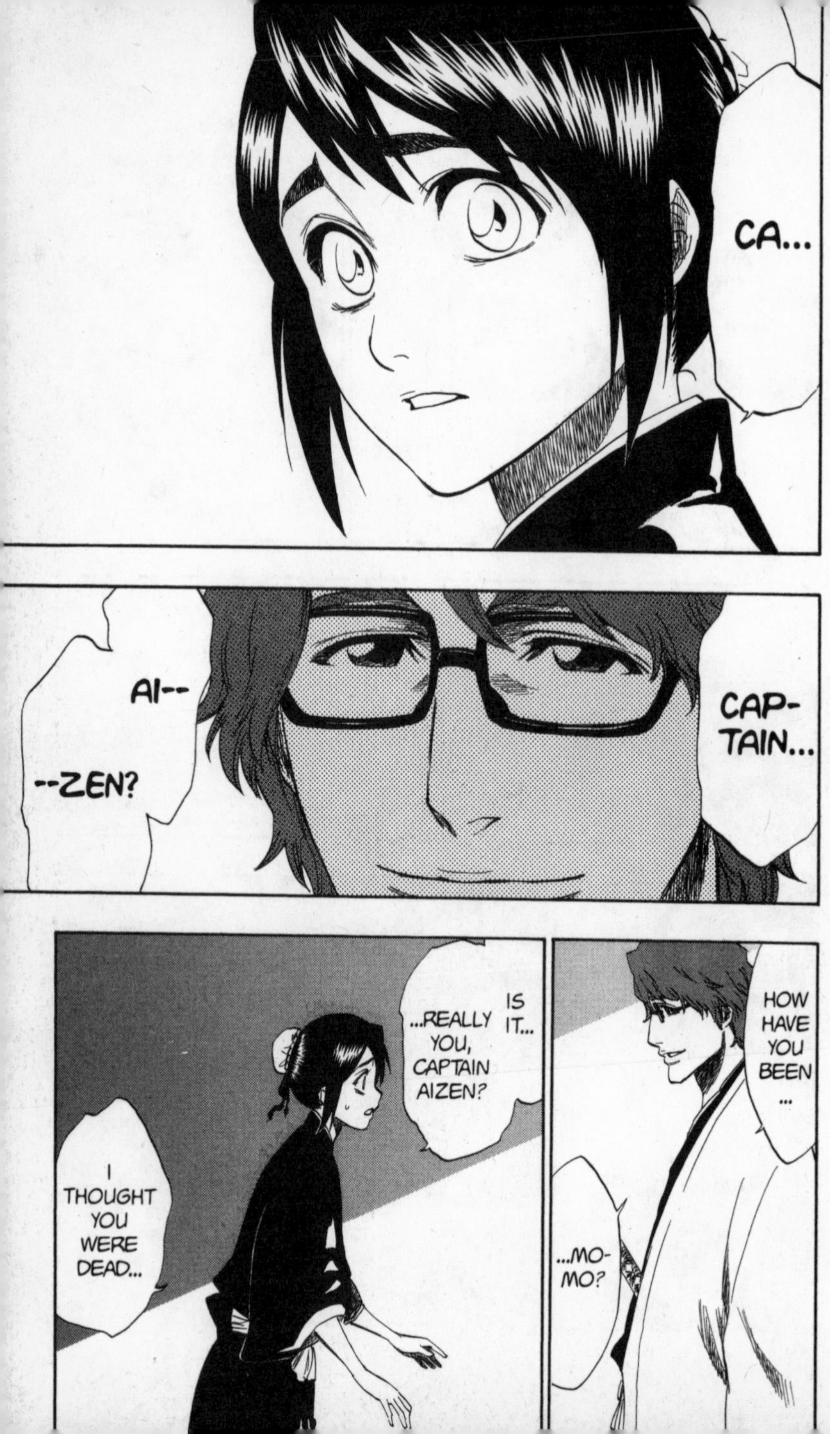
CA...
CAP-TAIN...
AI--
--ZEN?
HOW HAVE YOU BEEN ...
...MO-MO?
IS IT...
...REALLY YOU, CAPTAIN AIZEN?
I THOUGHT YOU WERE DEAD...

CA...

CAPTAIN AIZEN, I...

I...

CAP- TAIN AIZEN ...

I'M ALIVE...

...AS YOU CAN SEE.

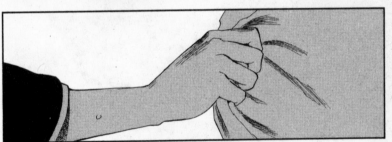

...CAP- TAIN...

...AI- ZEN...

26

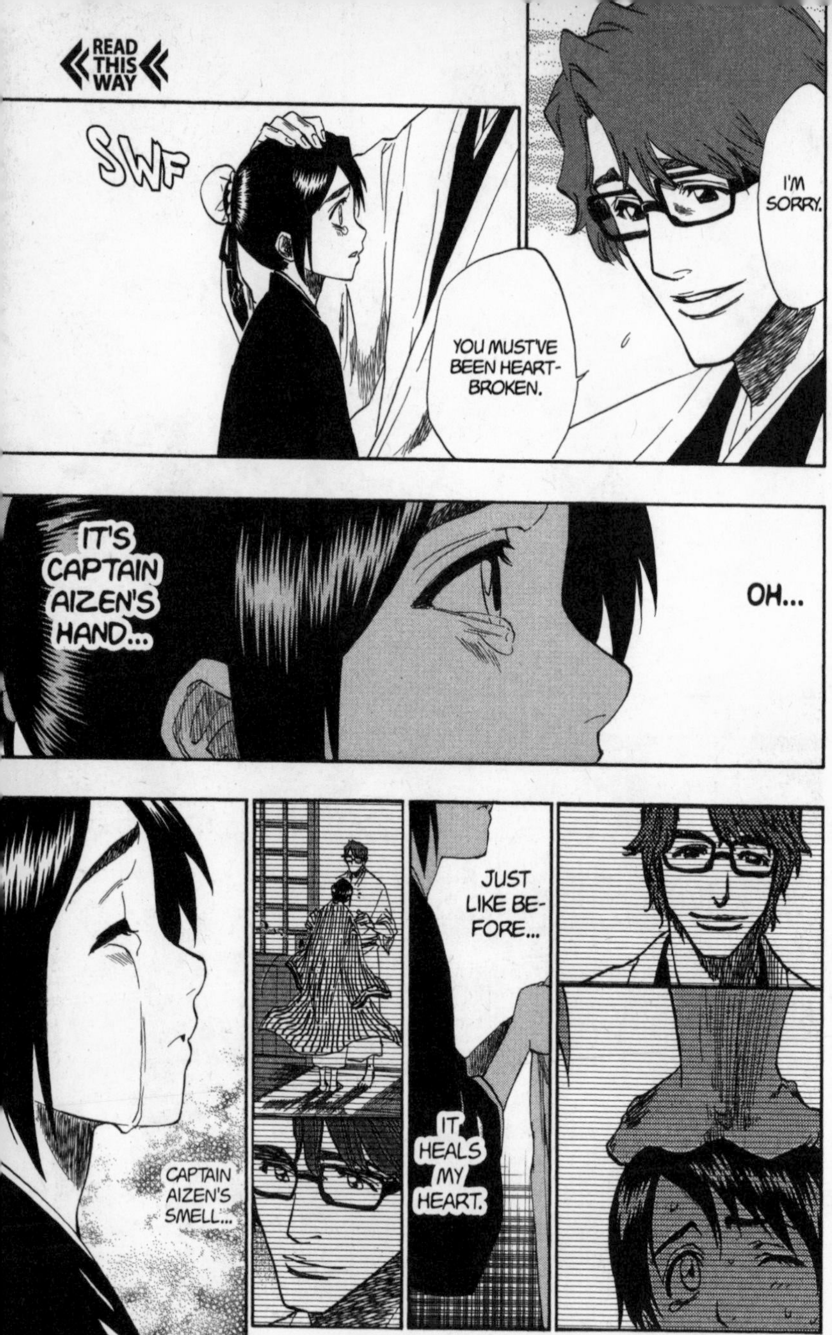
READ THIS WAY
I'M SORRY.
YOU MUST'VE BEEN HEART-BROKEN.
SWF
OH...
IT'S CAPTAIN AIZEN'S HAND...
JUST LIKE BE-FORE...
IT HEALS MY HEART.
CAPTAIN AIZEN'S SMELL...

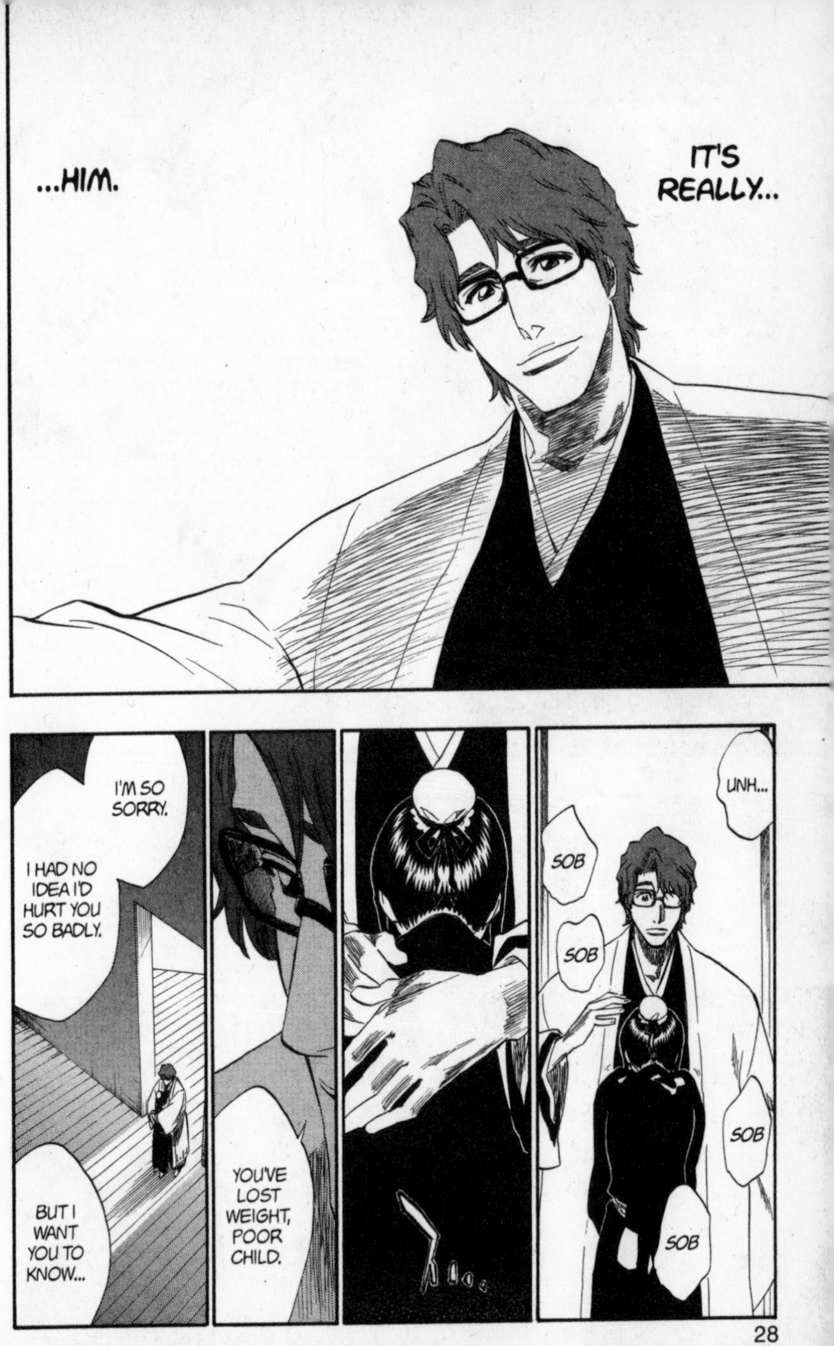
IT'S REALLY...
...HIM.
UNH...
SOB
SOB
SOB
SOB
YOU'VE LOST WEIGHT, POOR CHILD.
I'M SO SORRY.
I HAD NO IDEA I'D HURT YOU SO BADLY.
BUT I WANT YOU TO KNOW...

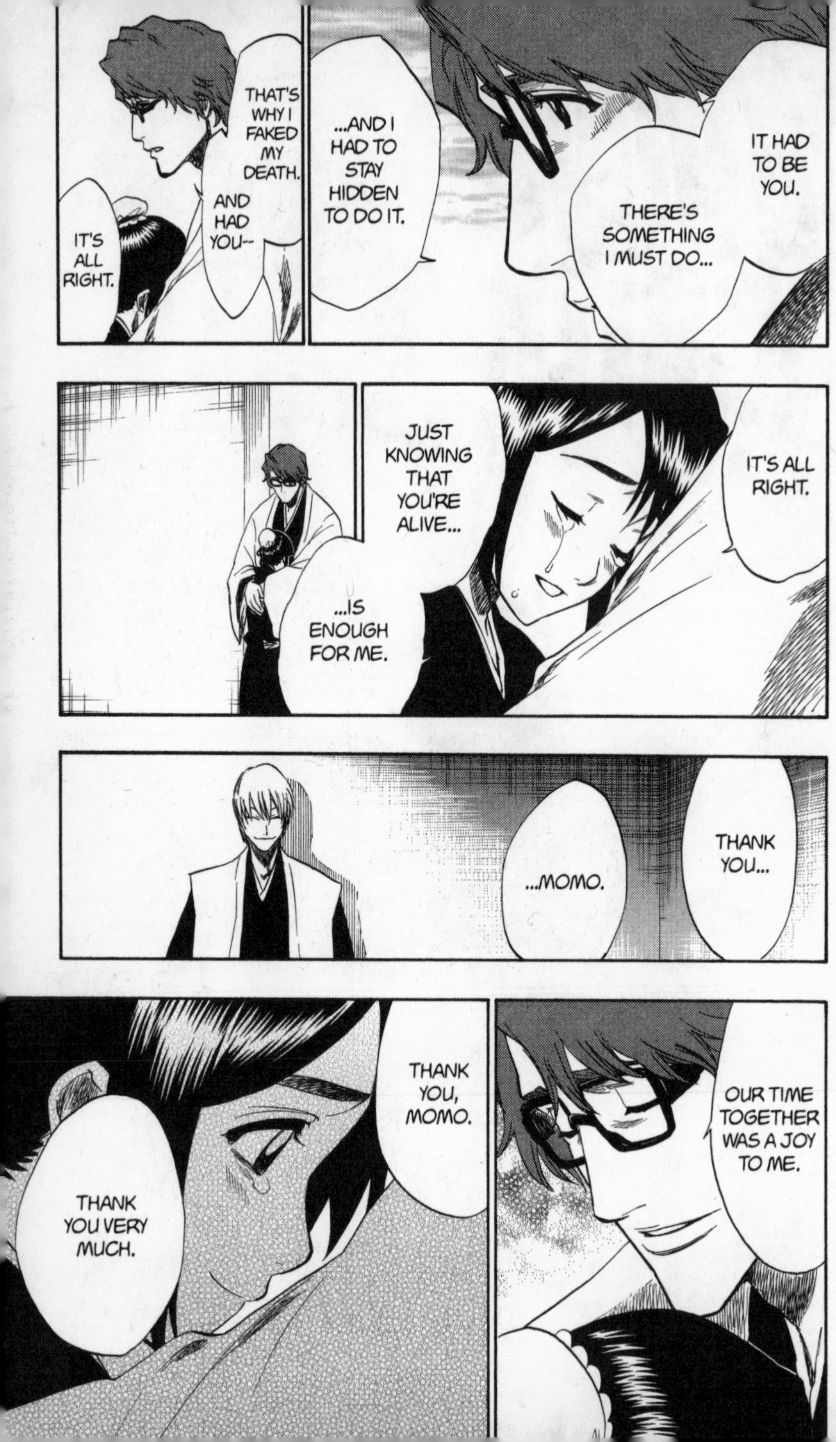
IT HAD TO BE YOU.
THERE'S SOMETHING I MUST DO...
...AND I HAD TO STAY HIDDEN TO DO IT.
THAT'S WHY I FAKED MY DEATH.
AND HAD YOU--
IT'S ALL RIGHT.
IT'S ALL RIGHT.
JUST KNOWING THAT YOU'RE ALIVE...
...IS ENOUGH FOR ME.
THANK YOU...
...MOMO.
OUR TIME TOGETHER WAS A JOY TO ME.
THANK YOU, MOMO.
THANK YOU VERY MUCH.

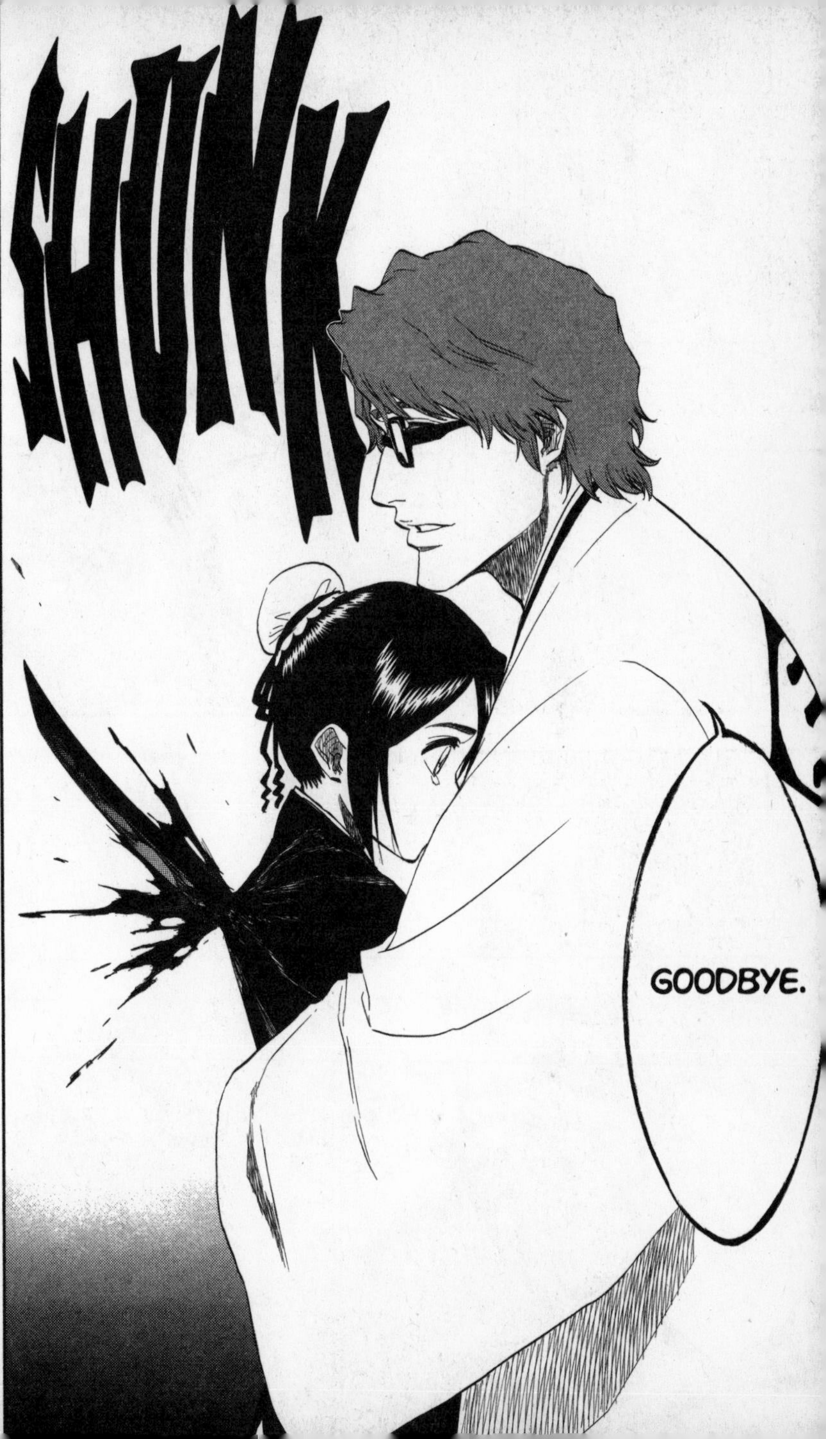
SHUNK
GOODBYE.

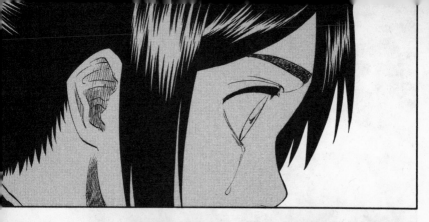

CAPTAIN...?

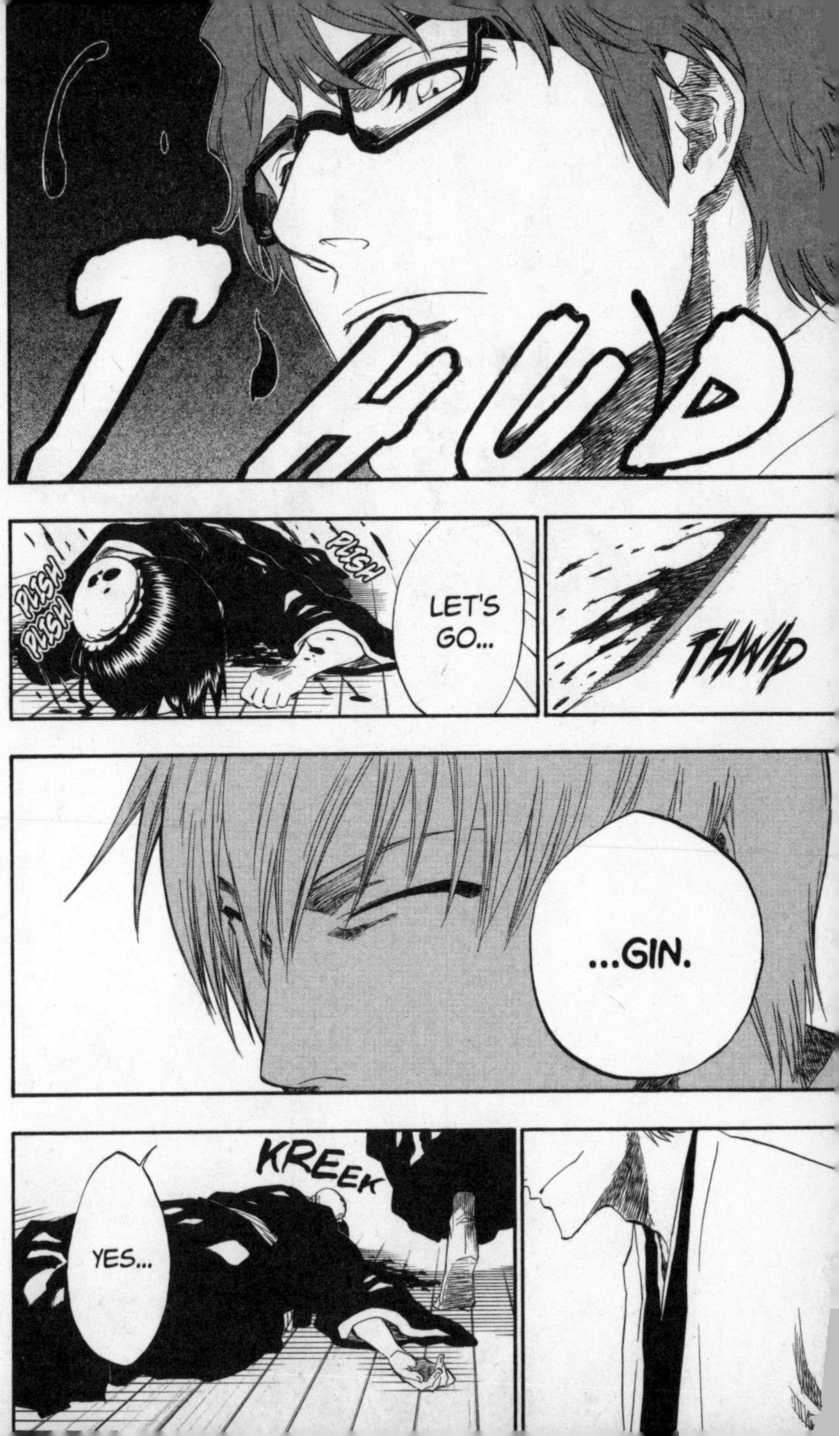
THUD
THWIP
LET'S GO...
PLISH
PLISH
PLISH
...GIN.
KREEK
YES...

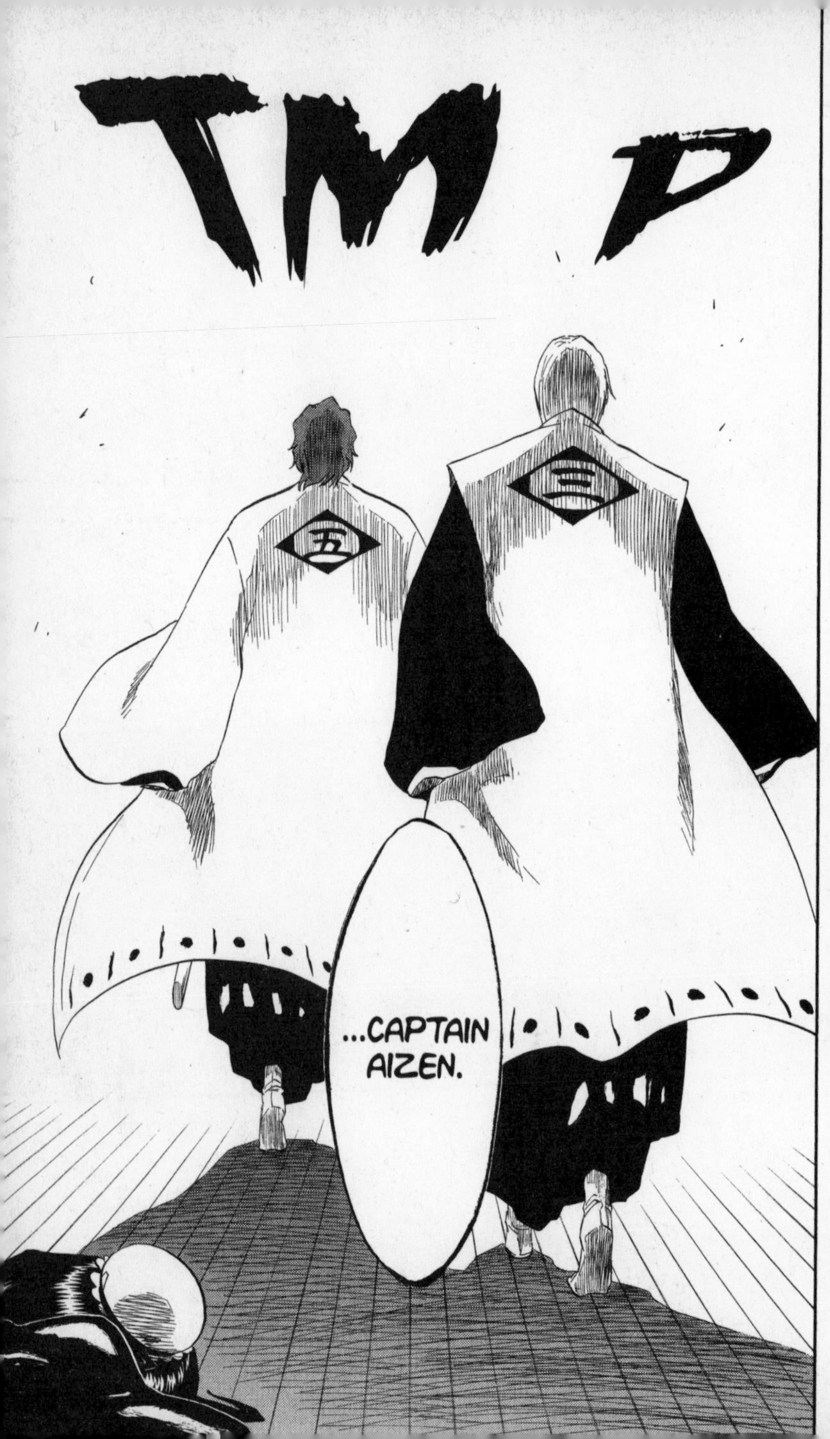
TMP
...CAPTAIN AIZEN.

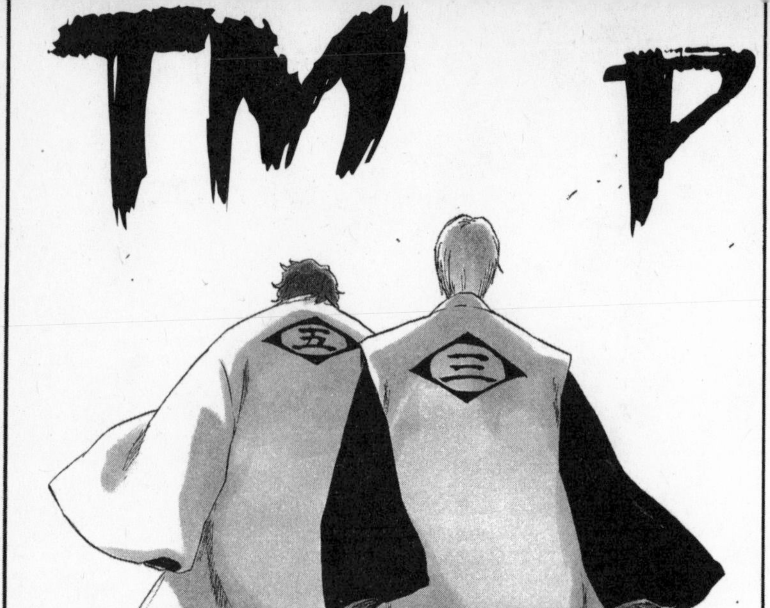
TMP

170. end of hypnosis2 (the Galvanizer)

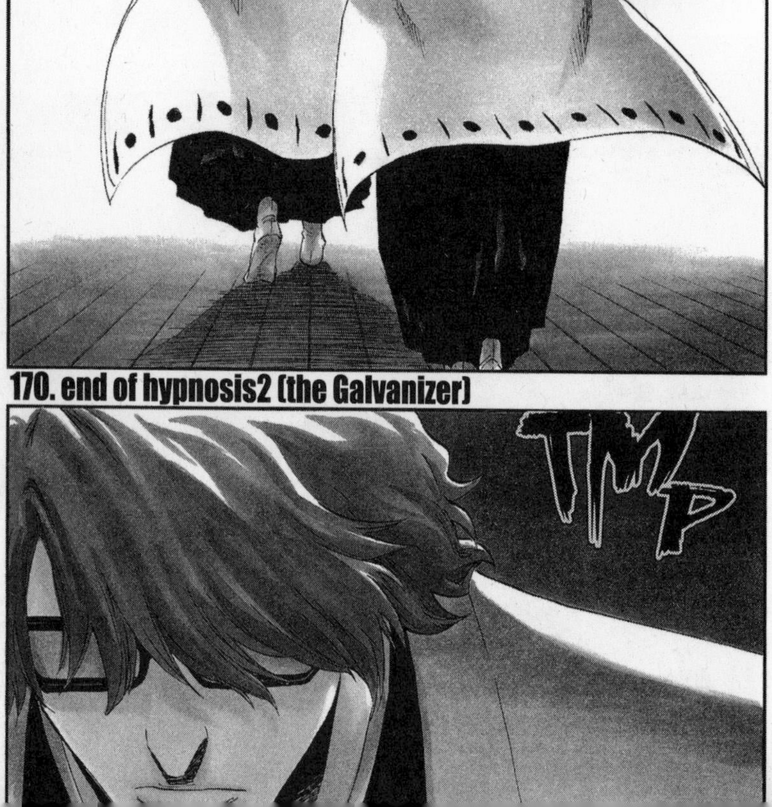
TMP

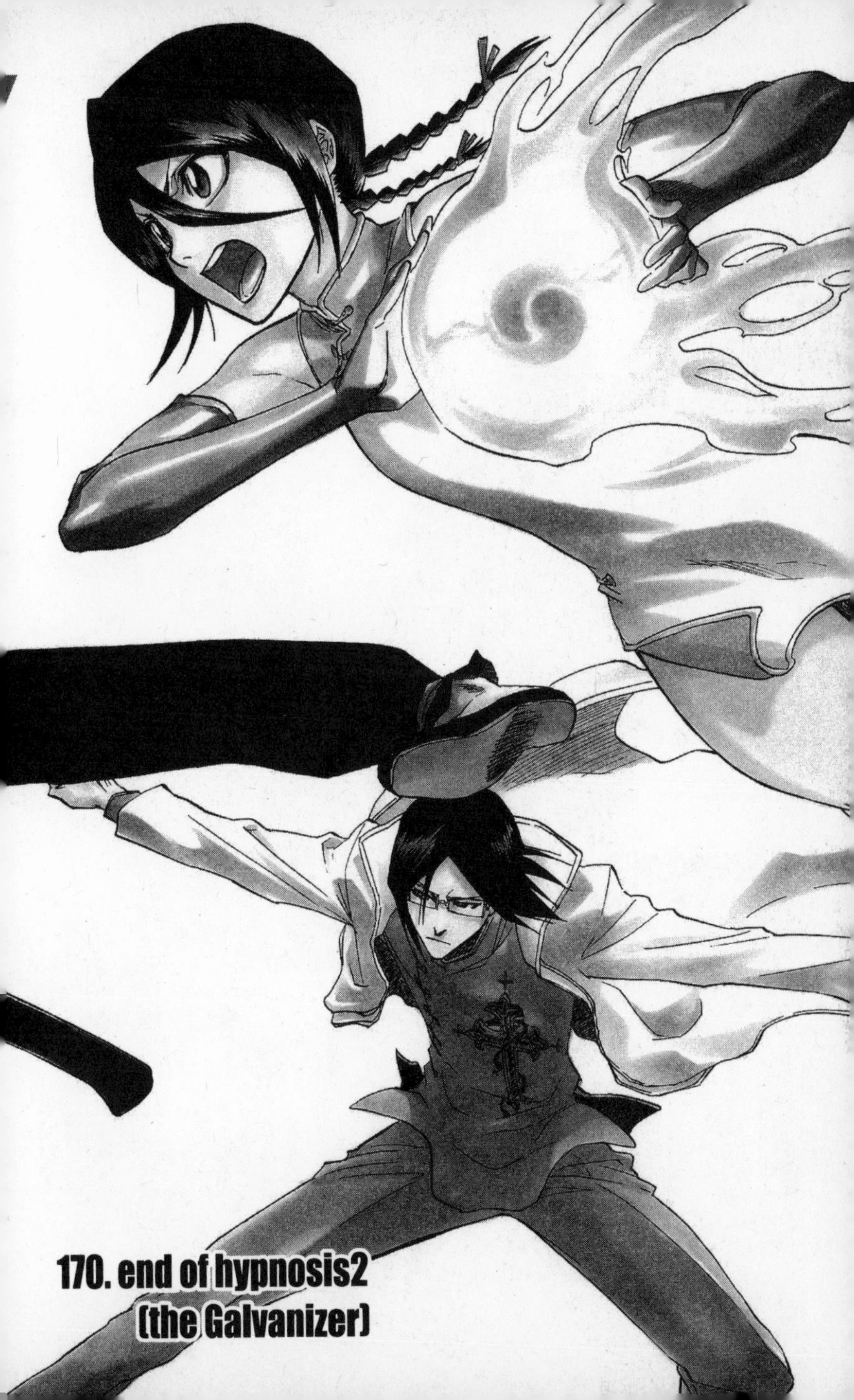

170. end of hypnosis2 (the Galvanizer)

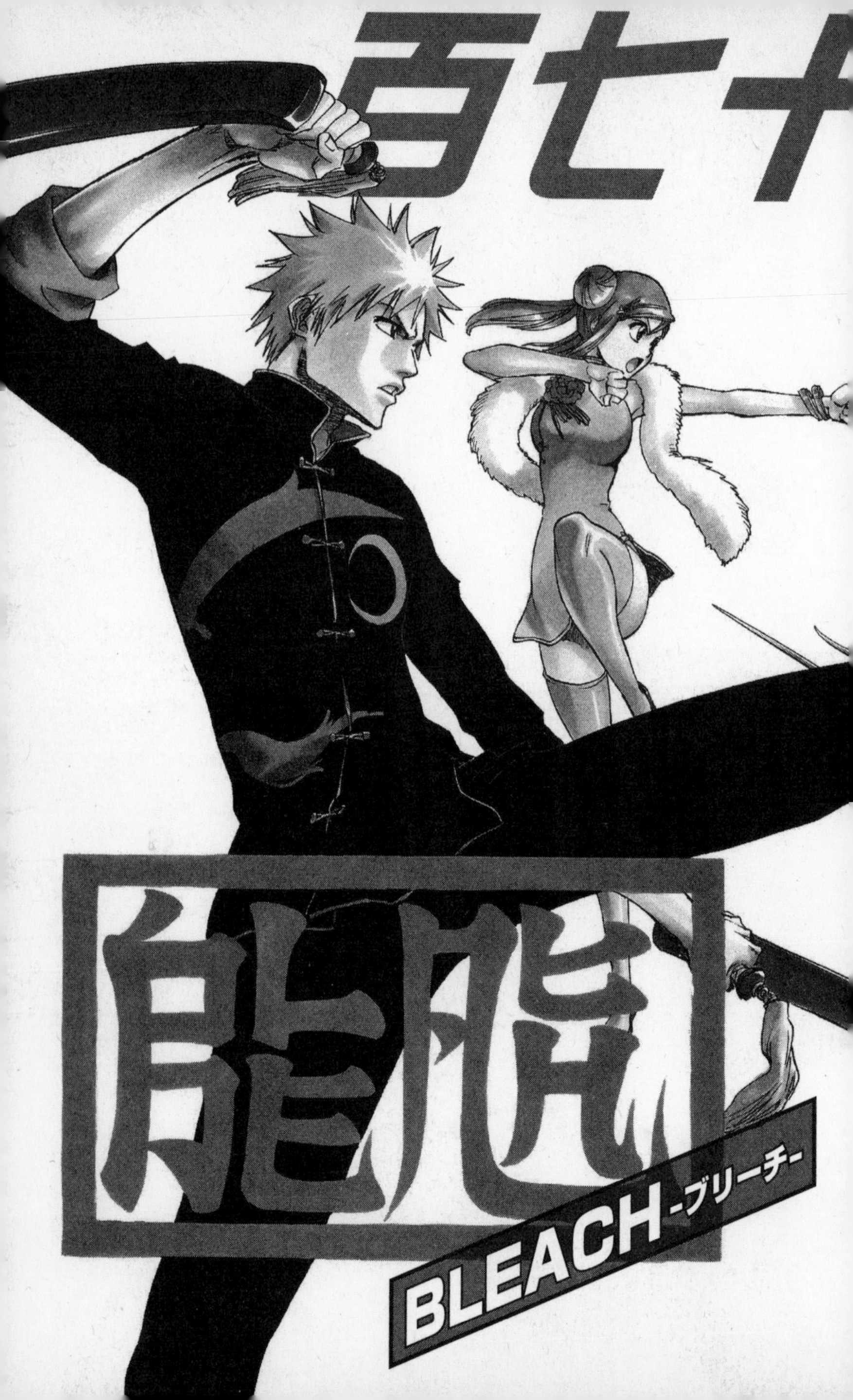
百七十
BLEACH-ブリーチ-

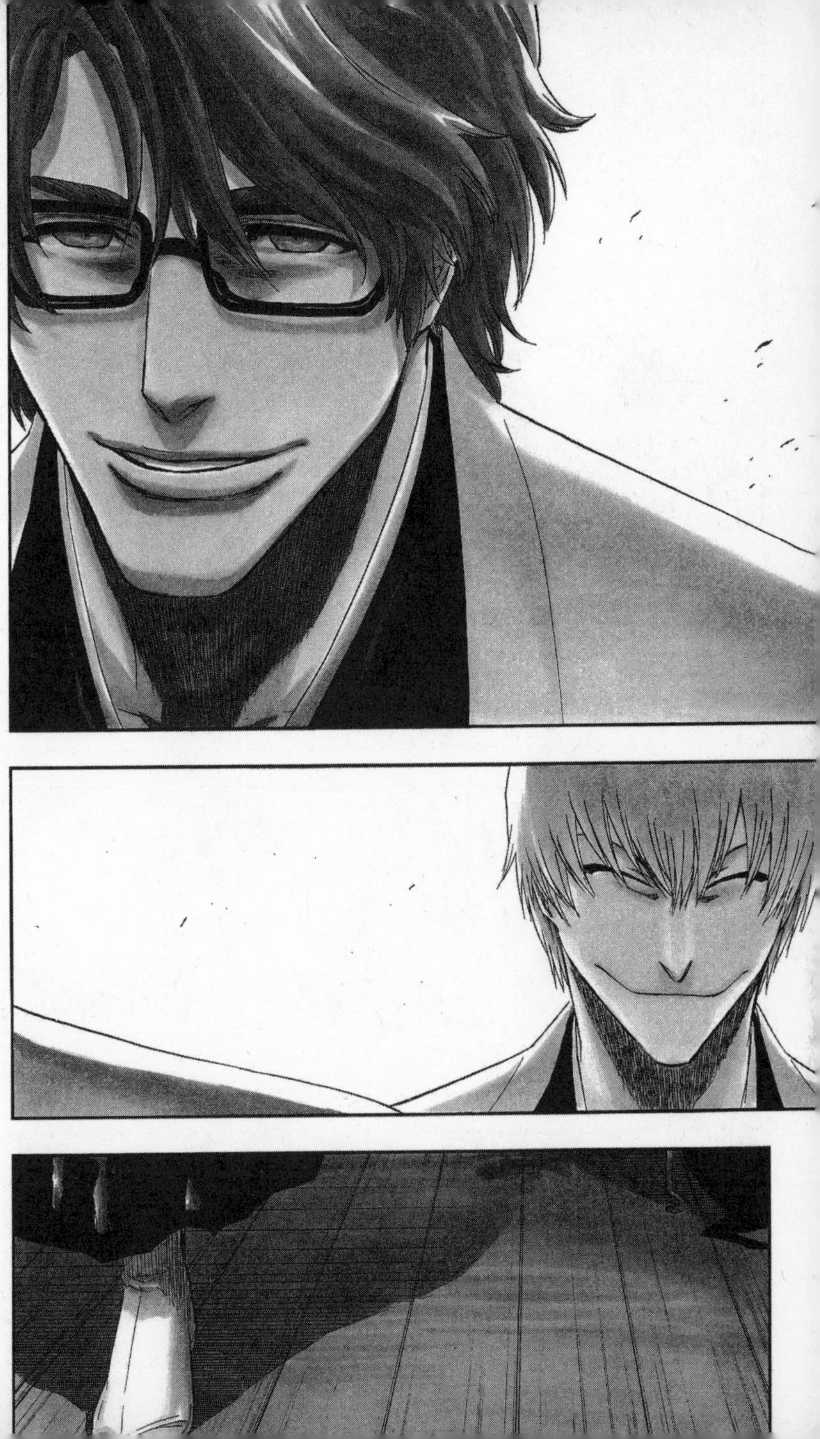

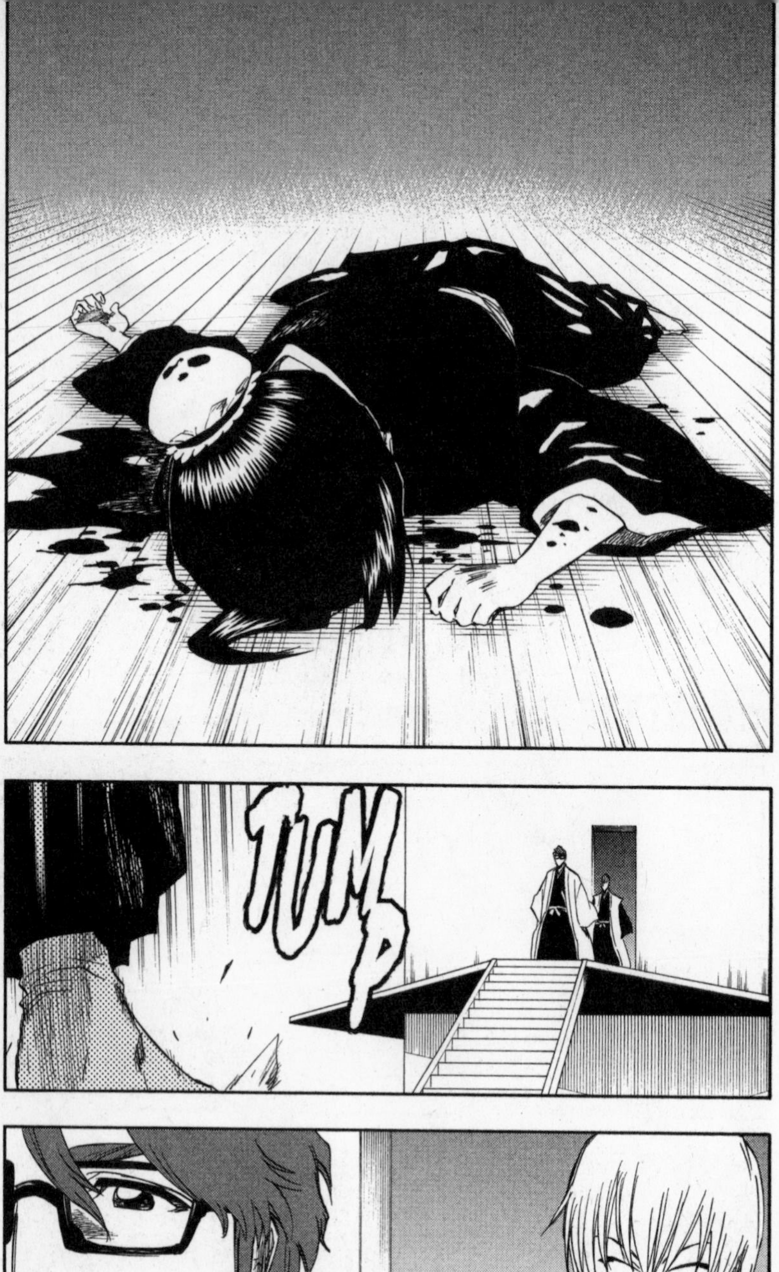
TUMP

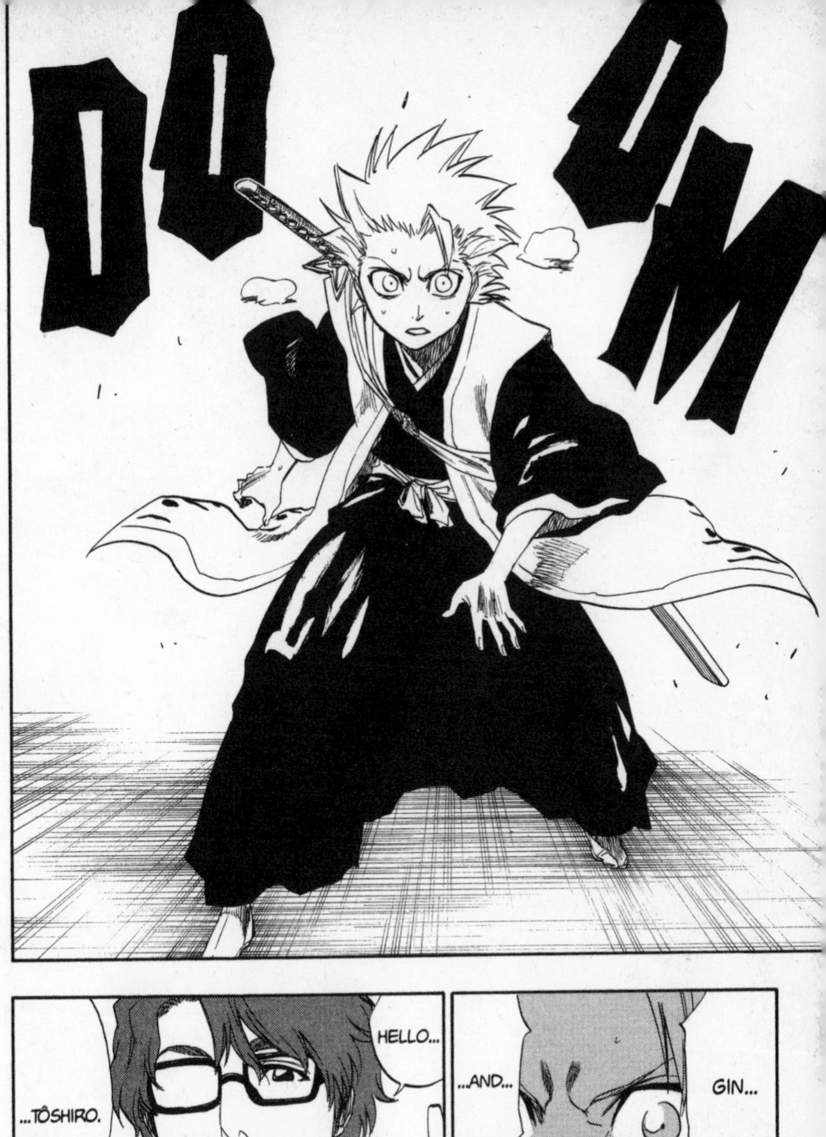
DOOM
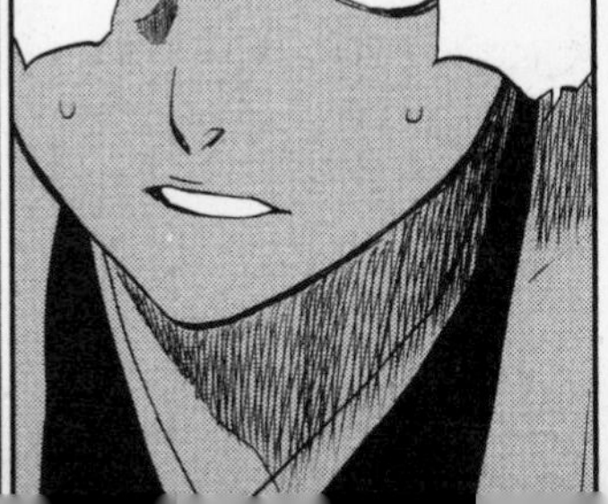
...AND...
GIN...
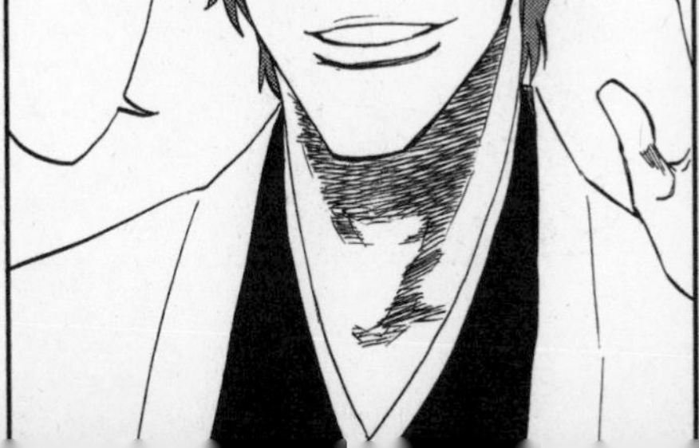
HELLO...
...TÔSHIRO.

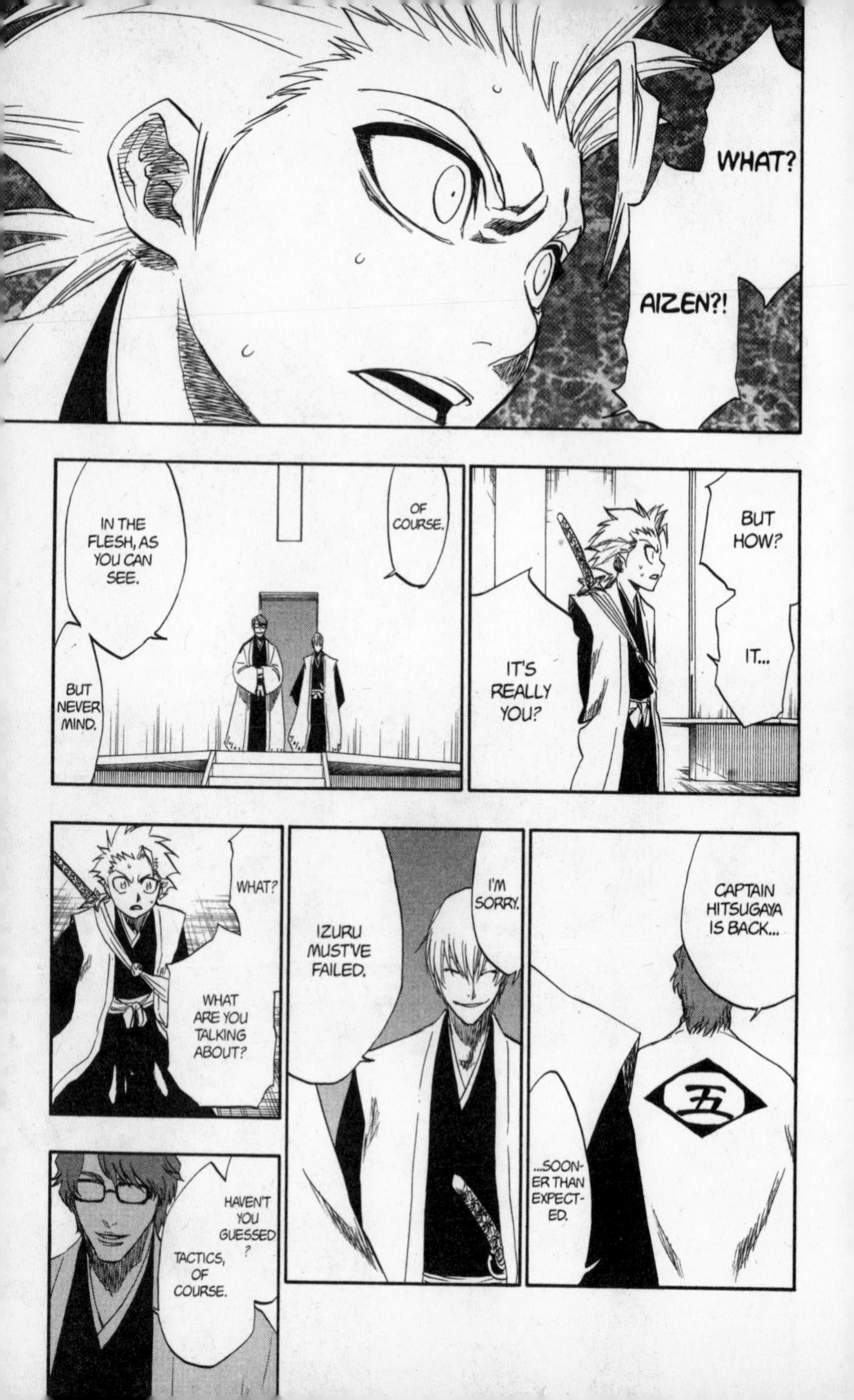
WHAT?
AIZEN?!
BUT HOW?
IT...
IT'S REALLY YOU?
OF COURSE.
IN THE FLESH, AS YOU CAN SEE.
BUT NEVER MIND.
CAPTAIN HITSUGAYA IS BACK...
...SOONER THAN EXPECTED.
I'M SORRY.
IZURU MUST'VE FAILED.
WHAT?
WHAT ARE YOU TALKING ABOUT?
HAVEN'T YOU GUESSED?
TACTICS, OF COURSE.

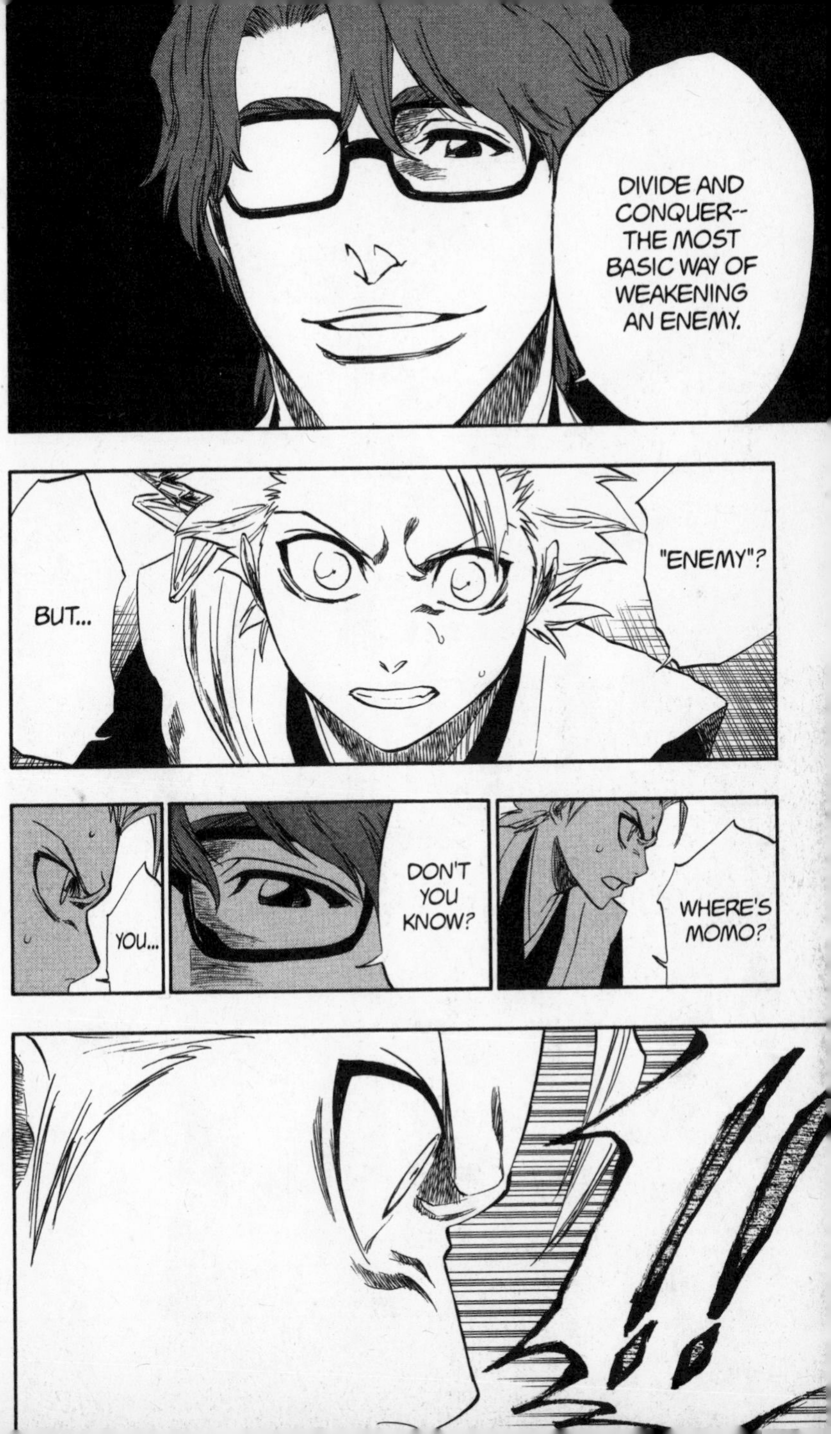
DIVIDE AND CONQUER-- THE MOST BASIC WAY OF WEAKENING AN ENEMY.
"ENEMY"?
BUT...
WHERE'S MOMO?
DON'T YOU KNOW?
YOU...

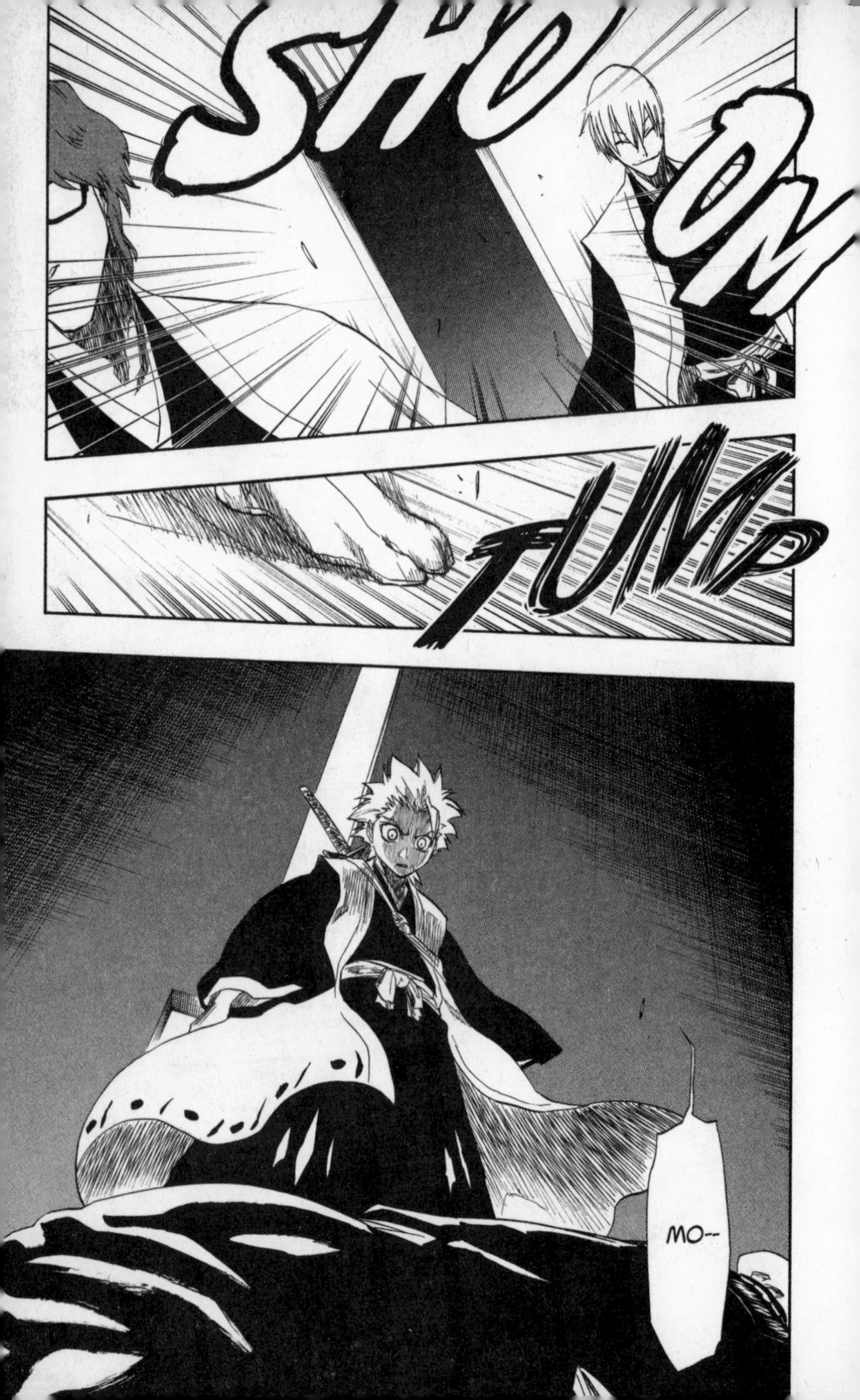
SHOOM
FUMP
MO--

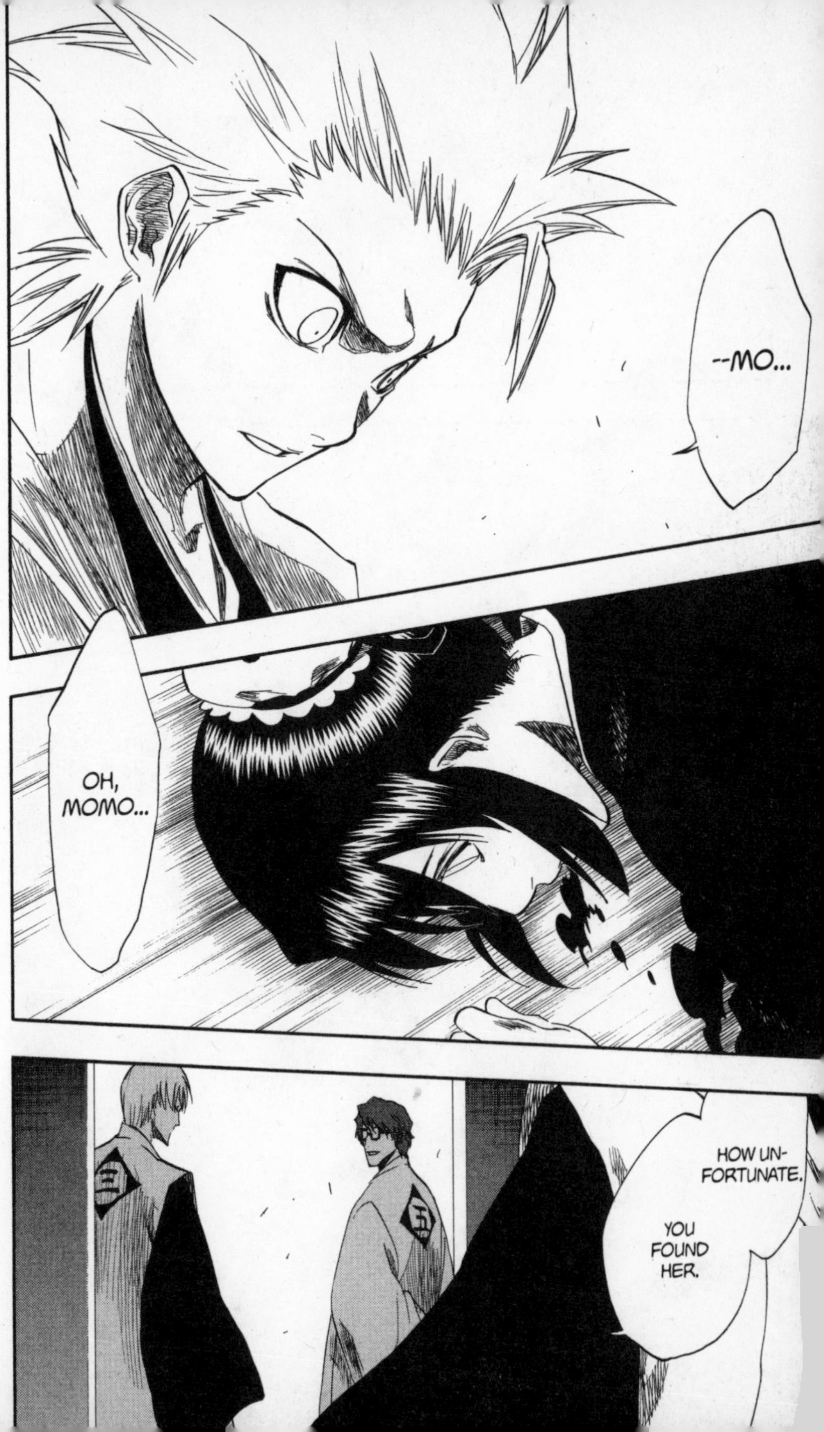
--MO...
OH, MOMO...
HOW UN-FORTUNATE.
YOU FOUND HER.

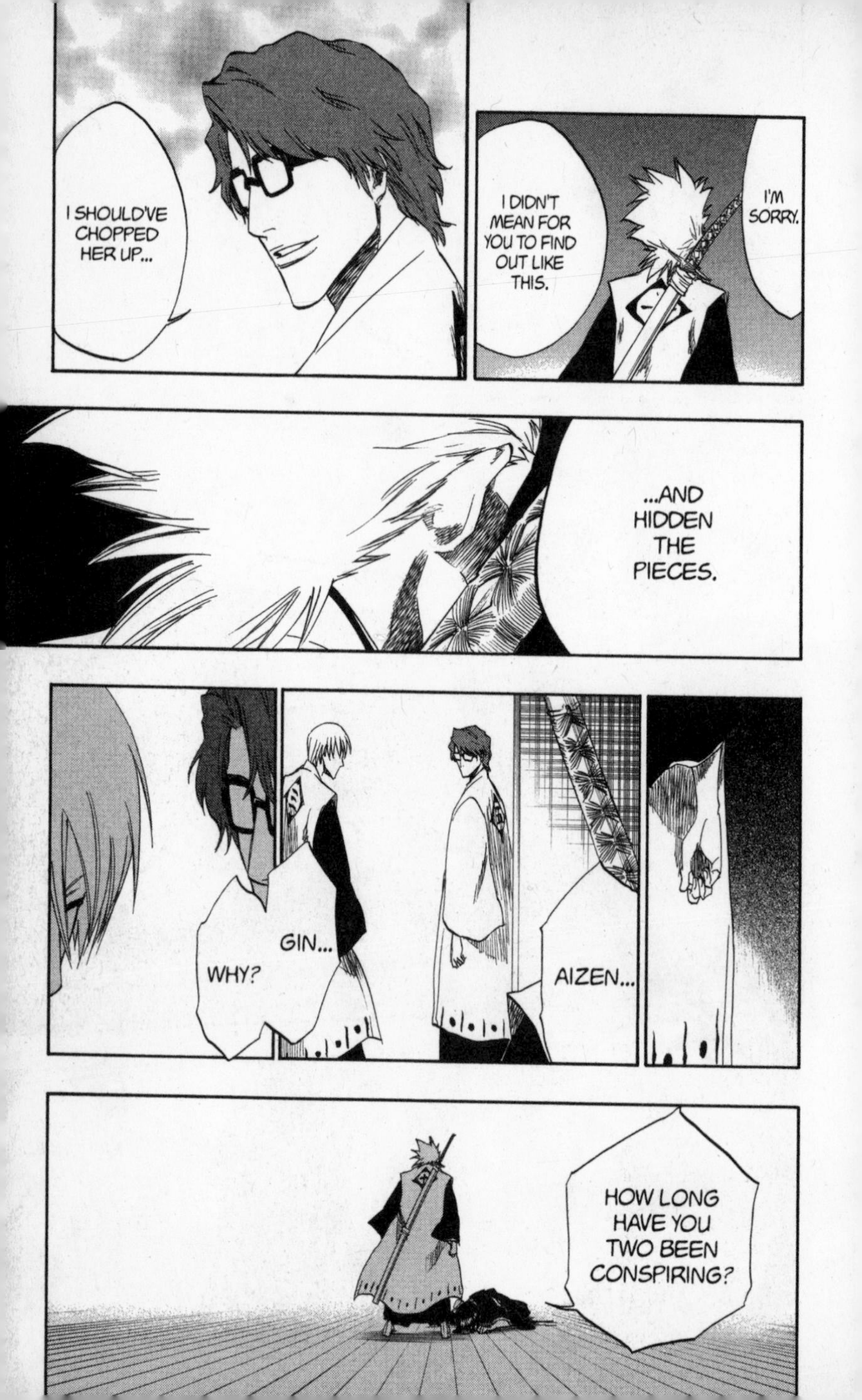
I'M SORRY.
I DIDN'T MEAN FOR YOU TO FIND OUT LIKE THIS.
I SHOULD'VE CHOPPED HER UP...
...AND HIDDEN THE PIECES.
AIZEN...
GIN...
WHY?
HOW LONG HAVE YOU TWO BEEN CONSPIRING?

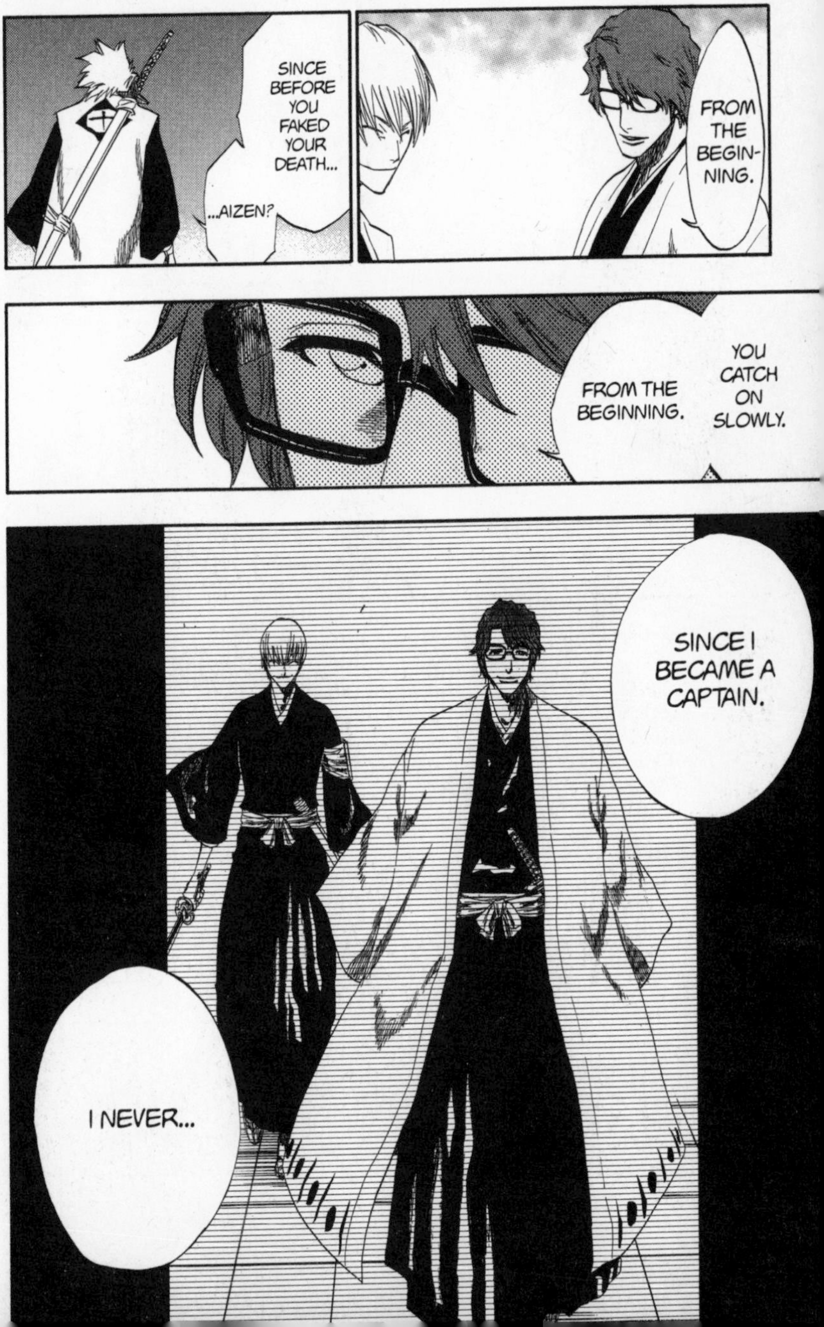
FROM THE BEGIN- NING.
SINCE BEFORE YOU FAKED YOUR DEATH...
...AIZEN?
YOU CATCH ON SLOWLY.
FROM THE BEGINNING.
SINCE I BECAME A CAPTAIN.
I NEVER...

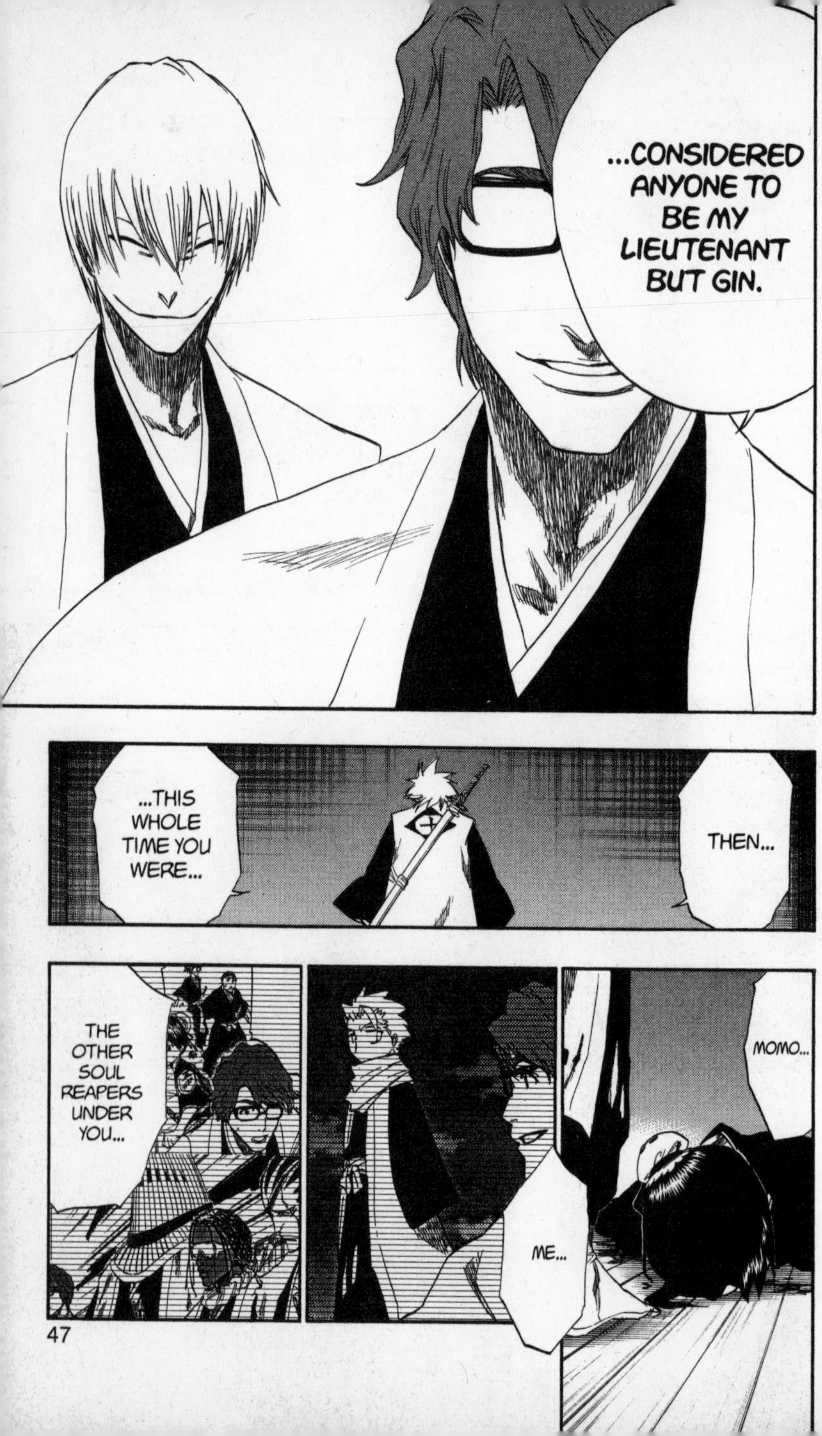
...CONSIDERED ANYONE TO BE MY LIEUTENANT BUT GIN.
THEN...
...THIS WHOLE TIME YOU WERE...
MOMO...
ME...
THE OTHER SOUL REAPERS UNDER YOU...

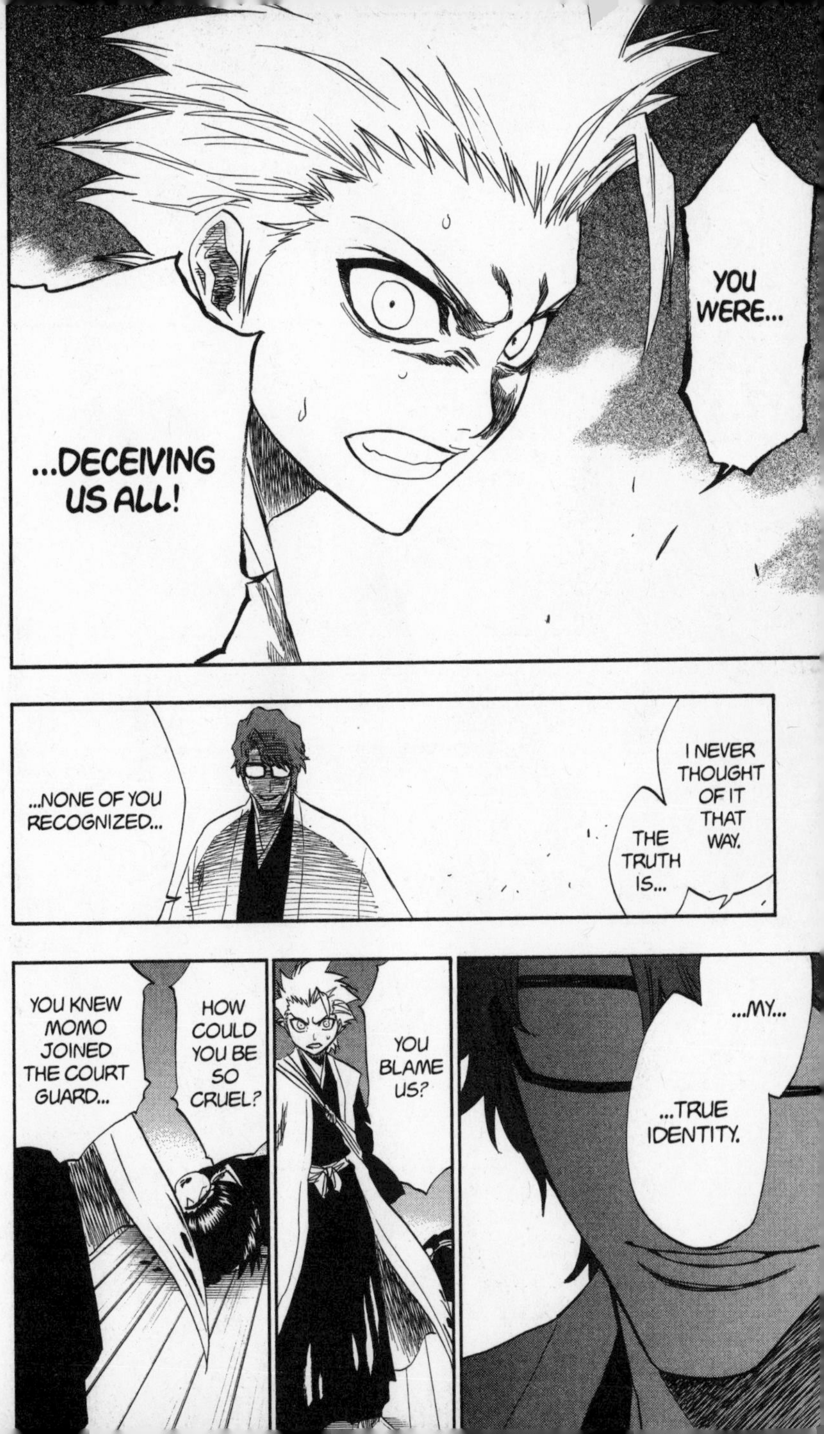
YOU WERE...
...DECEIVING US ALL!
I NEVER THOUGHT OF IT THAT WAY.
THE TRUTH IS...
...NONE OF YOU RECOGNIZED...
...MY...
...TRUE IDENTITY.
YOU BLAME US?
HOW COULD YOU BE SO CRUEL?
YOU KNEW MOMO JOINED THE COURT GUARD...

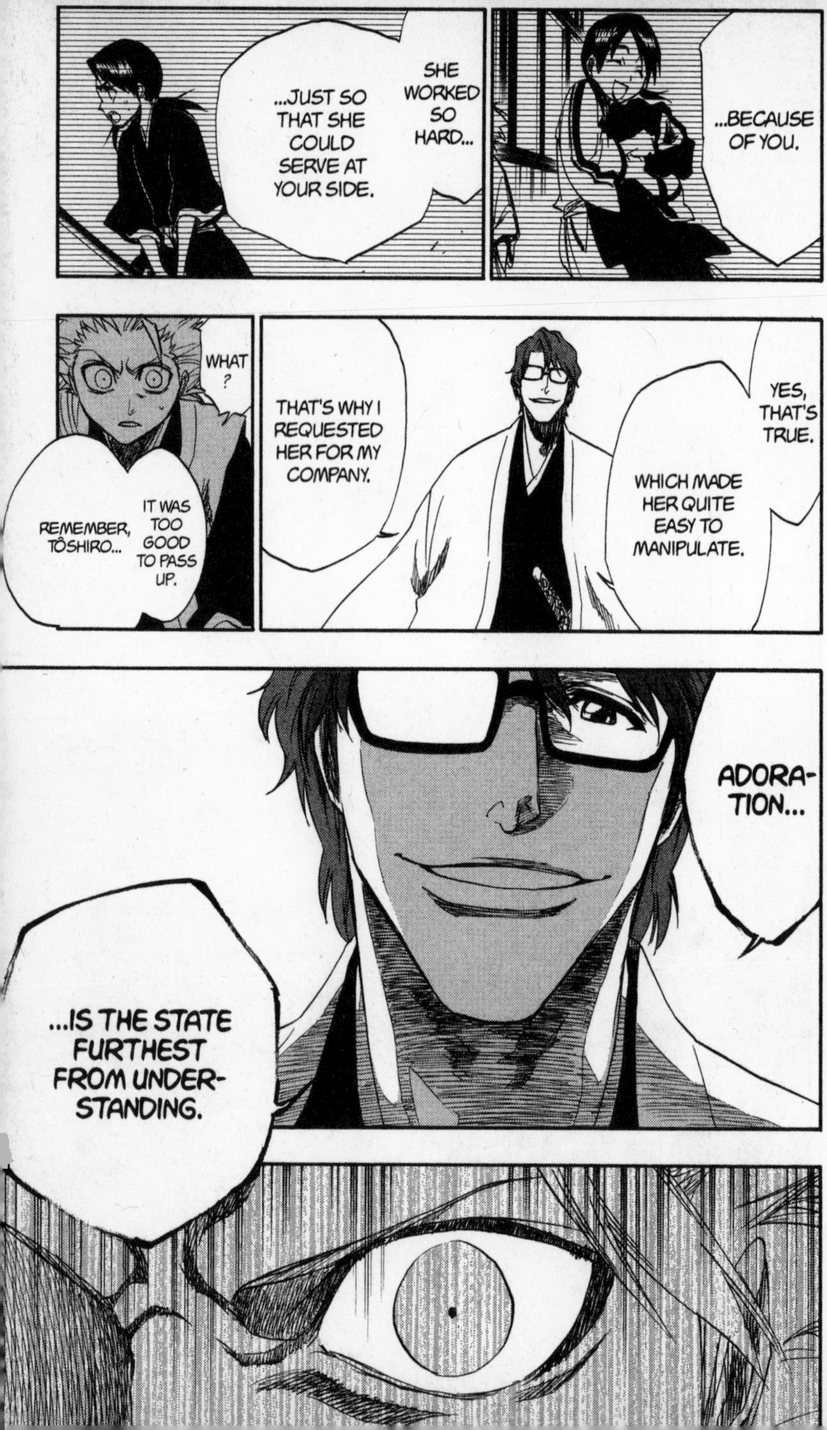
...BECAUSE OF YOU.
SHE WORKED SO HARD...
...JUST SO THAT SHE COULD SERVE AT YOUR SIDE.
YES, THAT'S TRUE.
WHICH MADE HER QUITE EASY TO MANIPULATE.
THAT'S WHY I REQUESTED HER FOR MY COMPANY.
WHAT?
IT WAS TOO GOOD TO PASS UP.
REMEMBER, TÔSHIRO...
ADORATION...
...IS THE STATE FURTHEST FROM UNDERSTANDING.

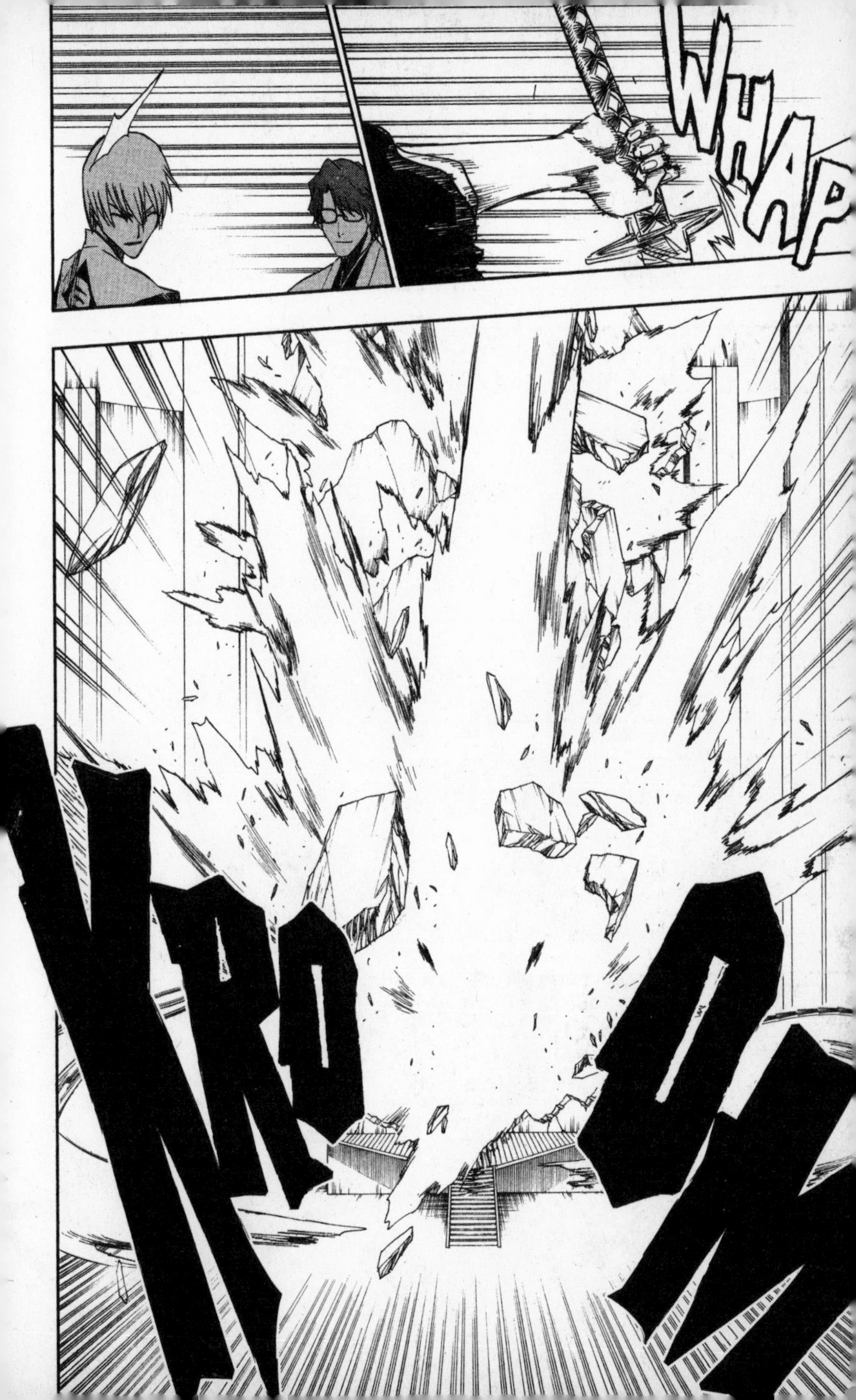
WHAP

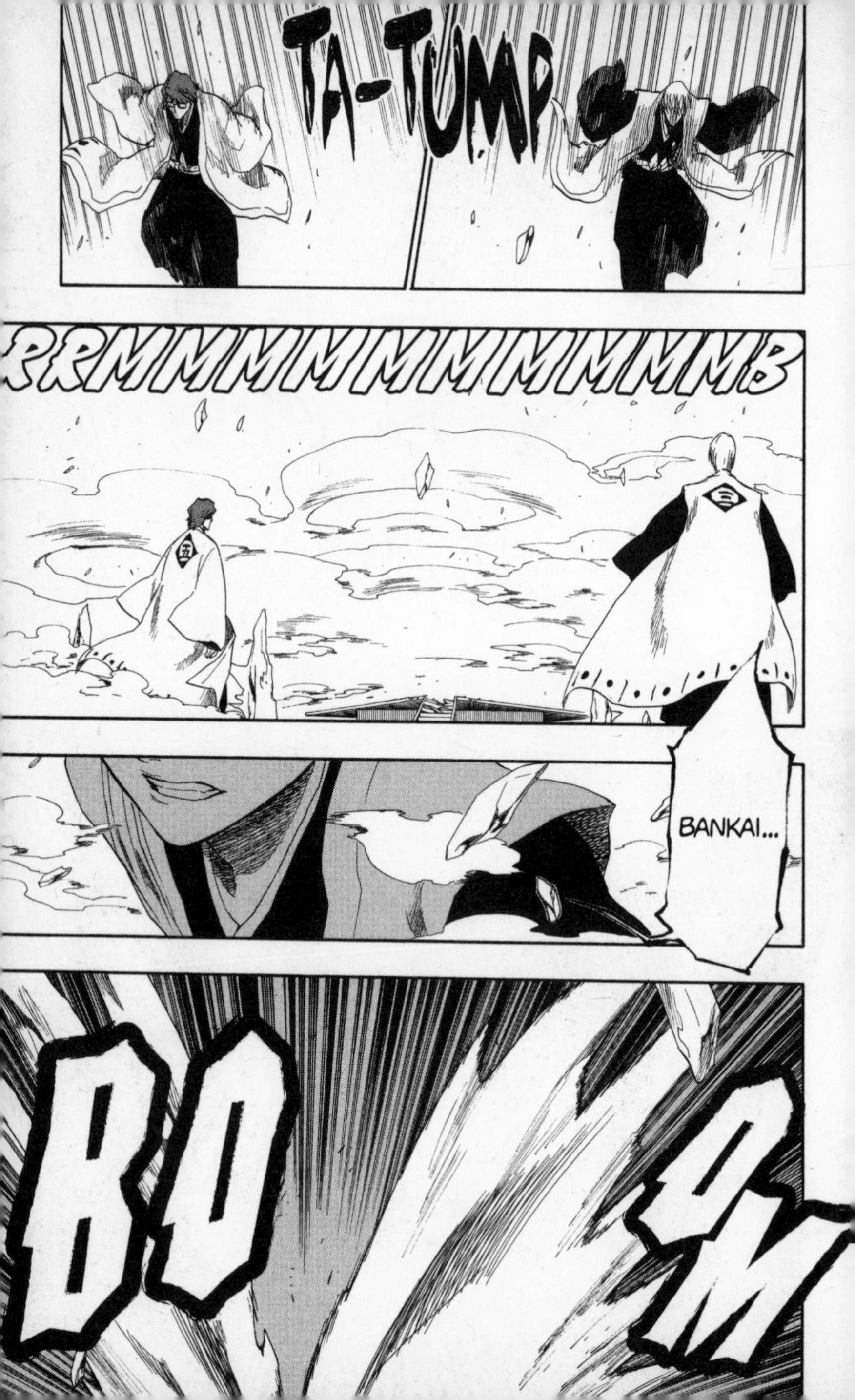
TA-TUMP
RRMMMMMMMMMMMMMB
BANKAI...
BOOM

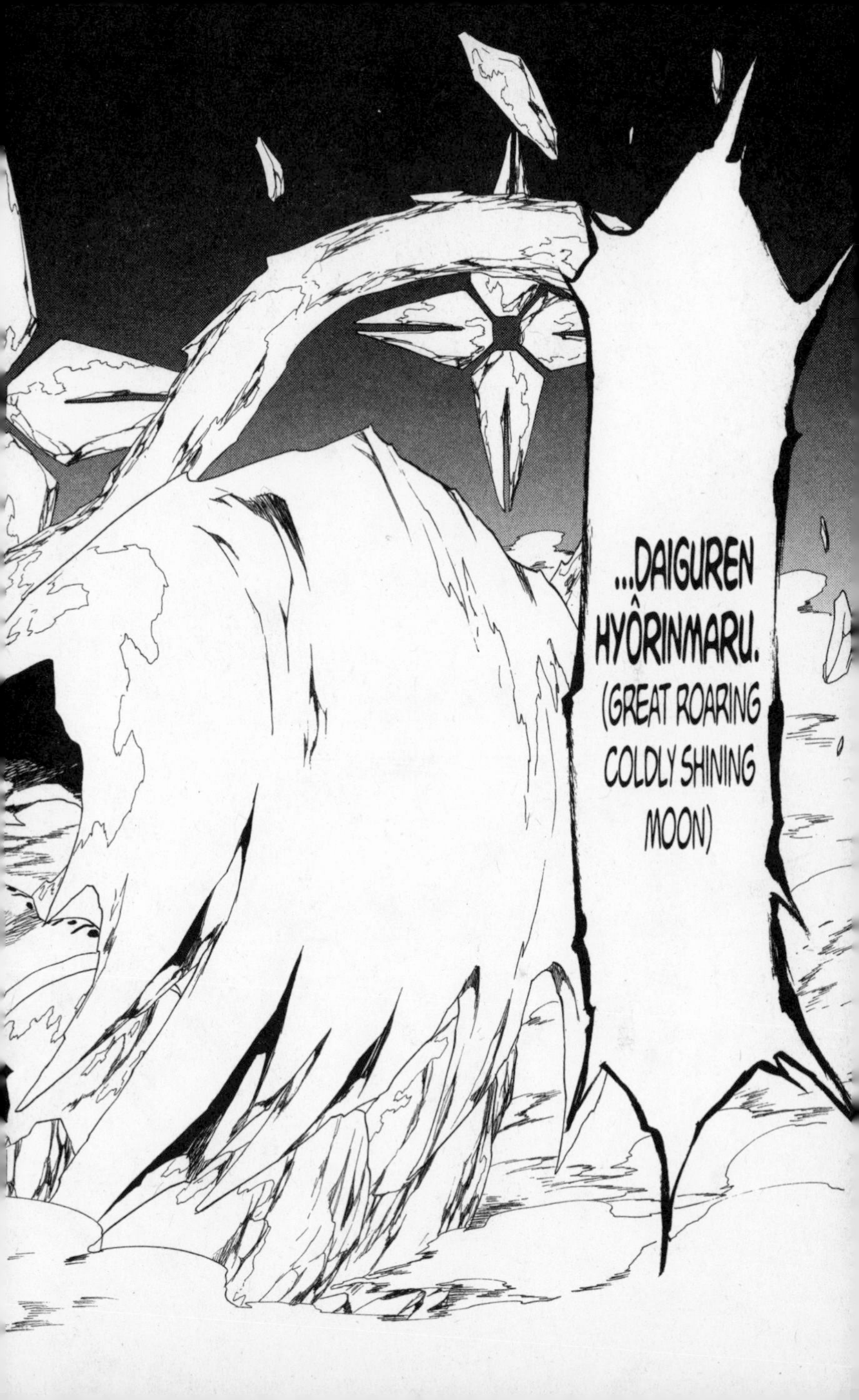
...DAIGUREN HYÔRINMARU.
(GREAT ROARING COLDLY SHINING MOON)

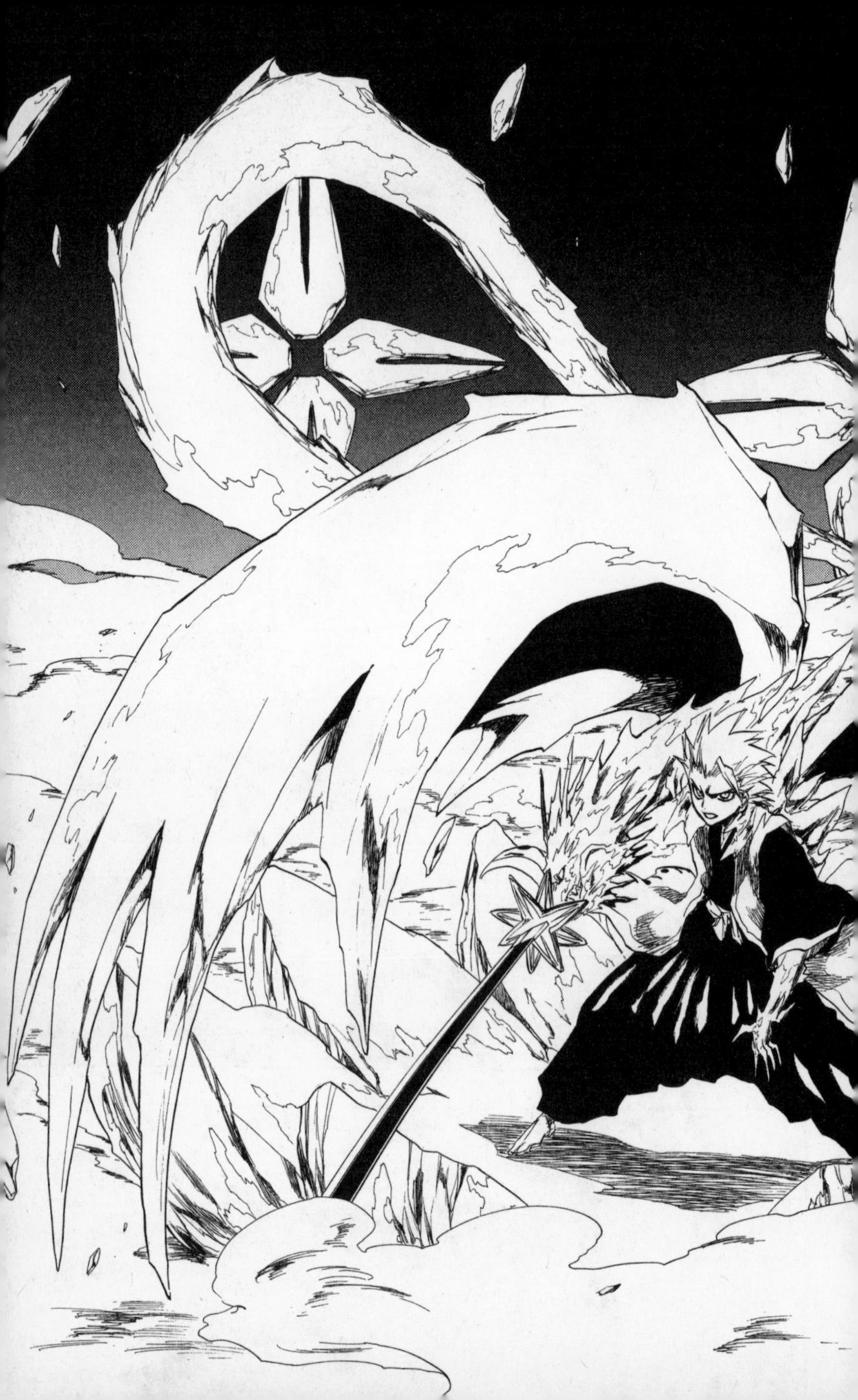

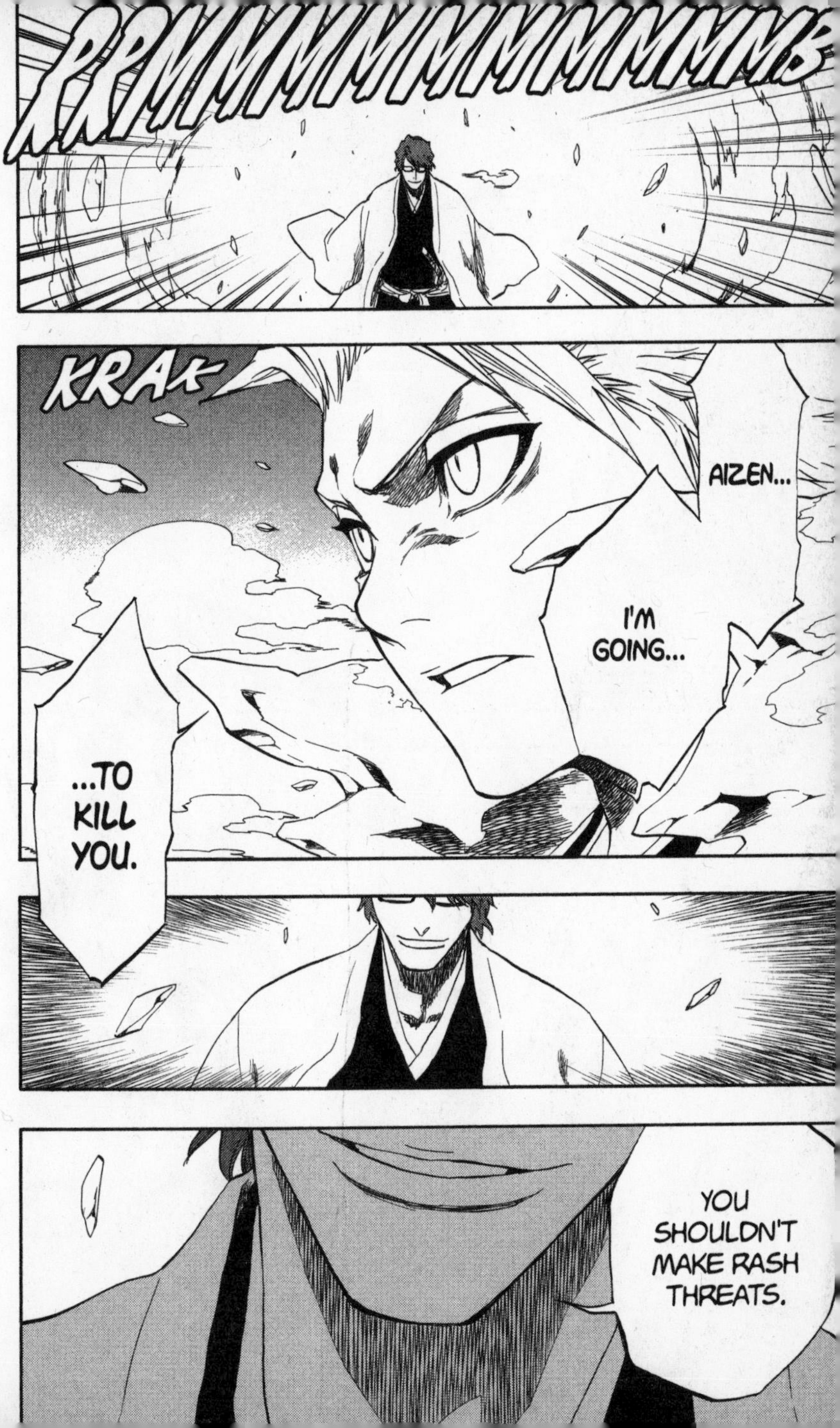
RRMMMMMMMMMMMMMB
KRAK
AIZEN...
I'M GOING...
...TO KILL YOU.
YOU SHOULDN'T MAKE RASH THREATS.

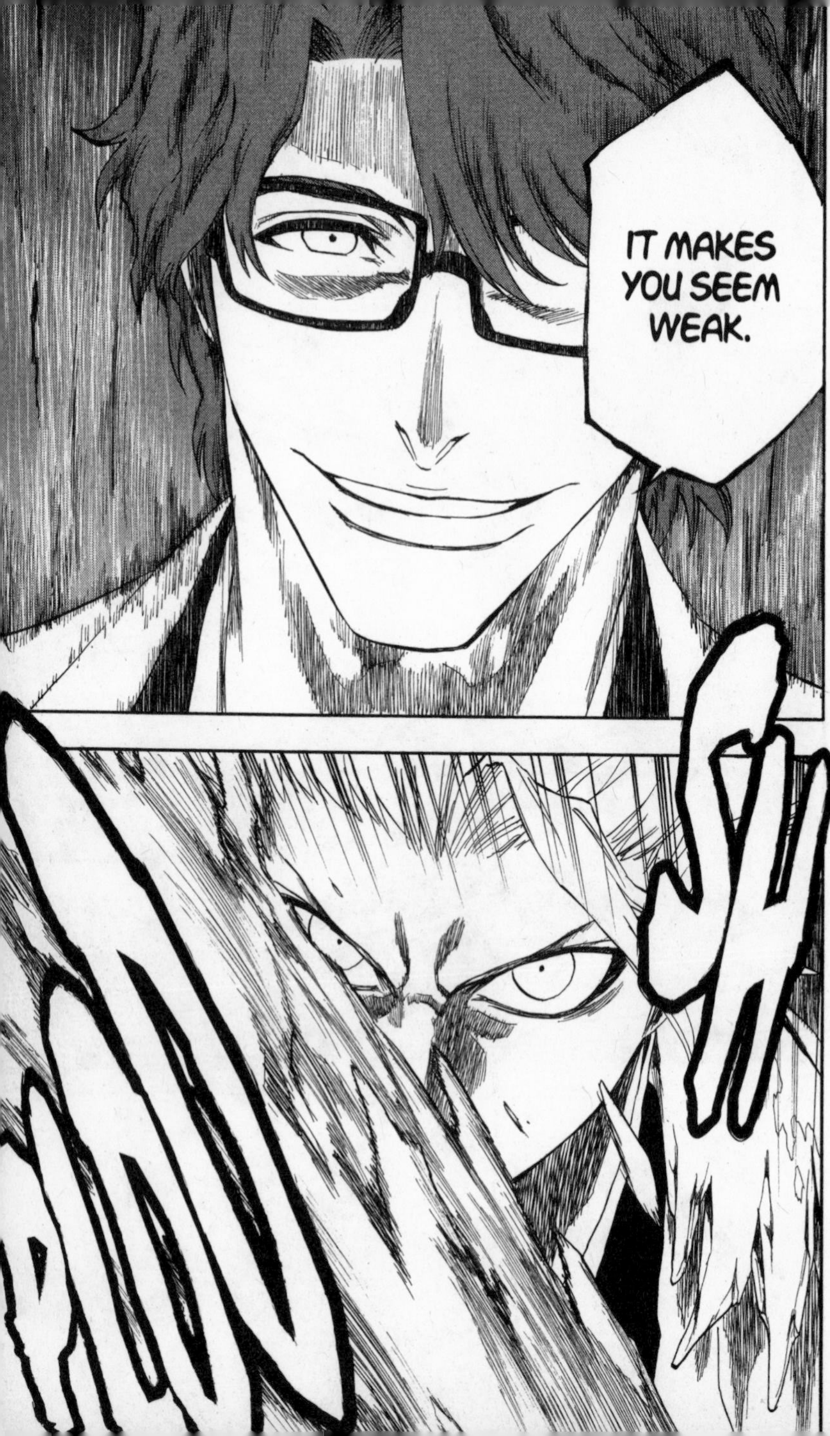
IT MAKES YOU SEEM WEAK.

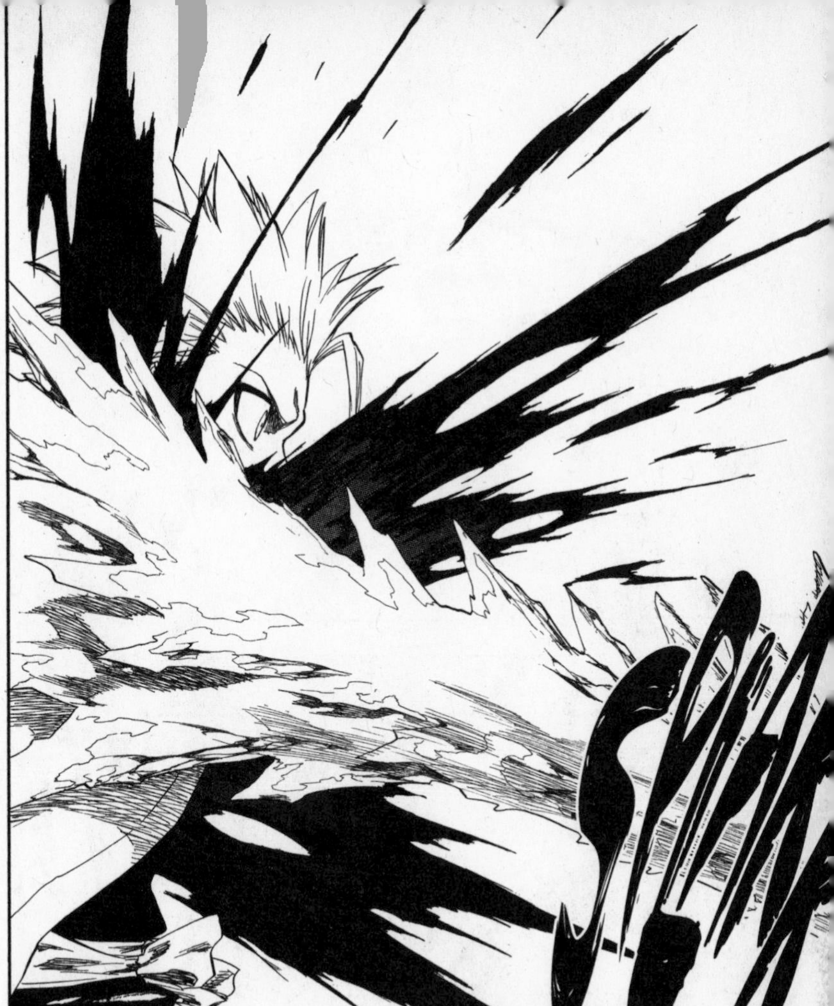
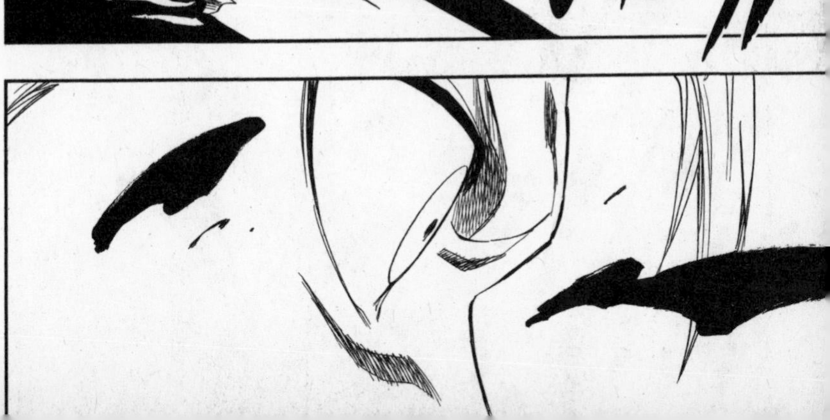

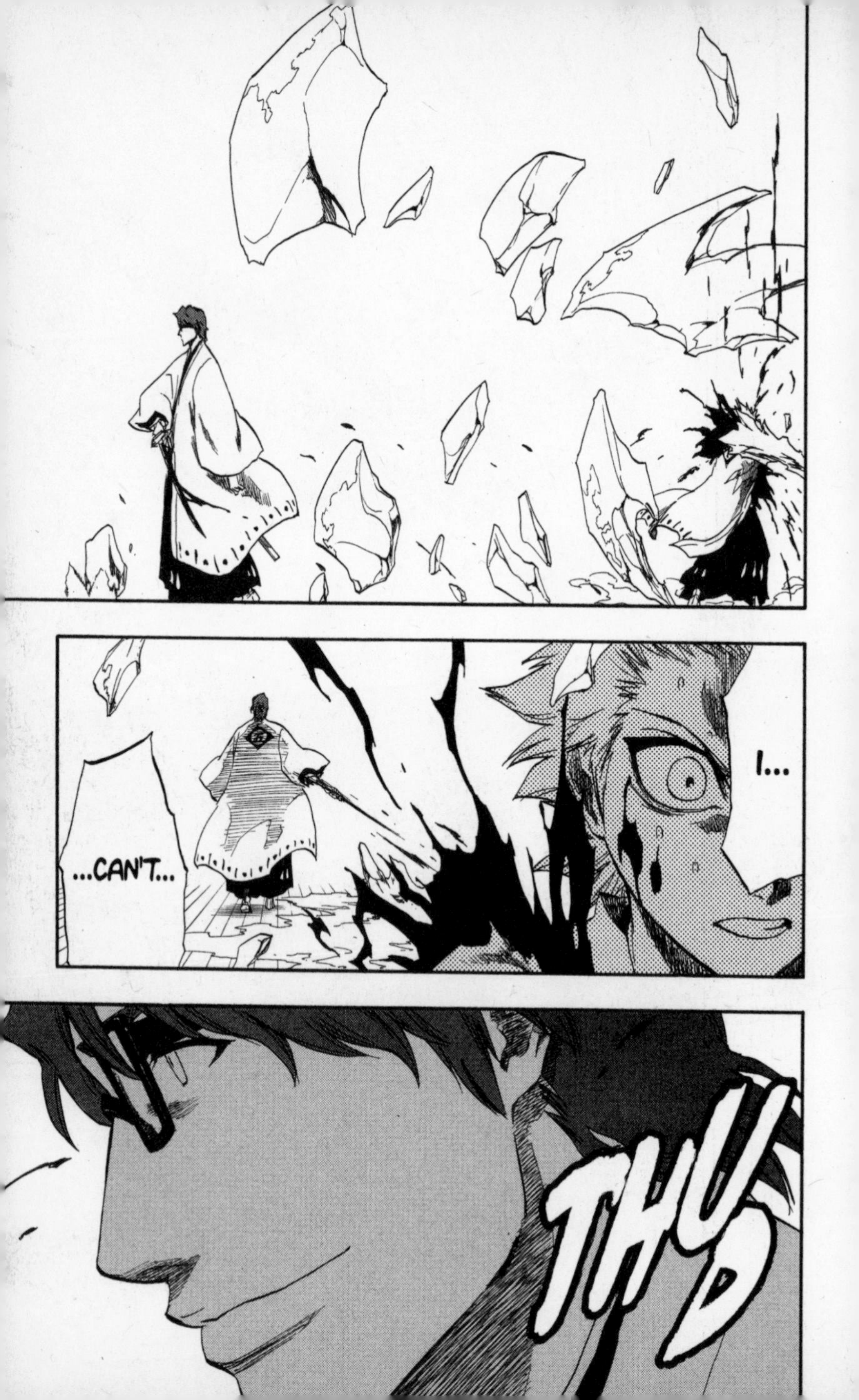
I...
...CAN'T...
THUD

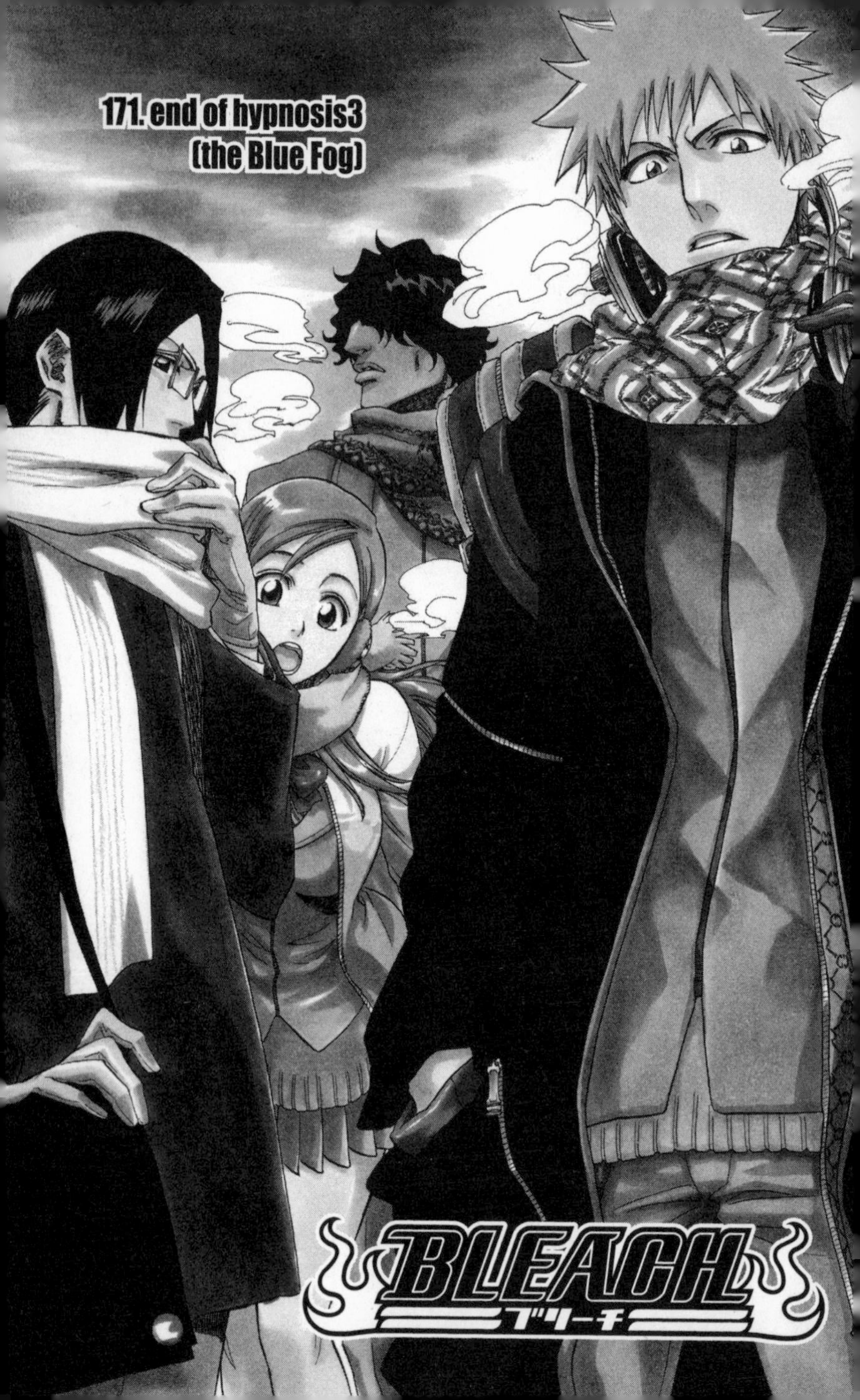
171. end of hypnosis3
(the Blue Fog)
BLEACH
ブリーチ

BLEACH
ブリーチ

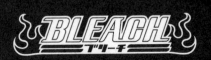

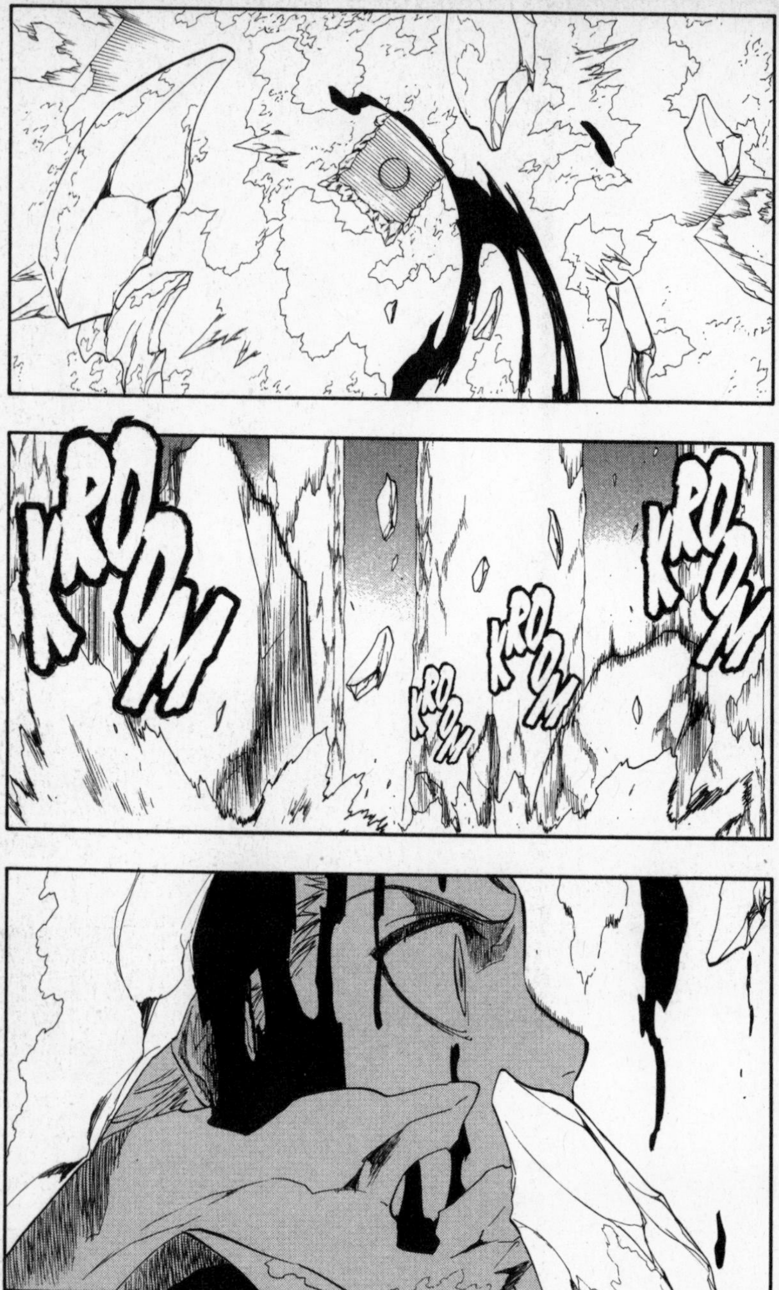
KROOM
KROOM
KROOM
KROOM

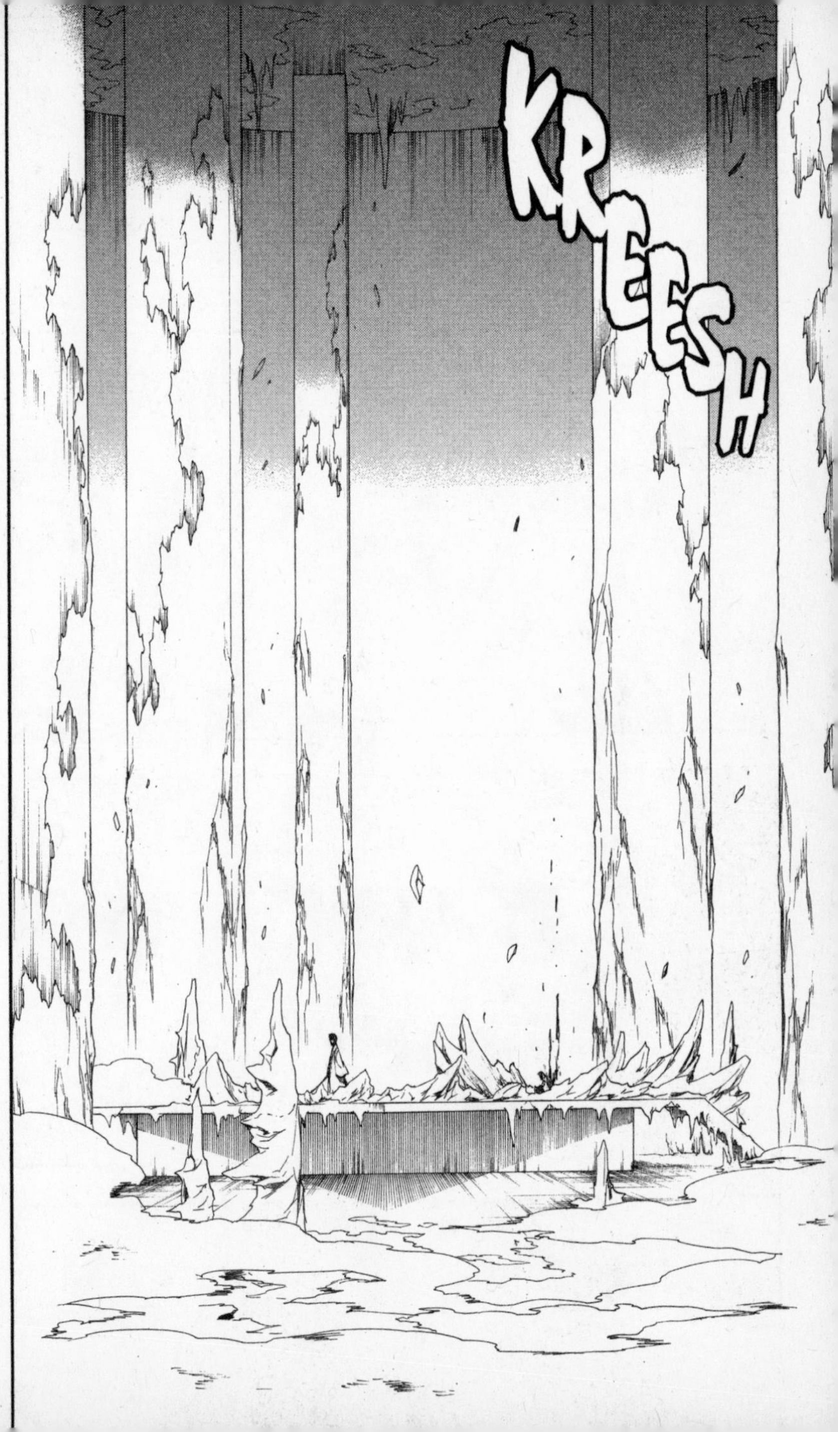
KREESH

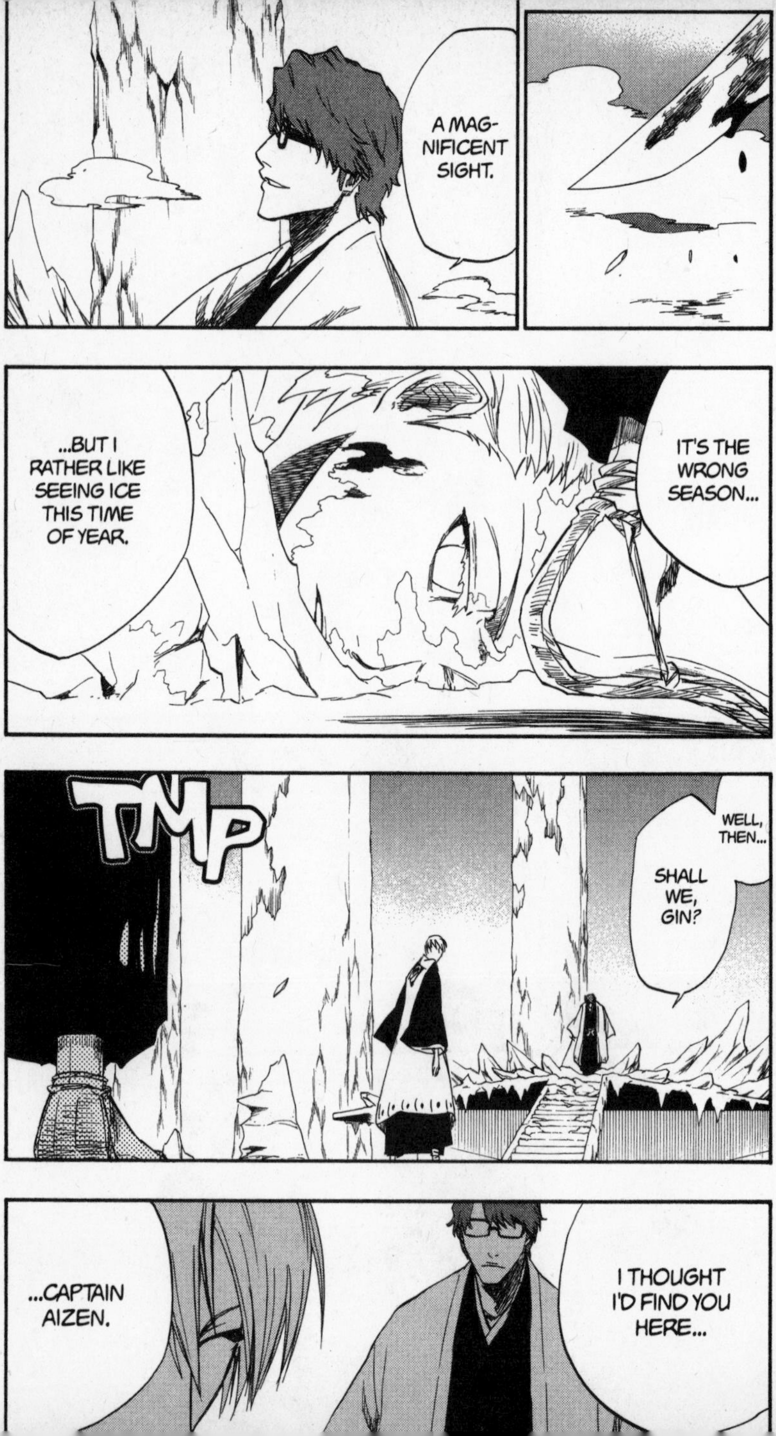
A MAG-
NIFICENT
SIGHT.
IT'S THE WRONG SEASON...
...BUT I RATHER LIKE SEEING ICE THIS TIME OF YEAR.
WELL, THEN...
SHALL WE, GIN?
TMP
I THOUGHT I'D FIND YOU HERE...
...CAPTAIN AIZEN.

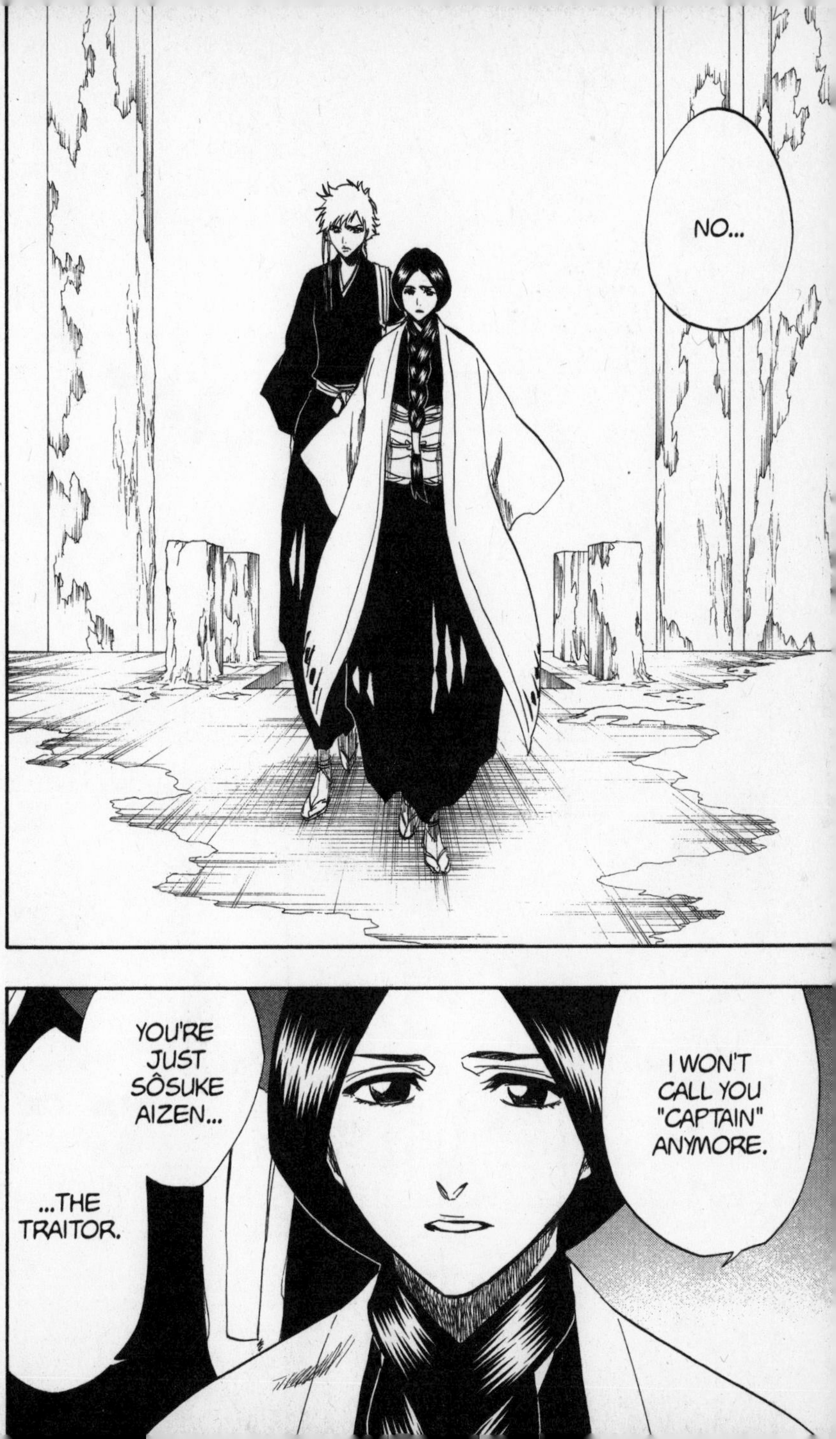
NO...
I WON'T CALL YOU "CAPTAIN" ANYMORE.
YOU'RE JUST SÔSUKE AIZEN...
...THE TRAITOR.

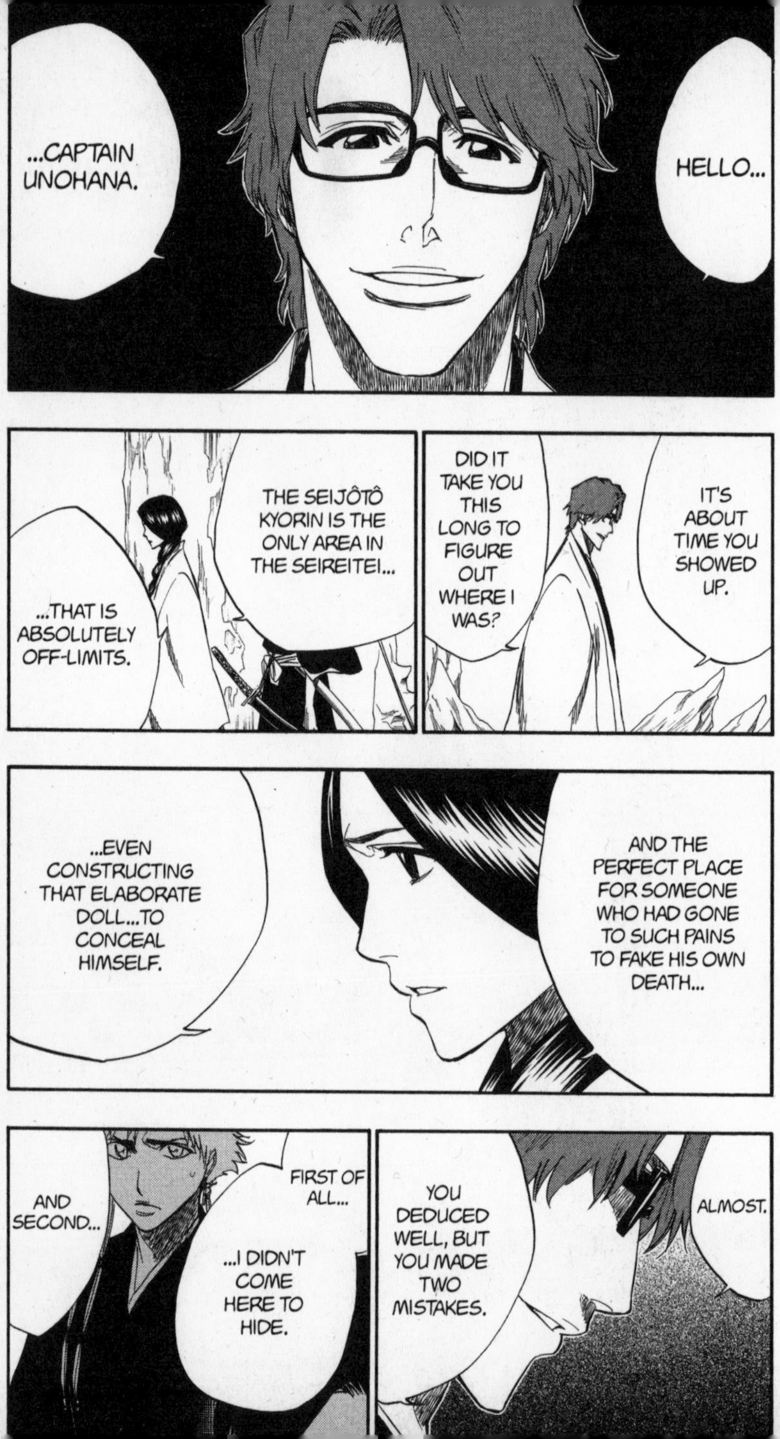
HELLO...
...CAPTAIN UNOHANA.
IT'S ABOUT TIME YOU SHOWED UP.
DID IT TAKE YOU THIS LONG TO FIGURE OUT WHERE I WAS?
THE SEIJÔTÔ KYORIN IS THE ONLY AREA IN THE SEIREITEI...
...THAT IS ABSOLUTELY OFF-LIMITS.
AND THE PERFECT PLACE FOR SOMEONE WHO HAD GONE TO SUCH PAINS TO FAKE HIS OWN DEATH...
...EVEN CONSTRUCTING THAT ELABORATE DOLL...TO CONCEAL HIMSELF.
ALMOST.
YOU DEDUCED WELL, BUT YOU MADE TWO MISTAKES.
FIRST OF ALL...
...I DIDN'T COME HERE TO HIDE.
AND SECOND...

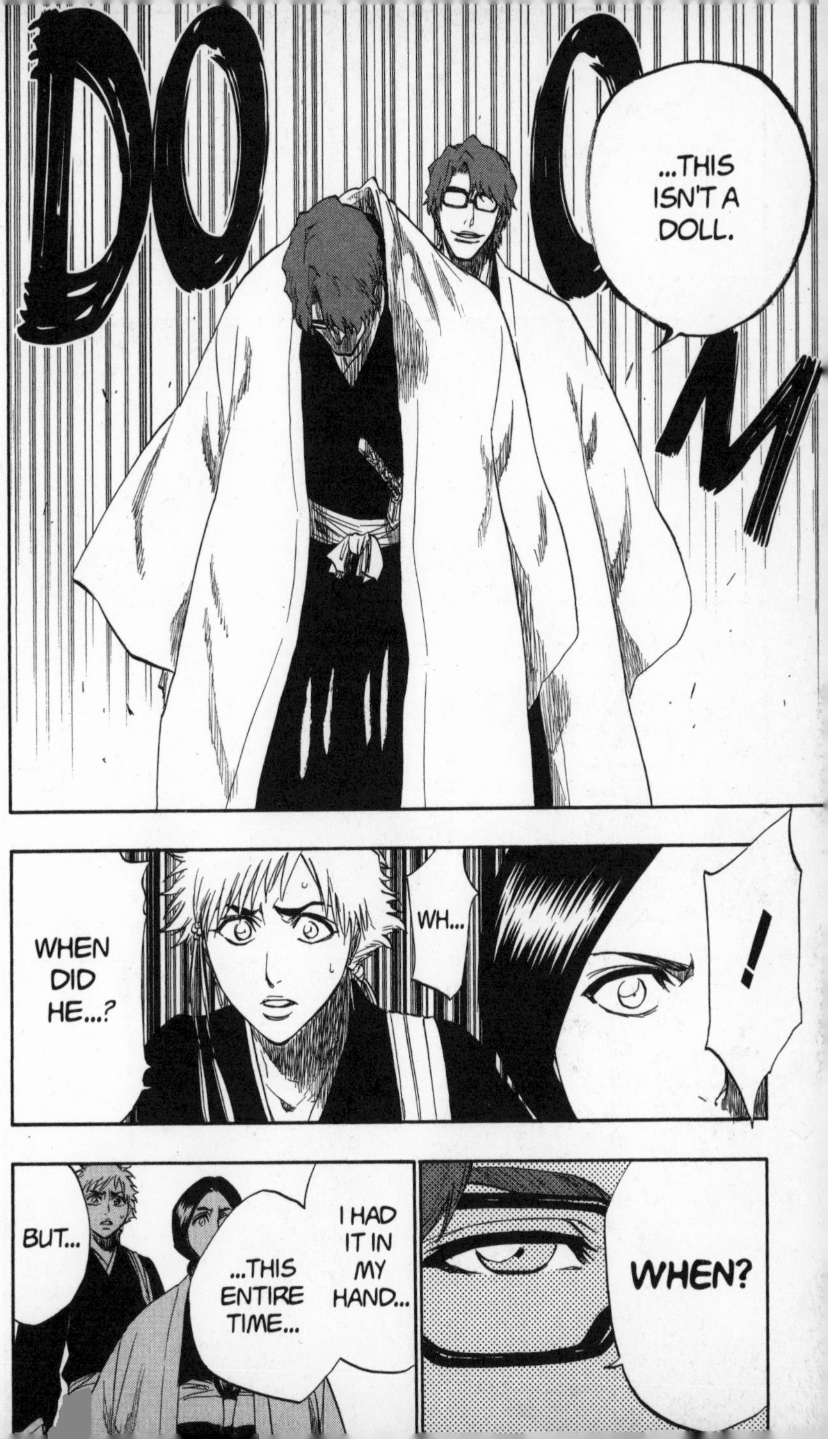

...THIS ISN'T A DOLL.
DOOM
!
WH...
WHEN DID HE...?
WHEN?
I HAD IT IN MY HAND...
...THIS ENTIRE TIME...
BUT...

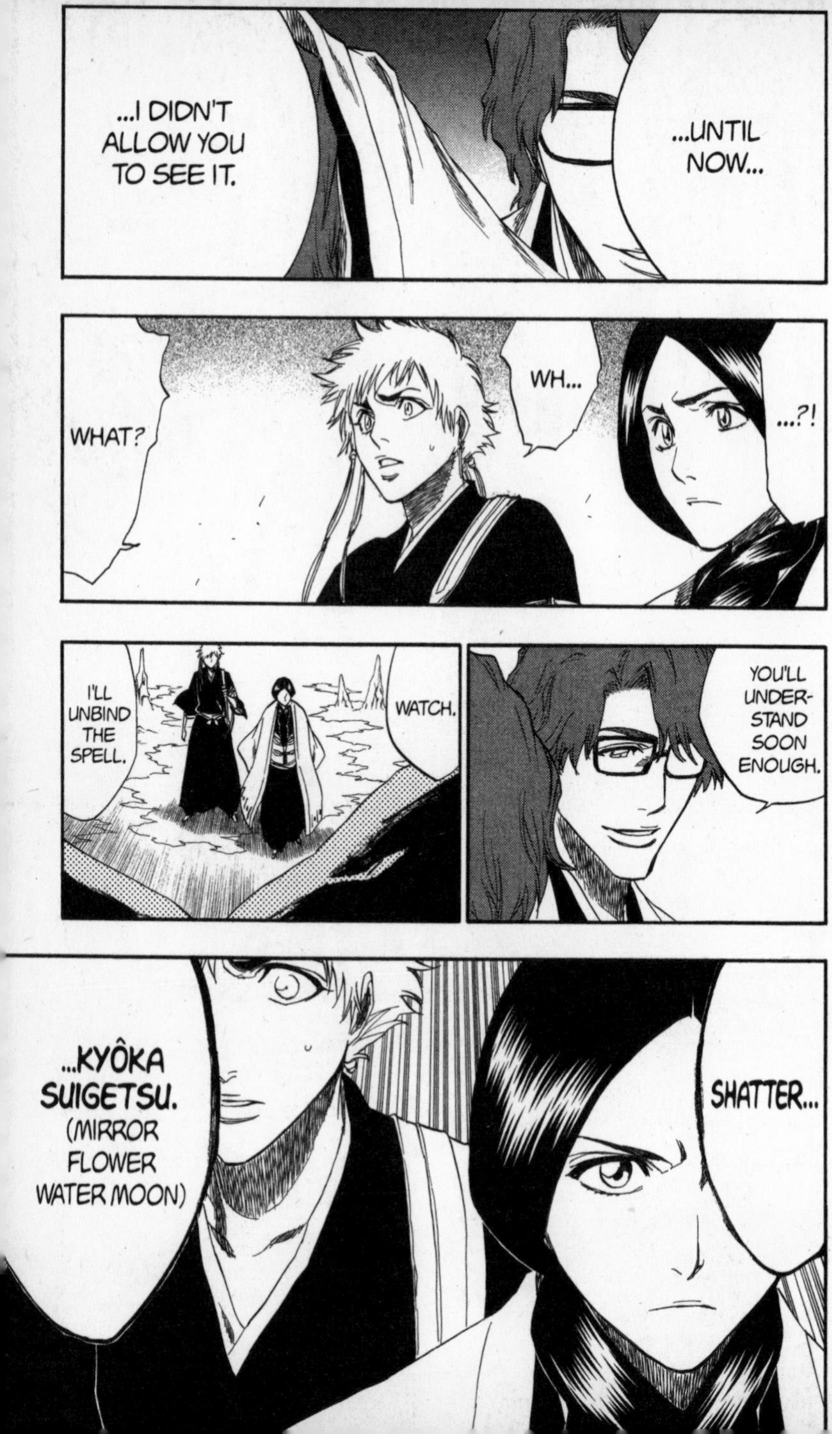
...UNTIL NOW...
...I DIDN'T ALLOW YOU TO SEE IT.
...?!
WH...
WHAT?
YOU'LL UNDER-STAND SOON ENOUGH.
WATCH.
I'LL UNBIND THE SPELL.
SHATTER...
...KYÔKA SUIGETSU. (MIRROR FLOWER WATER MOON)

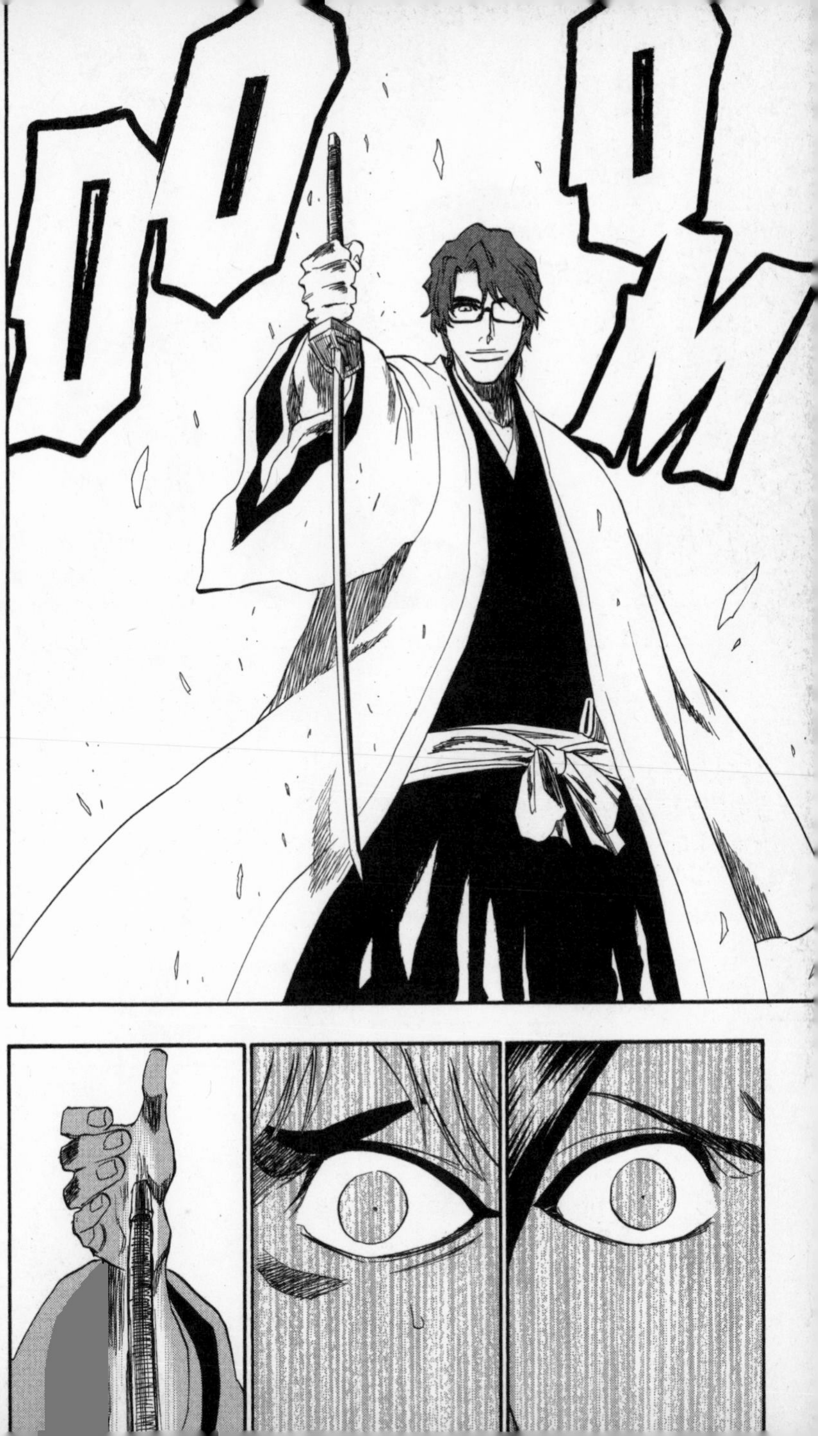
DOOM

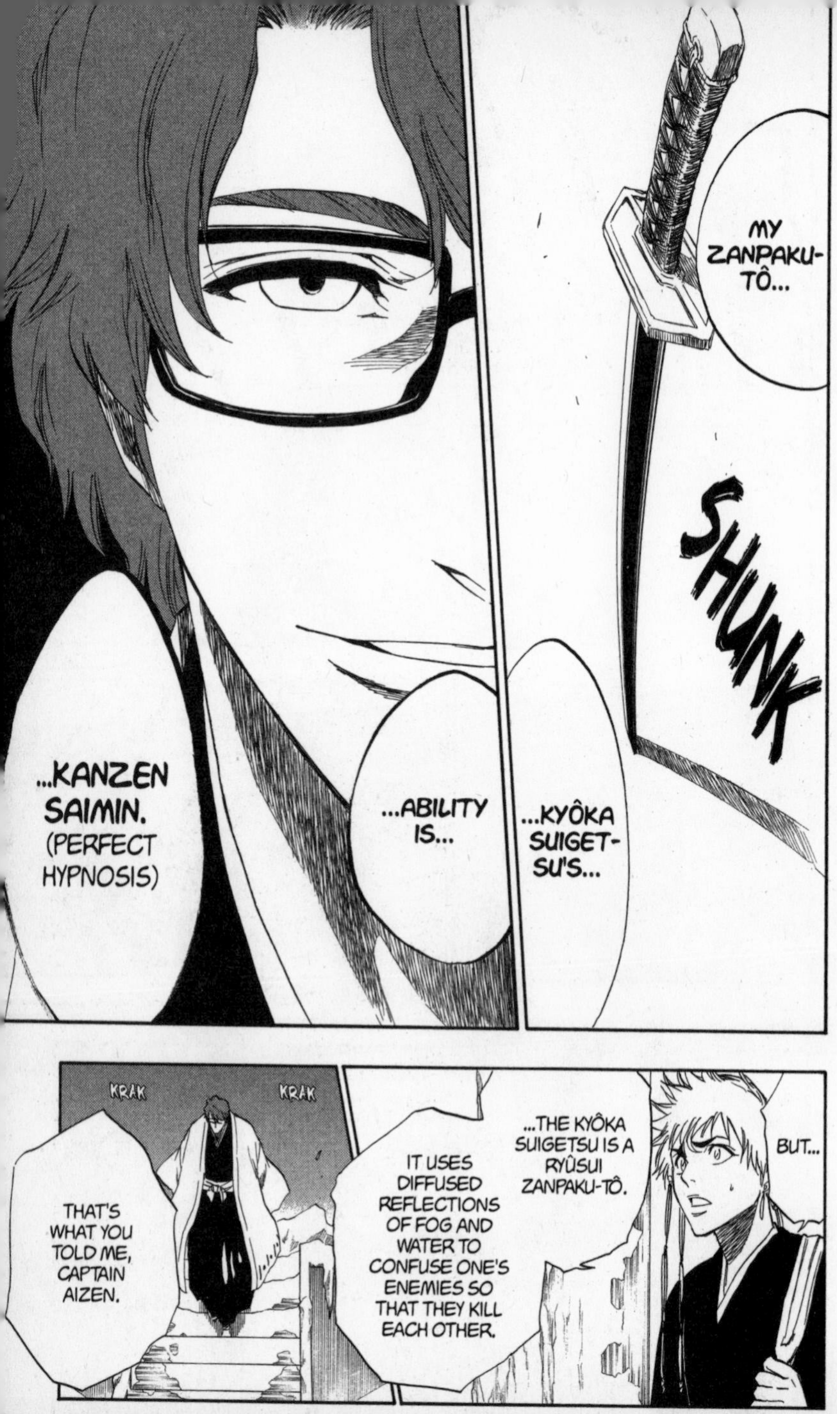
MY ZANPAKU-TÔ...
SHUNK
...KYÔKA SUIGET-SU'S...
...ABILITY IS...
...KANZEN SAIMIN. (PERFECT HYPNOSIS)
BUT...
...THE KYÔKA SUIGETSU IS A RYÛSUI ZANPAKU-TÔ.
IT USES DIFFUSED REFLECTIONS OF FOG AND WATER TO CONFUSE ONE'S ENEMIES SO THAT THEY KILL EACH OTHER.
KRAK
KRAK
THAT'S WHAT YOU TOLD ME, CAPTAIN AIZEN.

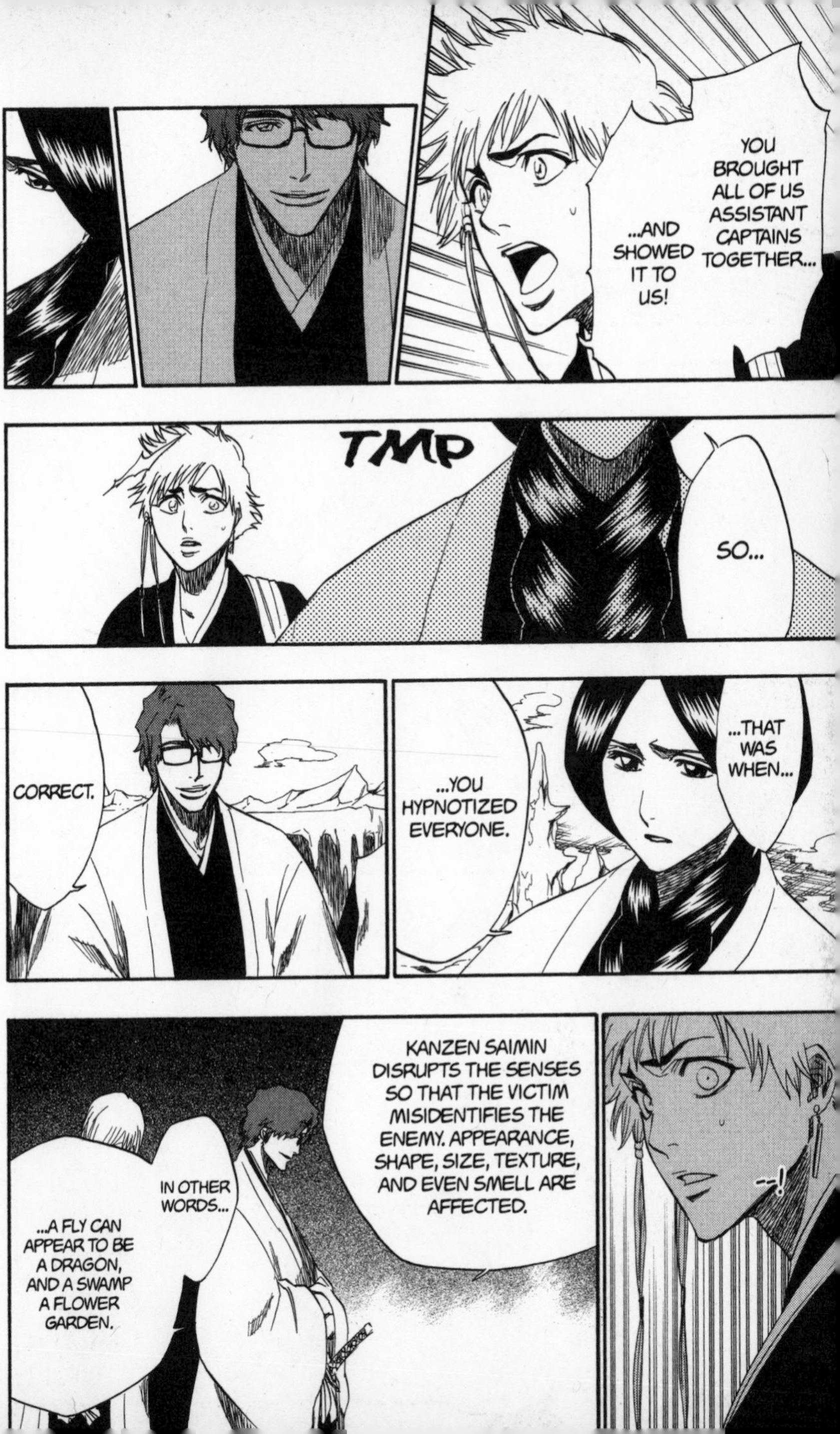
YOU BROUGHT ALL OF US ASSISTANT CAPTAINS TOGETHER...
...AND SHOWED IT TO US!
TMP
SO...
...THAT WAS WHEN...
...YOU HYPNOTIZED EVERYONE.
CORRECT.
--!
KANZEN SAIMIN DISRUPTS THE SENSES SO THAT THE VICTIM MISIDENTIFIES THE ENEMY. APPEARANCE, SHAPE, SIZE, TEXTURE, AND EVEN SMELL ARE AFFECTED.
IN OTHER WORDS...
...A FLY CAN APPEAR TO BE A DRAGON, AND A SWAMP A FLOWER GARDEN.

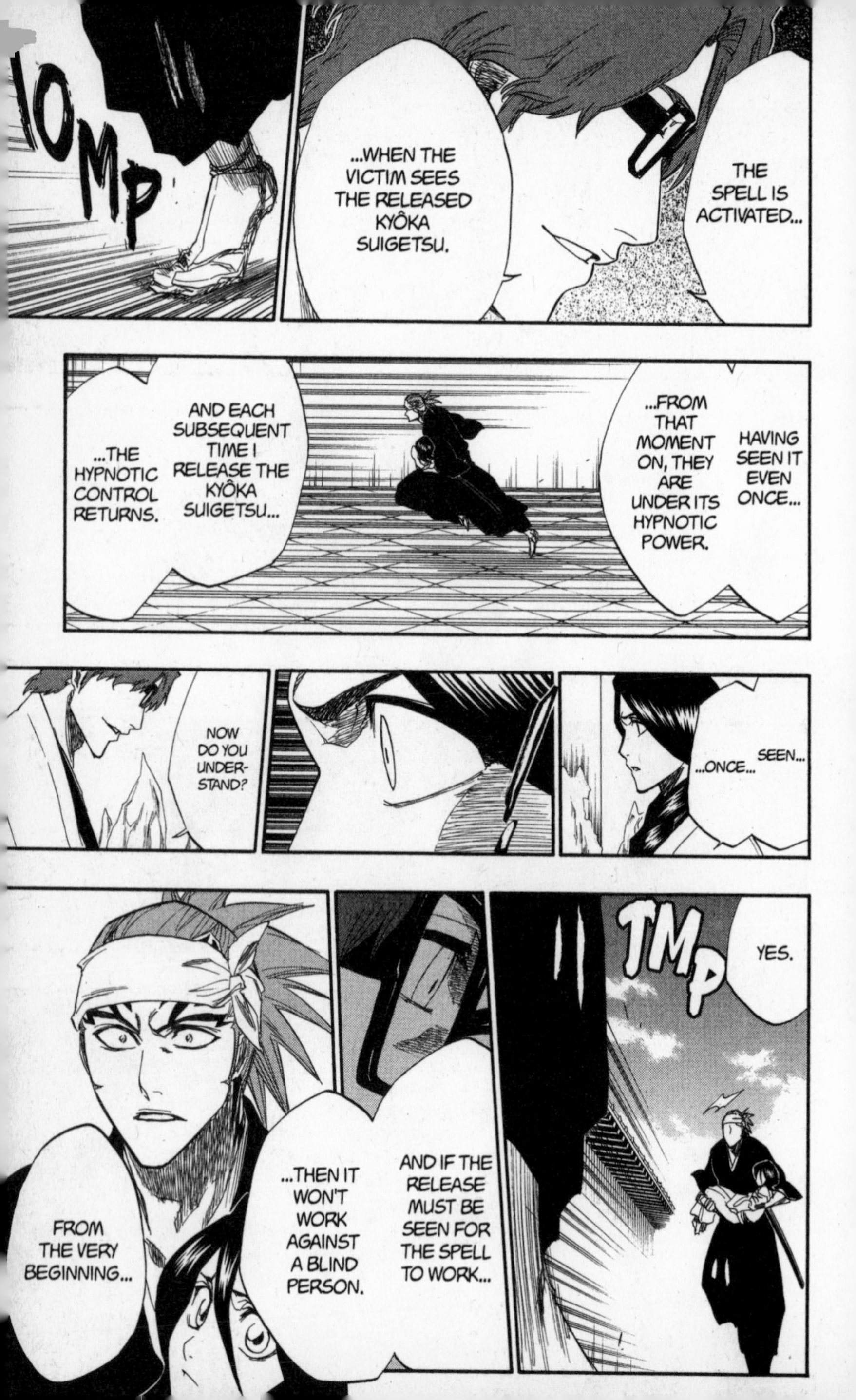

THE SPELL IS ACTIVATED...
...WHEN THE VICTIM SEES THE RELEASED KYÔKA SUIGETSU.
OMP
HAVING SEEN IT EVEN ONCE...
...FROM THAT MOMENT ON, THEY ARE UNDER ITS HYPNOTIC POWER.
AND EACH SUBSEQUENT TIME I RELEASE THE KYÔKA SUIGETSU...
...THE HYPNOTIC CONTROL RETURNS.
SEEN...
...ONCE...
NOW DO YOU UNDERSTAND?
TMP
YES.
AND IF THE RELEASE MUST BE SEEN FOR THE SPELL TO WORK...
...THEN IT WON'T WORK AGAINST A BLIND PERSON.
FROM THE VERY BEGINNING...

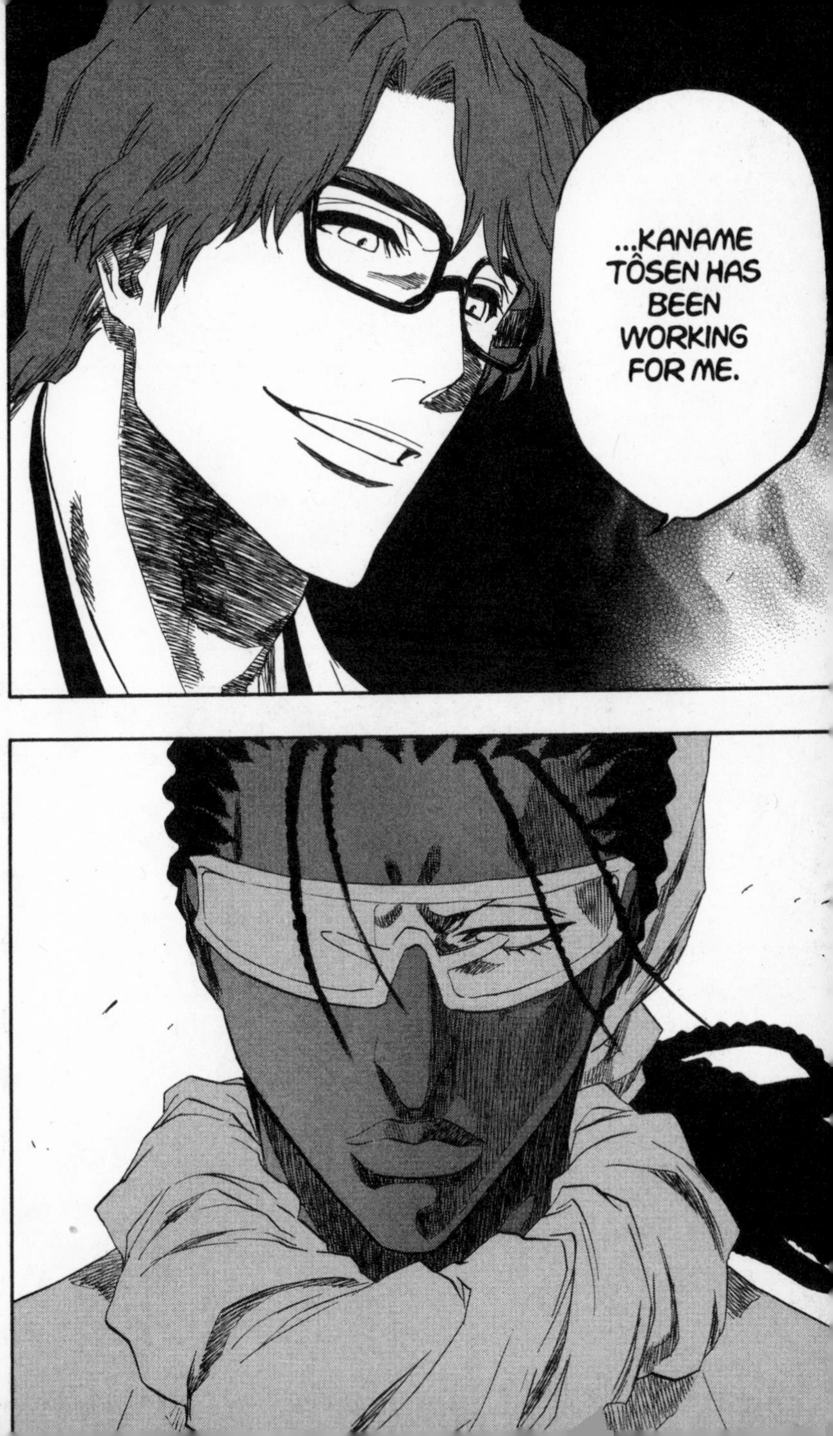
...KANAME TÔSEN HAS BEEN WORKING FOR ME.

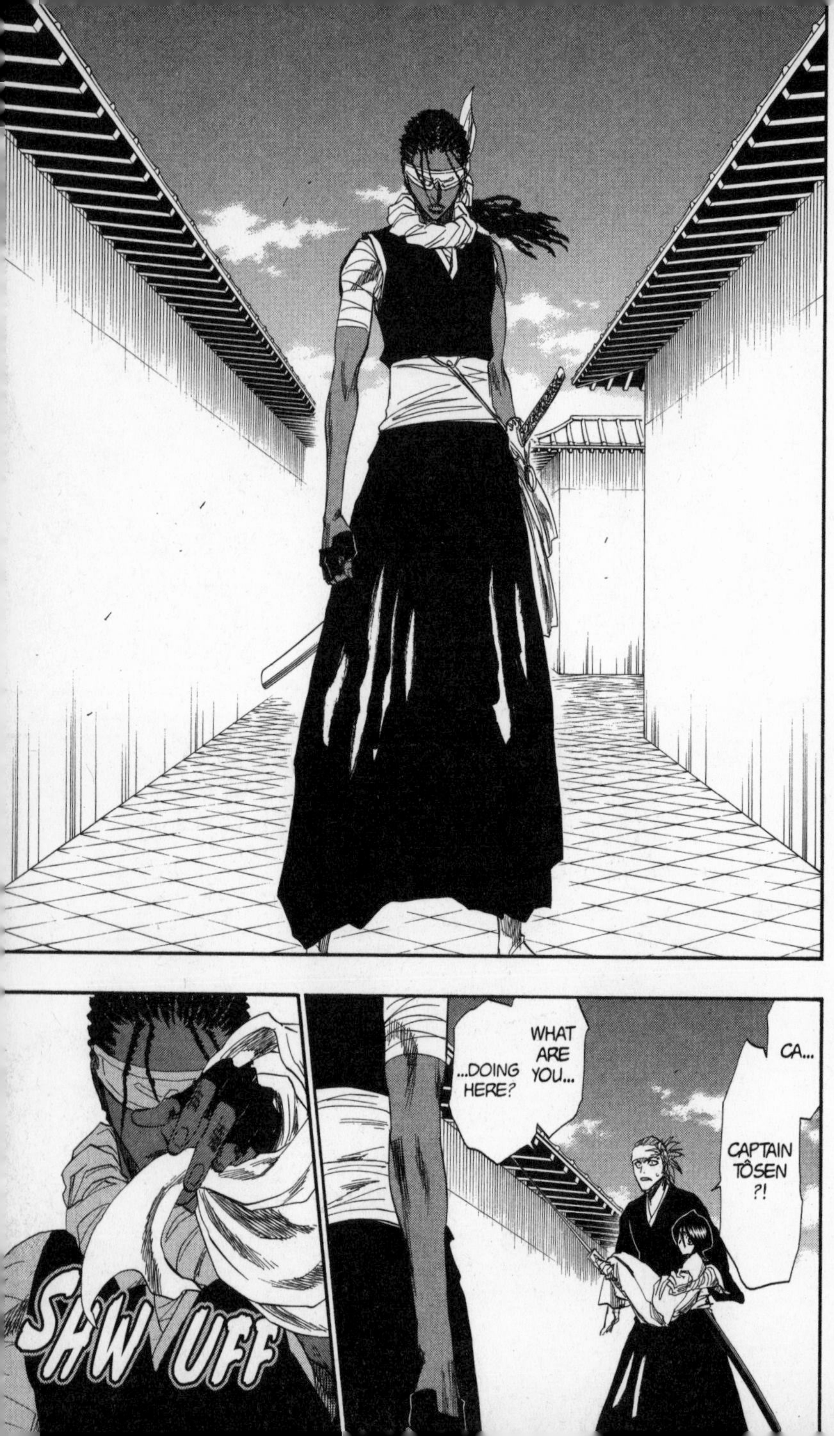
CA...
CAPTAIN TÔSEN ?!
WHAT ARE YOU...
...DOING HERE?
SHW UFF

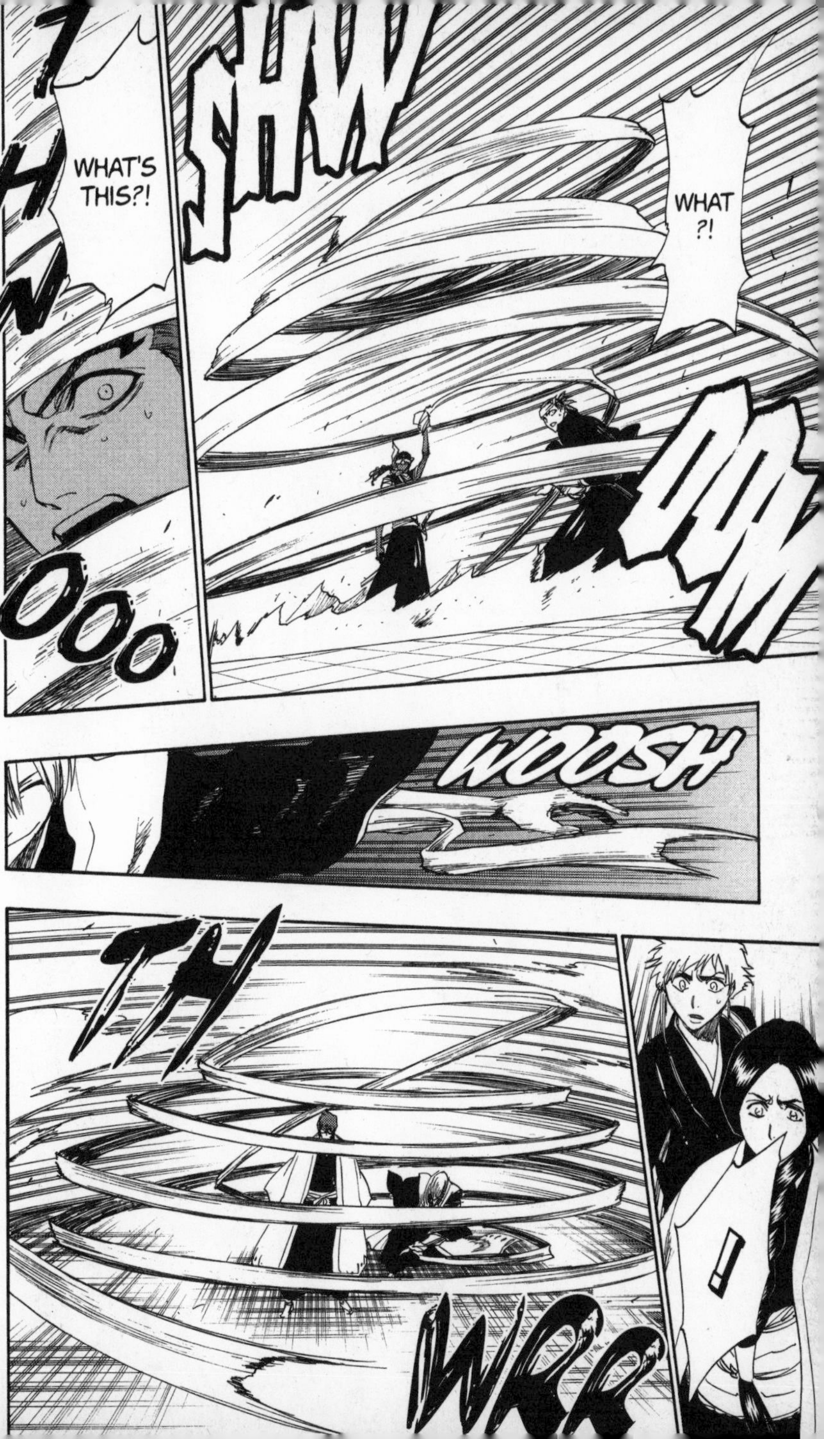

WHAT ?!
SHW
OOM
WHAT'S THIS?!
THW
OOO
WOOSH
!
WRR
TH

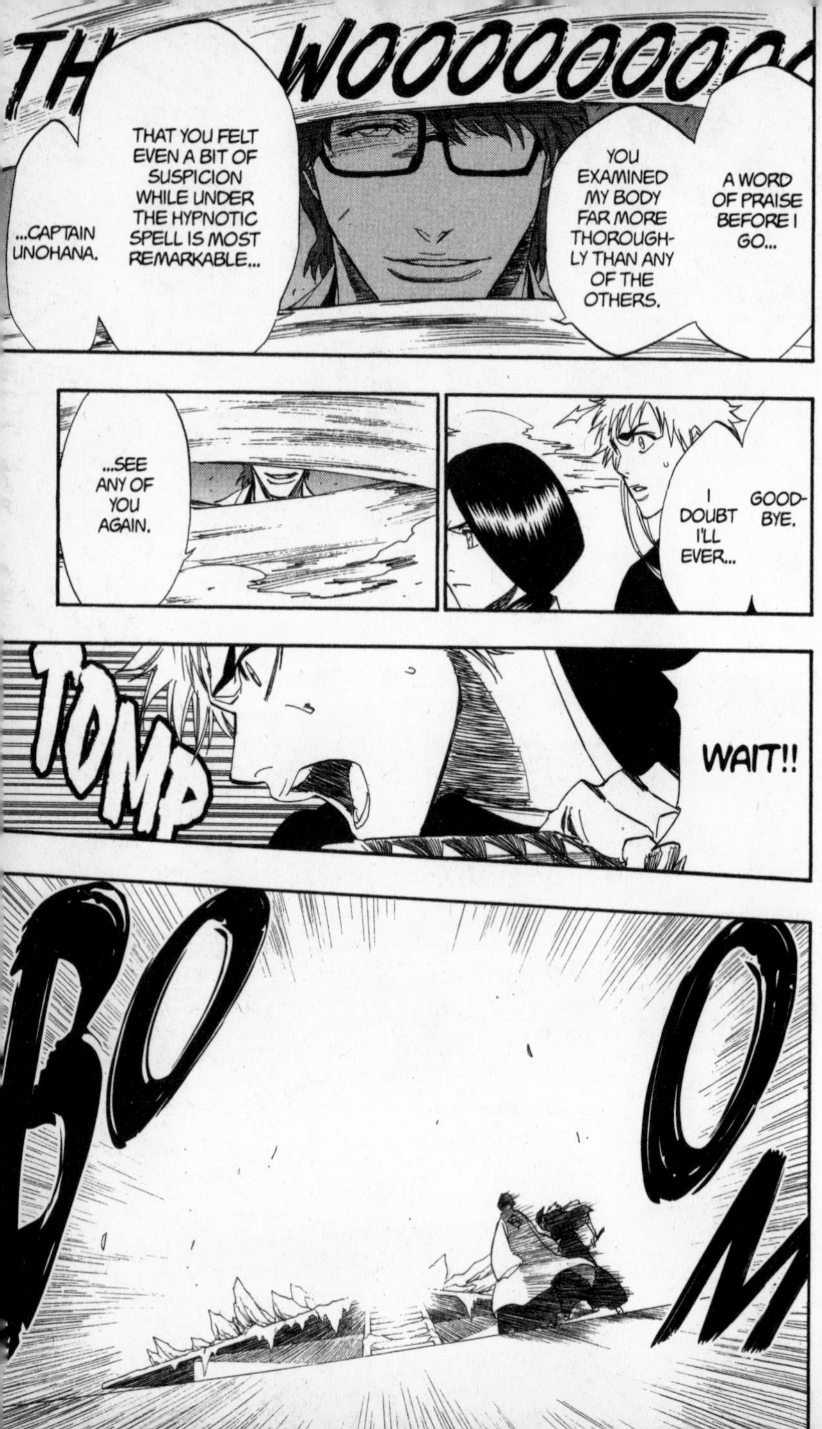
THWOOOOOOOO
A WORD OF PRAISE BEFORE I GO...
YOU EXAMINED MY BODY FAR MORE THOROUGH-LY THAN ANY OF THE OTHERS.
THAT YOU FELT EVEN A BIT OF SUSPICION WHILE UNDER THE HYPNOTIC SPELL IS MOST REMARKABLE...
...CAPTAIN UNOHANA.
GOOD-BYE.
I DOUBT I'LL EVER...
...SEE ANY OF YOU AGAIN.
WAIT!!
TOMP
BOOOM

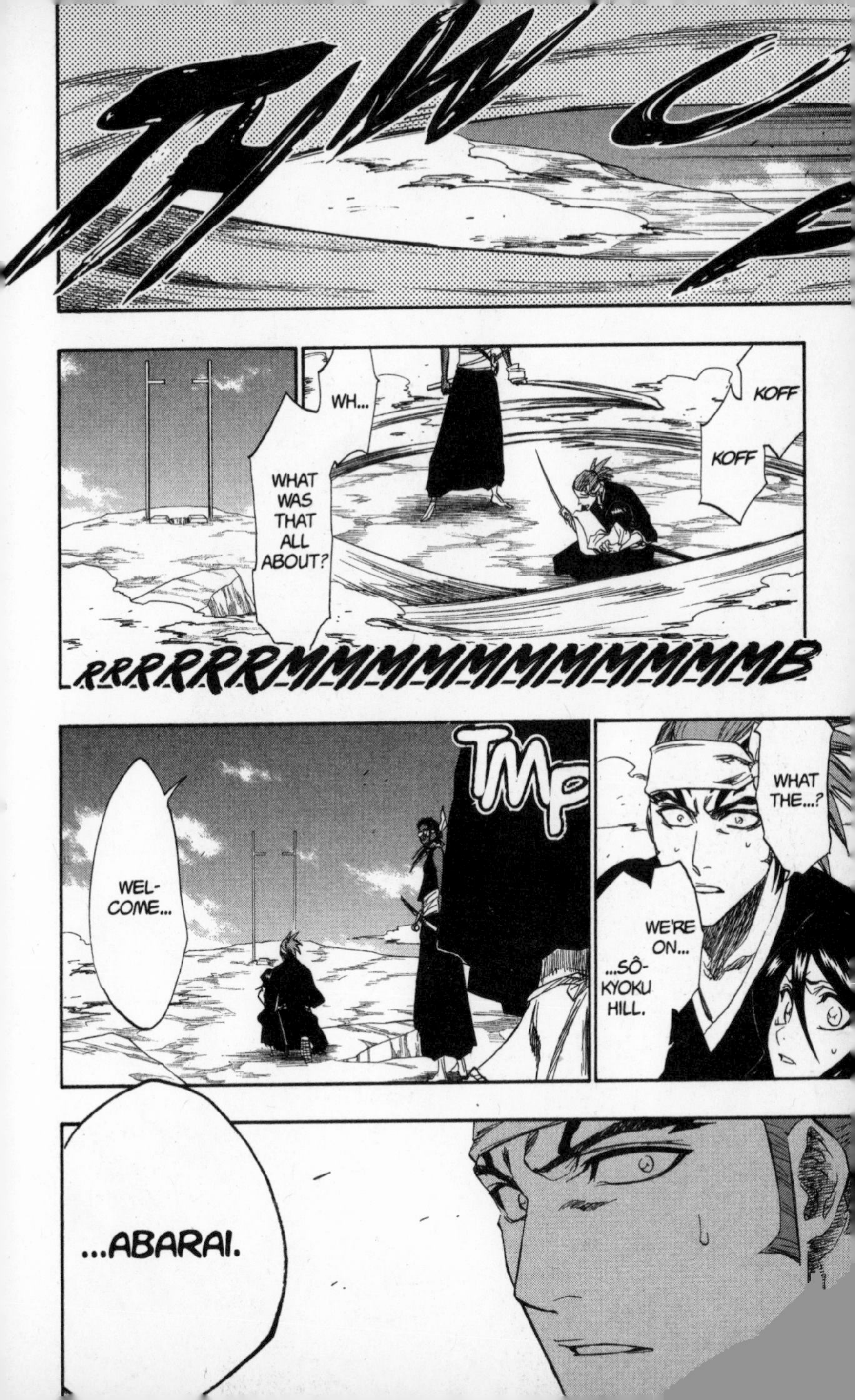
THWUP
KOFF
KOFF
WH...
WHAT WAS THAT ALL ABOUT?
RRRRRRMMMMMMMMMMMMMB
WHAT THE...?
WE'RE ON...
...SÔ-KYOKU HILL.
TMP
WEL-COME...
...ABARAI.

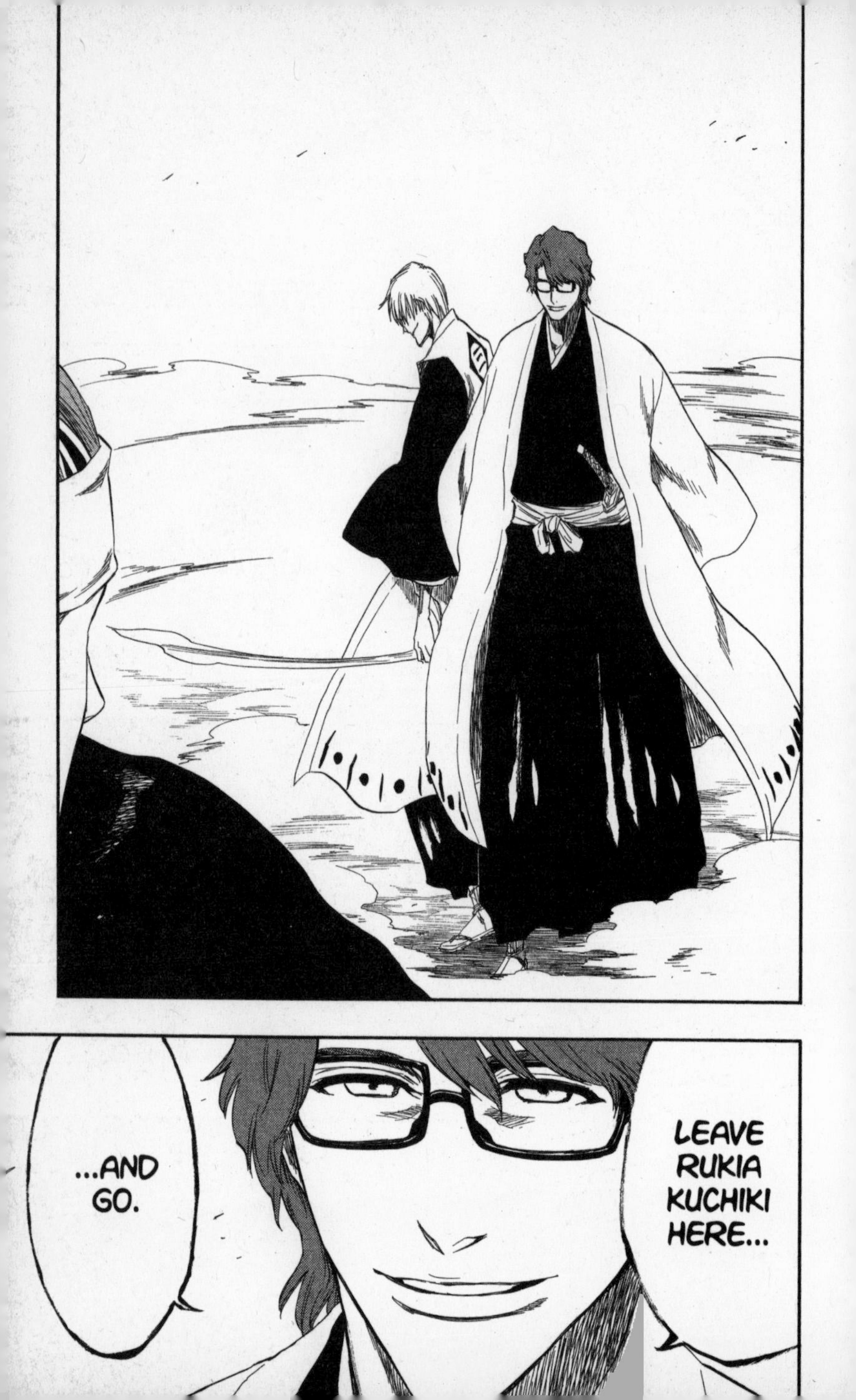
LEAVE RUKIA KUCHIKI HERE...
...AND GO.

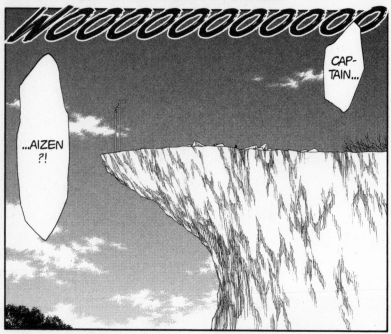

WOOOOOOOOOOOOOOOO

CAP-TAIN...

...AIZEN ?!

WOOOOOOOOOOOOOOOO

FORGET THAT.

WHAT DID YOU JUST ...?!

NO.

I THOUGHT YOU WERE...

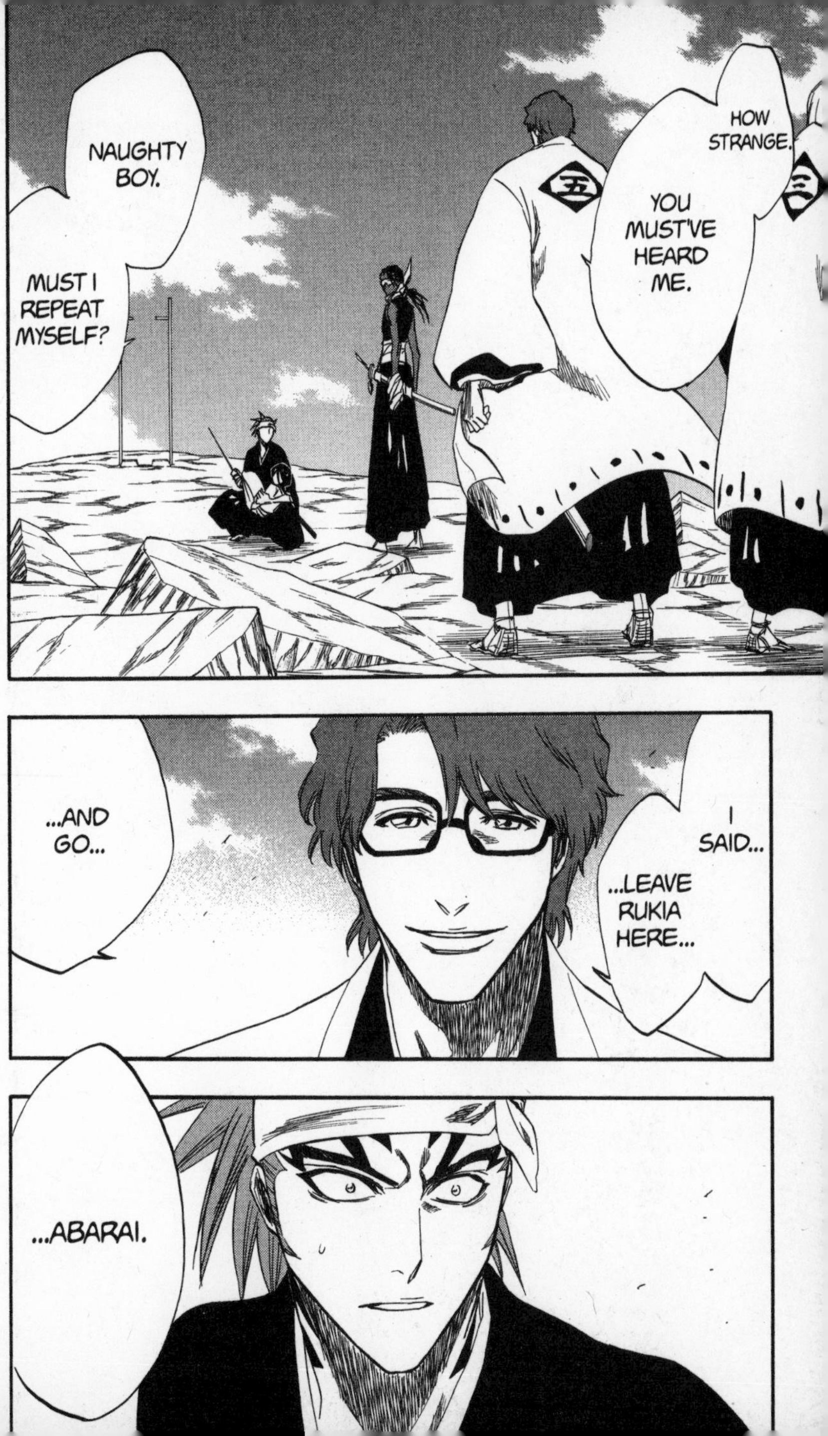
HOW STRANGE.
YOU MUST'VE HEARD ME.
NAUGHTY BOY.
MUST I REPEAT MYSELF?
I SAID...
...LEAVE RUKIA HERE...
...AND GO...
...ABARAI.

172. end of hypnosis4 (Prisoners in Paradise)

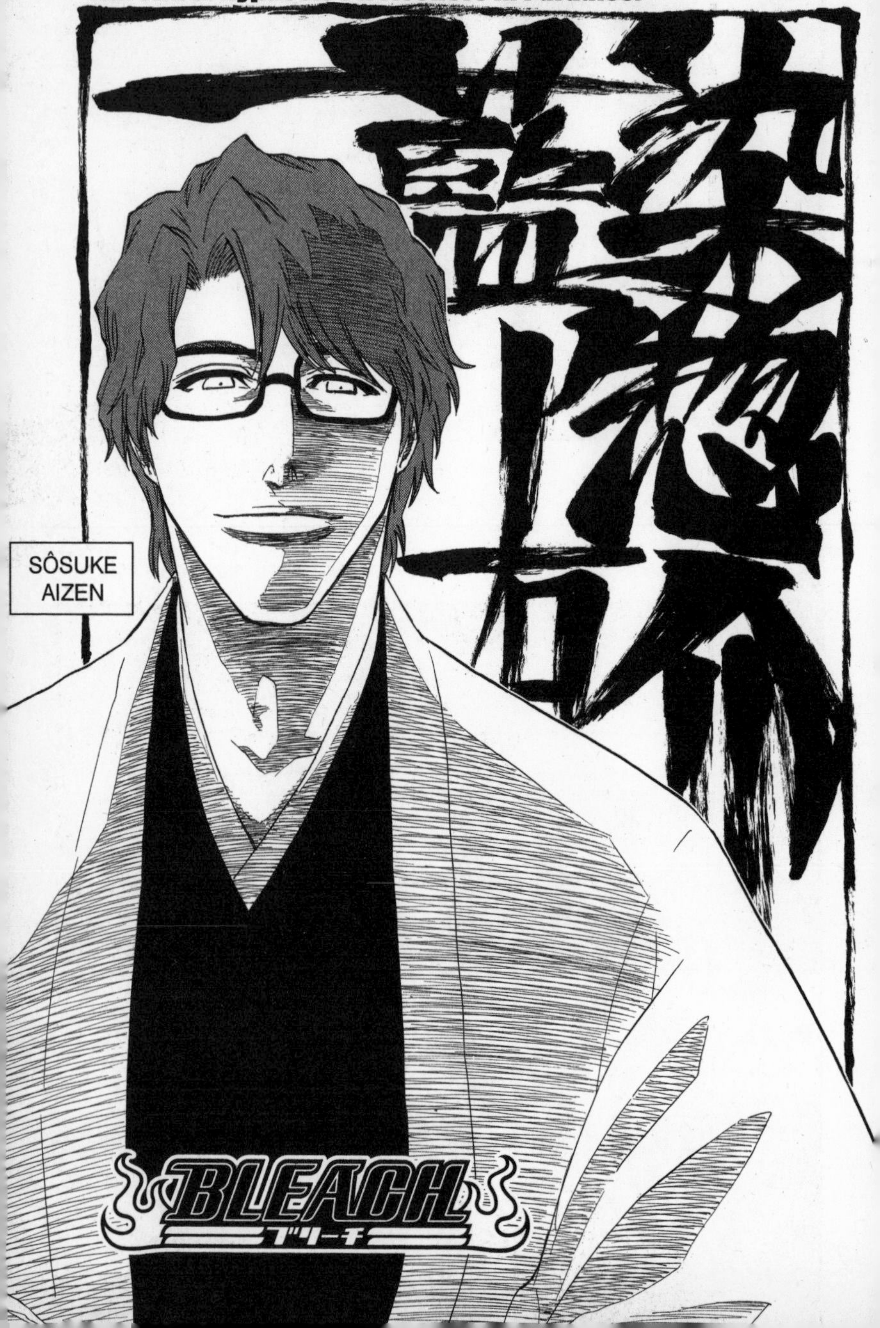
SÔSUKE AIZEN
BLEACH
ブリーチ

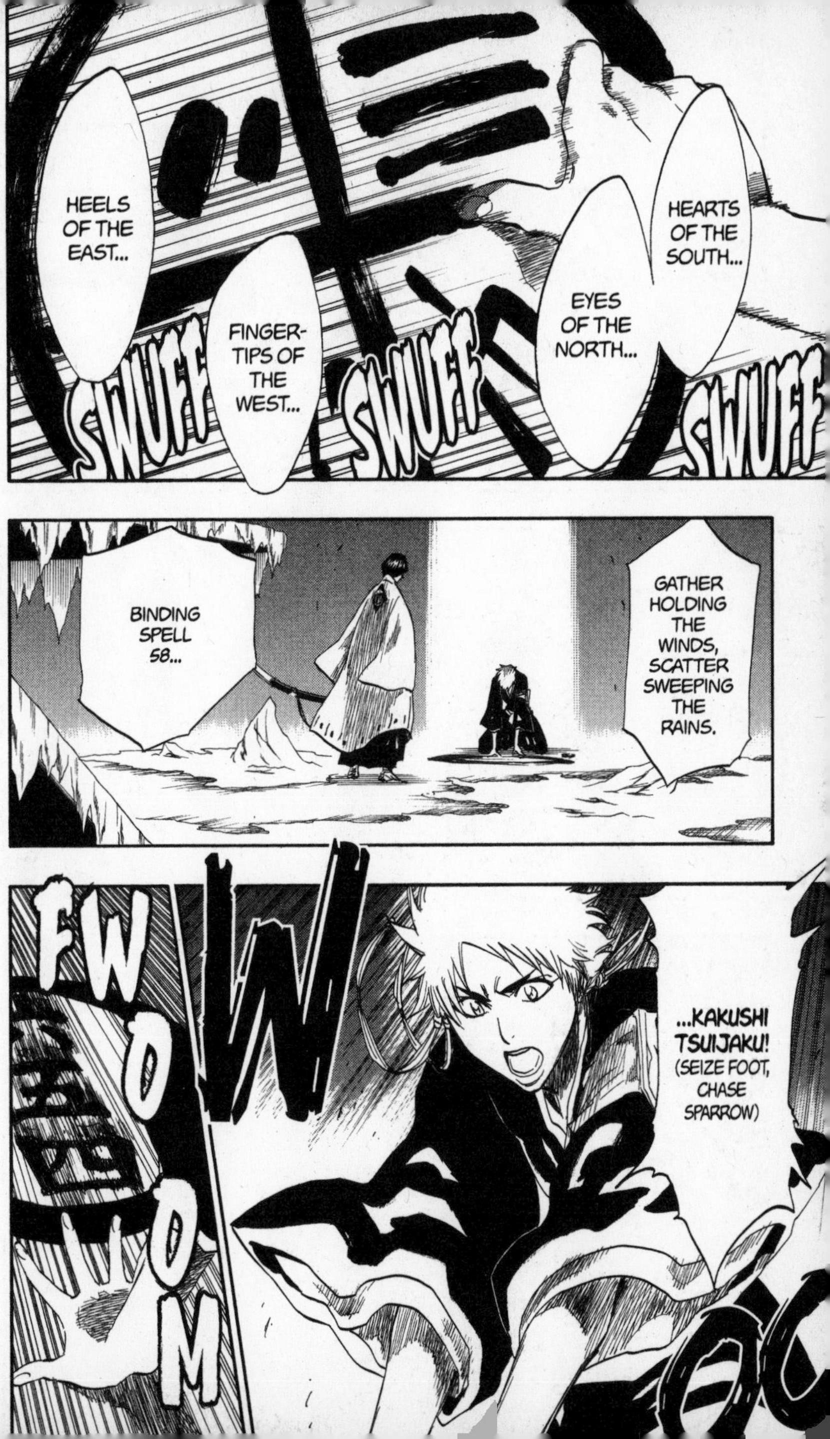
HEARTS OF THE SOUTH...
SWUFF
EYES OF THE NORTH...
SWUFF
FINGER-TIPS OF THE WEST...
HEELS OF THE EAST...
SWUFF
GATHER HOLDING THE WINDS, SCATTER SWEEPING THE RAINS.
BINDING SPELL 58...
...KAKUSHI TSUIJAKU! (SEIZE FOOT, CHASE SPARROW)
FWOOOM

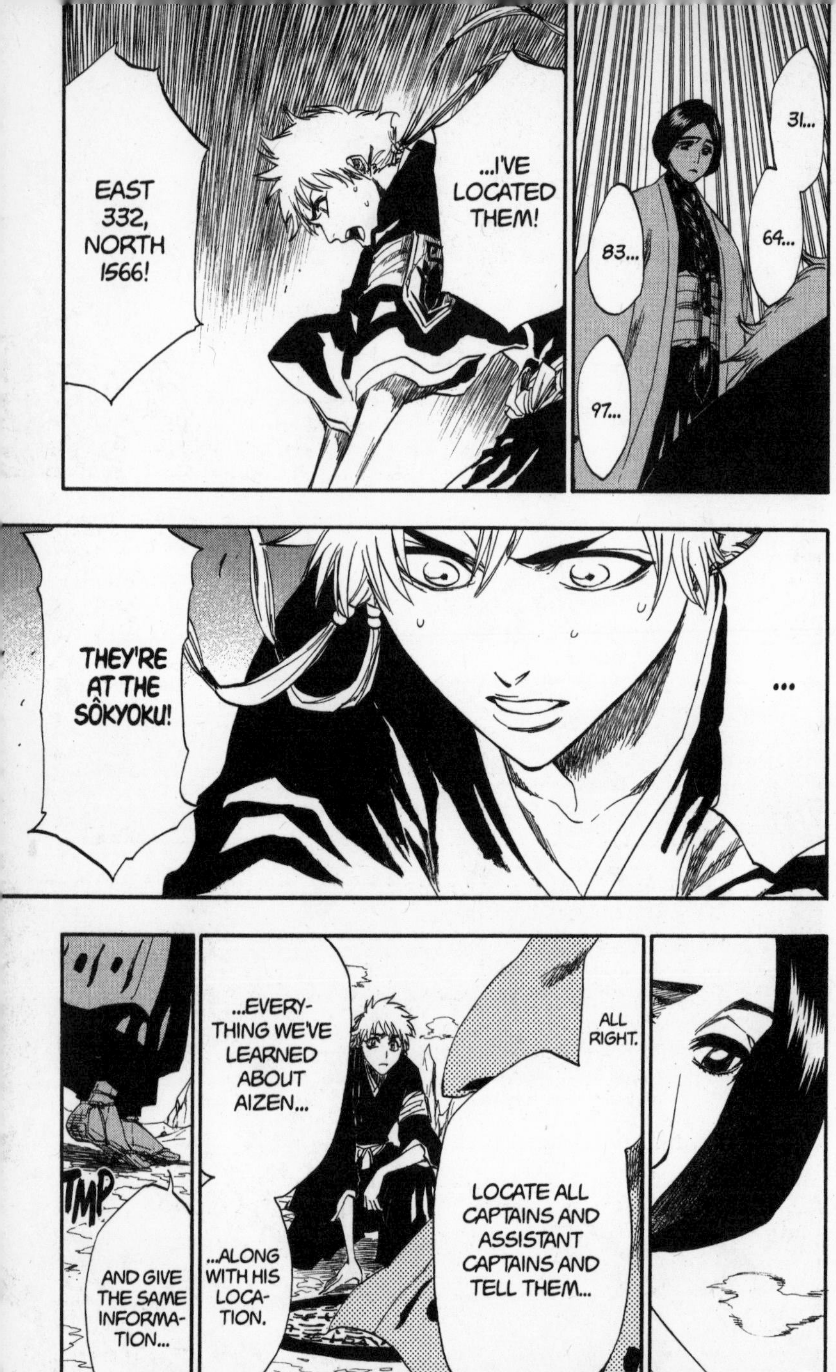
31...
64...
83...
97...
...I'VE LOCATED THEM!
EAST 332, NORTH 1566!
...
THEY'RE AT THE SÔKYOKU!
ALL RIGHT.
LOCATE ALL CAPTAINS AND ASSISTANT CAPTAINS AND TELL THEM...
...EVERY-THING WE'VE LEARNED ABOUT AIZEN...
...ALONG WITH HIS LOCA-TION.
TMP
AND GIVE THE SAME INFORMA-TION...

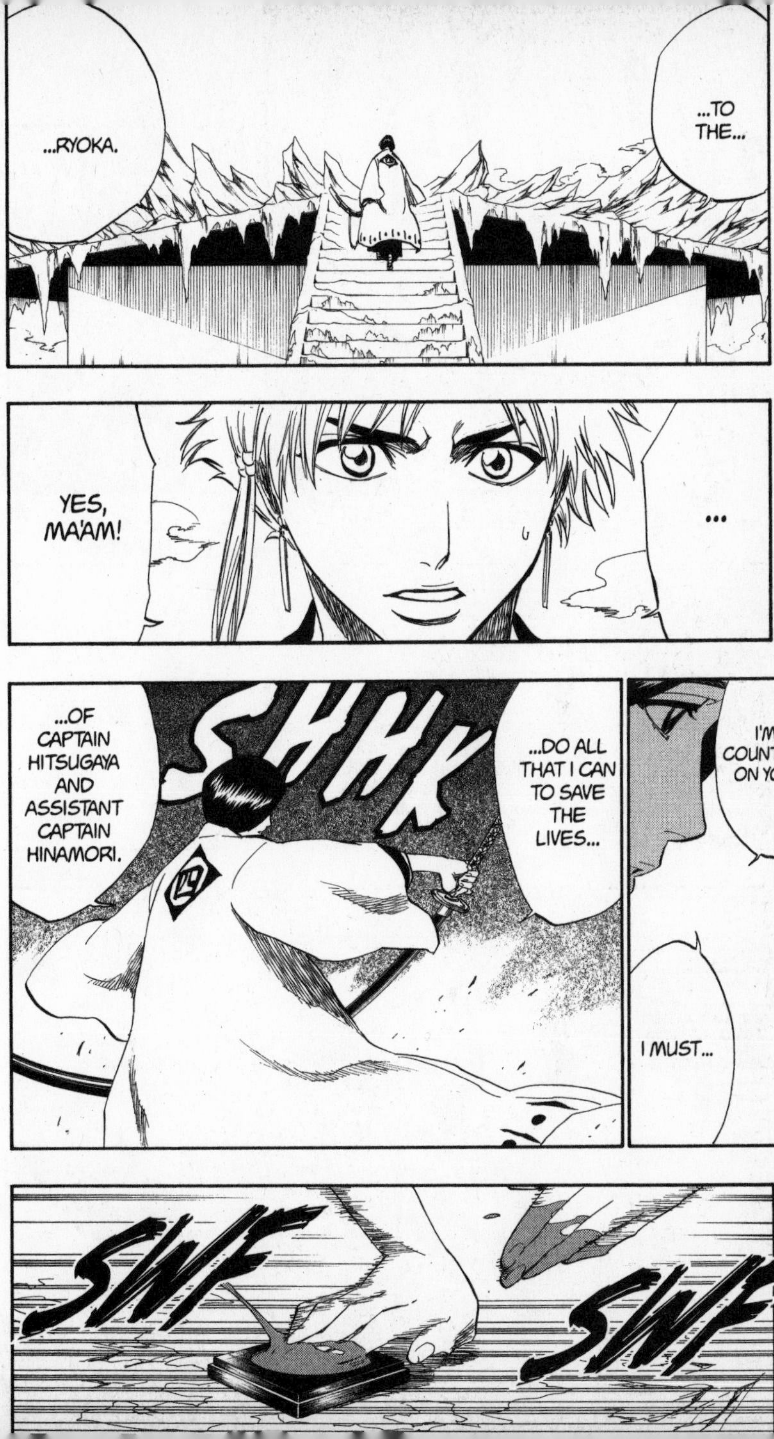

...TO THE...
...RYOKA.
...
YES, MA'AM!
I'M COUNTING ON YOU.
I MUST...
SHHK
...DO ALL THAT I CAN TO SAVE THE LIVES...
...OF CAPTAIN HITSUGAYA AND ASSISTANT CAPTAIN HINAMORI.
SWF
SWF

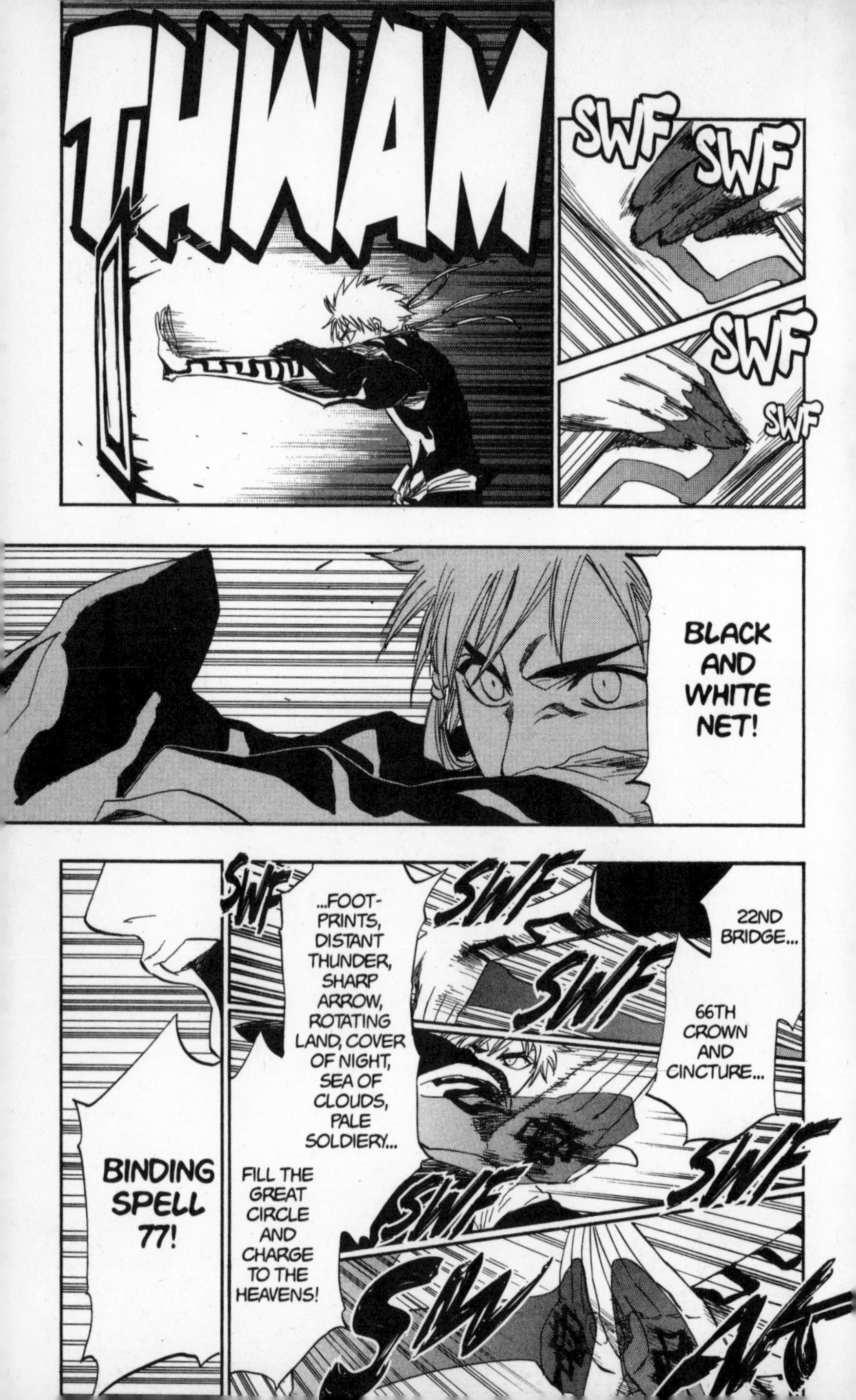
SWF
SWF
SWF
SWF
THWAM
BLACK AND WHITE NET!
22ND BRIDGE...
66TH CROWN AND CINCTURE...
SWF
SWF
SWF
SWF
SW
...FOOT-PRINTS, DISTANT THUNDER, SHARP ARROW, ROTATING LAND, COVER OF NIGHT, SEA OF CLOUDS, PALE SOLDIERY...
FILL THE GREAT CIRCLE AND CHARGE TO THE HEAVENS!
SWF
BINDING SPELL 77!

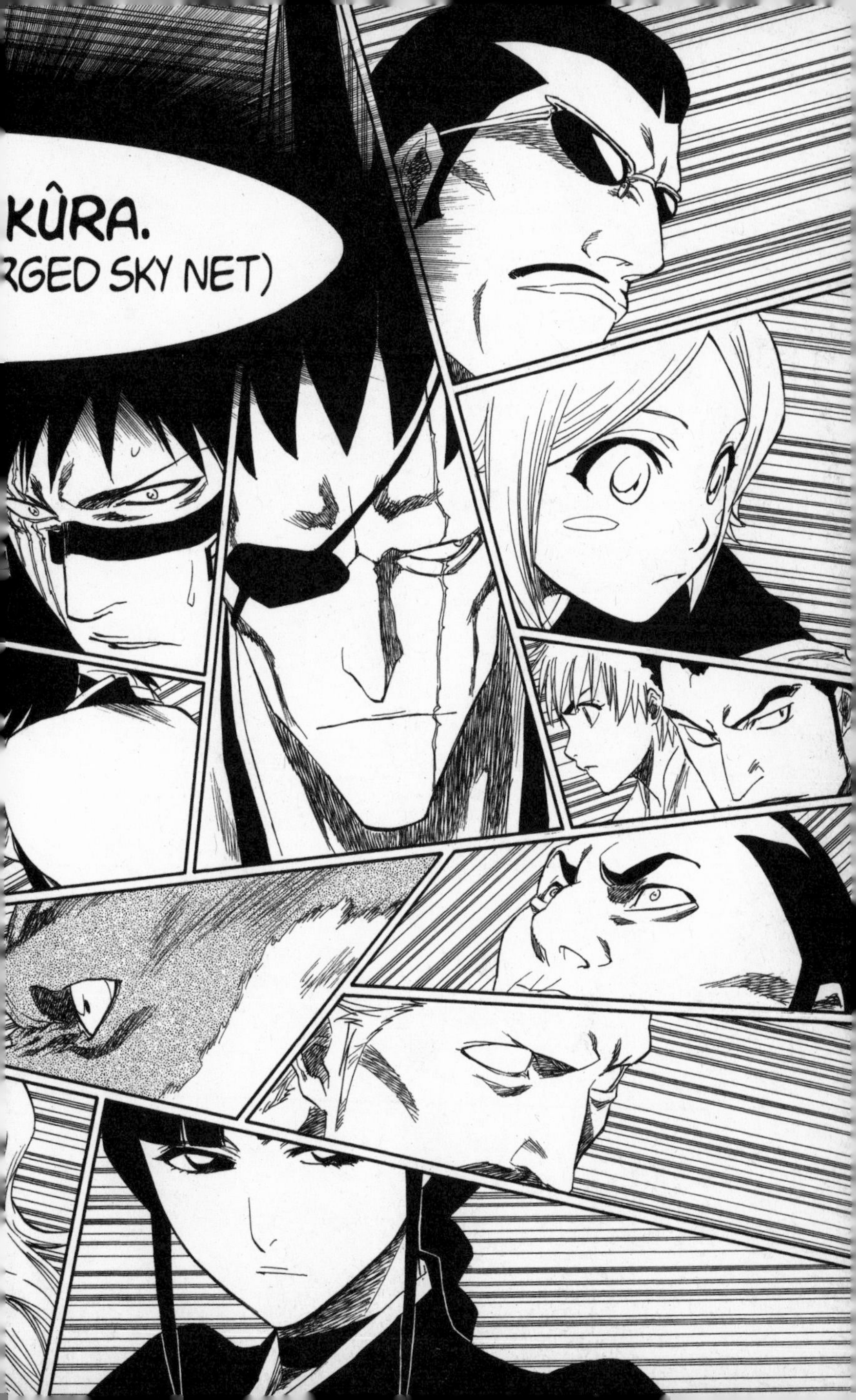
KÛRA.
RGED SKY NET)

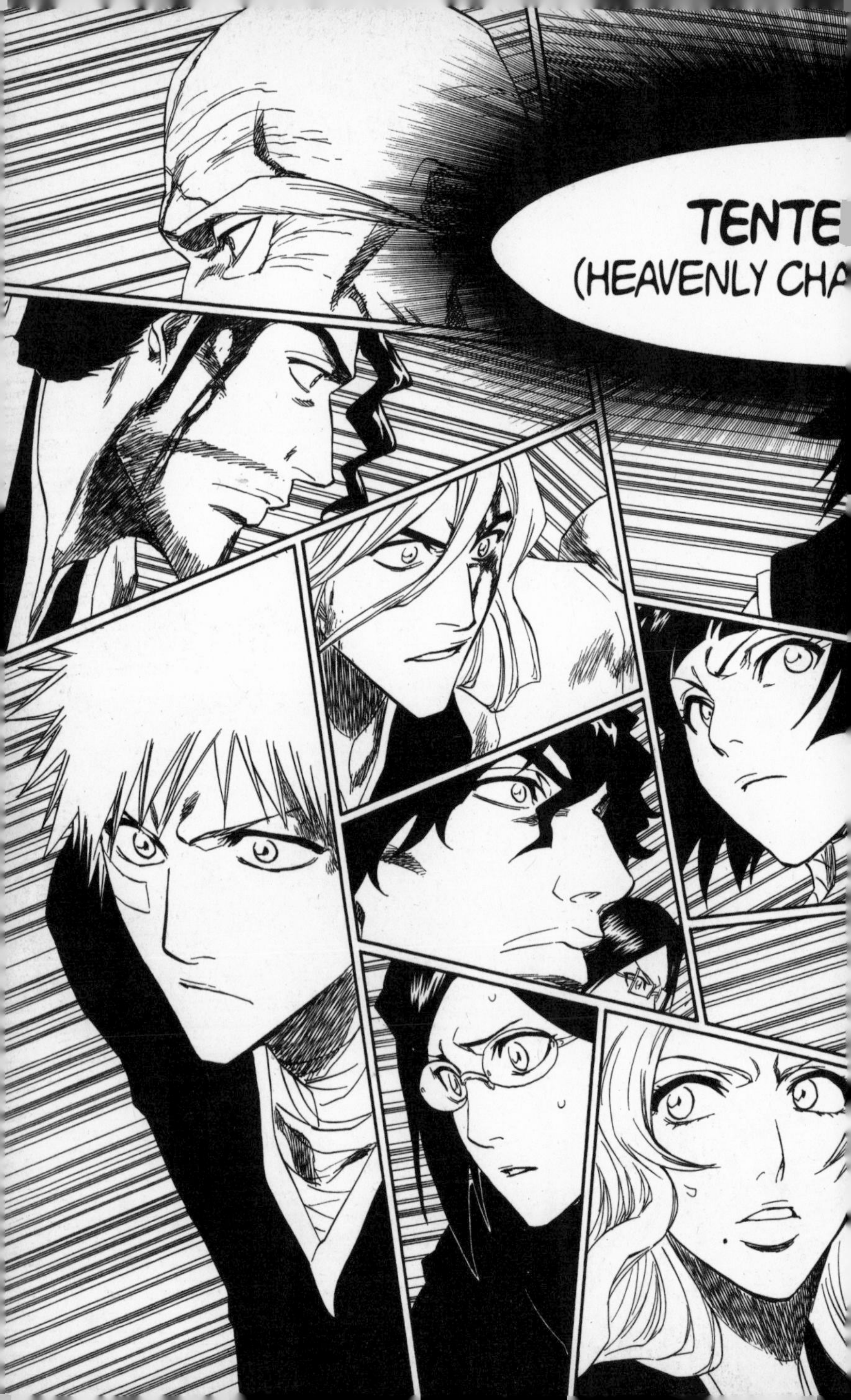
TENTE
(HEAVENLY CHA

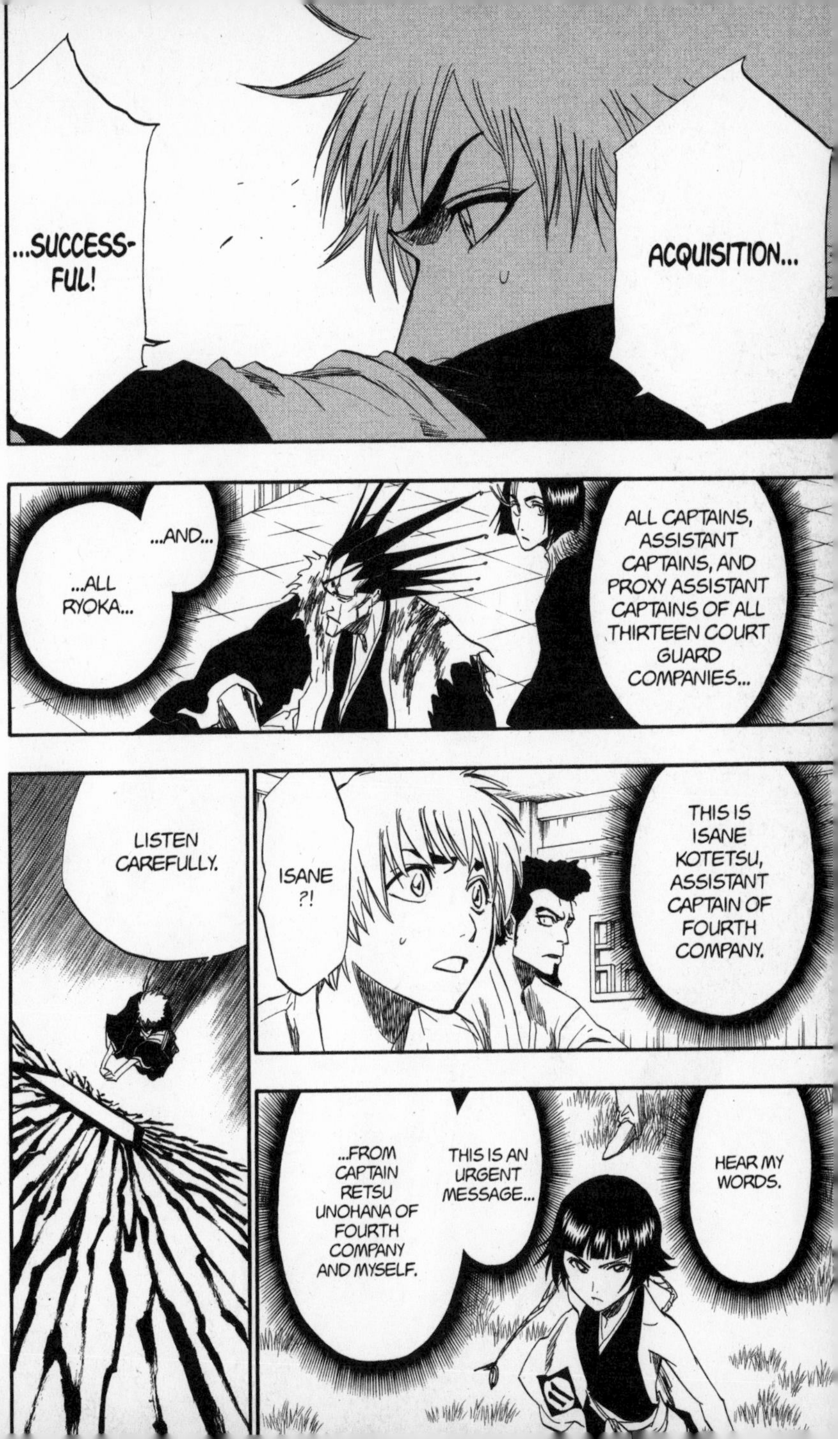
ACQUISITION...
...SUCCESSFUL!
ALL CAPTAINS, ASSISTANT CAPTAINS, AND PROXY ASSISTANT CAPTAINS OF ALL THIRTEEN COURT GUARD COMPANIES...
...AND...
...ALL RYOKA...
THIS IS ISANE KOTETSU, ASSISTANT CAPTAIN OF FOURTH COMPANY.
ISANE ?!
HEAR MY WORDS.
THIS IS AN URGENT MESSAGE...
...FROM CAPTAIN RETSU UNOHANA OF FOURTH COMPANY AND MYSELF.
LISTEN CAREFULLY.

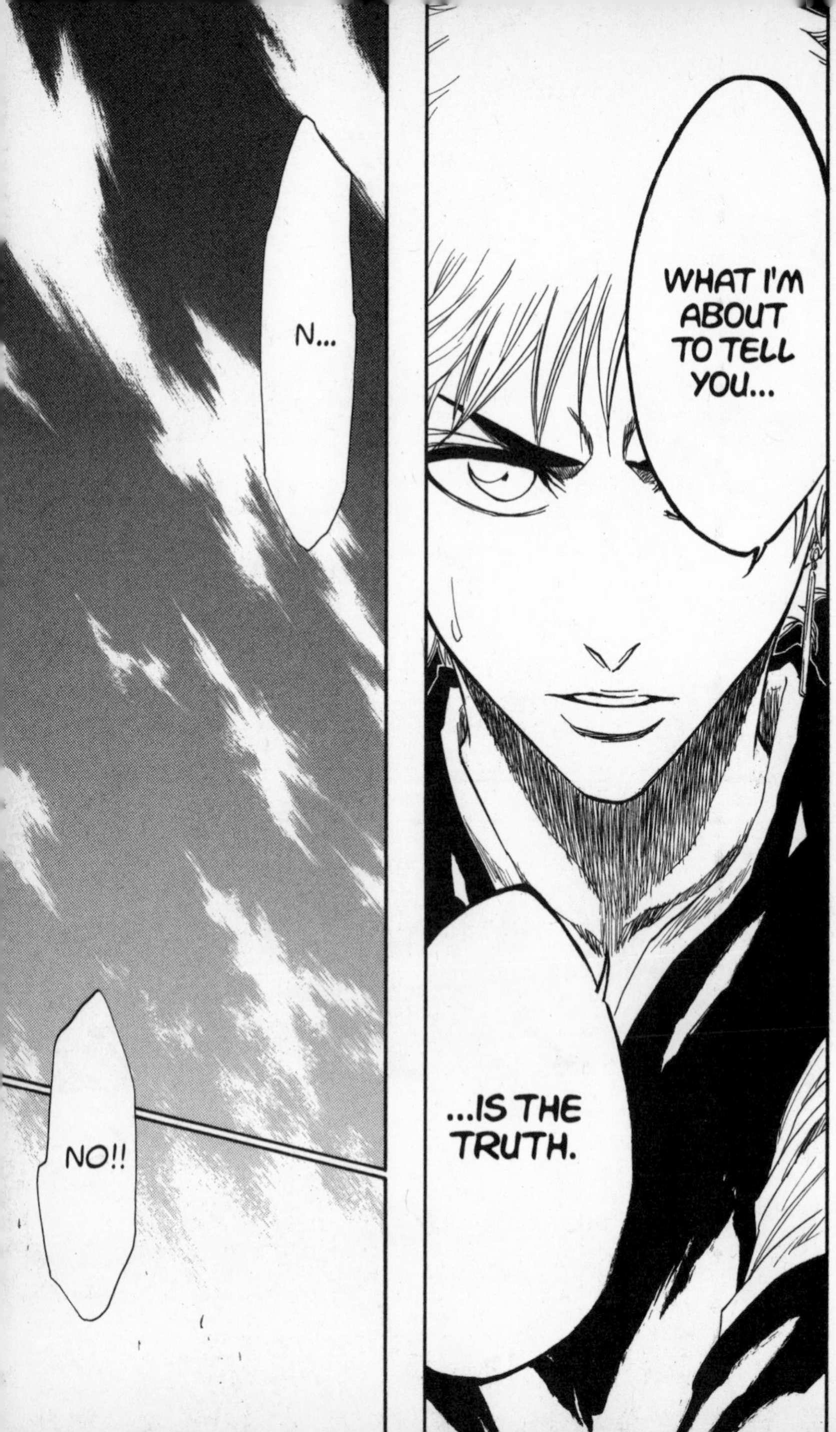
WHAT I'M ABOUT TO TELL YOU...
...IS THE TRUTH.
N...
NO!!

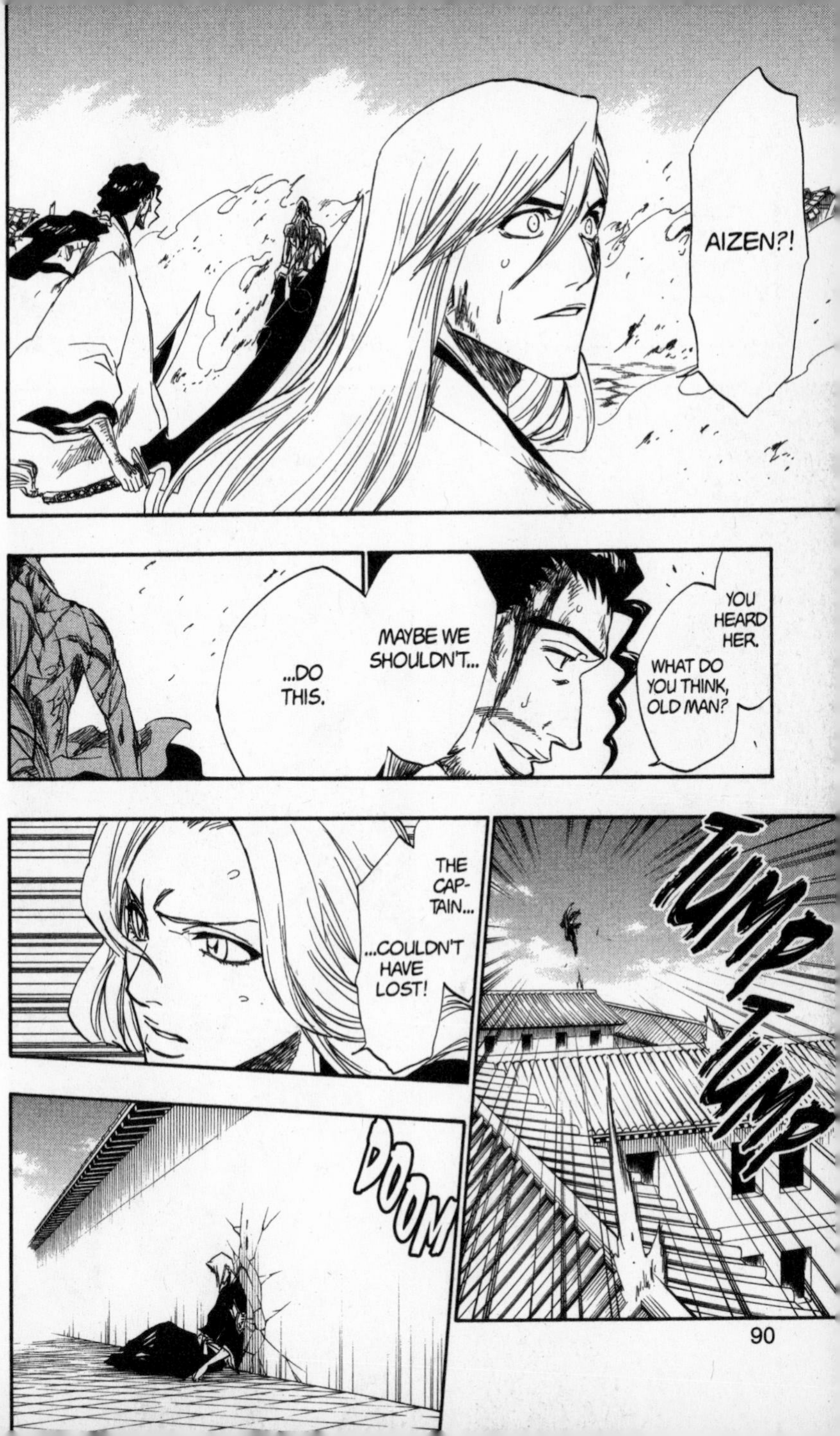
AIZEN?!
YOU HEARD HER.
WHAT DO YOU THINK, OLD MAN?
MAYBE WE SHOULDN'T...
...DO THIS.
TUMP TUMP
THE CAP-TAIN...
...COULDN'T HAVE LOST!
DOOM

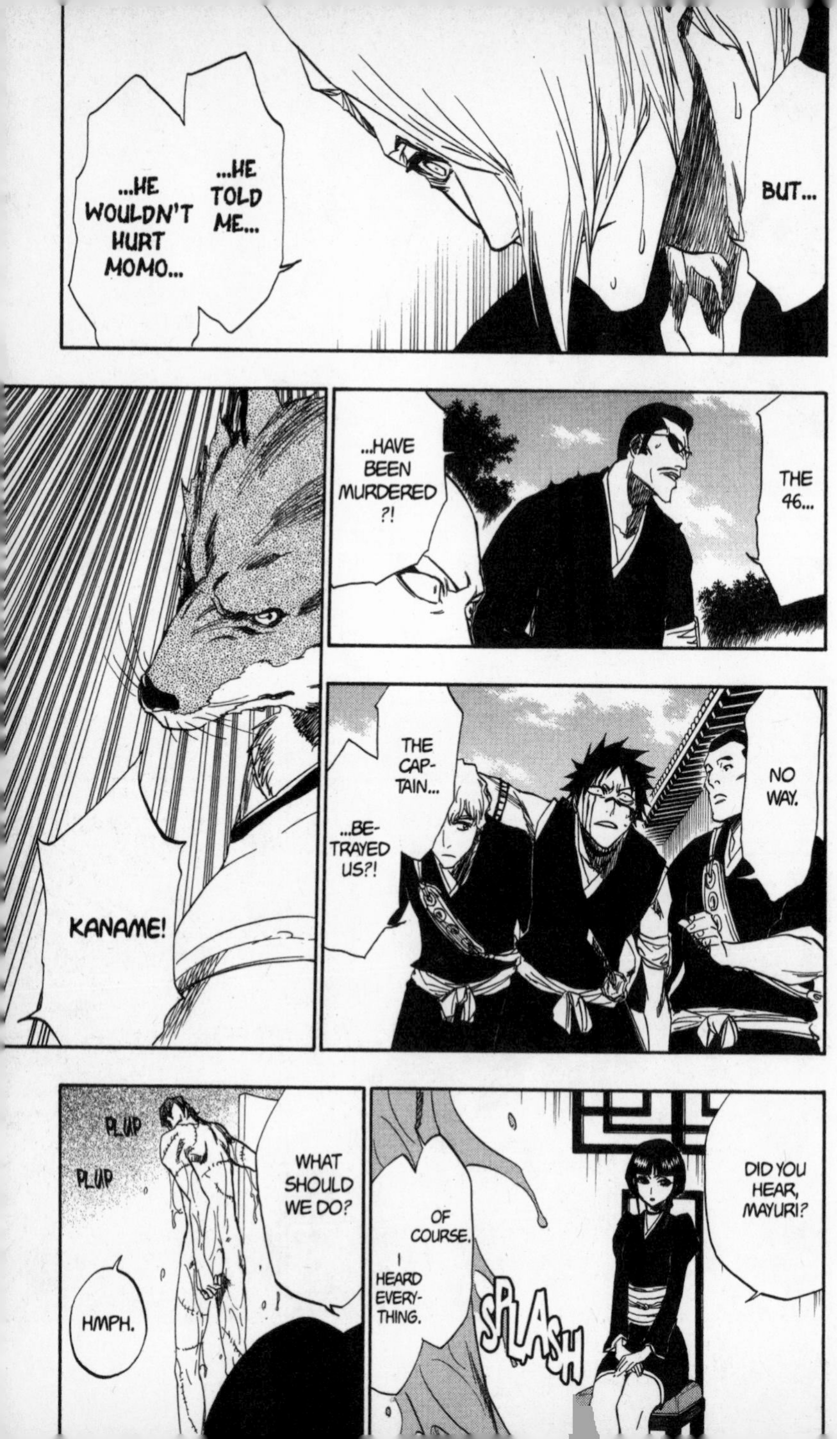
BUT...
...HE TOLD ME...
...HE WOULDN'T HURT MOMO...
THE 46...
...HAVE BEEN MURDERED?!
NO WAY.
THE CAPTAIN...
...BETRAYED US?!
KANAME!
DID YOU HEAR, MAYURI?
OF COURSE.
I HEARD EVERYTHING.
SPLASH
WHAT SHOULD WE DO?
PLUP
PLUP
HMPH.

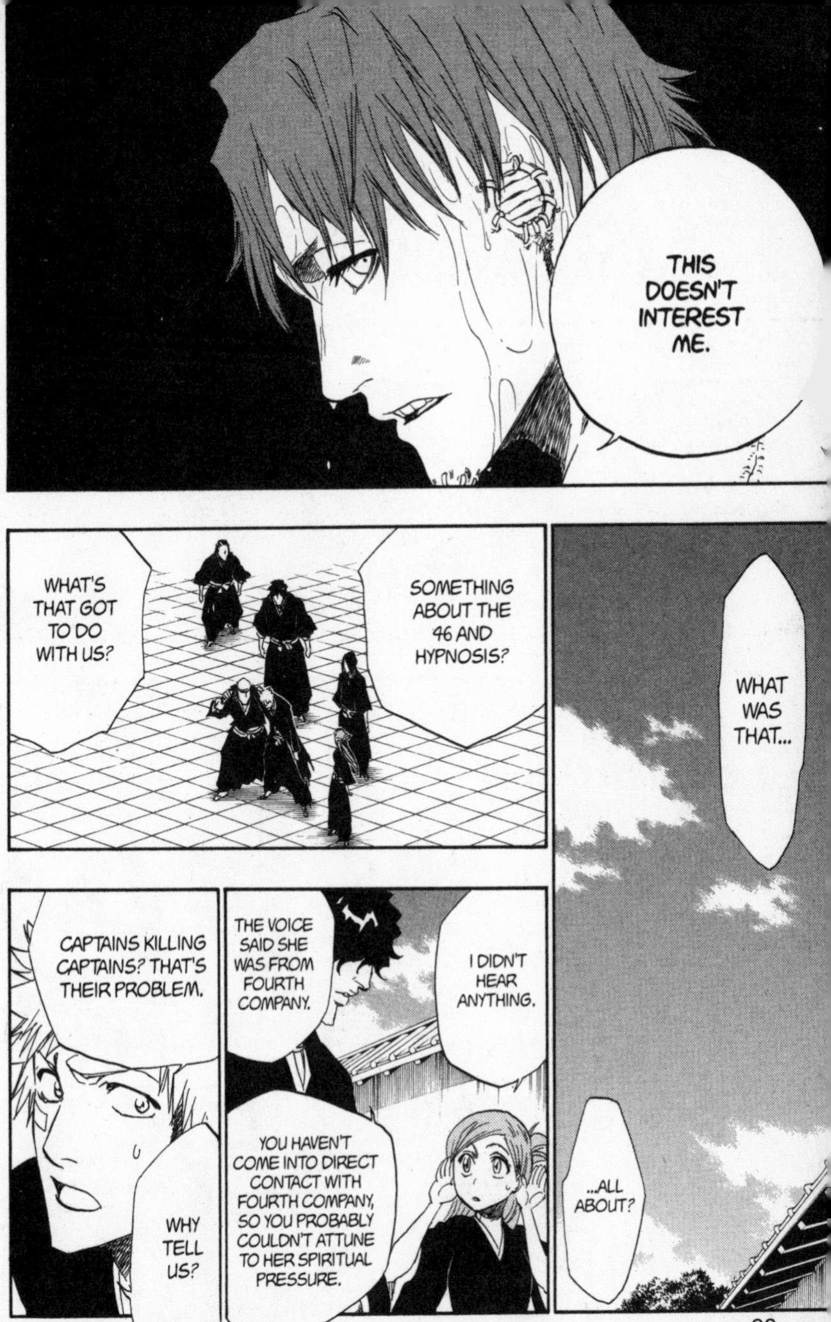
THIS DOESN'T INTEREST ME.
WHAT WAS THAT...
...ALL ABOUT?
SOMETHING ABOUT THE 46 AND HYPNOSIS?
WHAT'S THAT GOT TO DO WITH US?
I DIDN'T HEAR ANYTHING.
THE VOICE SAID SHE WAS FROM FOURTH COMPANY.
YOU HAVEN'T COME INTO DIRECT CONTACT WITH FOURTH COMPANY, SO YOU PROBABLY COULDN'T ATTUNE TO HER SPIRITUAL PRESSURE.
CAPTAINS KILLING CAPTAINS? THAT'S THEIR PROBLEM.
WHY TELL US?

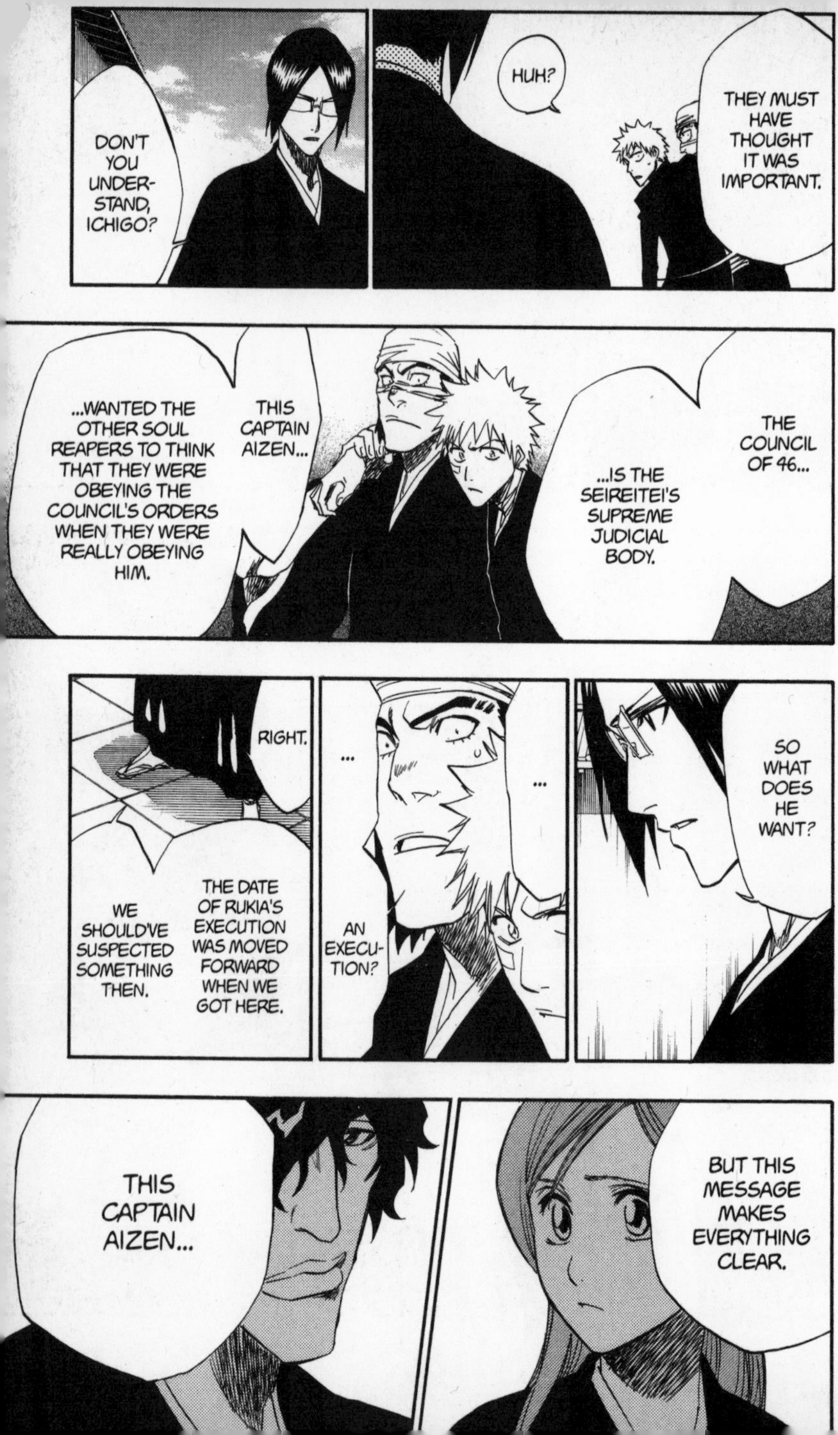
THEY MUST HAVE THOUGHT IT WAS IMPORTANT.
HUH?
DON'T YOU UNDER-STAND, ICHIGO?
THE COUNCIL OF 46...
...IS THE SEIREITEI'S SUPREME JUDICIAL BODY.
THIS CAPTAIN AIZEN...
...WANTED THE OTHER SOUL REAPERS TO THINK THAT THEY WERE OBEYING THE COUNCIL'S ORDERS WHEN THEY WERE REALLY OBEYING HIM.
SO WHAT DOES HE WANT?
...
...
AN EXECU-TION?
RIGHT.
THE DATE OF RUKIA'S EXECUTION WAS MOVED FORWARD WHEN WE GOT HERE.
WE SHOULD'VE SUSPECTED SOMETHING THEN.
BUT THIS MESSAGE MAKES EVERYTHING CLEAR.
THIS CAPTAIN AIZEN...

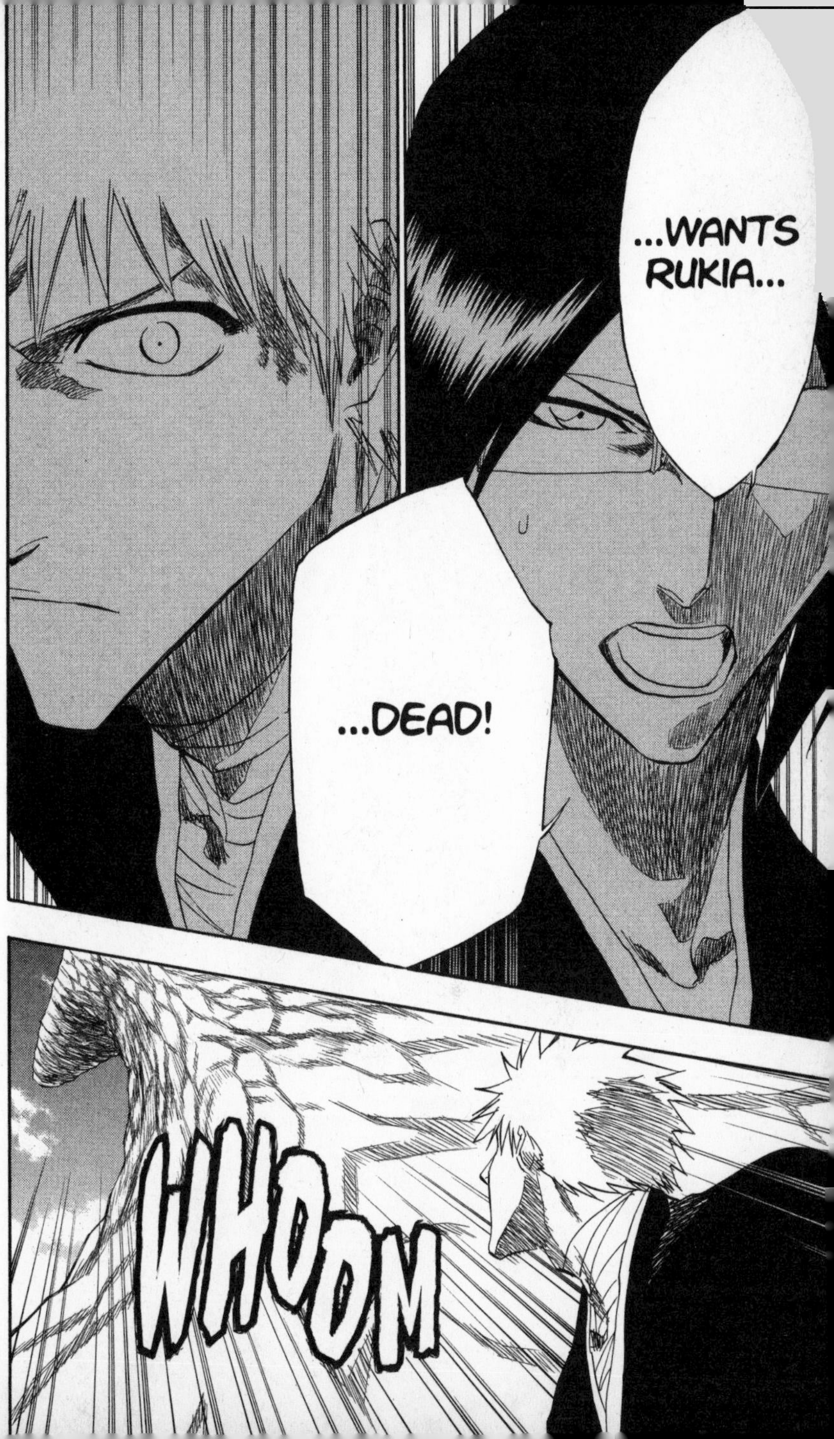
...WANTS RUKIA...
...DEAD!
WHOOM

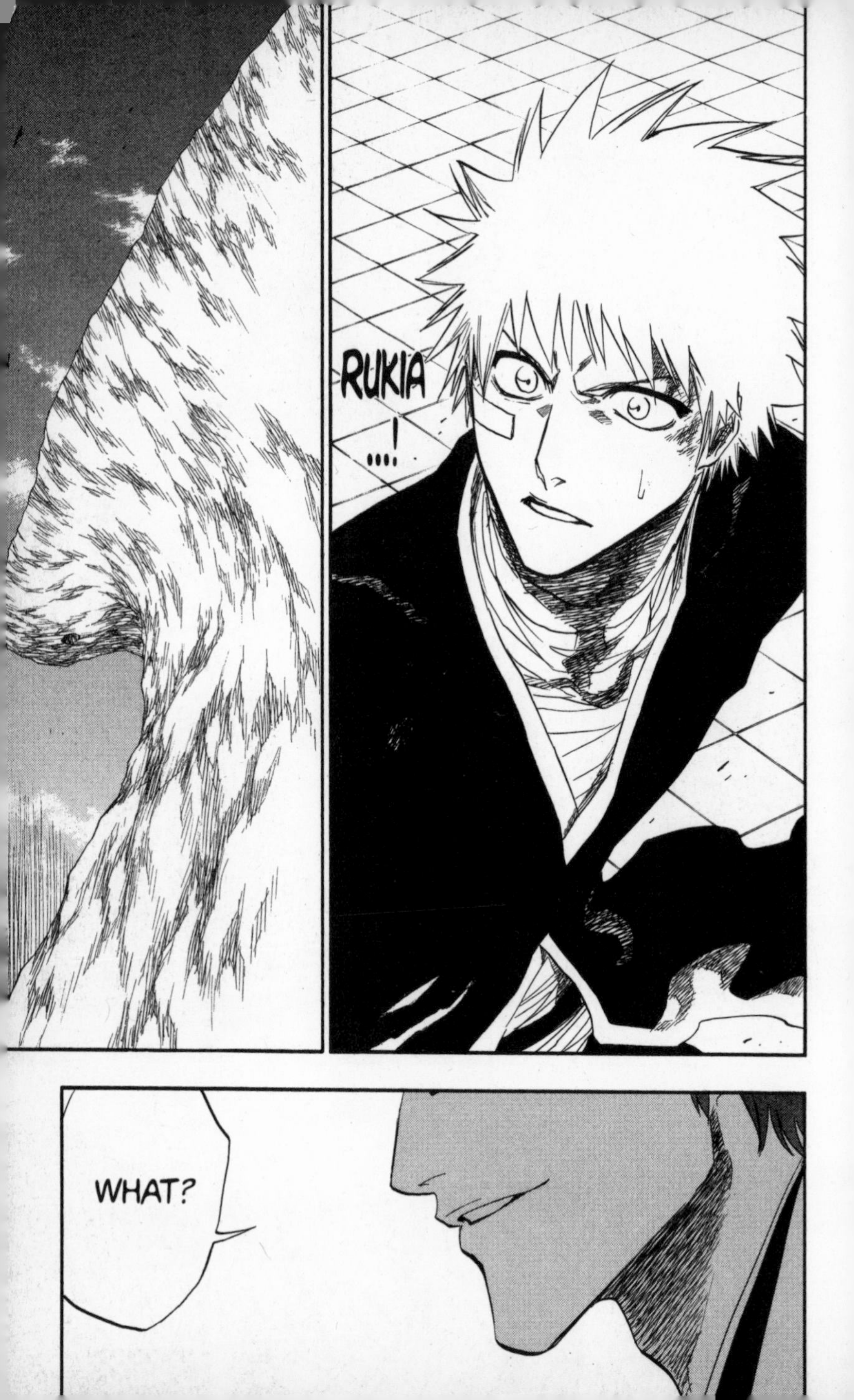

RUKIA ...!
WHAT?

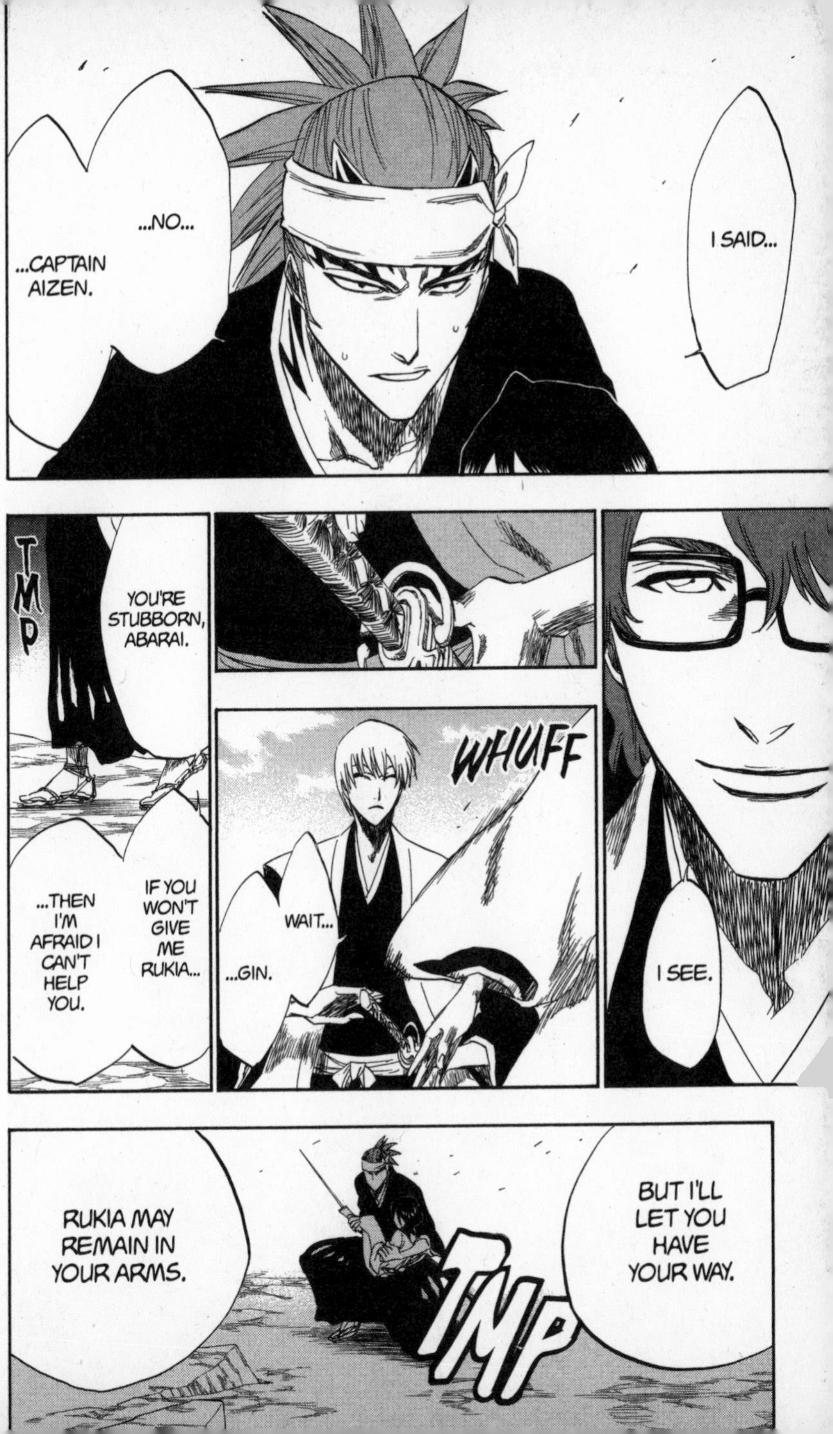
I SAID...
...NO...
...CAPTAIN AIZEN.
I SEE.
WHUFF
WAIT...
...GIN.
TMP
YOU'RE STUBBORN, ABARAI.
IF YOU WON'T GIVE ME RUKIA...
...THEN I'M AFRAID I CAN'T HELP YOU.
BUT I'LL LET YOU HAVE YOUR WAY.
TMP
RUKIA MAY REMAIN IN YOUR ARMS.

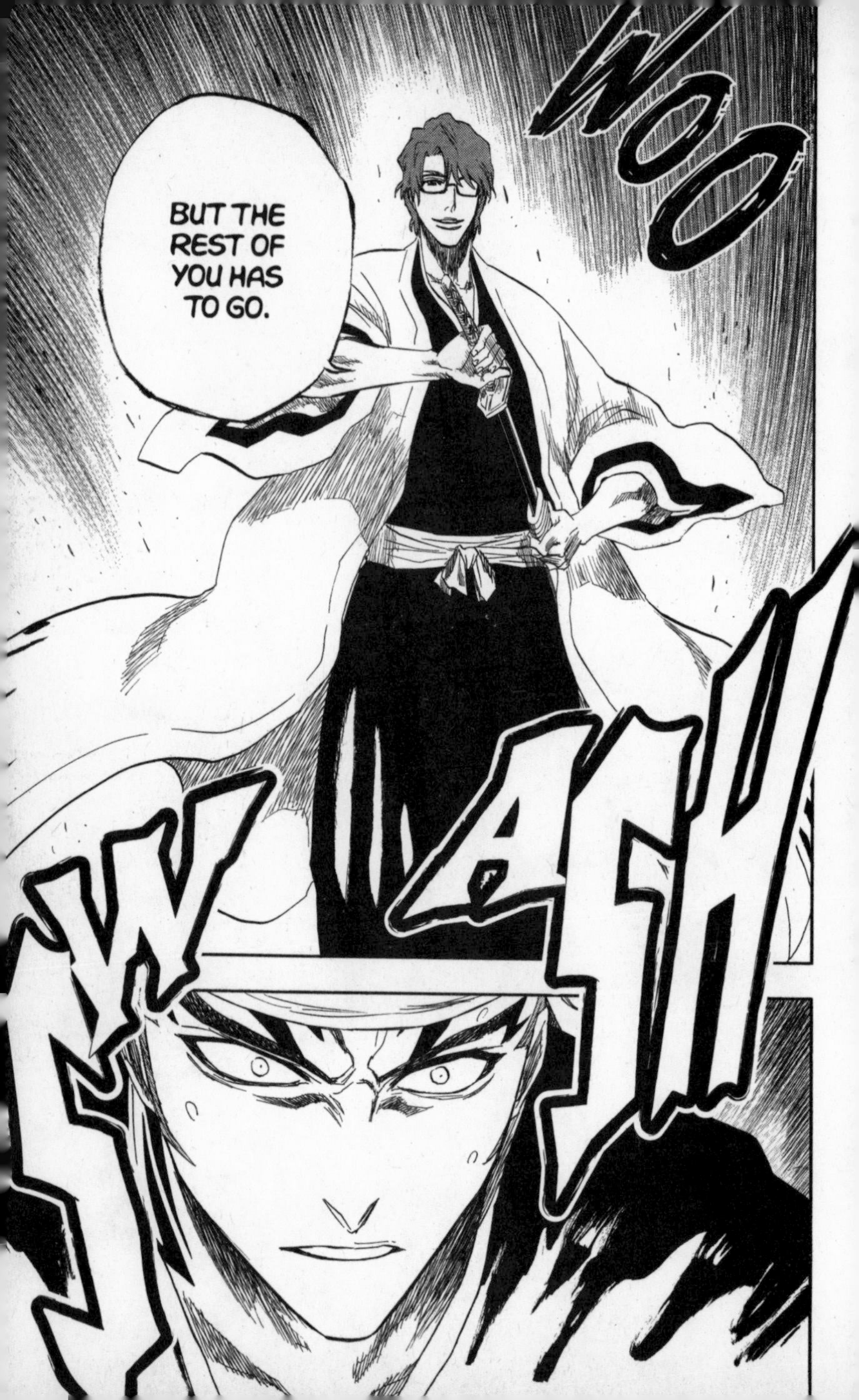
WOO
BUT THE REST OF YOU HAS TO GO.
WAAH

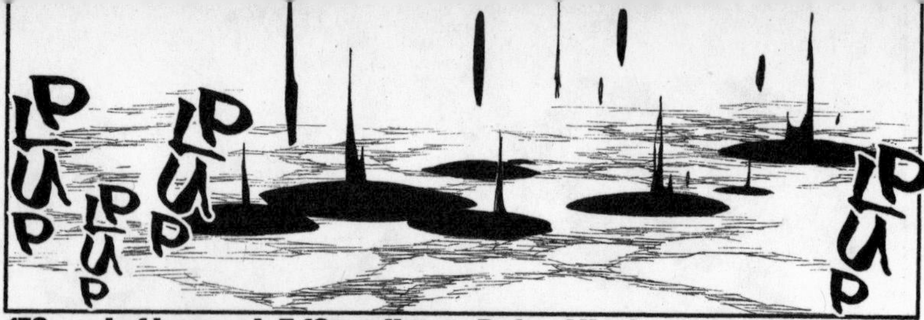
PLUP
PLUP
PLUP
PLUP

173. end of hypnosis5 (Standing to Defend You)

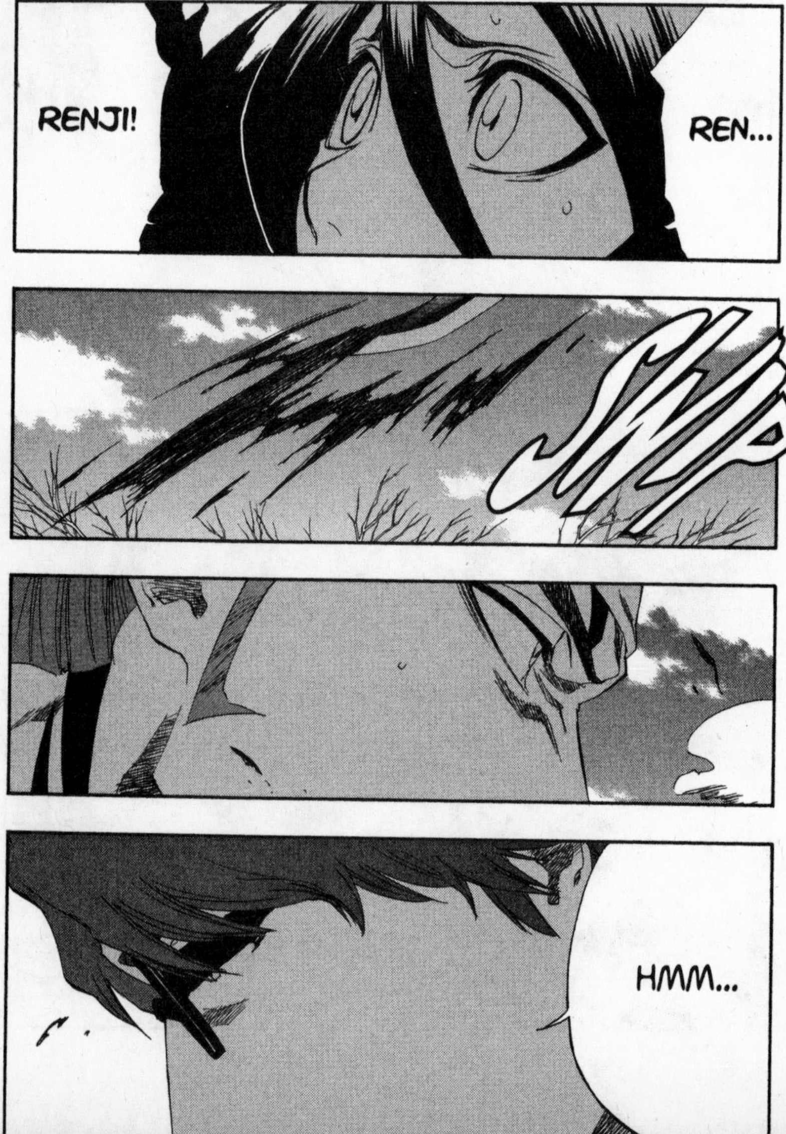
REN...
RENJI!
SHP
HMM...

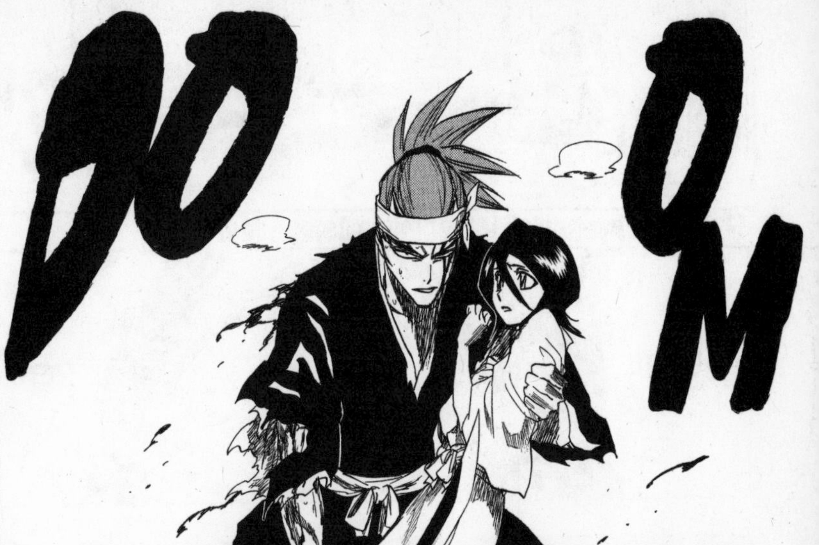
DOOM

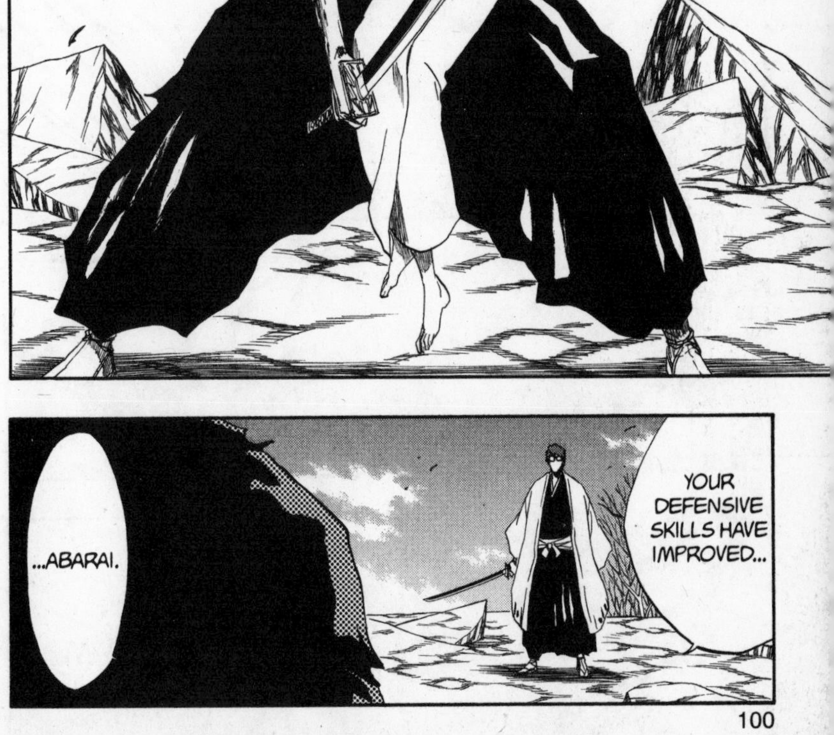
YOUR DEFENSIVE SKILLS HAVE IMPROVED...
...ABARAI.

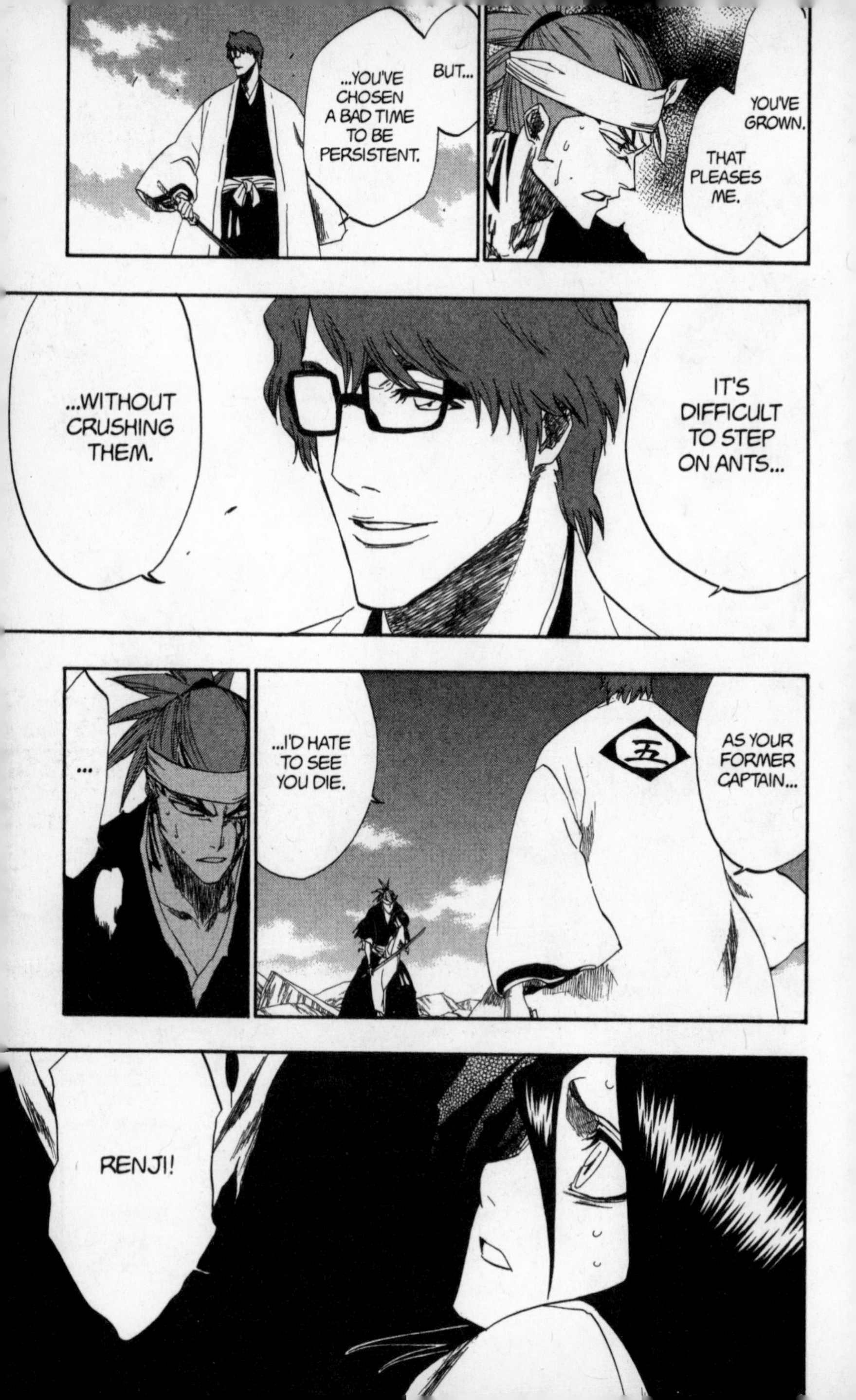
YOU'VE GROWN.
THAT PLEASES ME.
BUT...
...YOU'VE CHOSEN A BAD TIME TO BE PERSISTENT.
IT'S DIFFICULT TO STEP ON ANTS...
...WITHOUT CRUSHING THEM.
AS YOUR FORMER CAPTAIN...
...I'D HATE TO SEE YOU DIE.
...
RENJI!

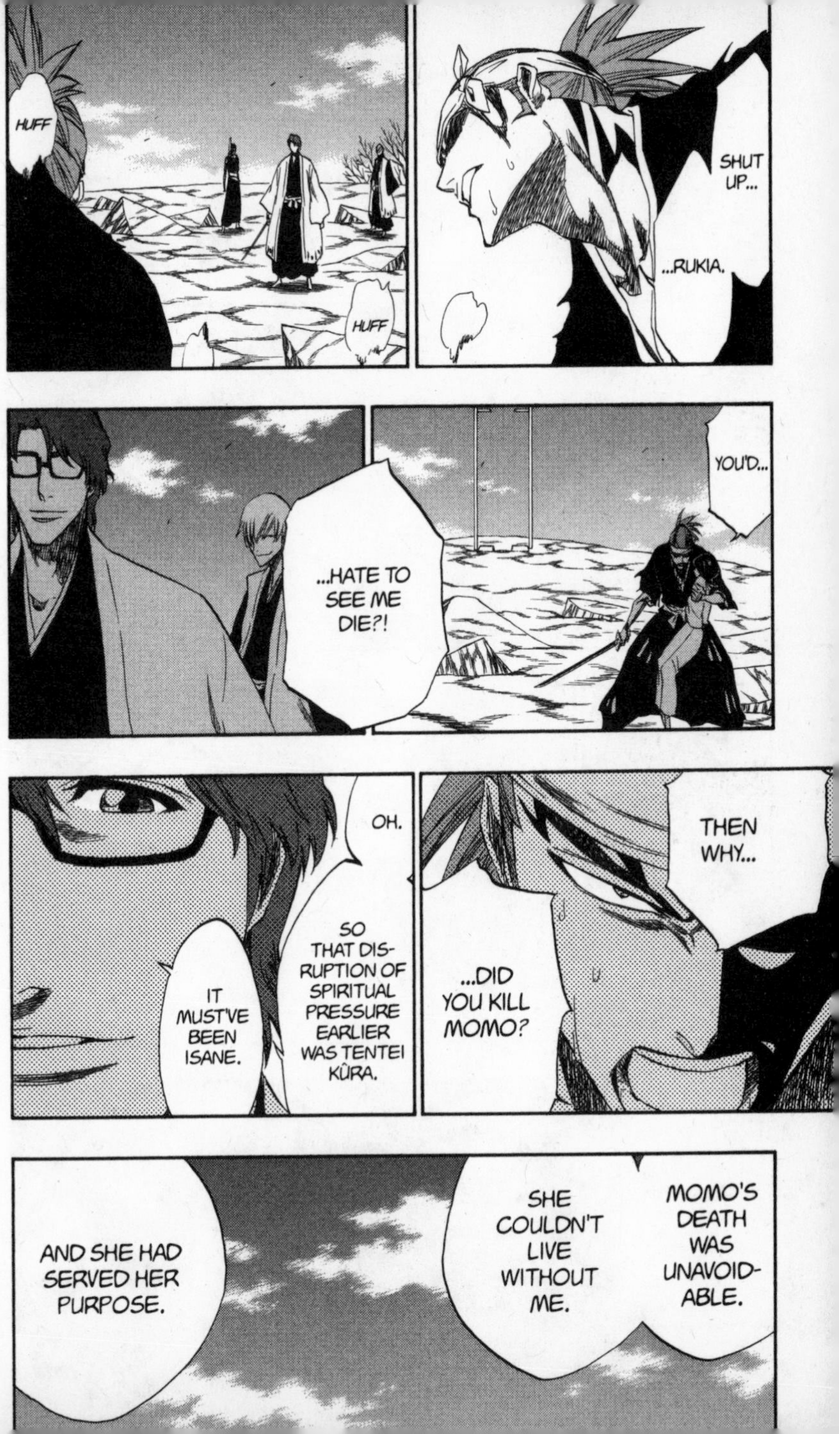
SHUT UP...
...RUKIA.
HUFF
HUFF
YOU'D...
...HATE TO SEE ME DIE?!
THEN WHY...
...DID YOU KILL MOMO?
OH.
SO THAT DISRUPTION OF SPIRITUAL PRESSURE EARLIER WAS TENTEI KŪRA.
IT MUST'VE BEEN ISANE.
MOMO'S DEATH WAS UNAVOIDABLE.
SHE COULDN'T LIVE WITHOUT ME.
AND SHE HAD SERVED HER PURPOSE.

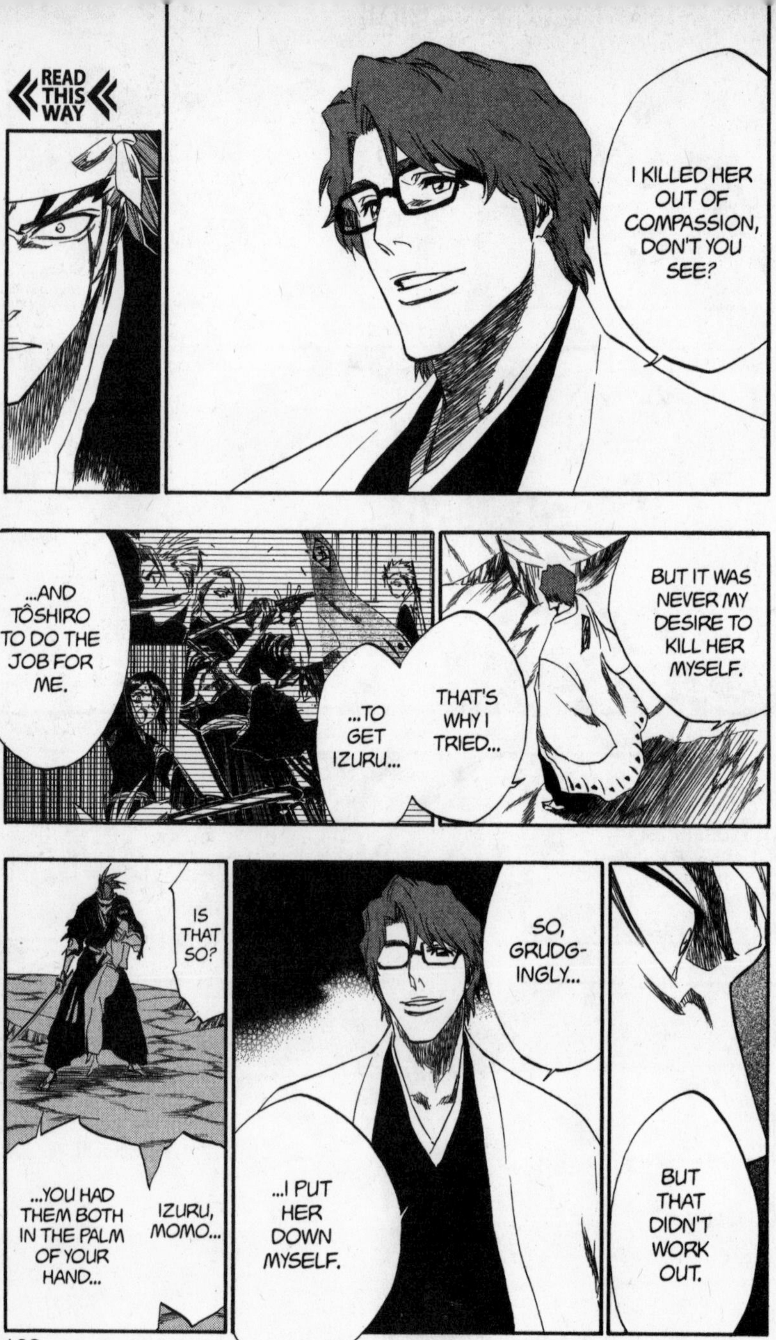
READ THIS WAY
I KILLED HER OUT OF COMPASSION, DON'T YOU SEE?
BUT IT WAS NEVER MY DESIRE TO KILL HER MYSELF.
THAT'S WHY I TRIED...
...TO GET IZURU...
...AND TÔSHIRO TO DO THE JOB FOR ME.
BUT THAT DIDN'T WORK OUT.
SO, GRUDGINGLY...
...I PUT HER DOWN MYSELF.
IS THAT SO?
IZURU, MOMO...
...YOU HAD THEM BOTH IN THE PALM OF YOUR HAND...

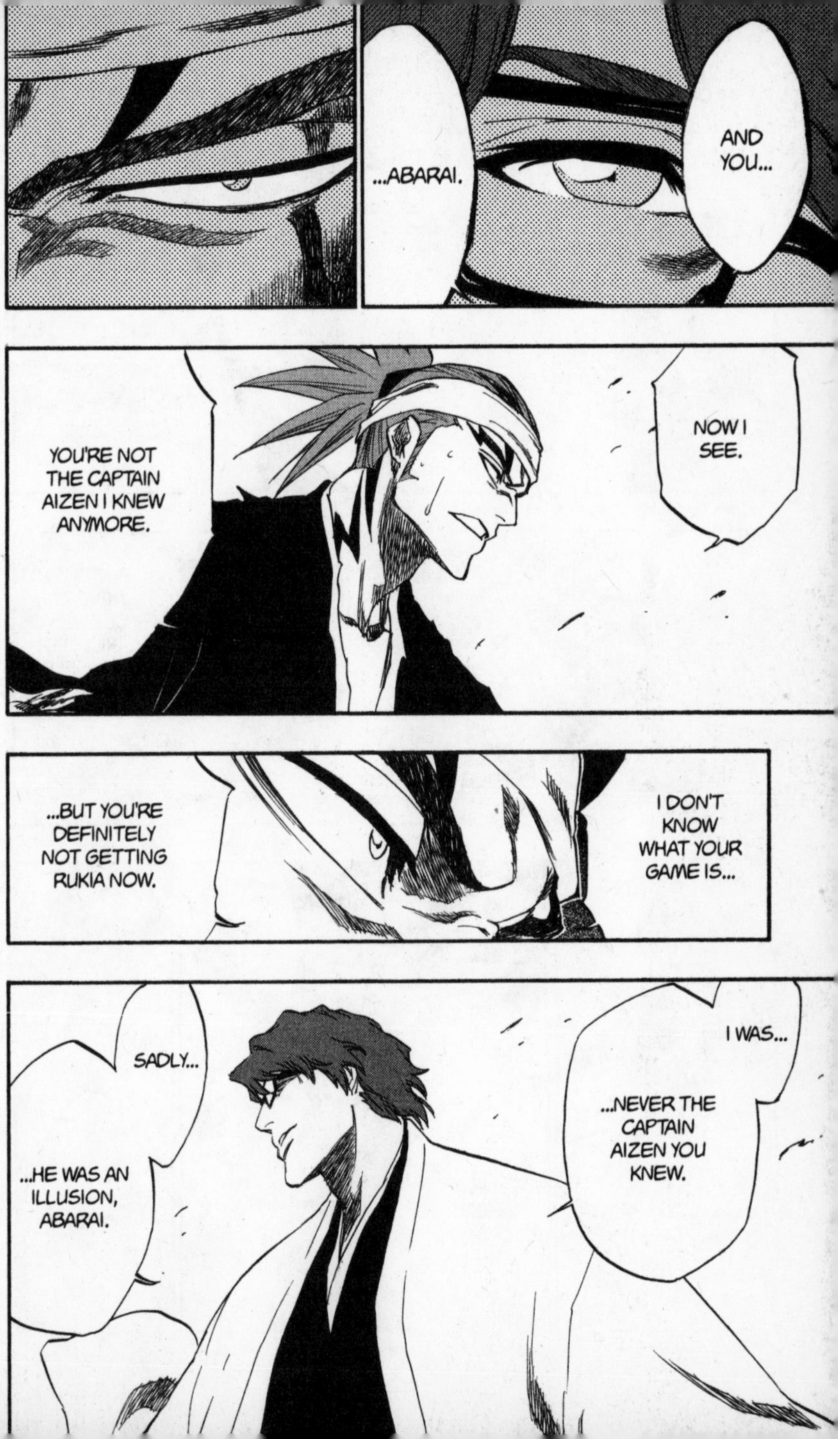
AND YOU...
...ABARAI.
NOW I SEE.
YOU'RE NOT THE CAPTAIN AIZEN I KNEW ANYMORE.
I DON'T KNOW WHAT YOUR GAME IS...
...BUT YOU'RE DEFINITELY NOT GETTING RUKIA NOW.
I WAS...
...NEVER THE CAPTAIN AIZEN YOU KNEW.
SADLY...
...HE WAS AN ILLUSION, ABARAI.

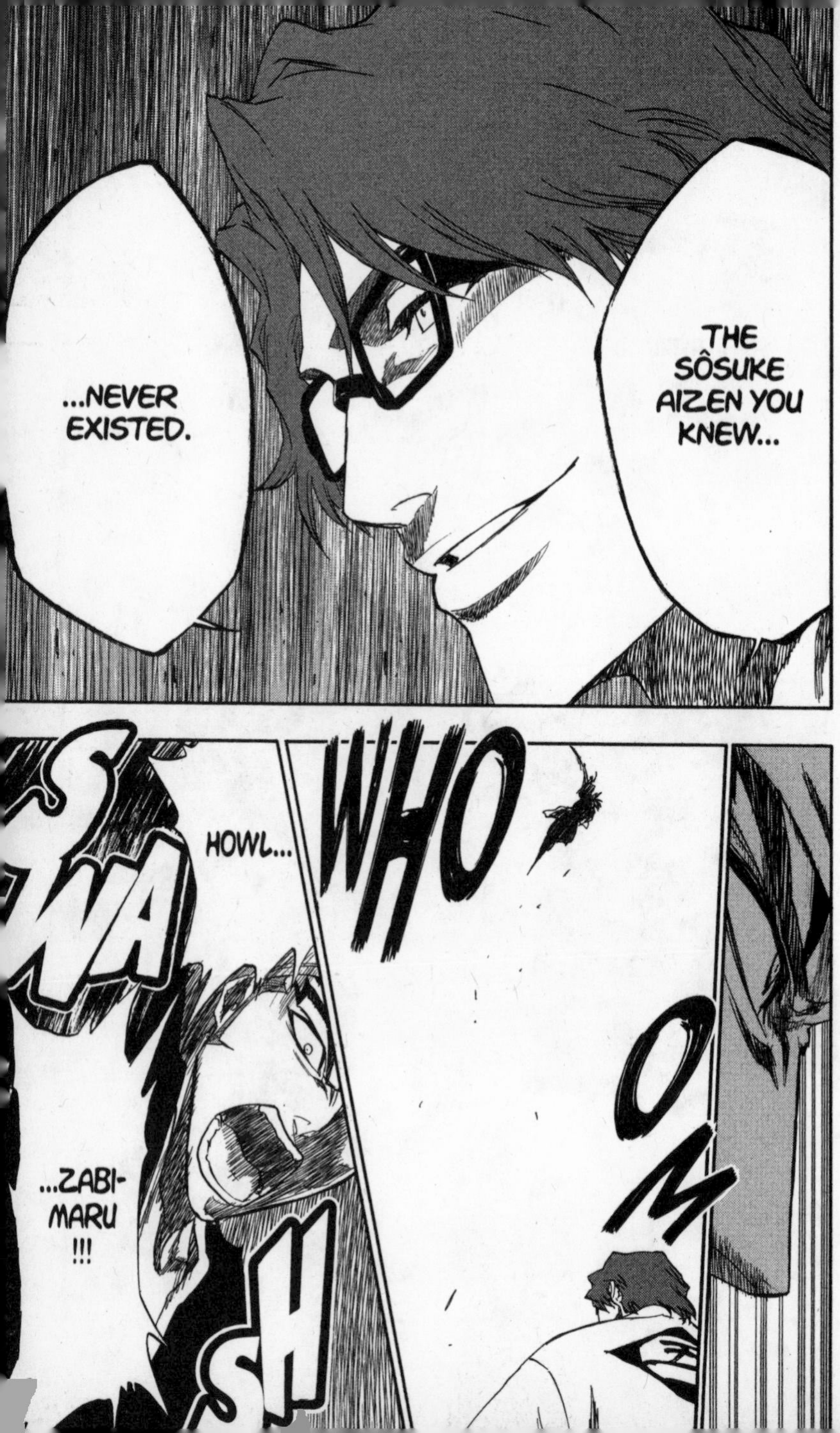
THE SÔSUKE AIZEN YOU KNEW...
...NEVER EXISTED.
WHOOM
HOWL...
...ZABI-MARU !!!
SWASH

百七十三
(173)

end of hypnosis 5
(Standing to Defend You)

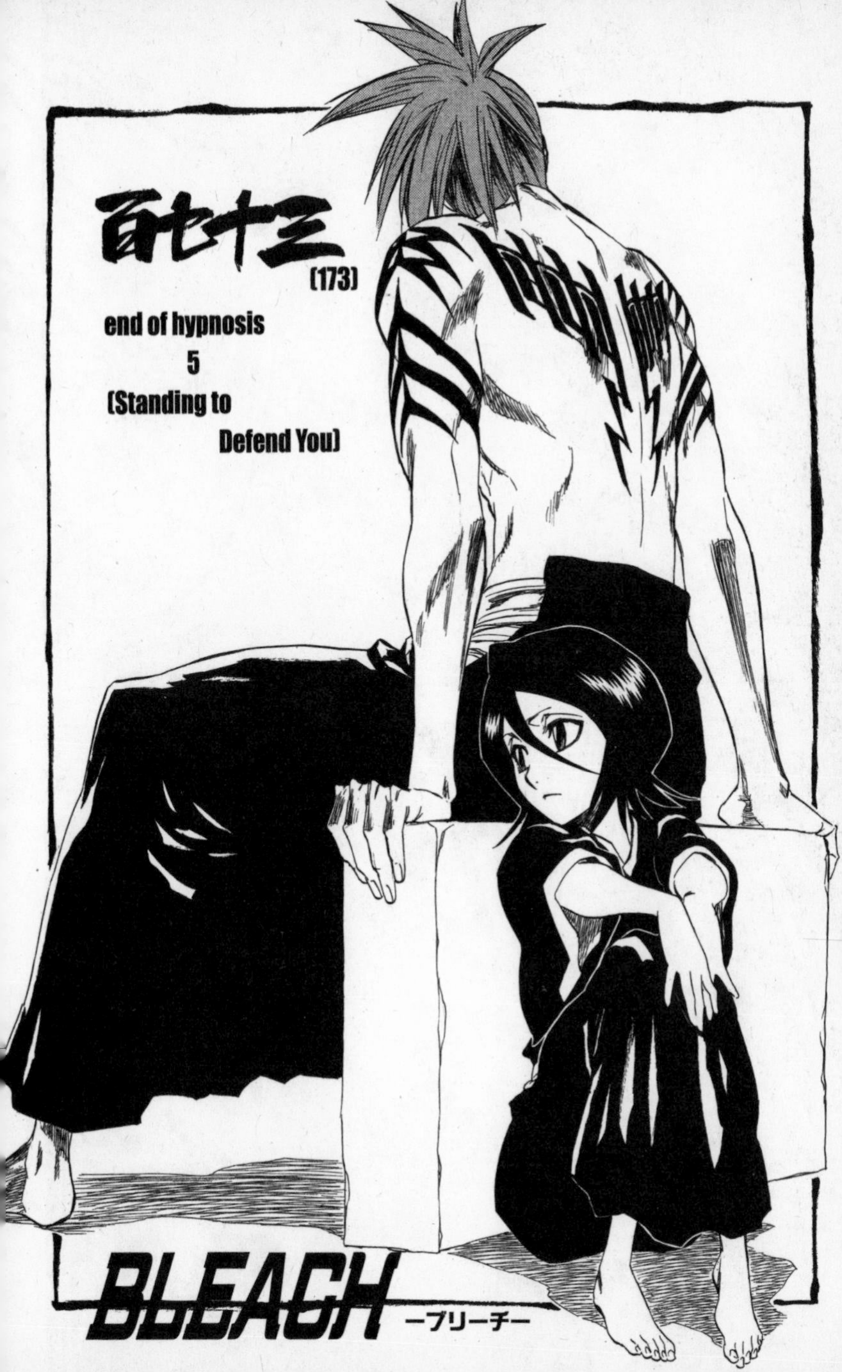

BLEACH
ーブリーチー

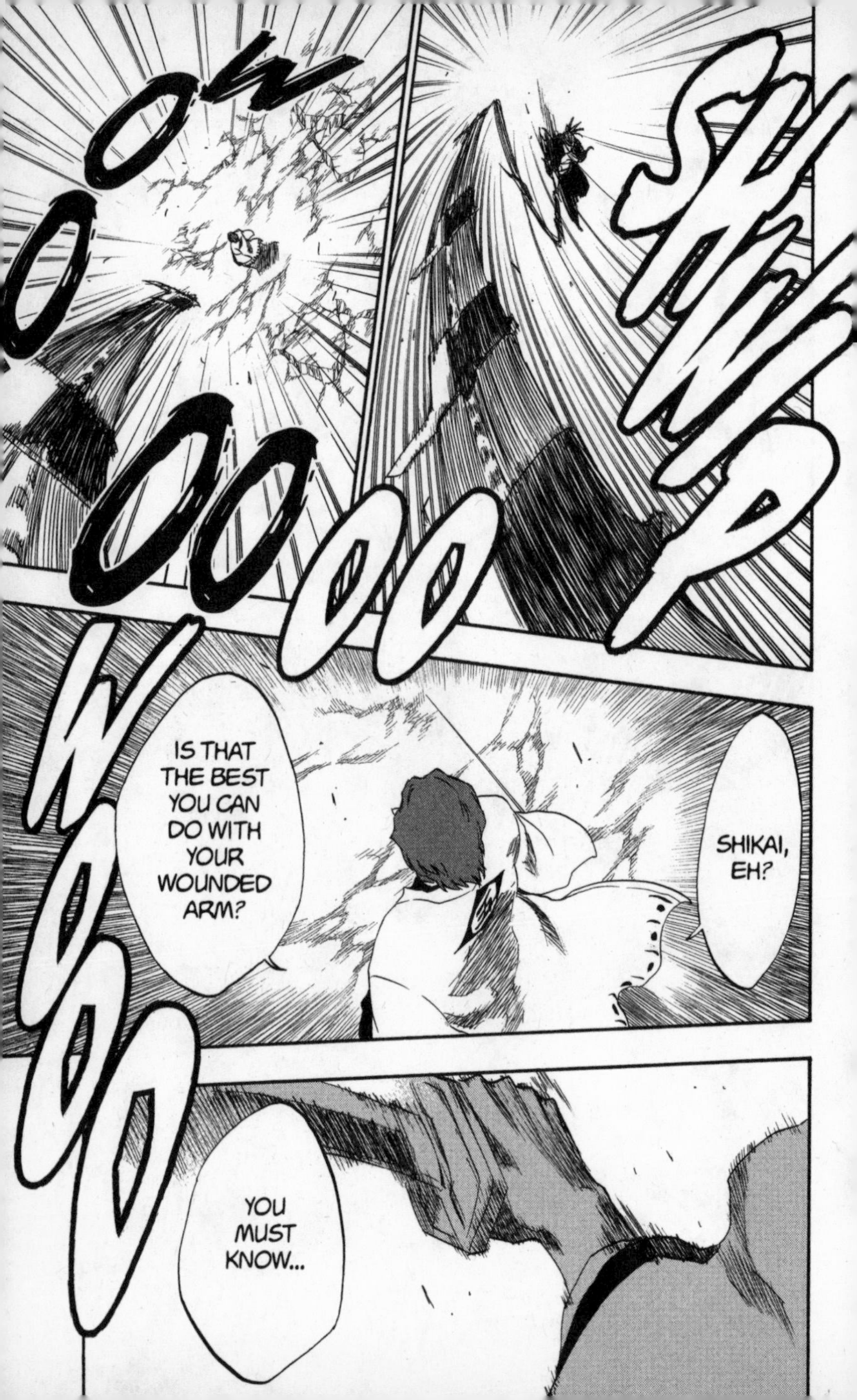
SHIKAI, EH?
IS THAT THE BEST YOU CAN DO WITH YOUR WOUNDED ARM?
YOU MUST KNOW...

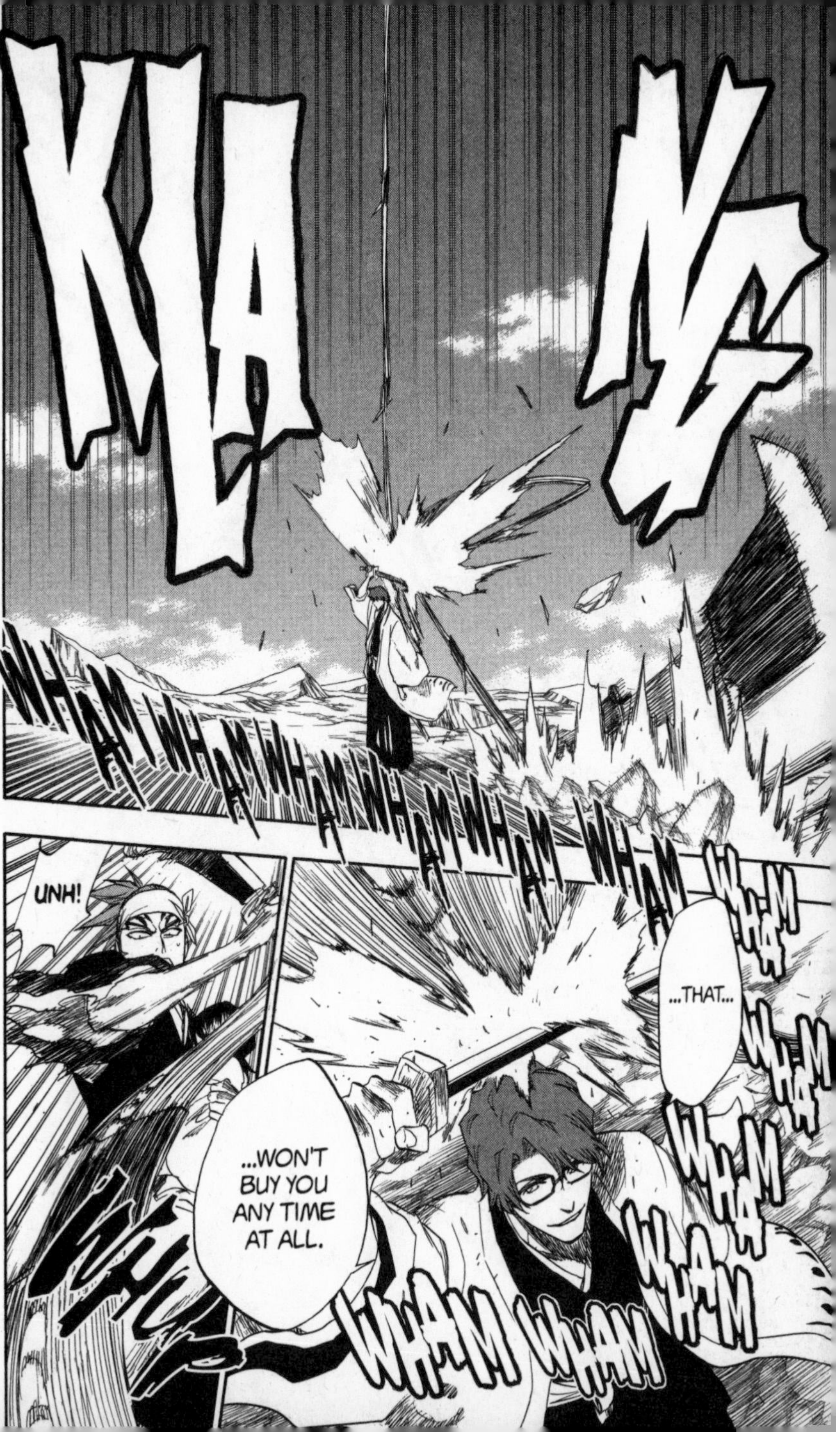
KLANG
WHAM WHAM WHAM WHAM WHAM WHAM
...THAT...
...WON'T BUY YOU ANY TIME AT ALL.
WHAM WHAM WHAM WHAM WHAM WHAM WHAM
UNH!

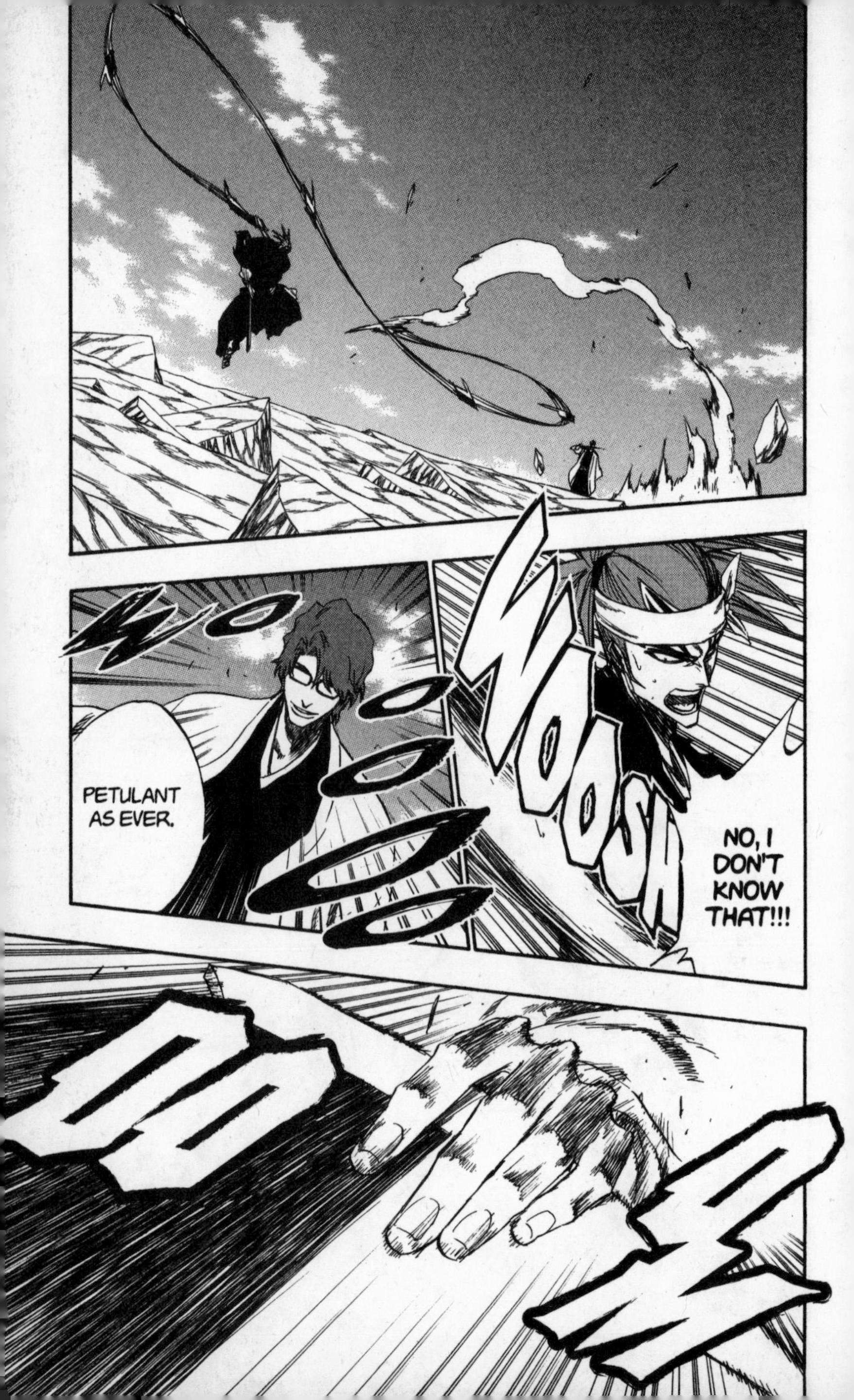
WOOSH
NO, I DON'T KNOW THAT!!!
PETULANT AS EVER.

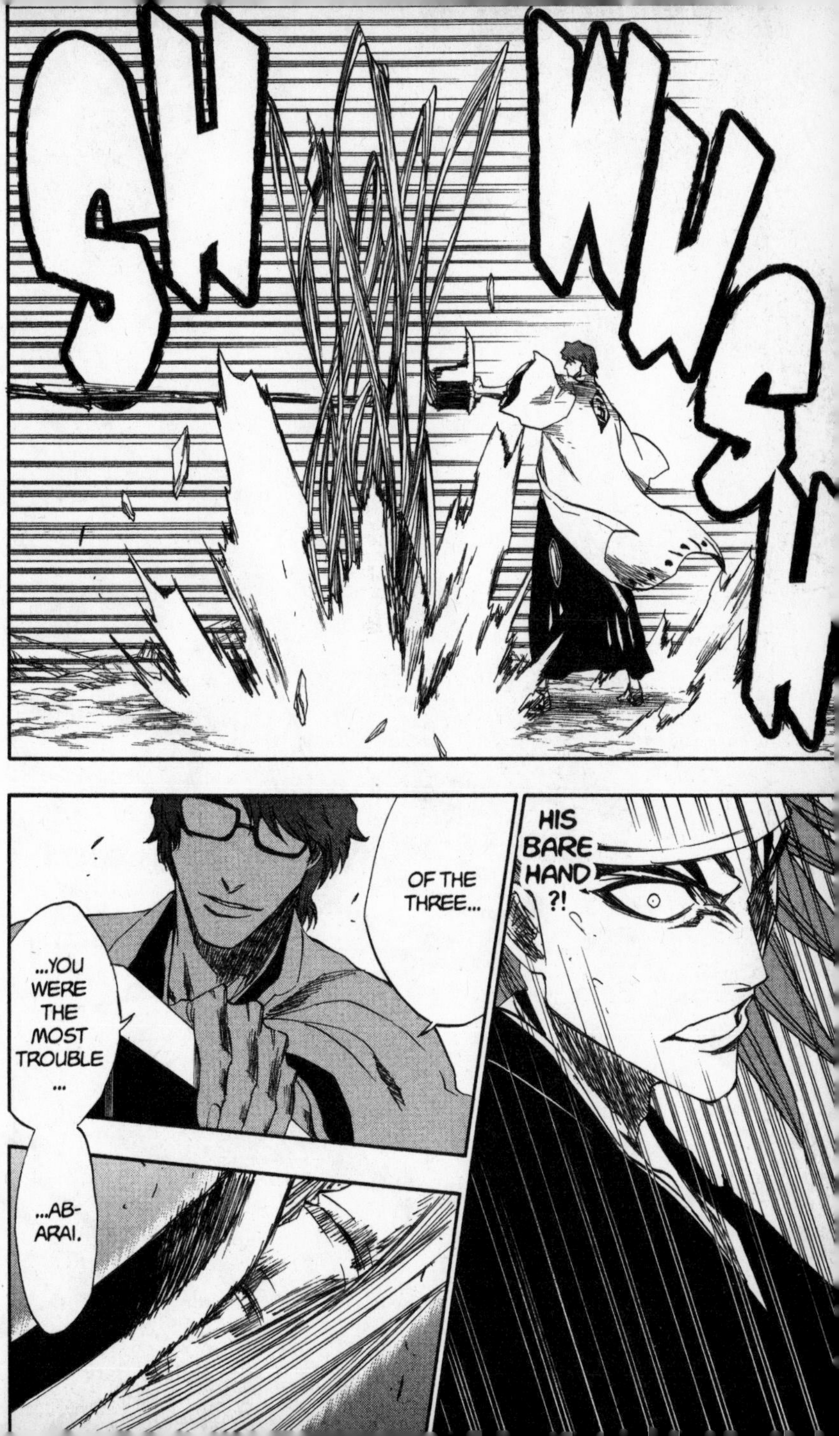

SHWHSH
HIS BARE HAND ?!
OF THE THREE...
...YOU WERE THE MOST TROUBLE ...
...AB-ARAI.

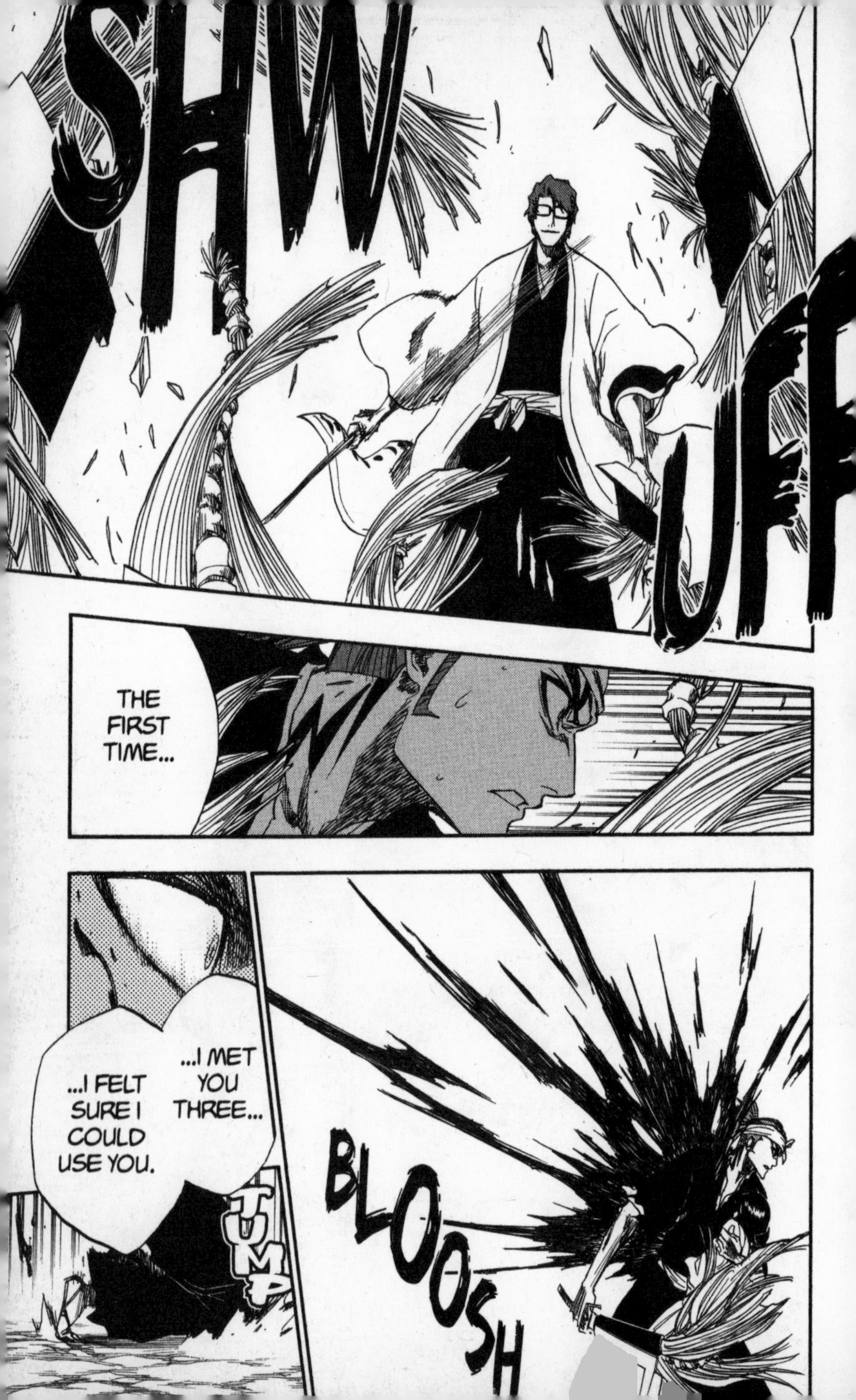
SHWUFF
THE FIRST TIME...
BLOOSH
...I MET YOU THREE...
...I FELT SURE I COULD USE YOU.
TUMP

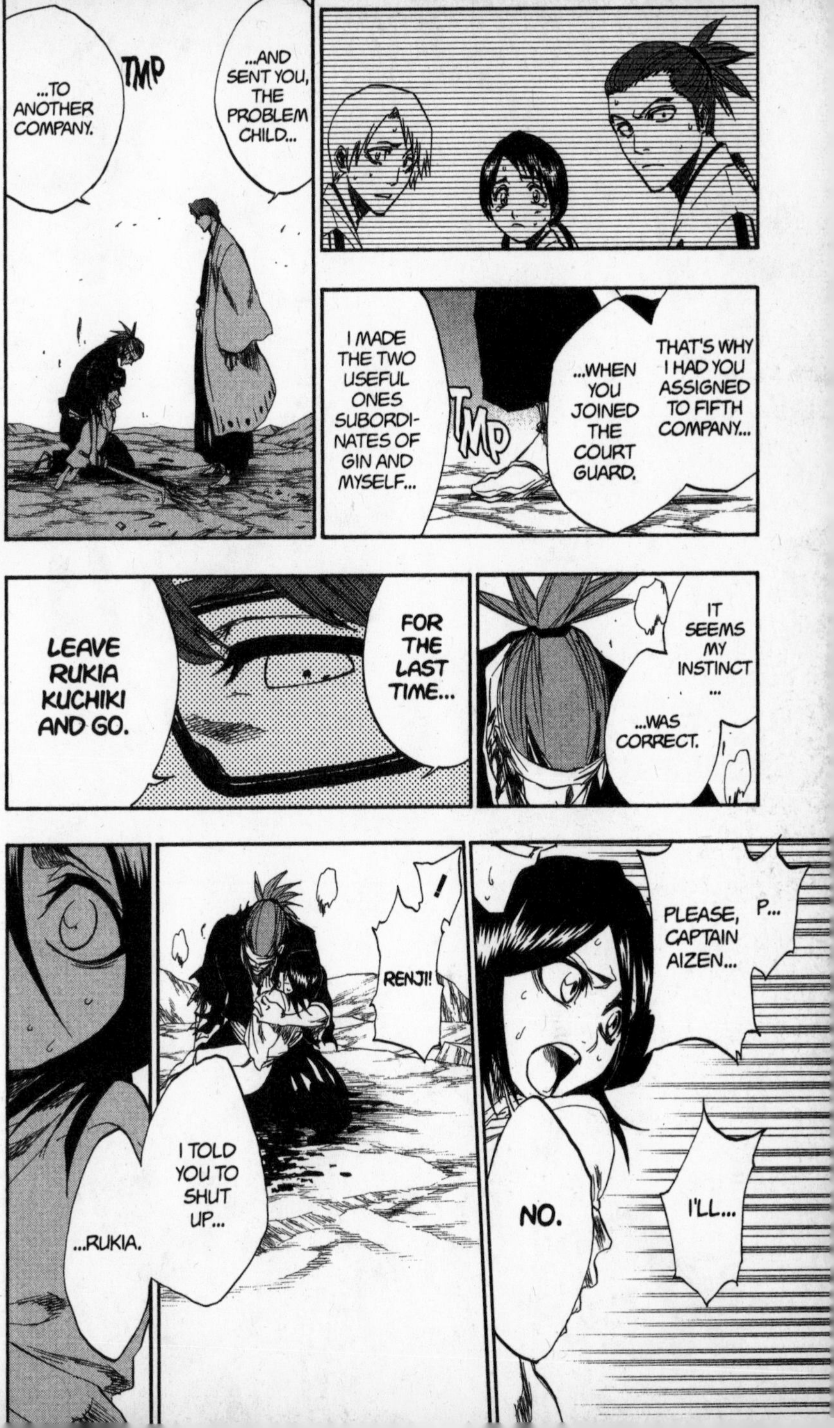
THAT'S WHY I HAD YOU ASSIGNED TO FIFTH COMPANY...
...WHEN YOU JOINED THE COURT GUARD.
TMP
I MADE THE TWO USEFUL ONES SUBORDINATES OF GIN AND MYSELF...
...AND SENT YOU, THE PROBLEM CHILD...
TMP
...TO ANOTHER COMPANY.
IT SEEMS MY INSTINCT...
...WAS CORRECT.
FOR THE LAST TIME...
LEAVE RUKIA KUCHIKI AND GO.
P...
PLEASE, CAPTAIN AIZEN...
I'LL...
NO.
RENJI!
I TOLD YOU TO SHUT UP...
...RUKIA.

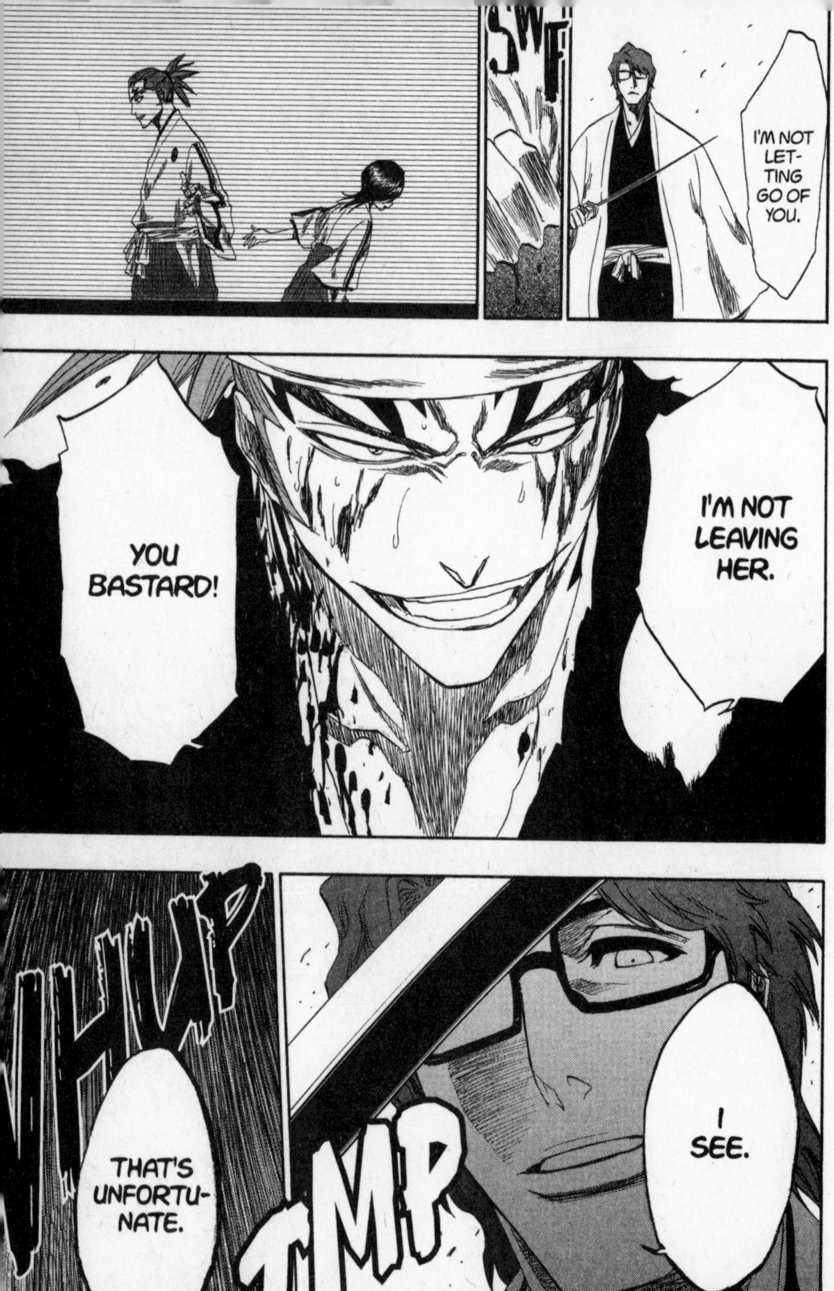
SWF
I'M NOT LETTING GO OF YOU.
I'M NOT LEAVING HER.
YOU BASTARD!
I SEE.
TMP
THAT'S UNFORTUNATE.

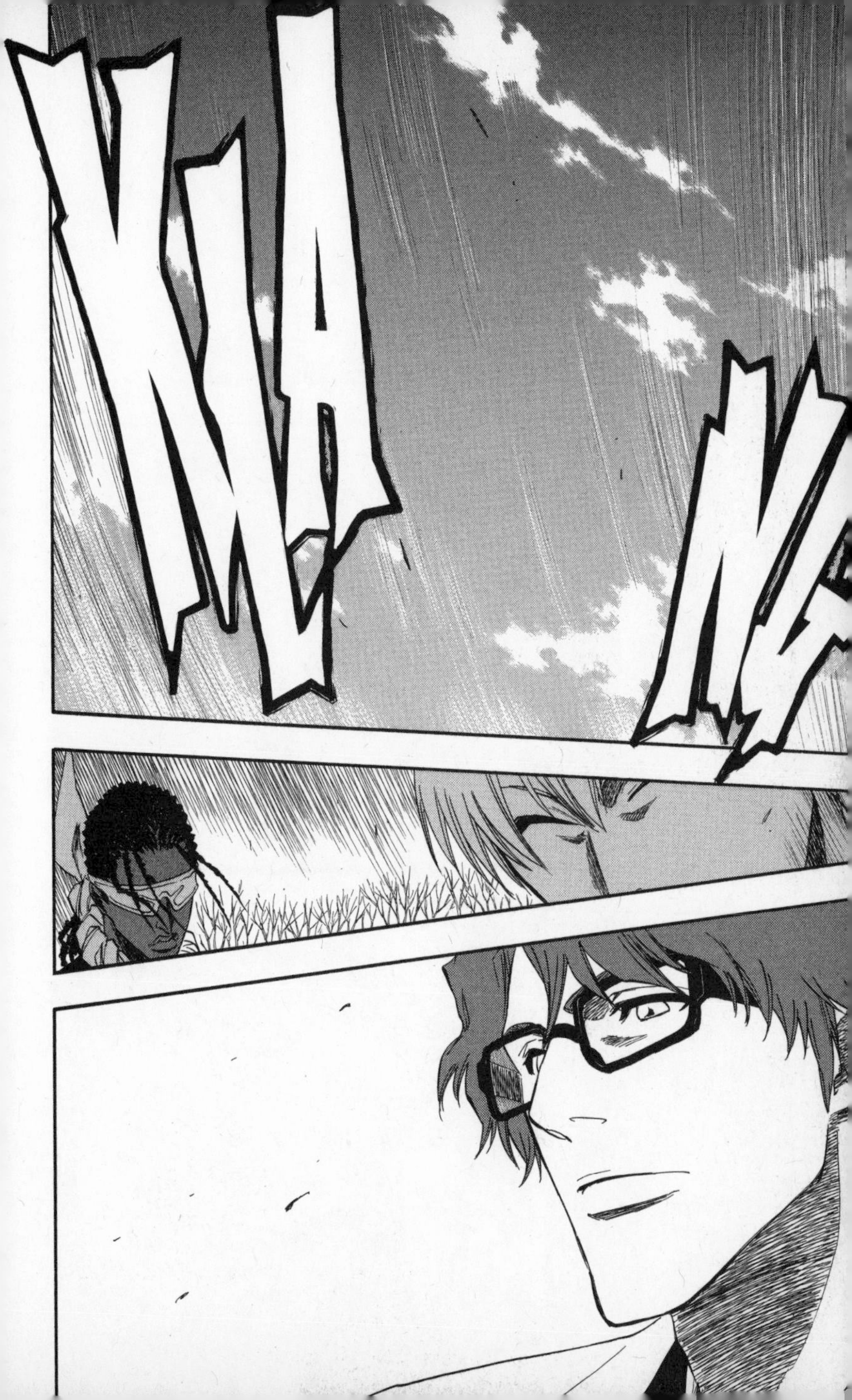
WA
N

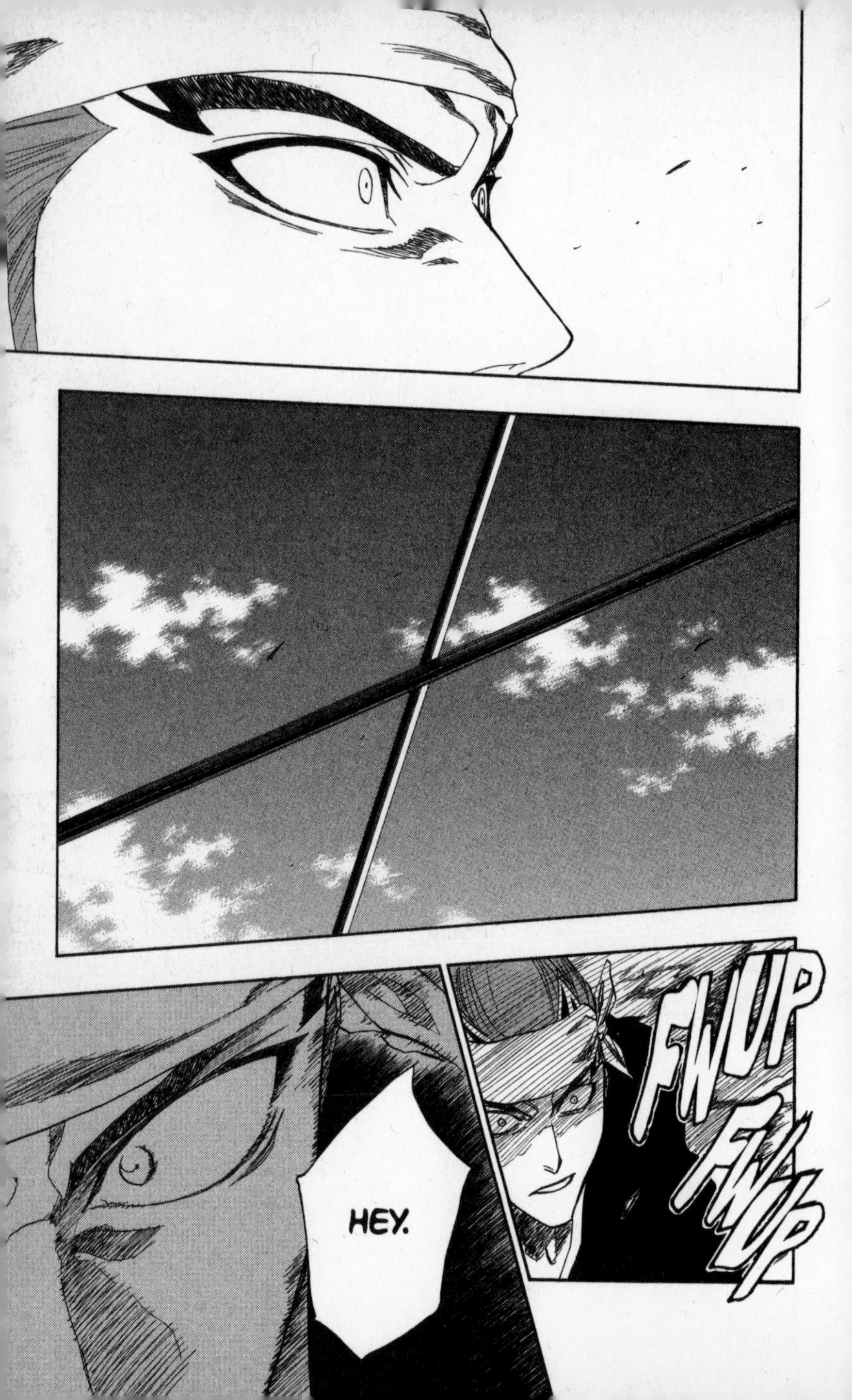

FWUP FWUP
HEY.

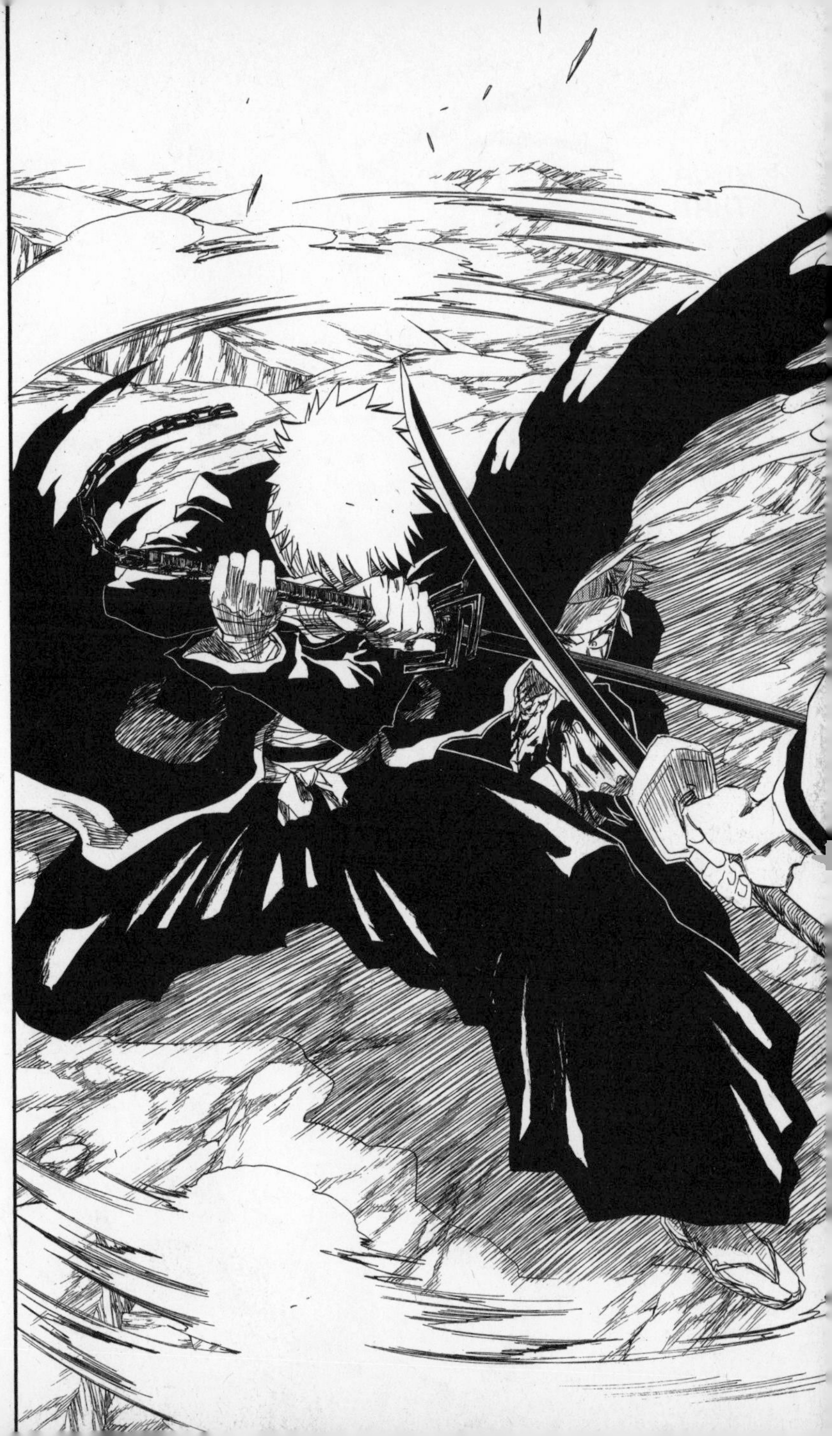

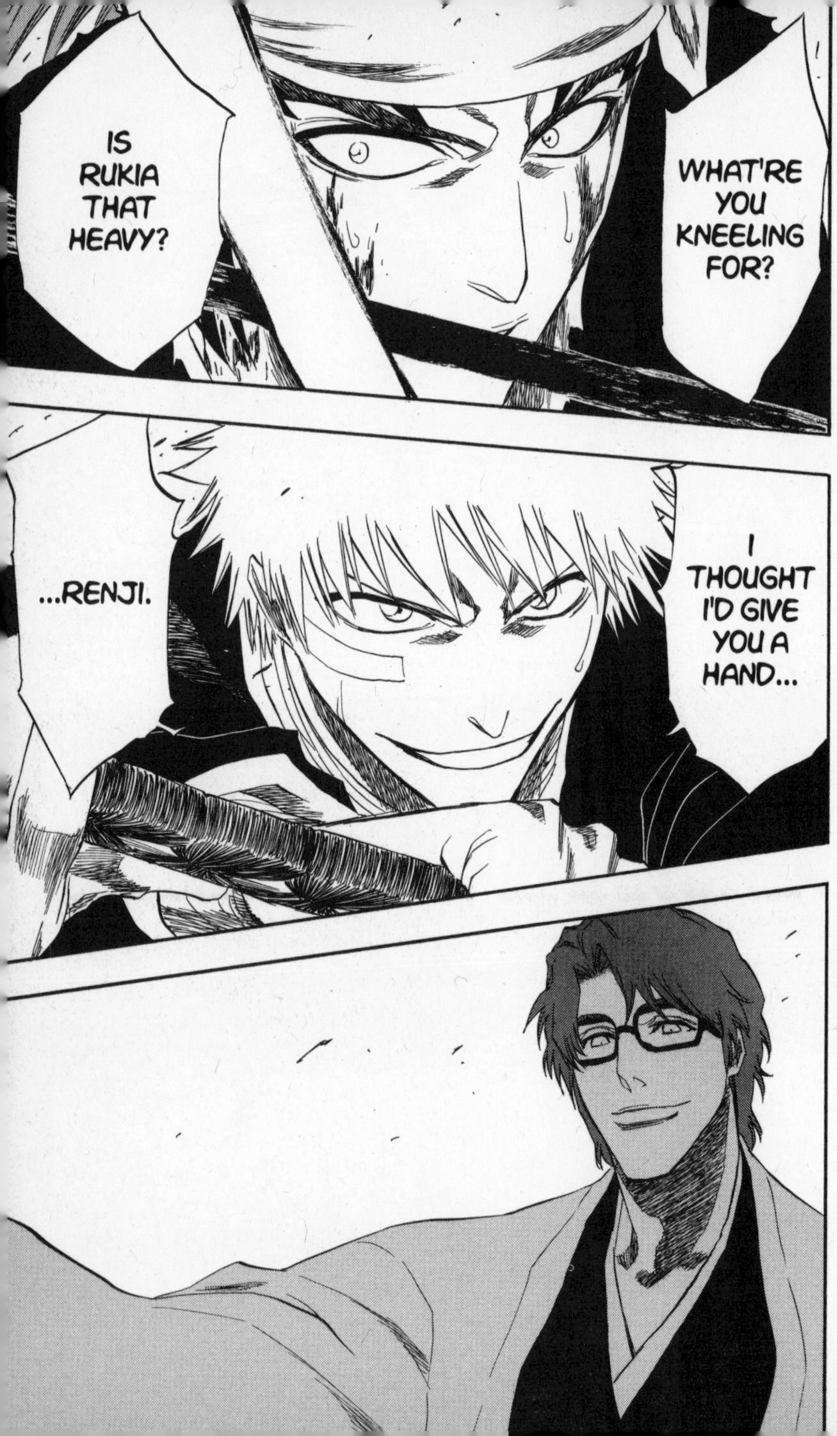
WHAT'RE YOU KNEELING FOR?
IS RUKIA THAT HEAVY?
I THOUGHT I'D GIVE YOU A HAND...
...RENJI.

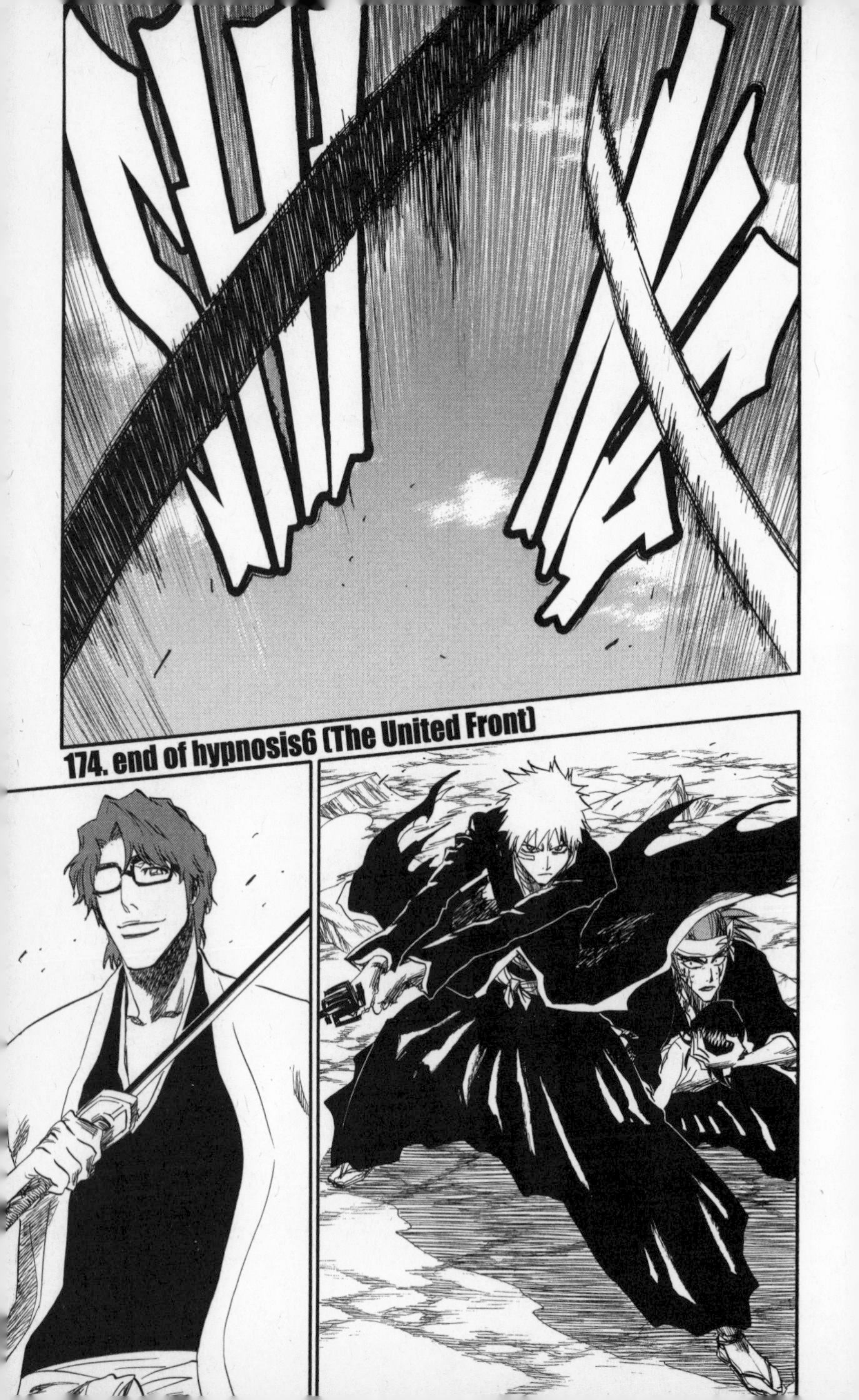
174. end of hypnosis6 (The United Front)

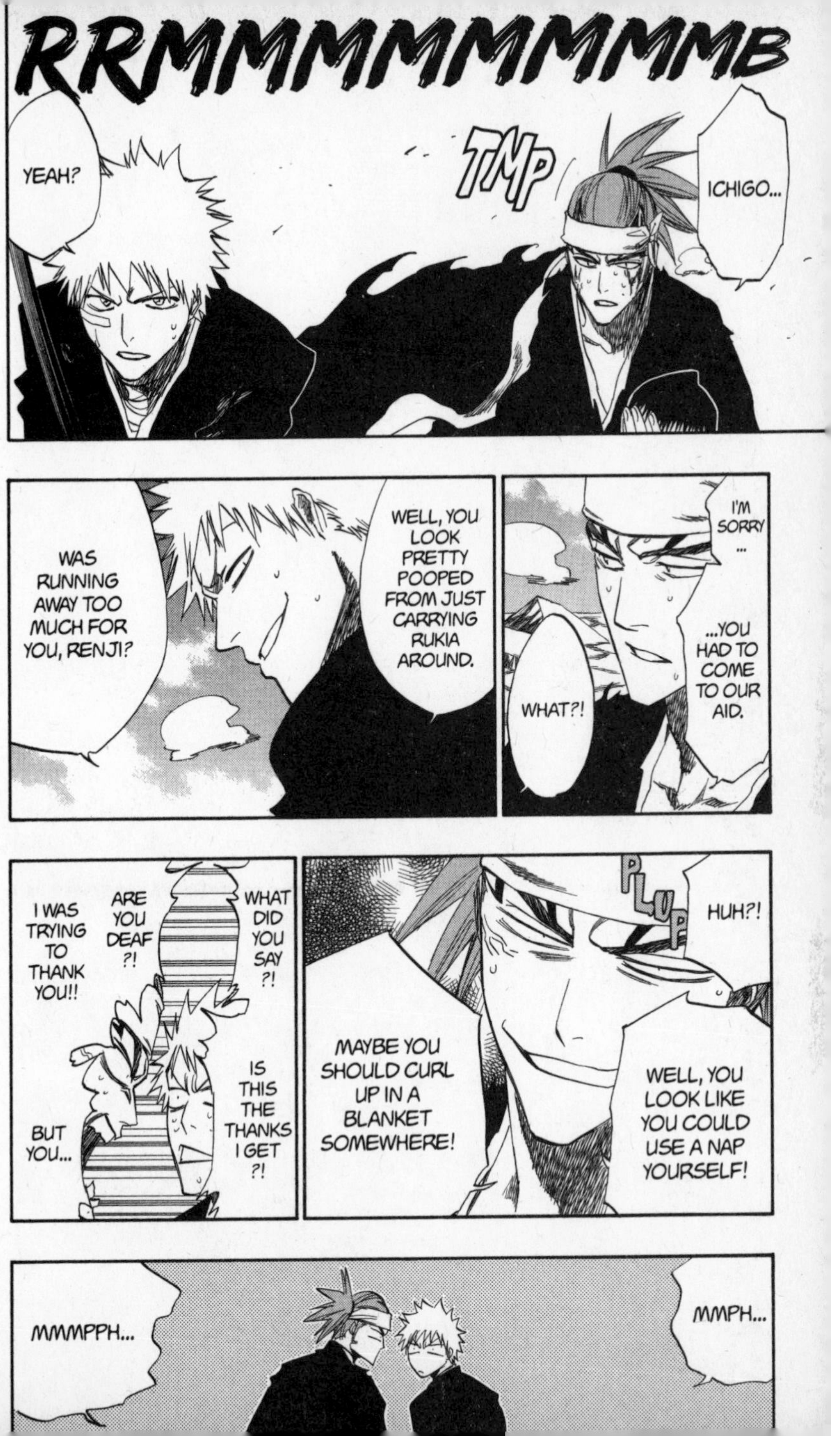
RRMMMMMMMMMB
ICHIGO...
TMP
YEAH?
I'M SORRY ...
...YOU HAD TO COME TO OUR AID.
WHAT?!
WELL, YOU LOOK PRETTY POOPED FROM JUST CARRYING RUKIA AROUND.
WAS RUNNING AWAY TOO MUCH FOR YOU, RENJI?
PLUP
HUH?!
WELL, YOU LOOK LIKE YOU COULD USE A NAP YOURSELF!
MAYBE YOU SHOULD CURL UP IN A BLANKET SOMEWHERE!
WHAT DID YOU SAY ?!
ARE YOU DEAF ?!
I WAS TRYING TO THANK YOU!!
IS THIS THE THANKS I GET ?!
BUT YOU...
MMPH...
MMMPPH...

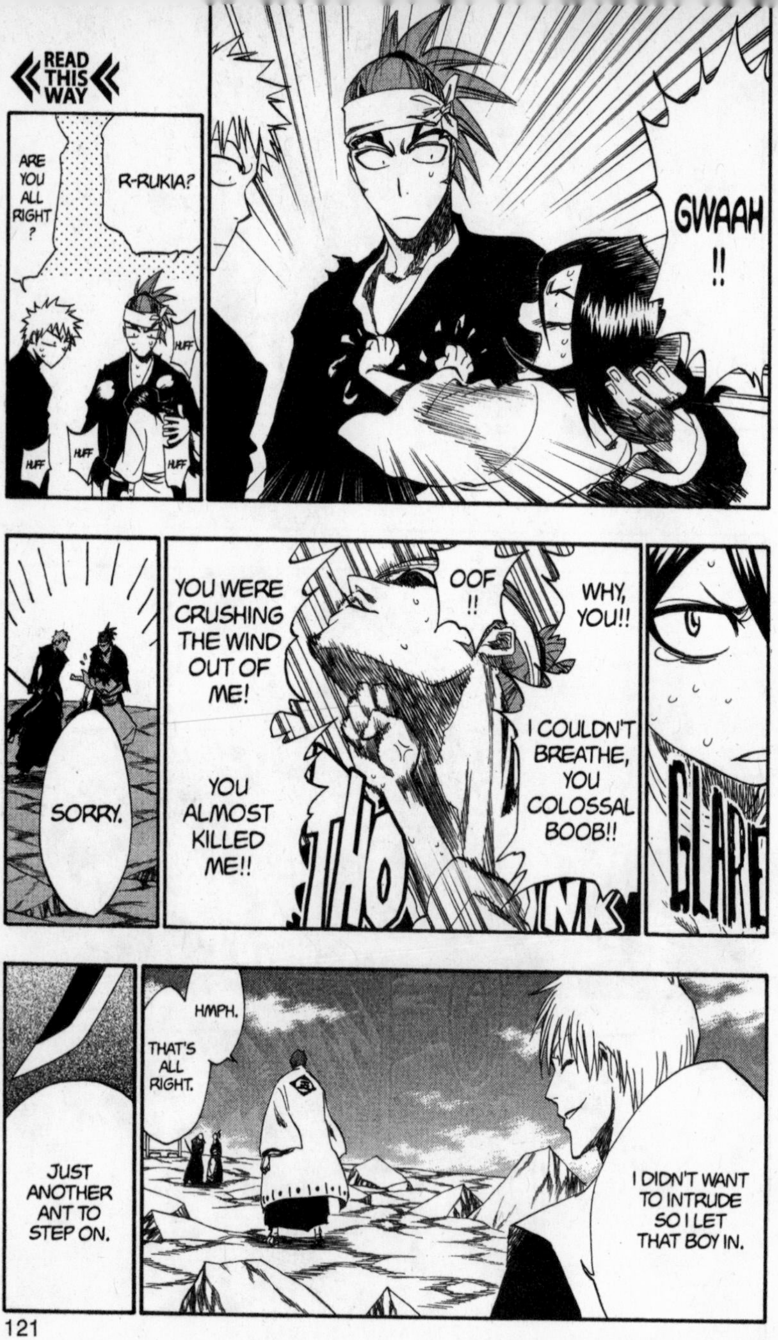
READ THIS WAY
GWAAH!!
R-RUKIA?
ARE YOU ALL RIGHT?
HUFF
HUFF
HUFF
HUFF
GLARE
WHY, YOU!!
OOF!!
YOU WERE CRUSHING THE WIND OUT OF ME!
I COULDN'T BREATHE, YOU COLOSSAL BOOB!!
YOU ALMOST KILLED ME!!
SORRY.
I DIDN'T WANT TO INTRUDE SO I LET THAT BOY IN.
HMPH.
THAT'S ALL RIGHT.
JUST ANOTHER ANT TO STEP ON.

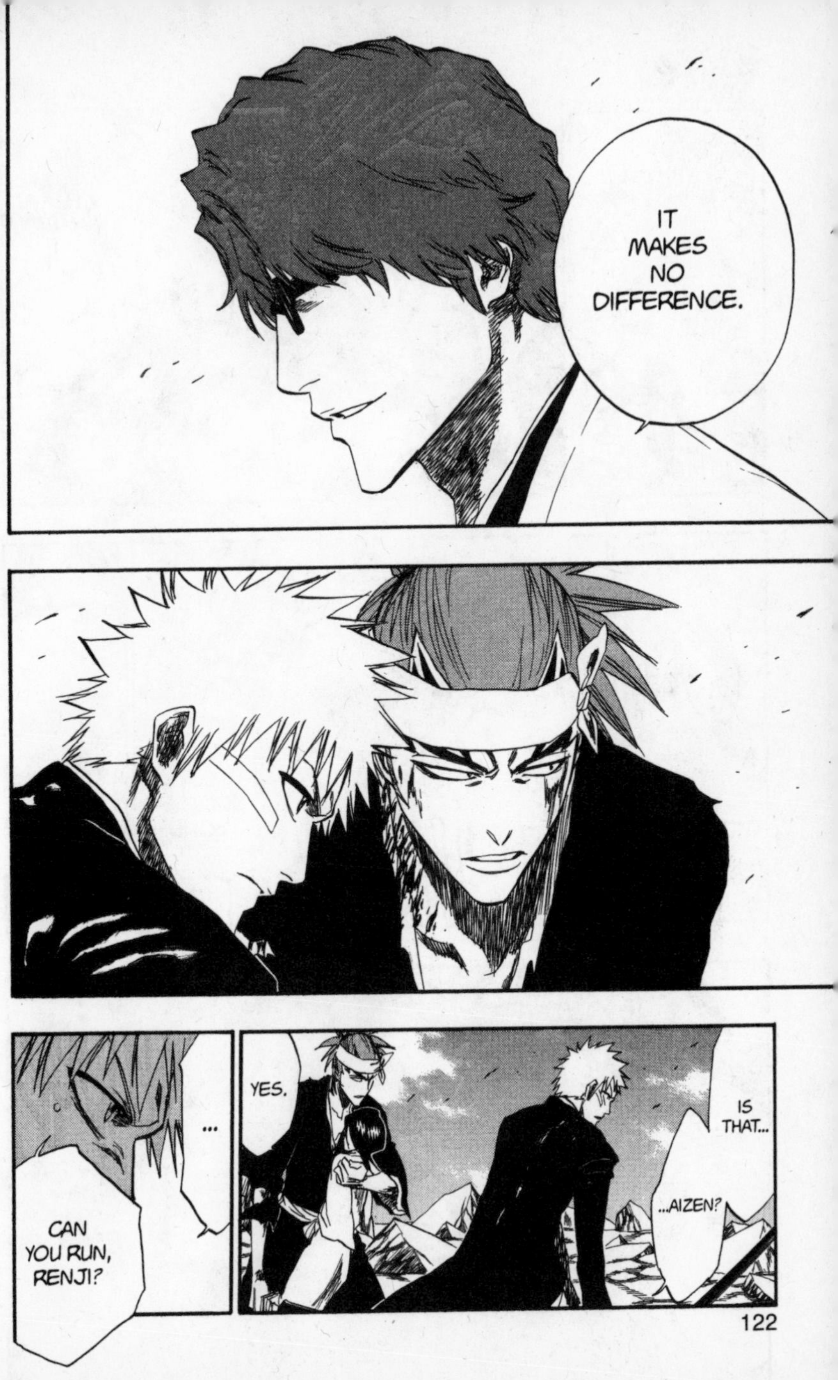
IT MAKES NO DIFFERENCE.
IS THAT...
...AIZEN?
YES.
...
CAN YOU RUN, RENJI?

READ THIS WAY

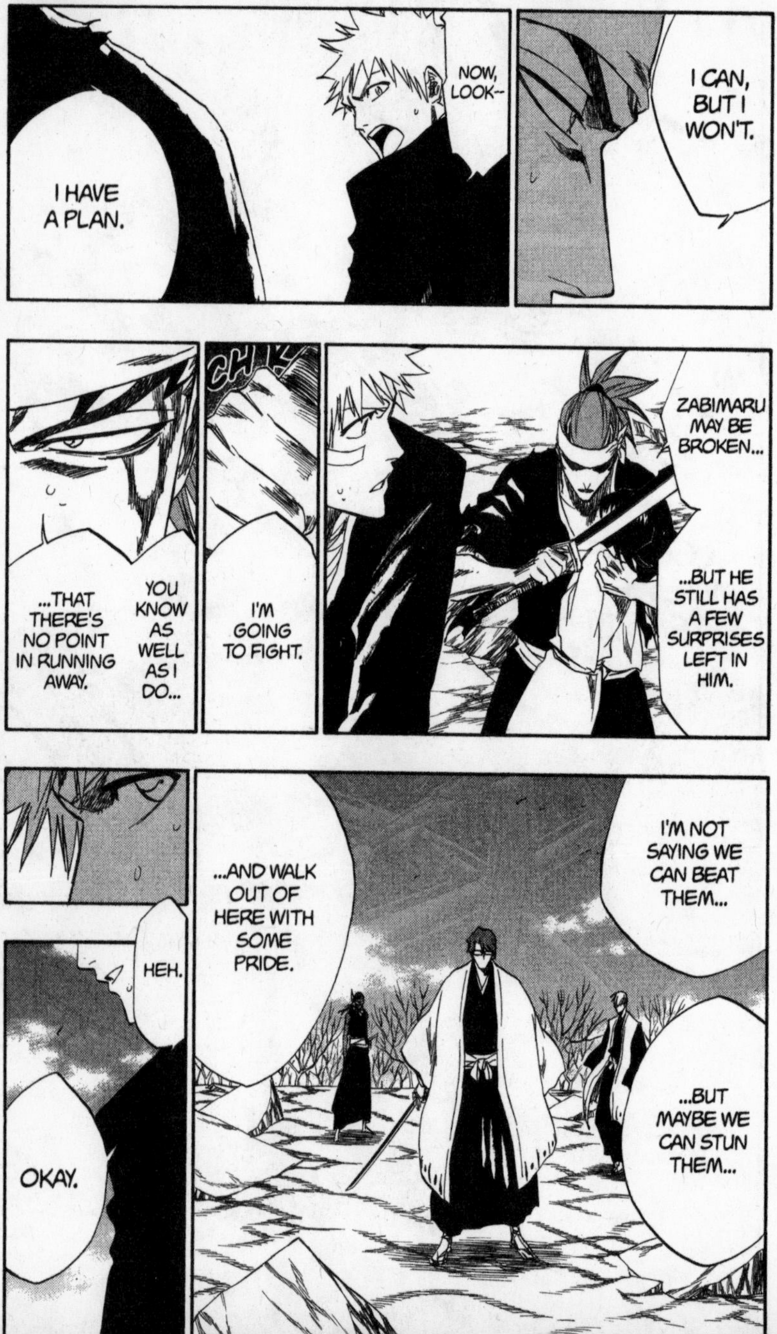
I CAN, BUT I WON'T.
NOW, LOOK--
I HAVE A PLAN.
ZABIMARU MAY BE BROKEN...
...BUT HE STILL HAS A FEW SURPRISES LEFT IN HIM.
I'M GOING TO FIGHT.
YOU KNOW AS WELL AS I DO...
...THAT THERE'S NO POINT IN RUNNING AWAY.
I'M NOT SAYING WE CAN BEAT THEM...
...BUT MAYBE WE CAN STUN THEM...
...AND WALK OUT OF HERE WITH SOME PRIDE.
HEH.
OKAY.

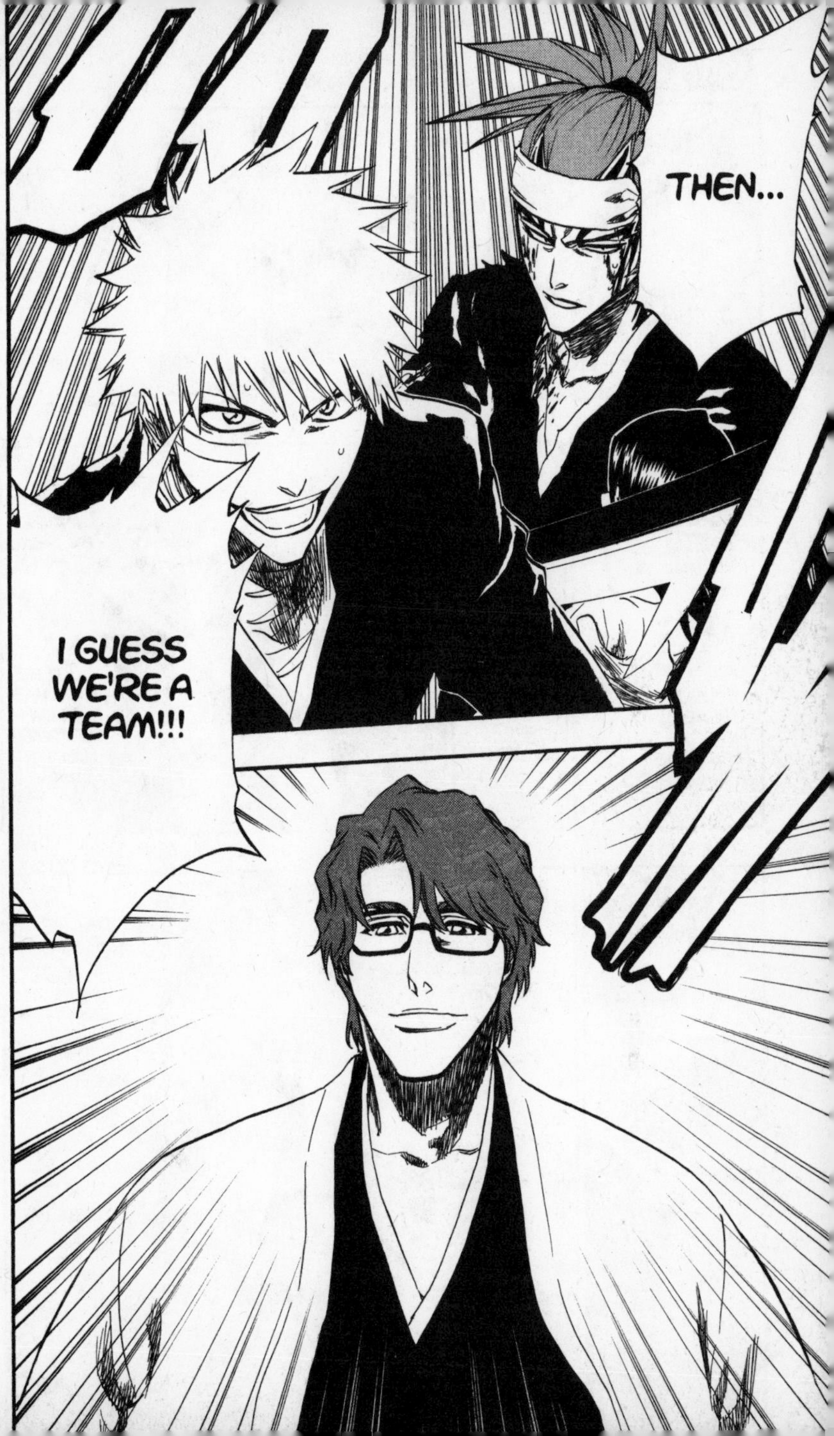
THEN...
I GUESS WE'RE A TEAM!!!

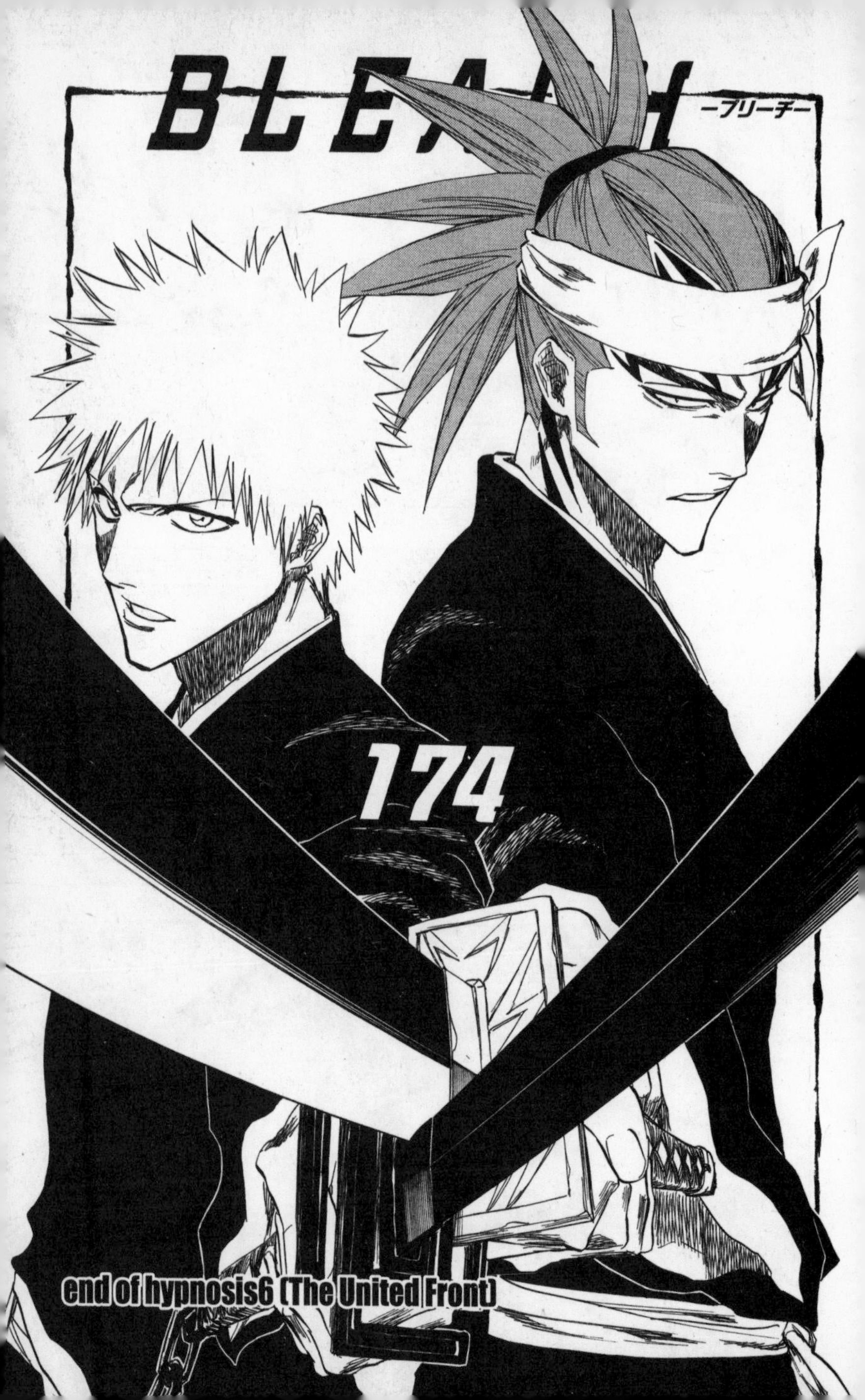
BLEACH
ーブリーチー
174
end of hypnosis6 (The United Front)

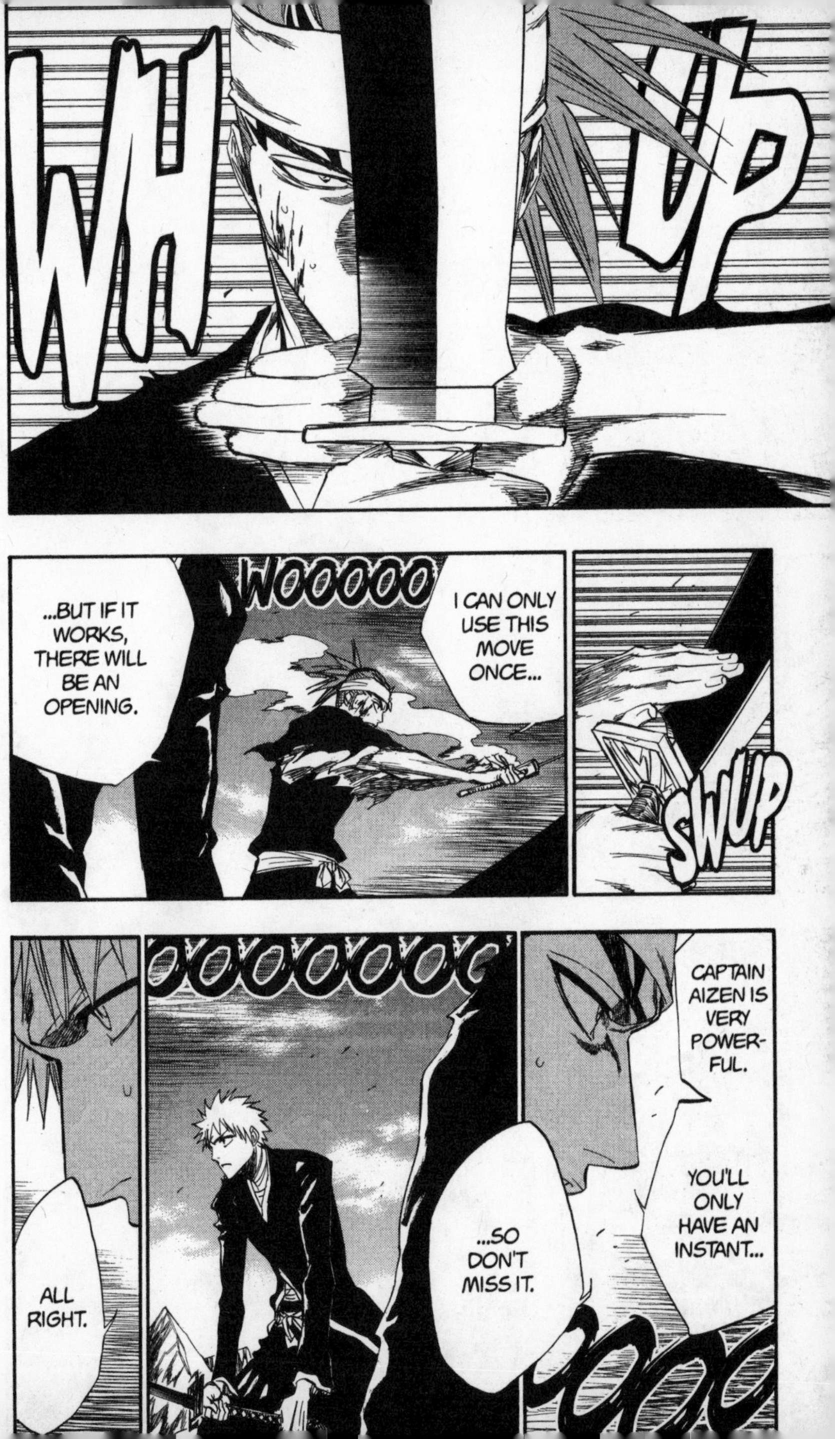
WHUP
SWUP
I CAN ONLY USE THIS MOVE ONCE...
...BUT IF IT WORKS, THERE WILL BE AN OPENING.
WOOOOO
CAPTAIN AIZEN IS VERY POWER-FUL.
YOU'LL ONLY HAVE AN INSTANT...
OOOOOOOOO
...SO DON'T MISS IT.
ALL RIGHT.

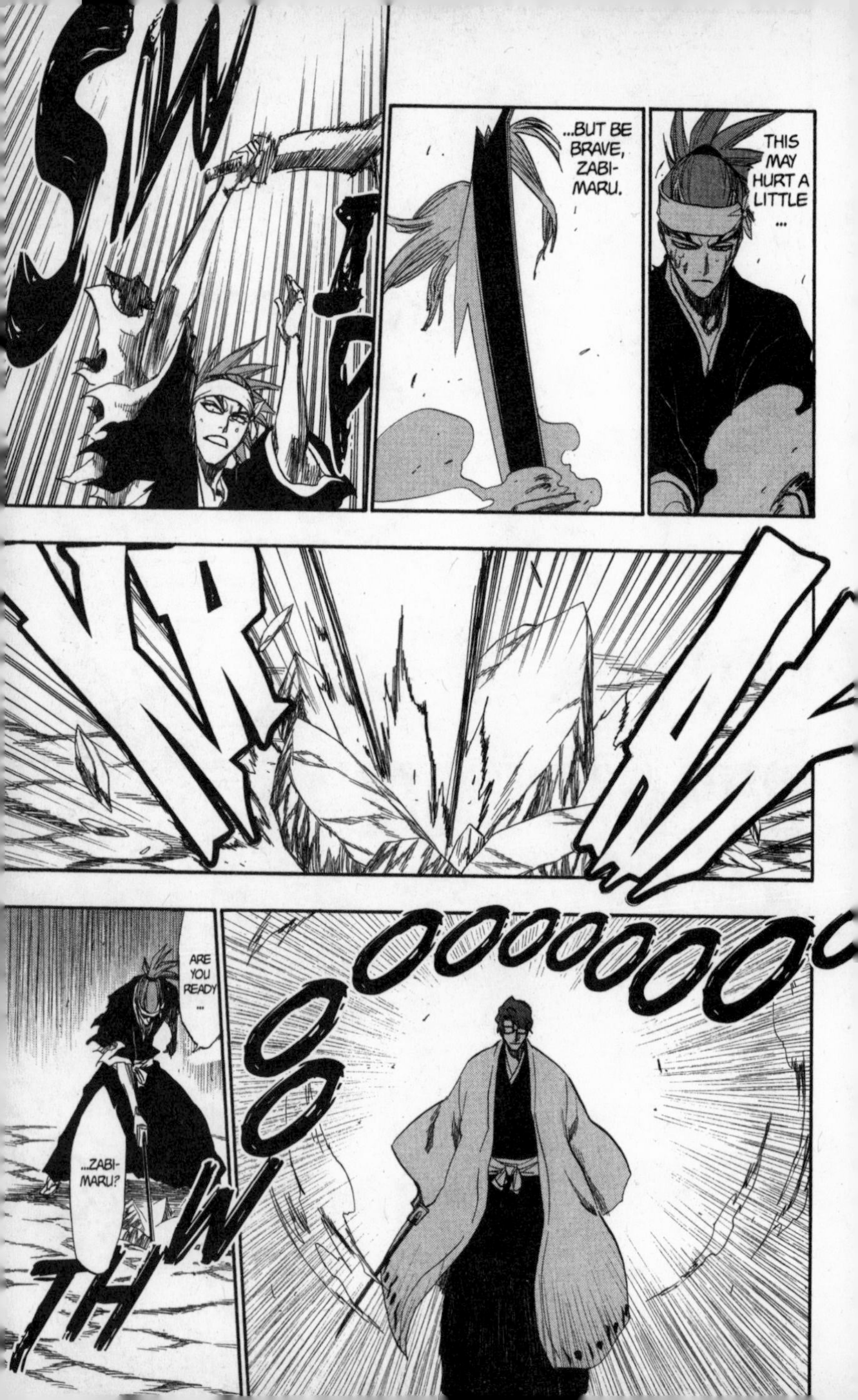
THIS MAY HURT A LITTLE ...
...BUT BE BRAVE, ZABI-MARU.
ARE YOU READY ...
...ZABI-MARU?

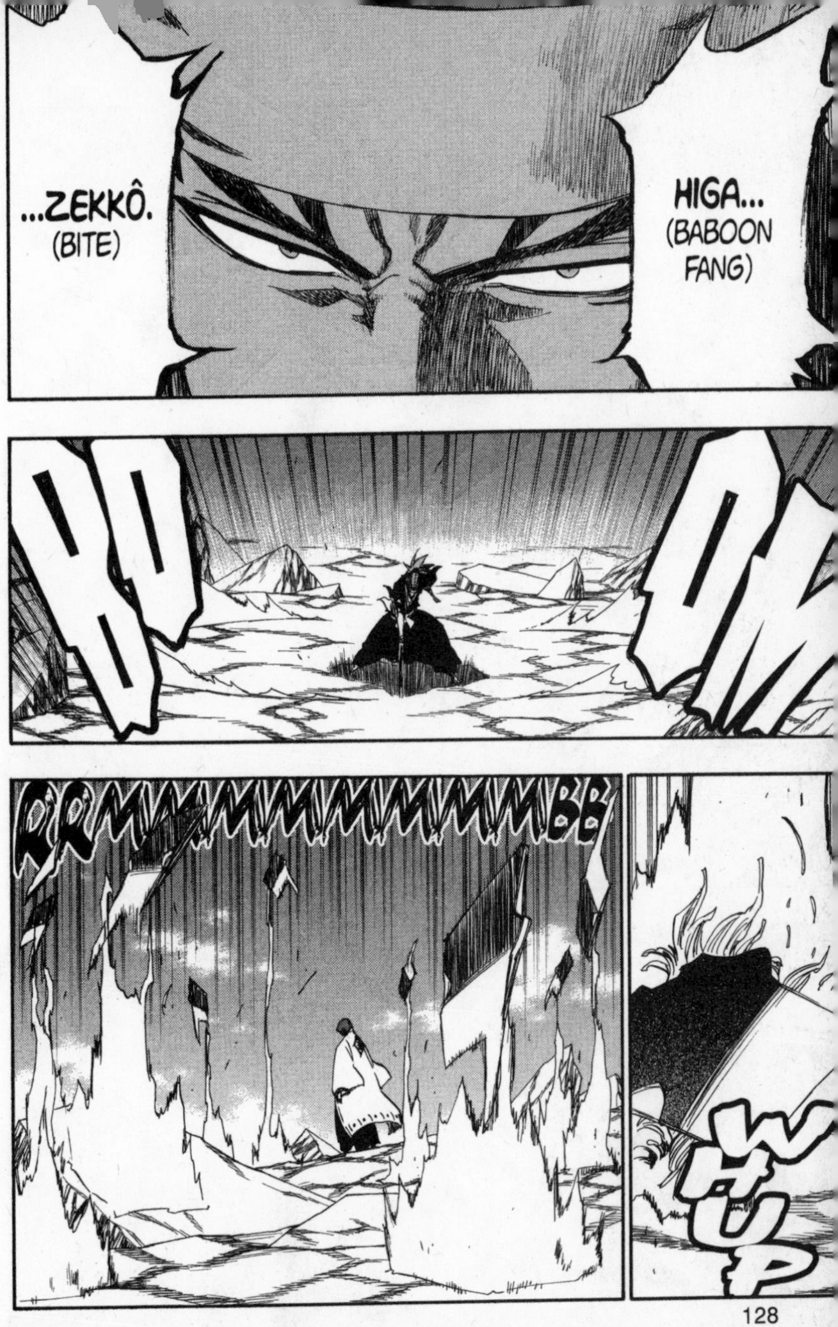
HIGA...
(BABOON FANG)
...ZEKKÔ.
(BITE)
WHUP

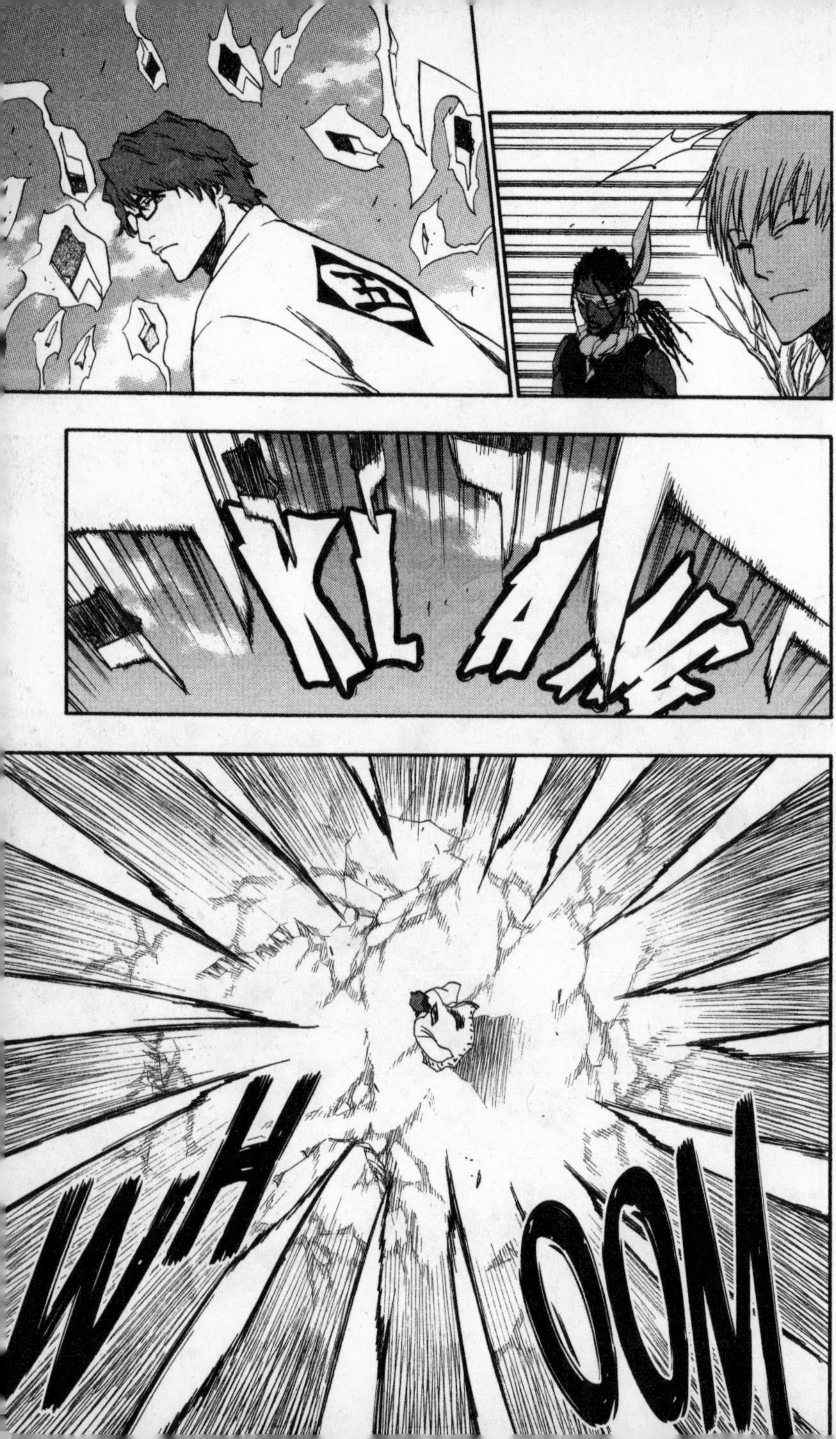
WHOOM

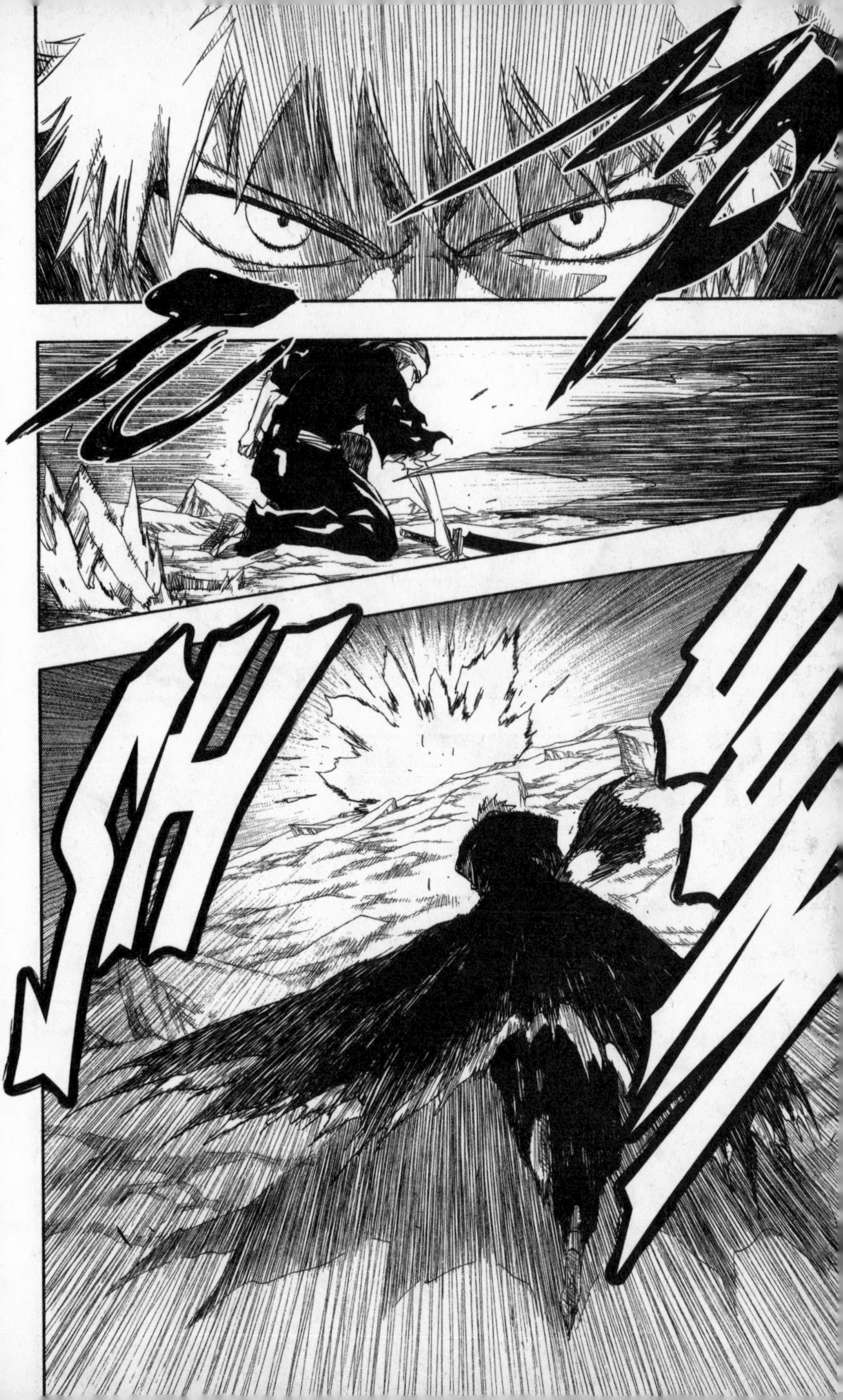
SH

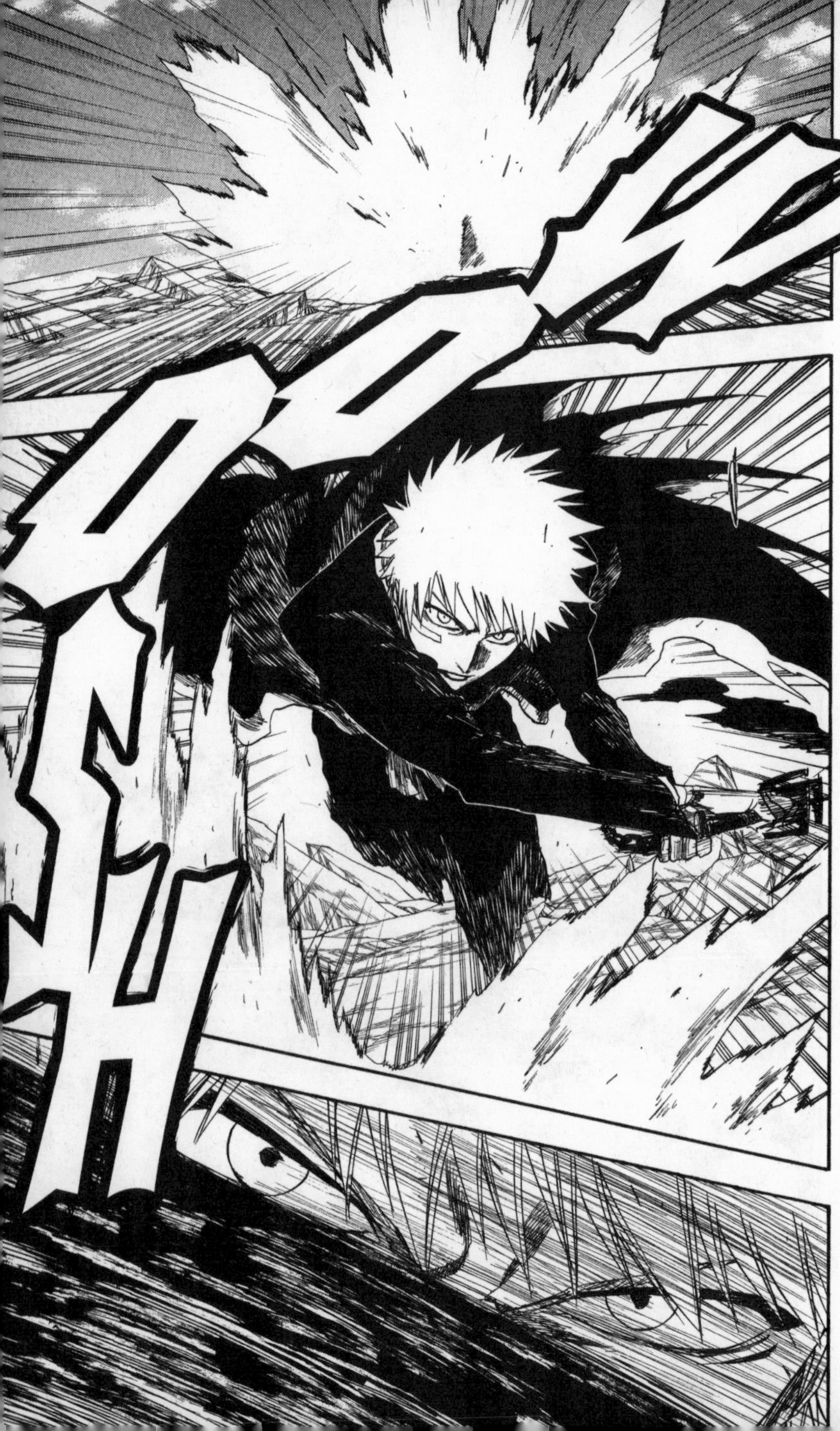

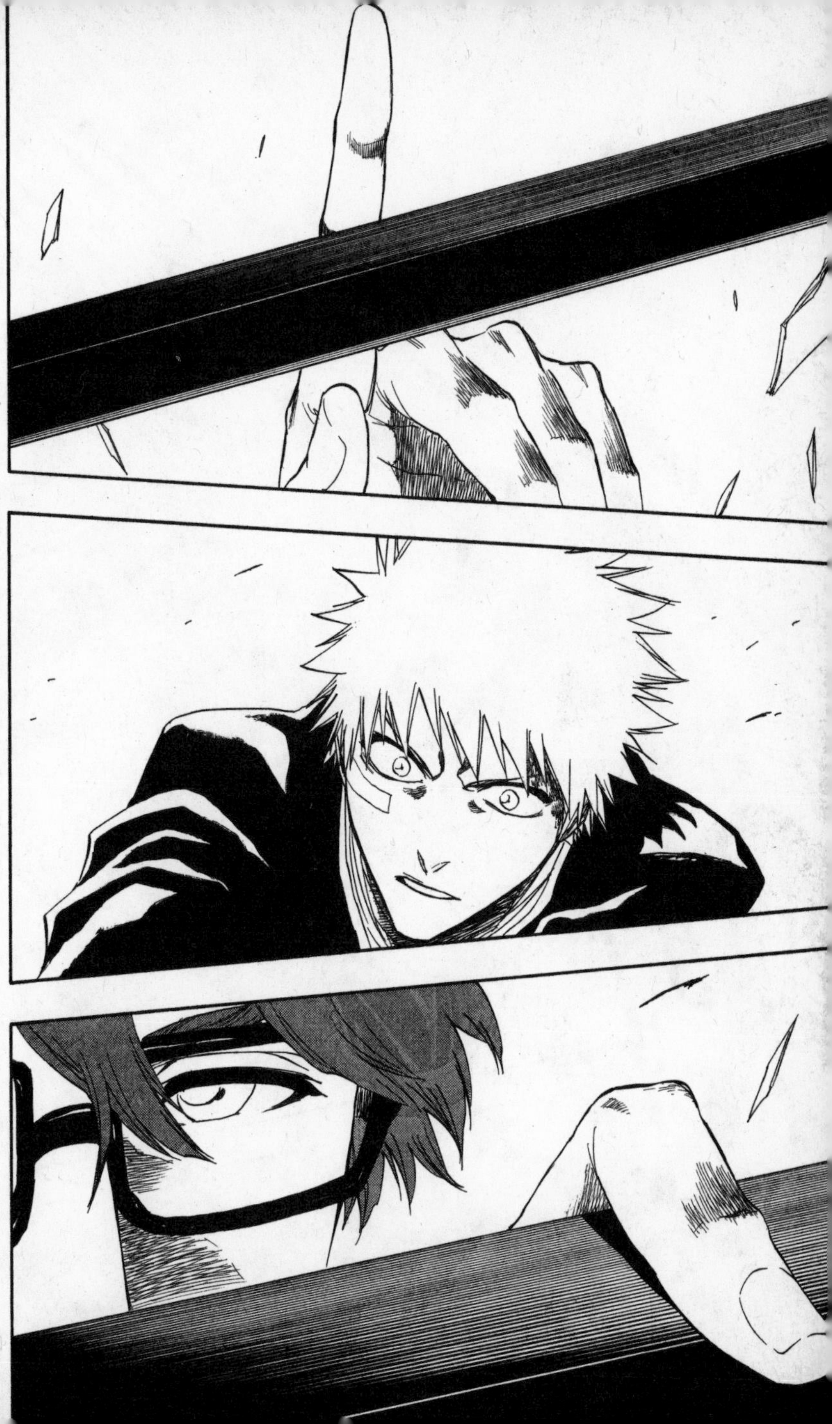

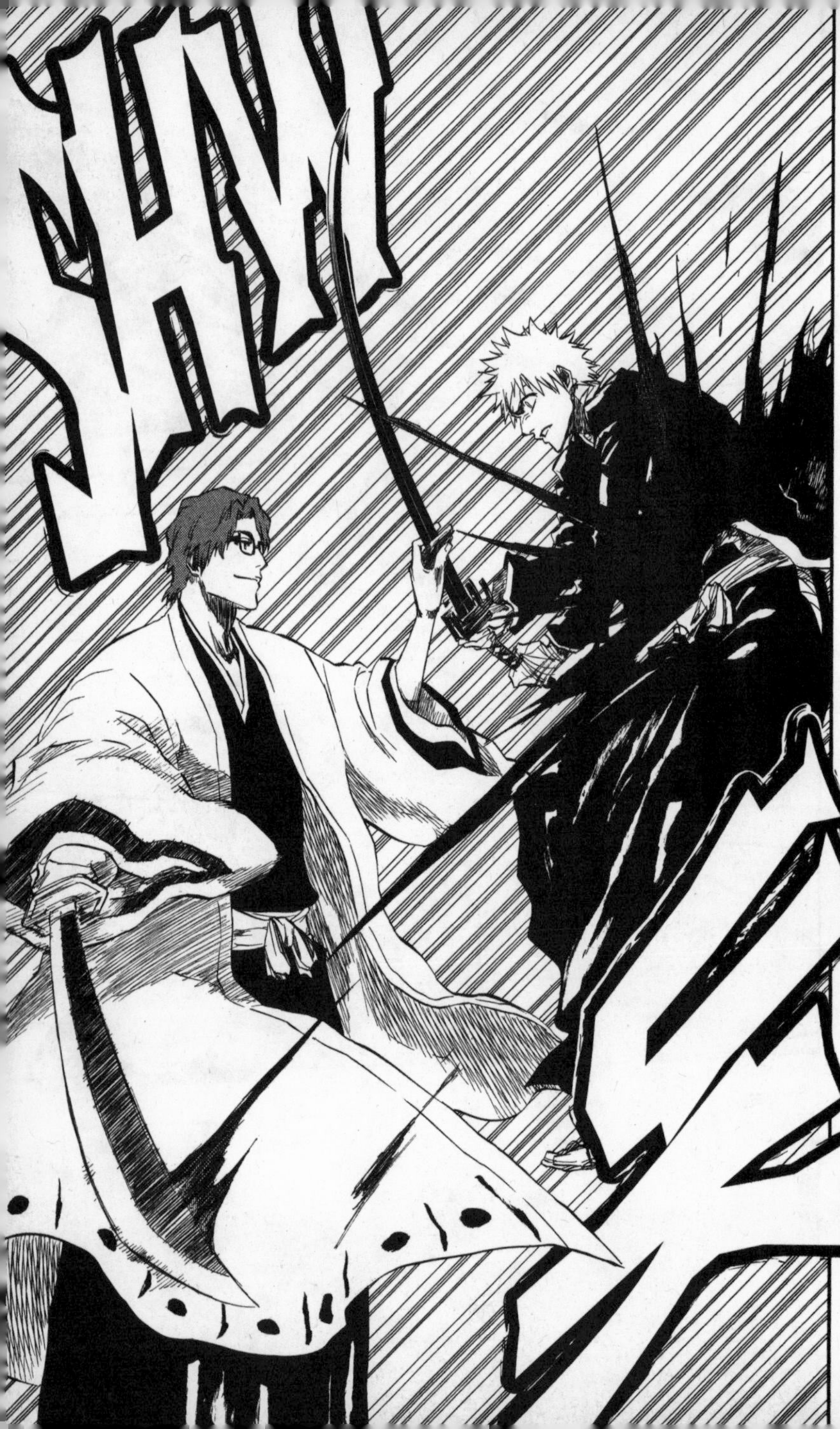

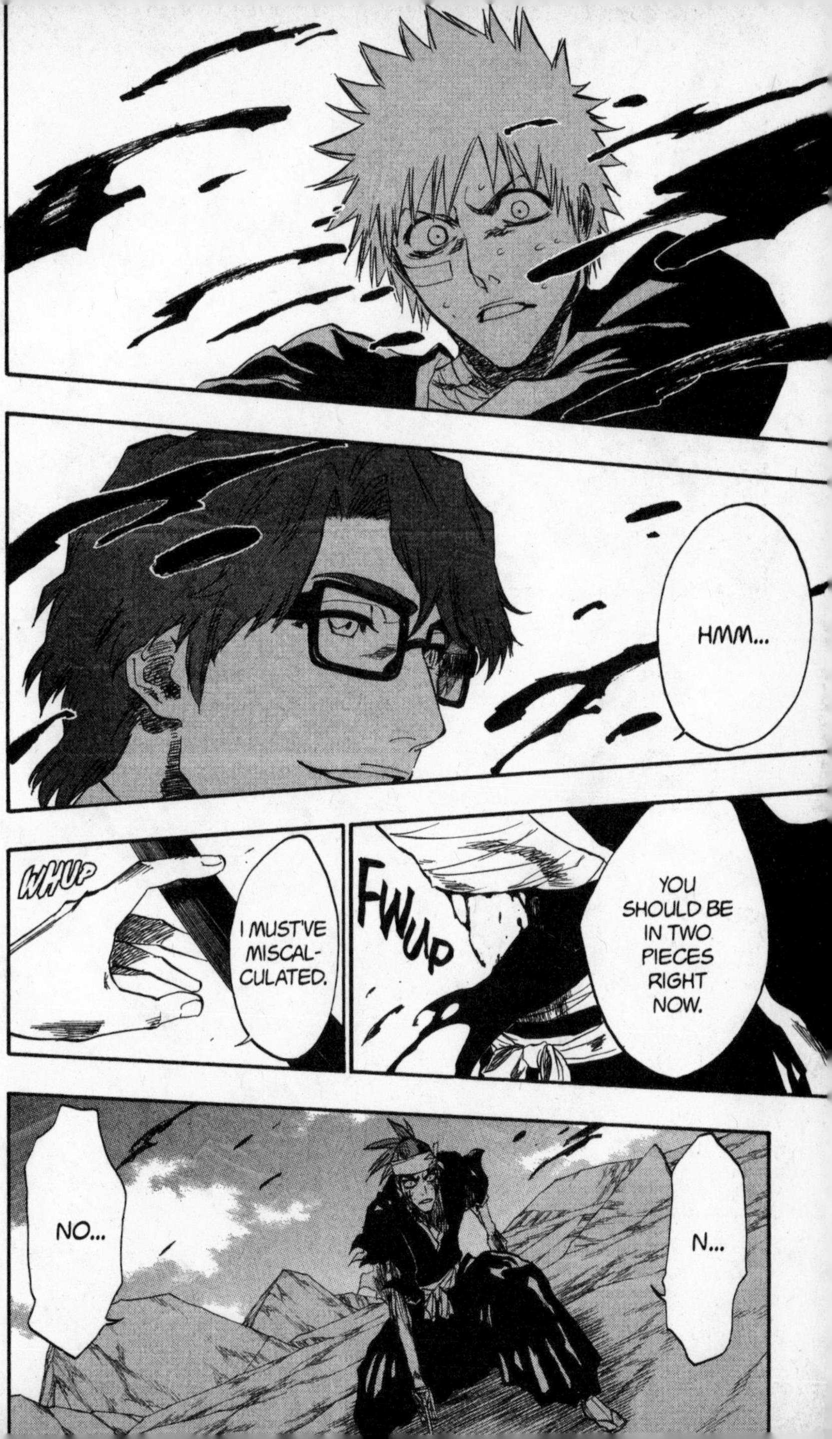
HMM...
YOU SHOULD BE IN TWO PIECES RIGHT NOW.
FWUP
I MUST'VE MISCAL-CULATED.
WHUP
N...
NO...

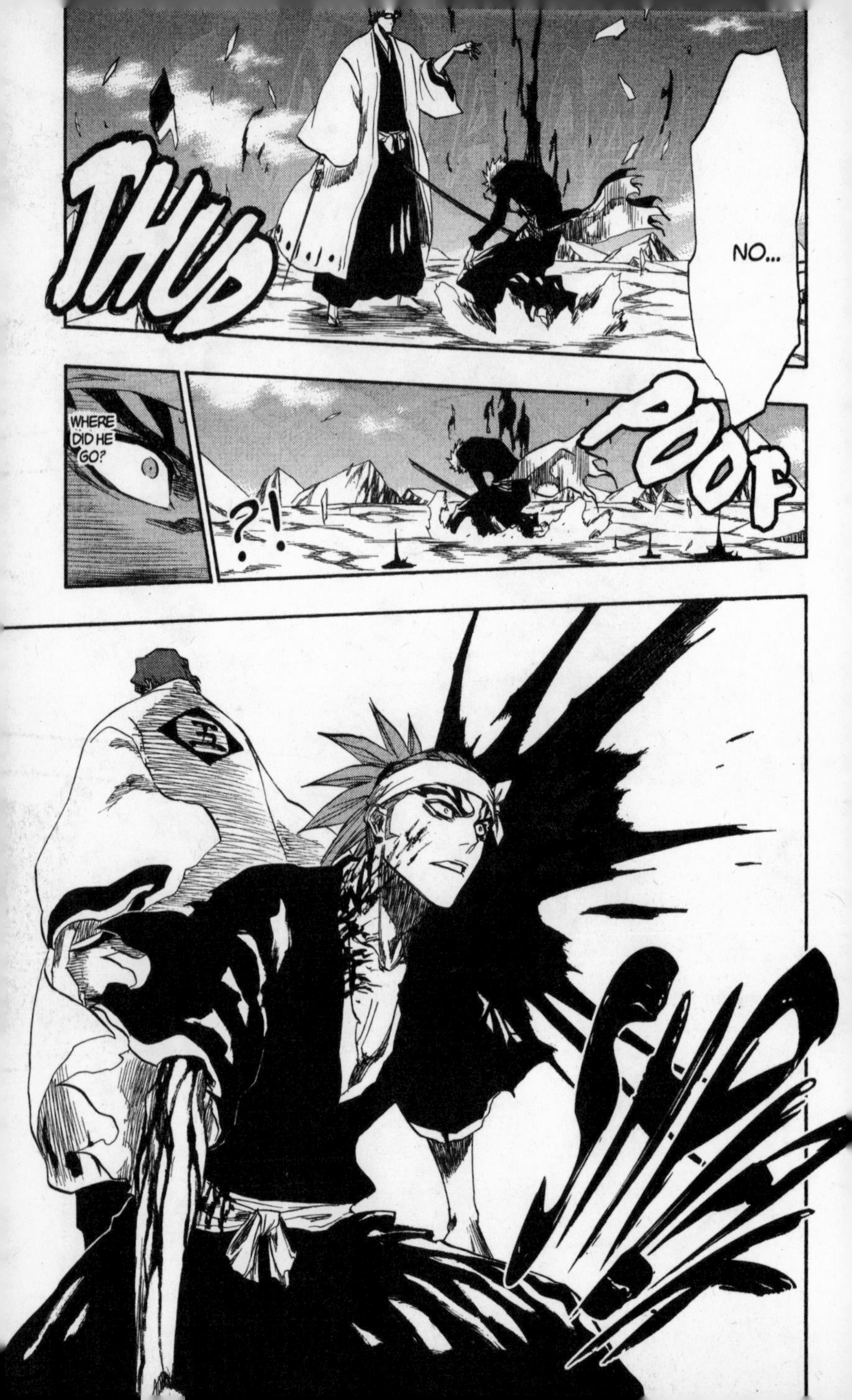
NO...
THUD
POOF
?!
WHERE DID HE GO?

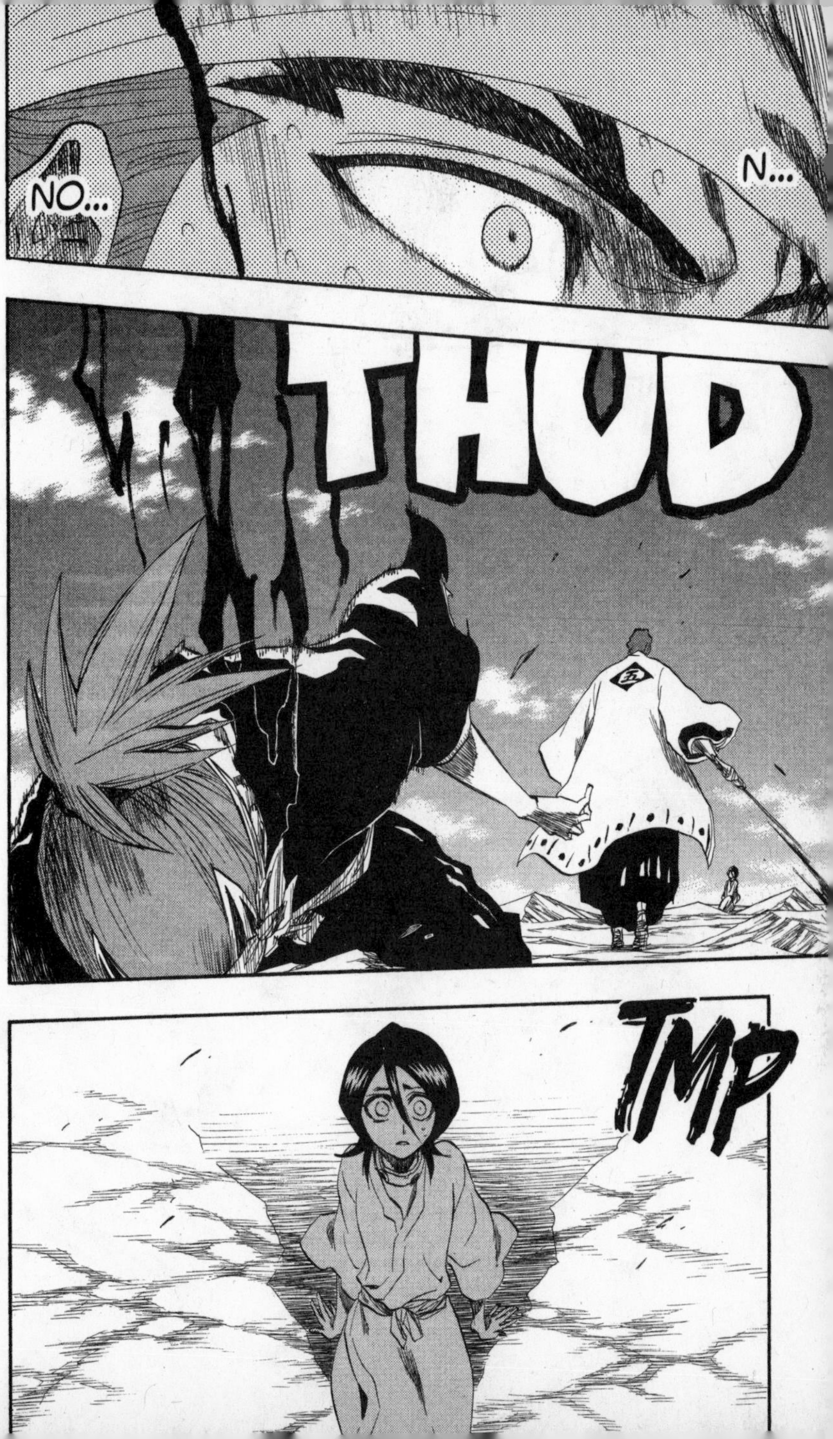
N...
NO...
THUD
TMP

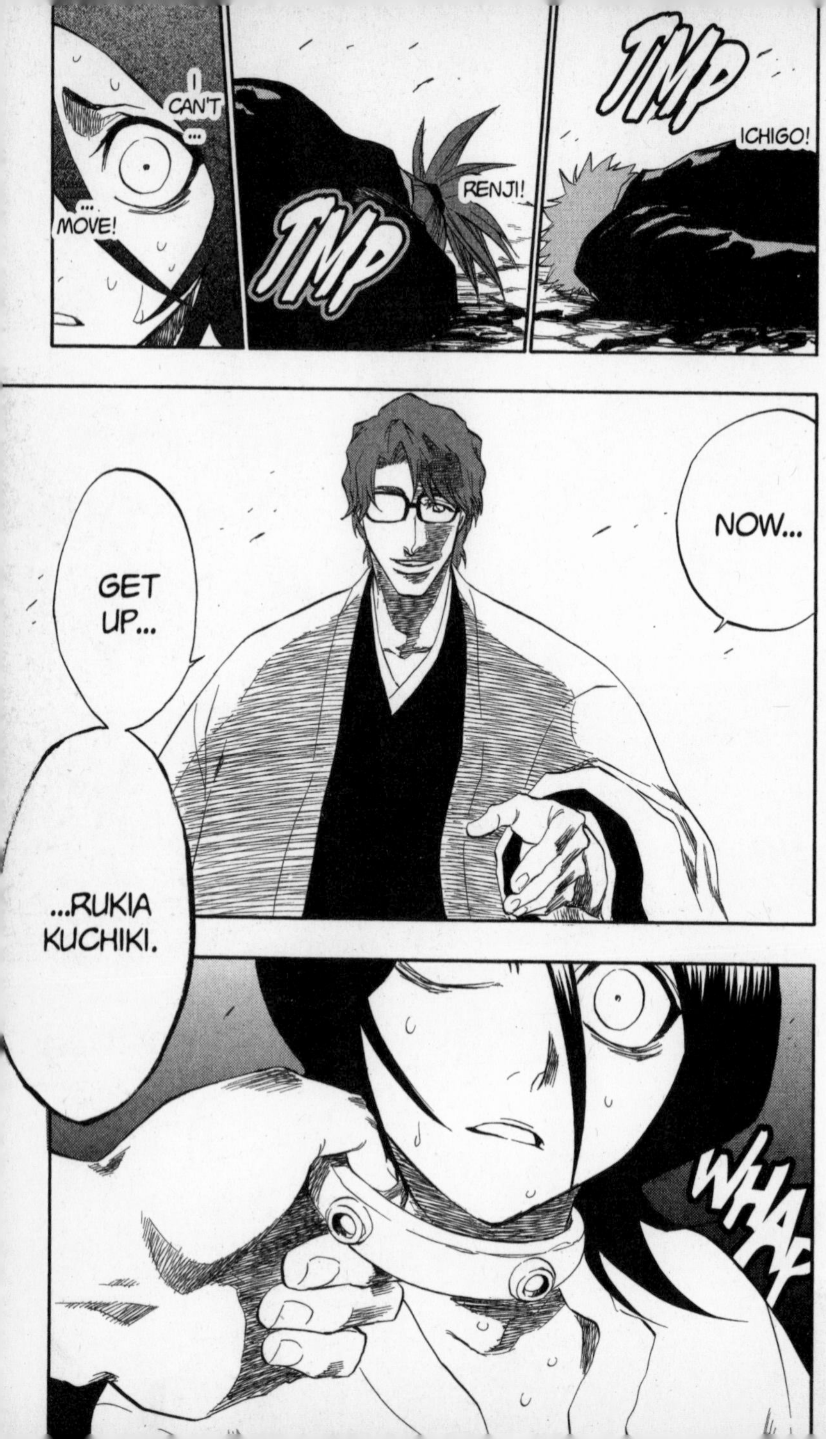
TMP
ICHIGO!
RENJI!
TMP
I CAN'T ...
... MOVE!
NOW...
GET UP...
...RUKIA KUCHIKI.
WHAK

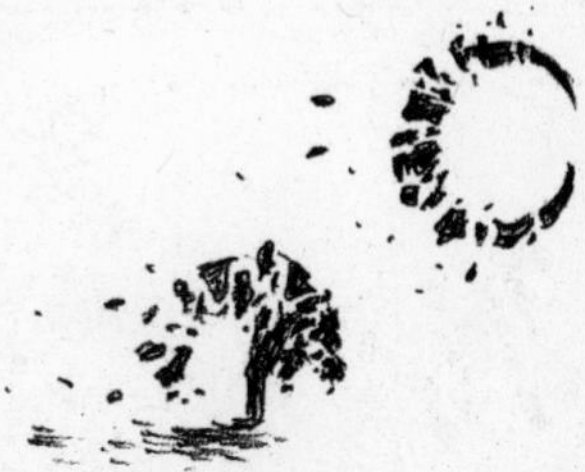

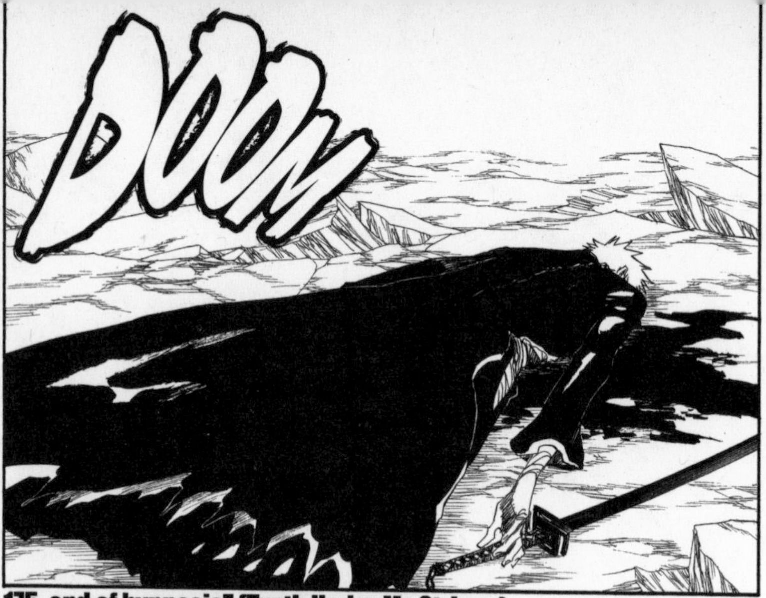
DOOM

175. end of hypnosis7 (Truth Under My Strings)

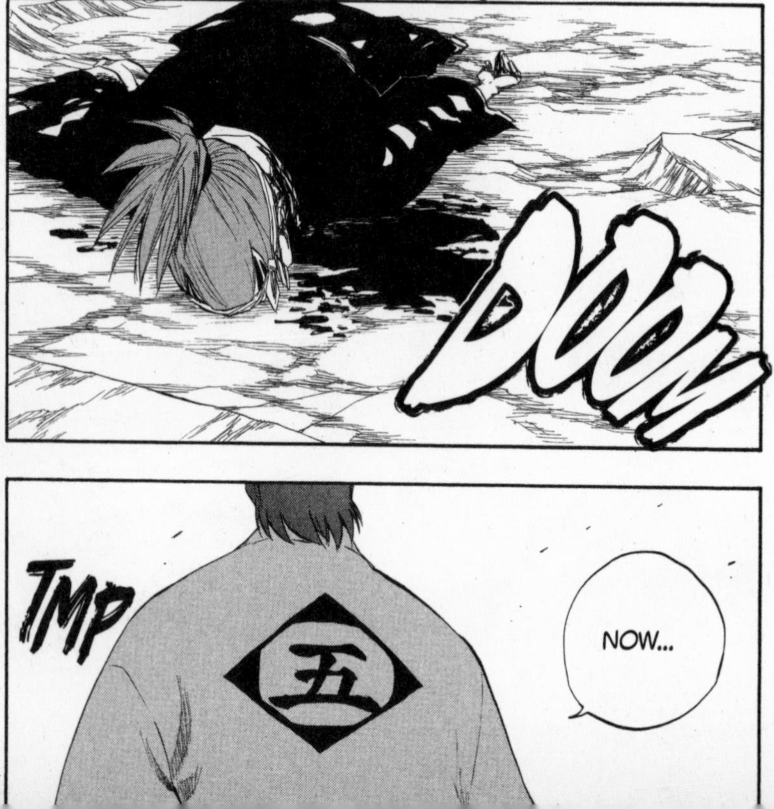
DOOM
TMP
NOW...

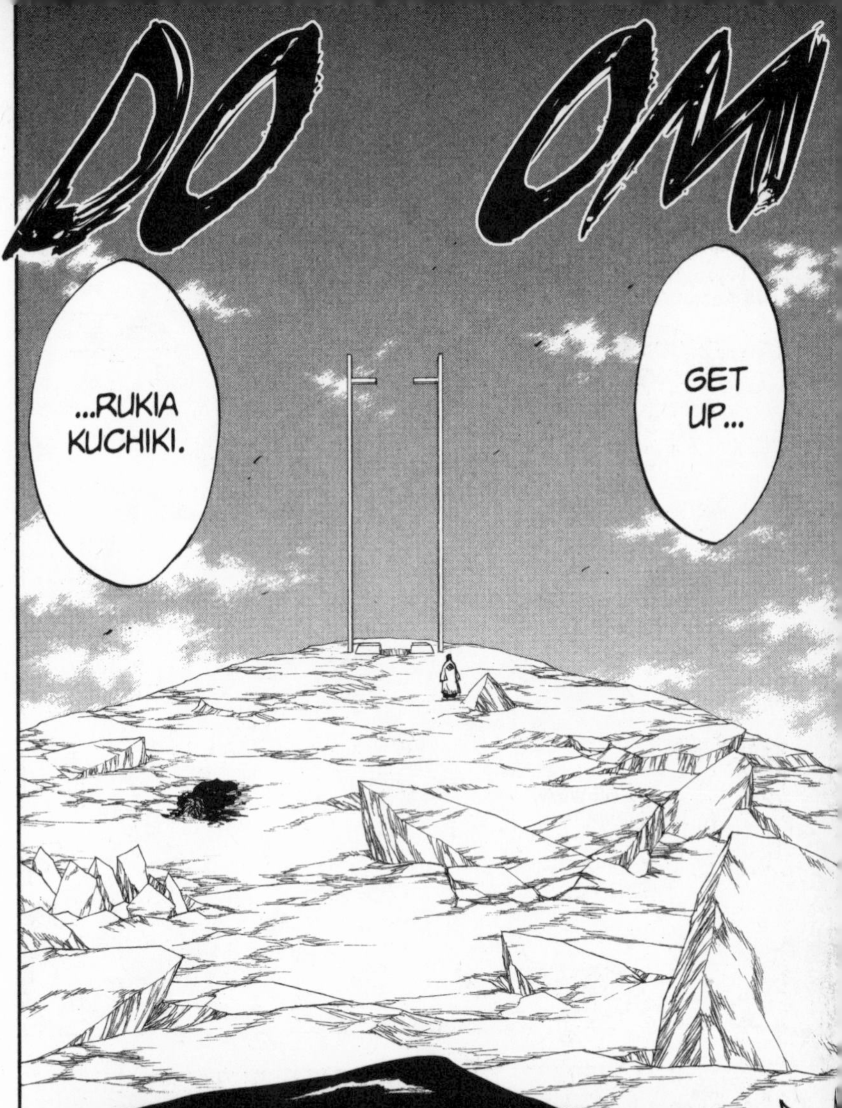

[redacted]

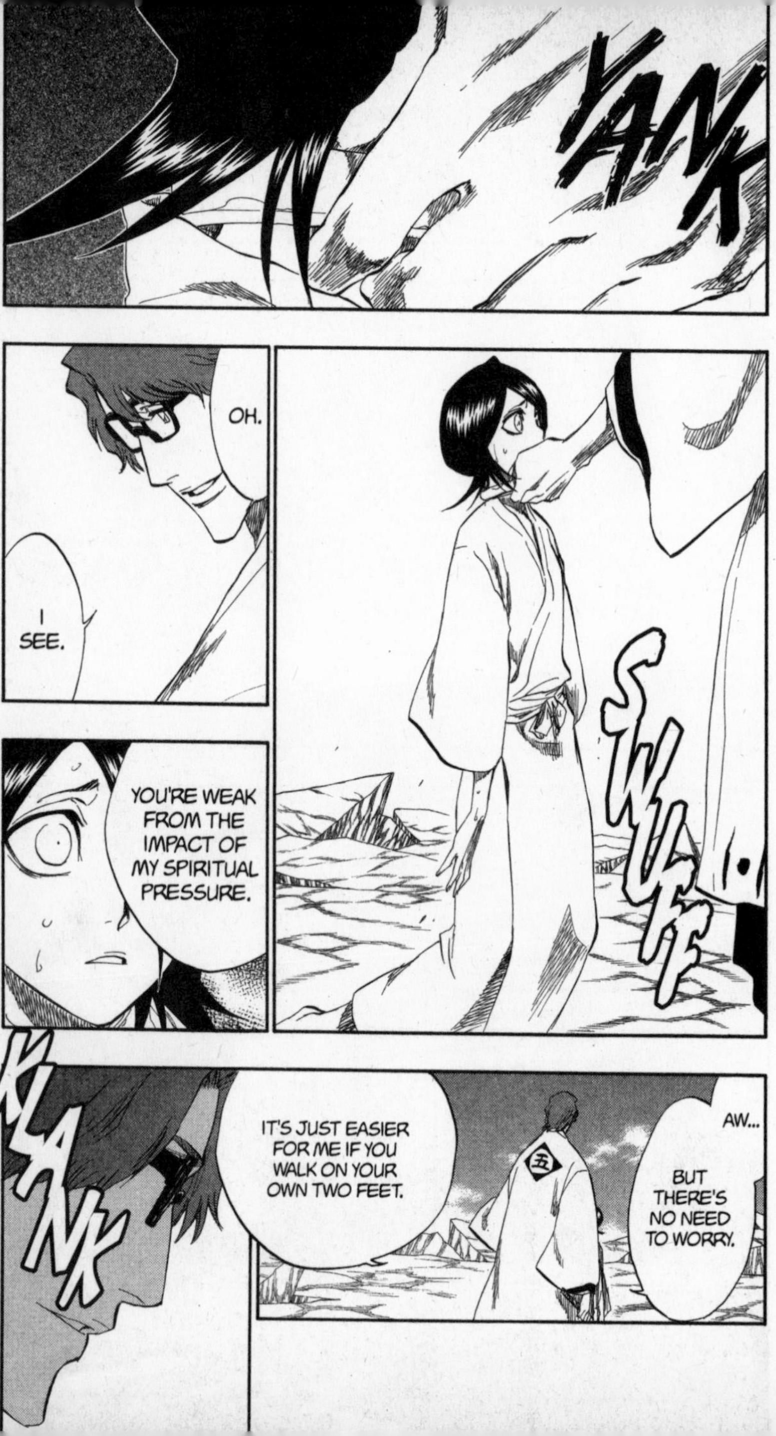
YANK
SWUFF
OH.
I SEE.
YOU'RE WEAK FROM THE IMPACT OF MY SPIRITUAL PRESSURE.
AW...
BUT THERE'S NO NEED TO WORRY.
IT'S JUST EASIER FOR ME IF YOU WALK ON YOUR OWN TWO FEET.
KLANK

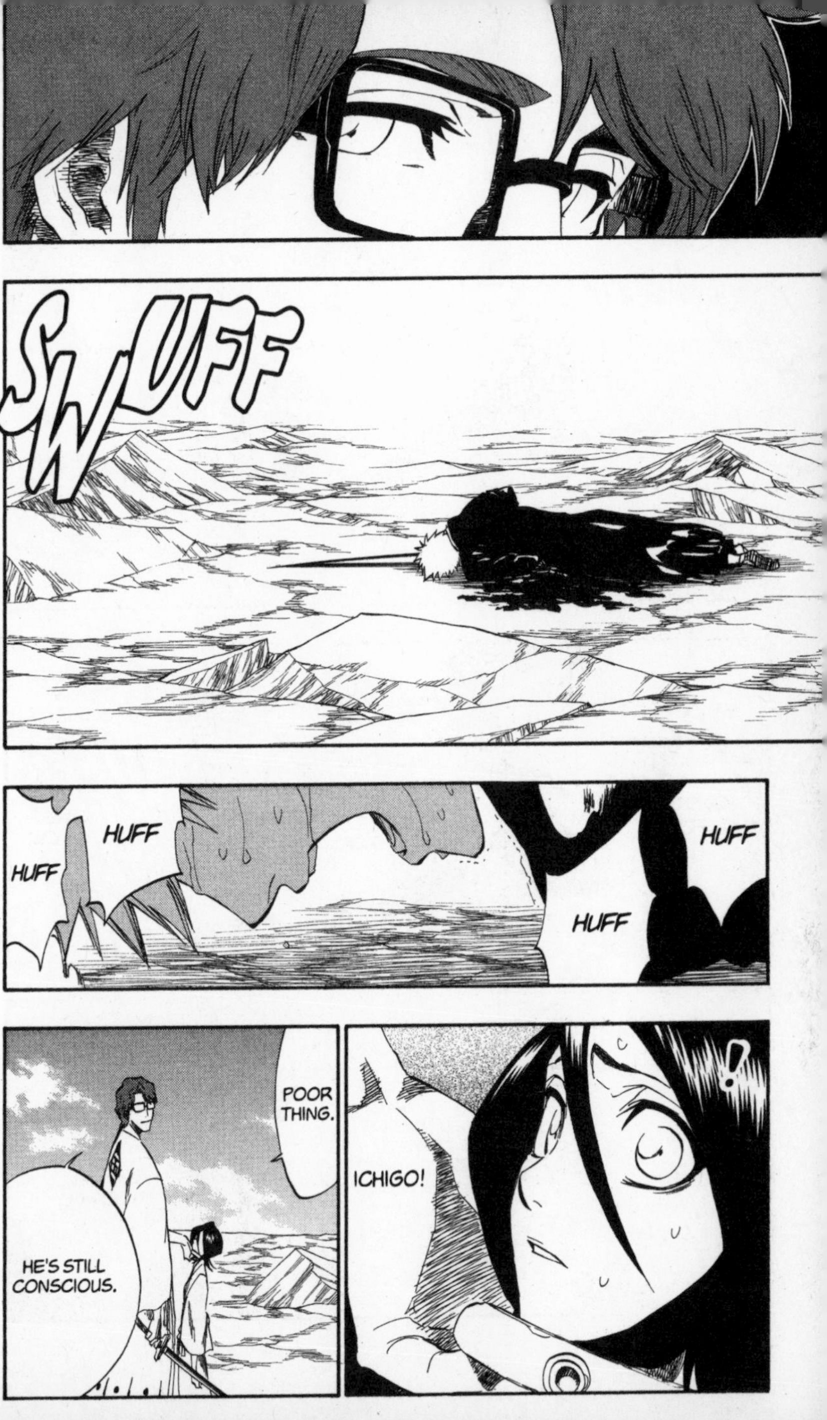
SWUFF
HUFF
HUFF
HUFF
HUFF
ICHIGO!
POOR THING.
HE'S STILL CONSCIOUS.

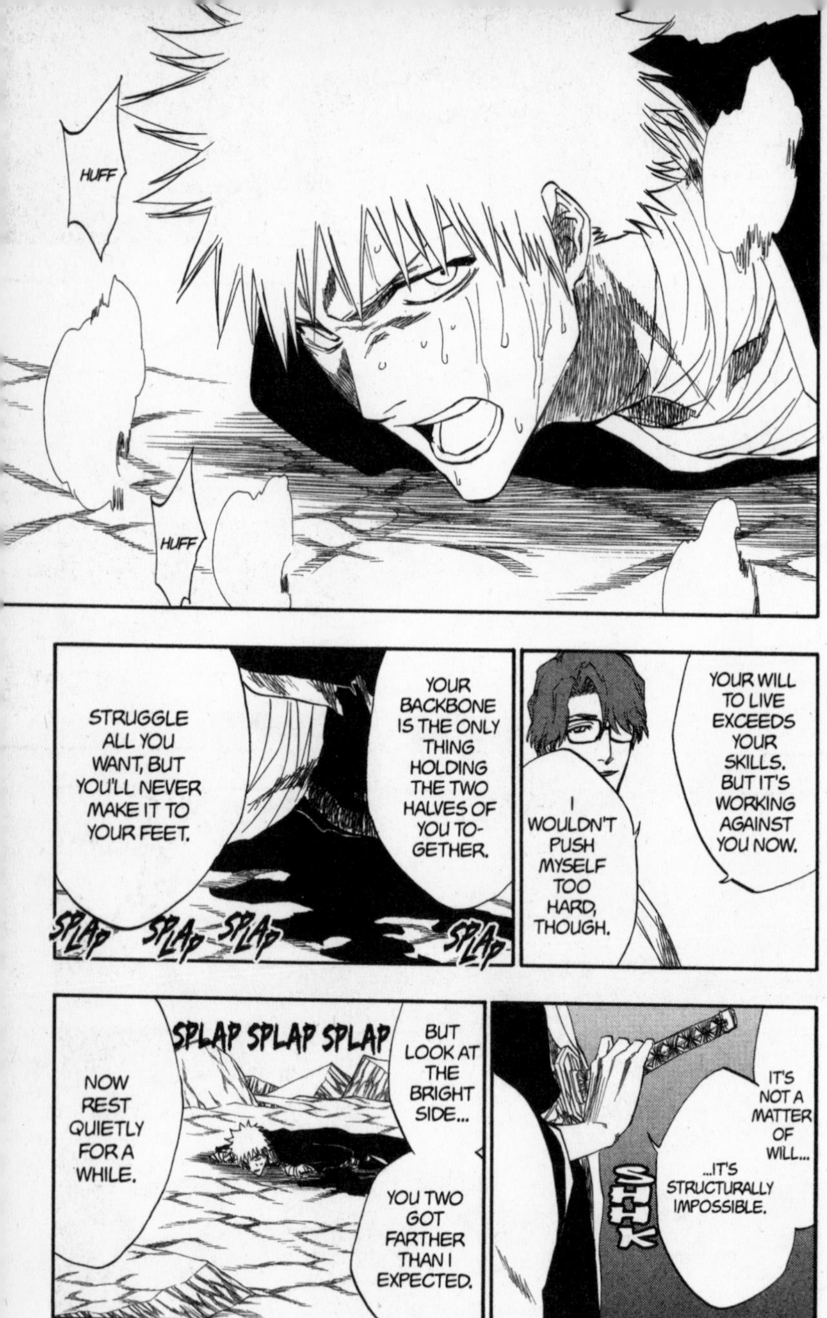
HUFF
HUFF
YOUR WILL TO LIVE EXCEEDS YOUR SKILLS. BUT IT'S WORKING AGAINST YOU NOW.
I WOULDN'T PUSH MYSELF TOO HARD, THOUGH.
YOUR BACKBONE IS THE ONLY THING HOLDING THE TWO HALVES OF YOU TO-GETHER.
STRUGGLE ALL YOU WANT, BUT YOU'LL NEVER MAKE IT TO YOUR FEET.
SPLAP
SPLAP
SPLAP
SPLAP
IT'S NOT A MATTER OF WILL...
...IT'S STRUCTURALLY IMPOSSIBLE.
SHIK
SPLAP SPLAP SPLAP
BUT LOOK AT THE BRIGHT SIDE...
YOU TWO GOT FARTHER THAN I EXPECTED.
NOW REST QUIETLY FOR A WHILE.

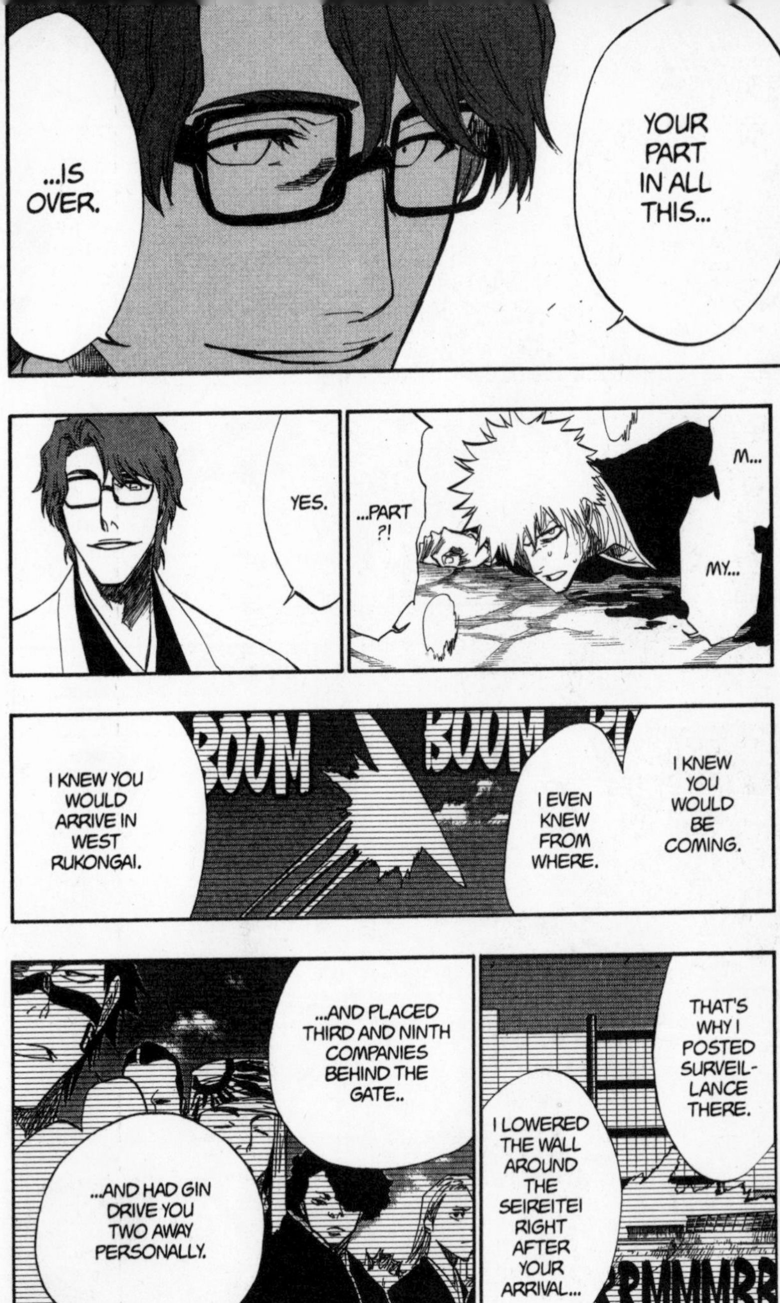
YOUR PART IN ALL THIS...
...IS OVER.
M...
MY...
...PART ?!
YES.
I KNEW YOU WOULD BE COMING.
I EVEN KNEW FROM WHERE.
BOOM
BOOM
I KNEW YOU WOULD ARRIVE IN WEST RUKONGAI.
THAT'S WHY I POSTED SURVEIL-LANCE THERE.
I LOWERED THE WALL AROUND THE SEIREITEI RIGHT AFTER YOUR ARRIVAL...
RRMMMRB
...AND PLACED THIRD AND NINTH COMPANIES BEHIND THE GATE..
...AND HAD GIN DRIVE YOU TWO AWAY PERSONALLY.

READ THIS WAY

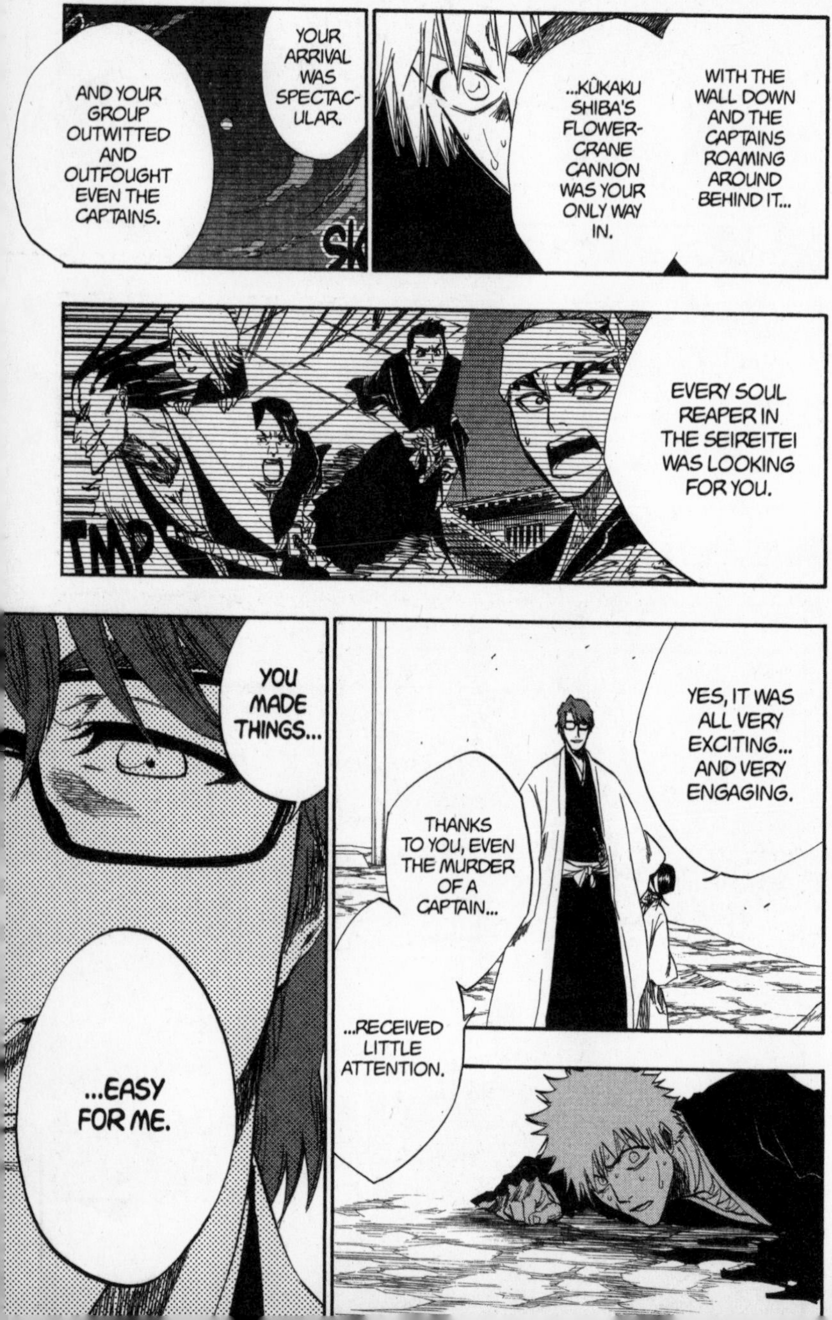
WITH THE WALL DOWN AND THE CAPTAINS ROAMING AROUND BEHIND IT...
...KÛKAKU SHIBA'S FLOWER-CRANE CANNON WAS YOUR ONLY WAY IN.
YOUR ARRIVAL WAS SPECTAC-ULAR.
AND YOUR GROUP OUTWITTED AND OUTFOUGHT EVEN THE CAPTAINS.
SK
EVERY SOUL REAPER IN THE SEIREITEI WAS LOOKING FOR YOU.
TMP
YES, IT WAS ALL VERY EXCITING... AND VERY ENGAGING.
THANKS TO YOU, EVEN THE MURDER OF A CAPTAIN...
...RECEIVED LITTLE ATTENTION.
YOU MADE THINGS...
...EASY FOR ME.

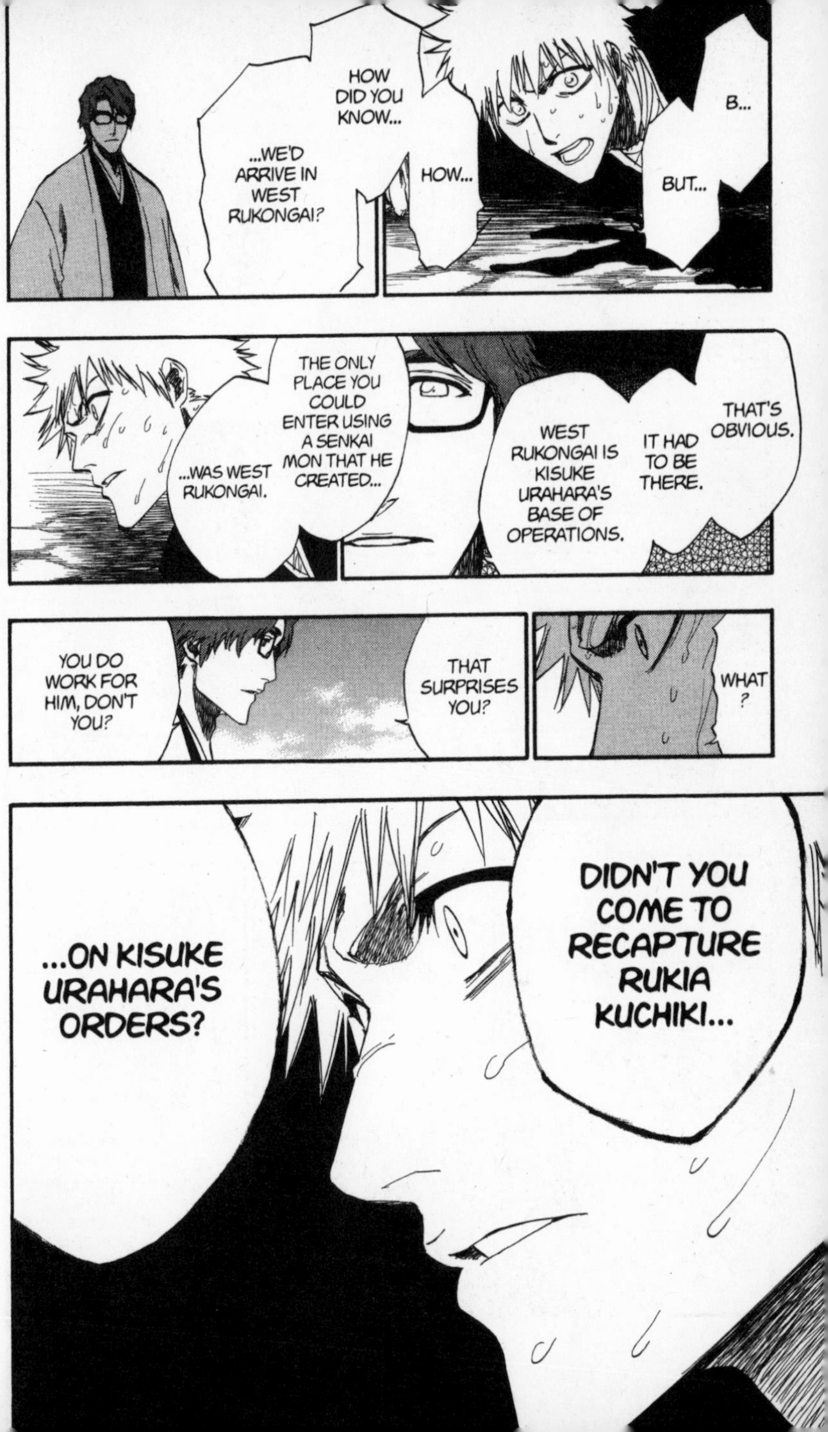
B...
BUT...
HOW...
HOW DID YOU KNOW...
...WE'D ARRIVE IN WEST RUKONGAI?
THAT'S OBVIOUS.
IT HAD TO BE THERE.
WEST RUKONGAI IS KISUKE URAHARA'S BASE OF OPERATIONS.
THE ONLY PLACE YOU COULD ENTER USING A SENKAI MON THAT HE CREATED...
...WAS WEST RUKONGAI.
WHAT?
THAT SURPRISES YOU?
YOU DO WORK FOR HIM, DON'T YOU?
DIDN'T YOU COME TO RECAPTURE RUKIA KUCHIKI...
...ON KISUKE URAHARA'S ORDERS?

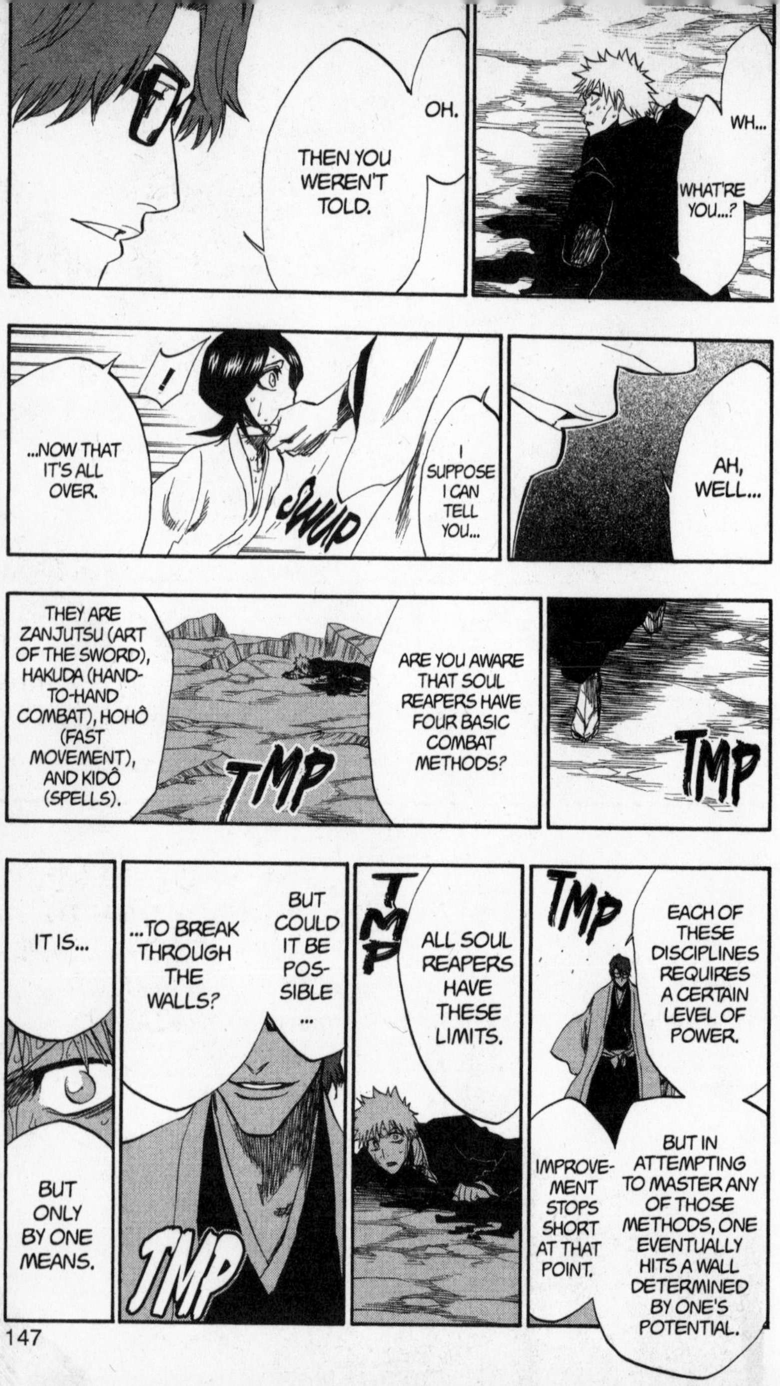
WH...
WHAT'RE YOU...?
OH.
THEN YOU WEREN'T TOLD.
AH, WELL...
I SUPPOSE I CAN TELL YOU...
SWUP
!
...NOW THAT IT'S ALL OVER.
TMP
ARE YOU AWARE THAT SOUL REAPERS HAVE FOUR BASIC COMBAT METHODS?
TMP
THEY ARE ZANJUTSU (ART OF THE SWORD), HAKUDA (HAND-TO-HAND COMBAT), HOHÔ (FAST MOVEMENT), AND KIDÔ (SPELLS).
TMP
EACH OF THESE DISCIPLINES REQUIRES A CERTAIN LEVEL OF POWER.
BUT IN ATTEMPTING TO MASTER ANY OF THOSE METHODS, ONE EVENTUALLY HITS A WALL DETERMINED BY ONE'S POTENTIAL.
IMPROVE-MENT STOPS SHORT AT THAT POINT.
TMP
ALL SOUL REAPERS HAVE THESE LIMITS.
BUT COULD IT BE POS-SIBLE...
...TO BREAK THROUGH THE WALLS?
TMP
IT IS...
BUT ONLY BY ONE MEANS.

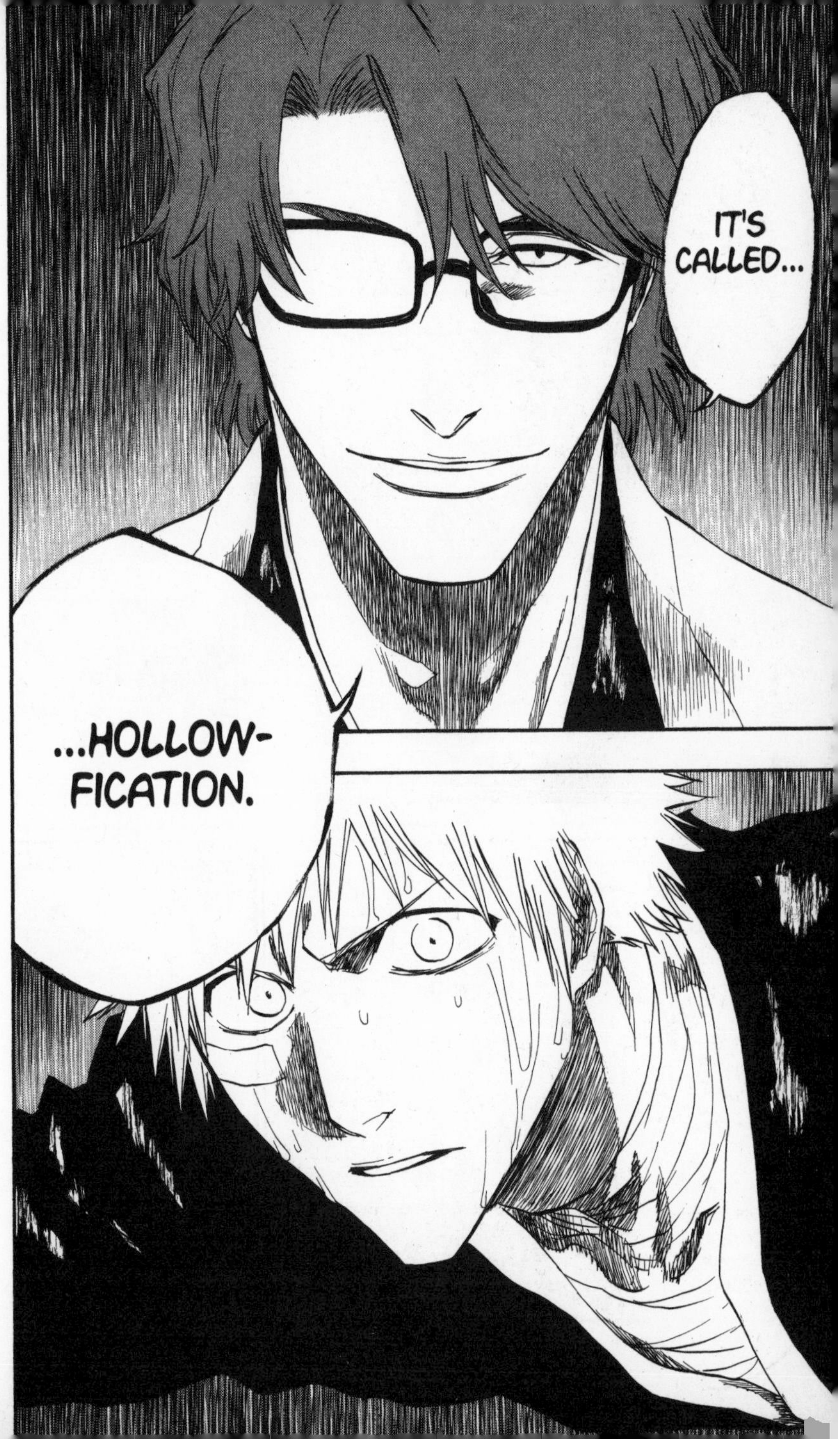
IT'S CALLED...
...HOLLOW-FICATION.

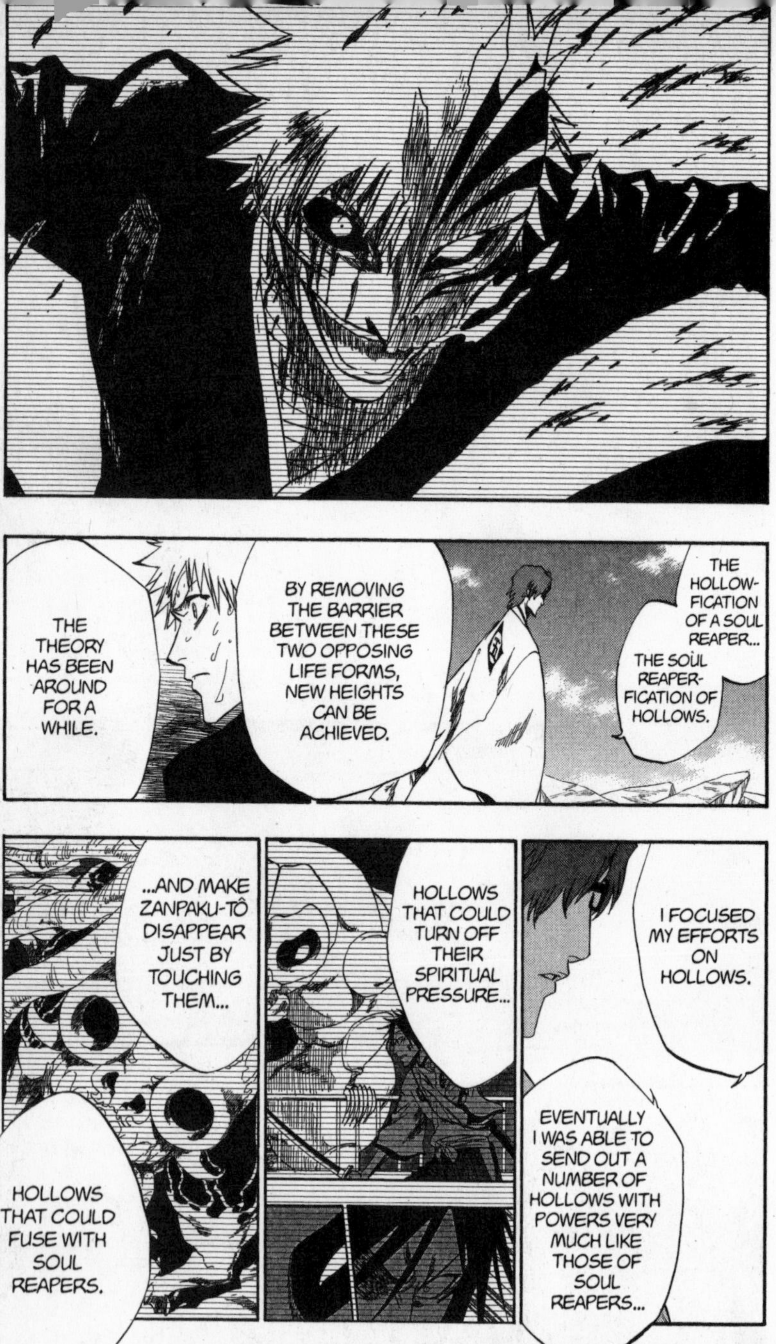
THE HOLLOWFICATION OF A SOUL REAPER... THE SOUL REAPERFICATION OF HOLLOWS.
BY REMOVING THE BARRIER BETWEEN THESE TWO OPPOSING LIFE FORMS, NEW HEIGHTS CAN BE ACHIEVED.
THE THEORY HAS BEEN AROUND FOR A WHILE.
I FOCUSED MY EFFORTS ON HOLLOWS.
EVENTUALLY I WAS ABLE TO SEND OUT A NUMBER OF HOLLOWS WITH POWERS VERY MUCH LIKE THOSE OF SOUL REAPERS...
HOLLOWS THAT COULD TURN OFF THEIR SPIRITUAL PRESSURE...
...AND MAKE ZANPAKU-TÔ DISAPPEAR JUST BY TOUCHING THEM...
HOLLOWS THAT COULD FUSE WITH SOUL REAPERS.

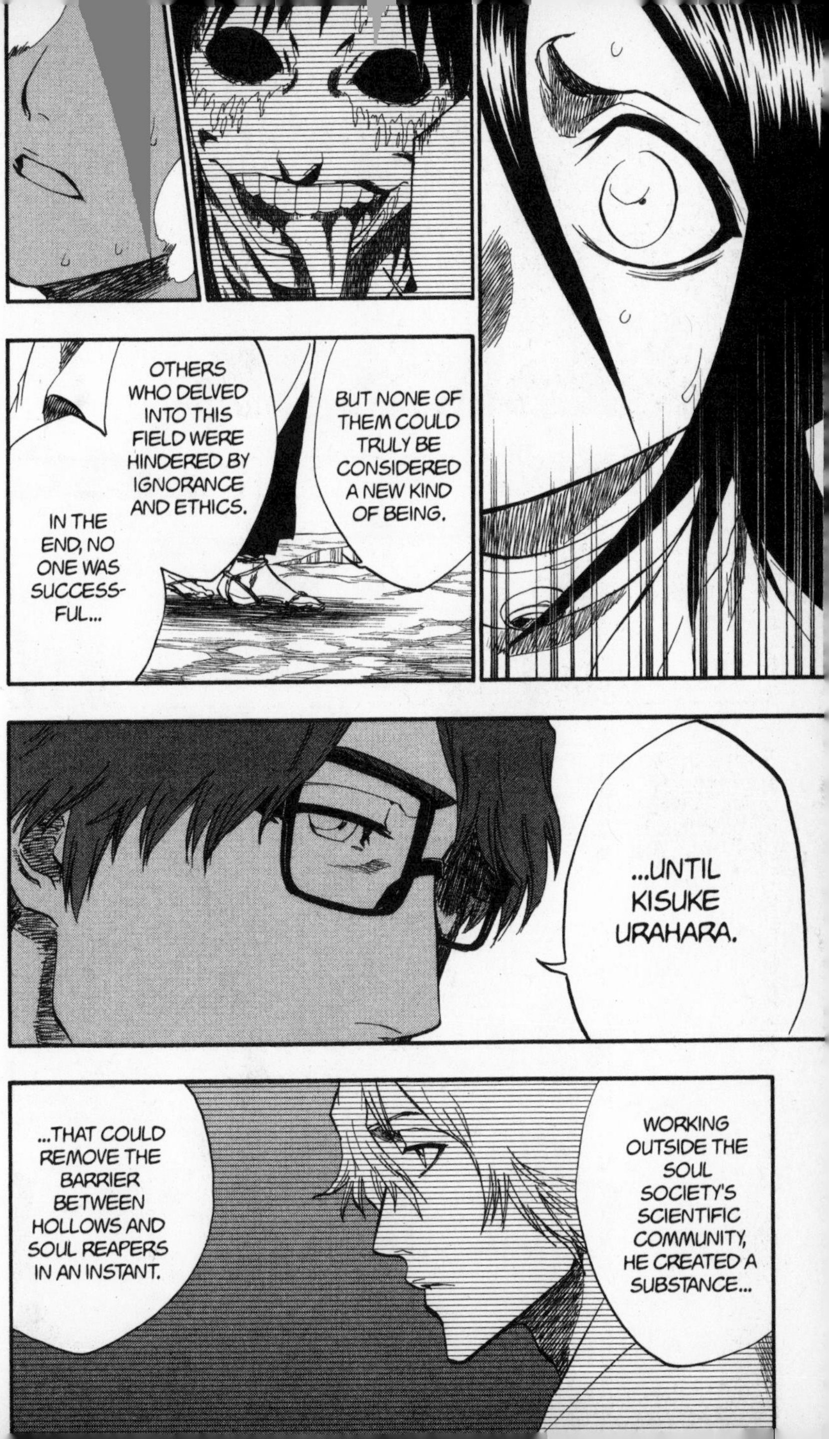
BUT NONE OF THEM COULD TRULY BE CONSIDERED A NEW KIND OF BEING.
OTHERS WHO DELVED INTO THIS FIELD WERE HINDERED BY IGNORANCE AND ETHICS.
IN THE END, NO ONE WAS SUCCESS-FUL...
...UNTIL KISUKE URAHARA.
WORKING OUTSIDE THE SOUL SOCIETY'S SCIENTIFIC COMMUNITY, HE CREATED A SUBSTANCE...
...THAT COULD REMOVE THE BARRIER BETWEEN HOLLOWS AND SOUL REAPERS IN AN INSTANT.

READ THIS WAY

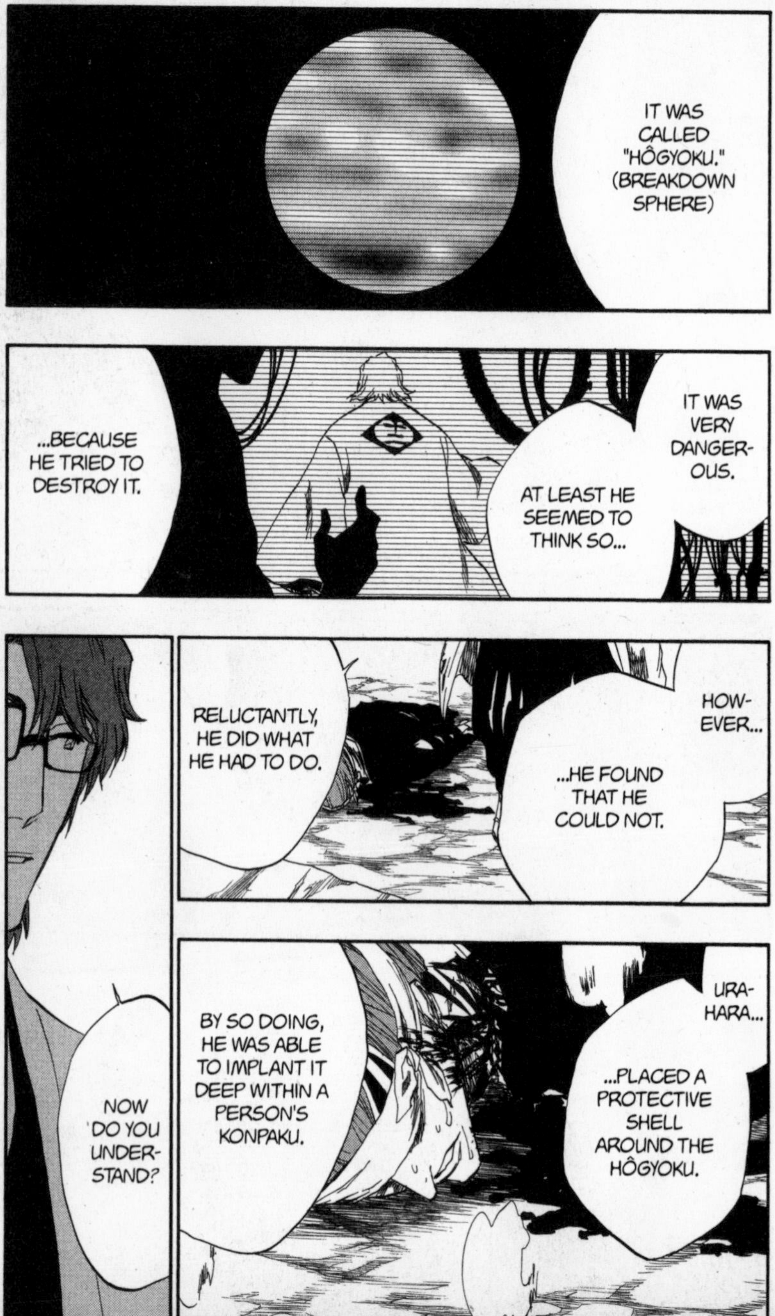
IT WAS CALLED "HÔGYOKU." (BREAKDOWN SPHERE)
IT WAS VERY DANGER-OUS.
AT LEAST HE SEEMED TO THINK SO...
...BECAUSE HE TRIED TO DESTROY IT.
HOW-EVER...
...HE FOUND THAT HE COULD NOT.
RELUCTANTLY, HE DID WHAT HE HAD TO DO.
URA-HARA...
...PLACED A PROTECTIVE SHELL AROUND THE HÔGYOKU.
BY SO DOING, HE WAS ABLE TO IMPLANT IT DEEP WITHIN A PERSON'S KONPAKU.
NOW DO YOU UNDER-STAND?

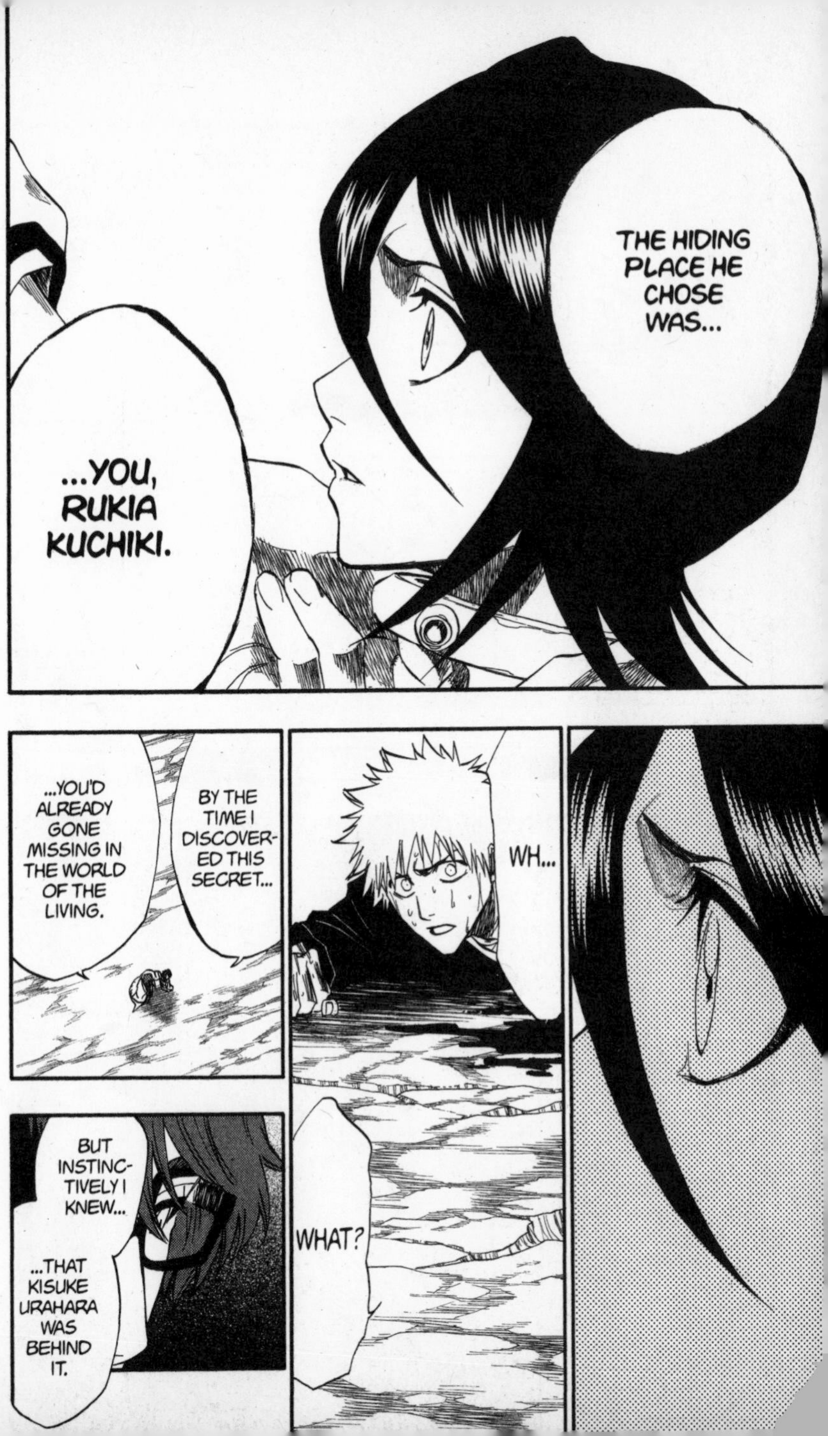
THE HIDING PLACE HE CHOSE WAS...
...YOU, RUKIA KUCHIKI.
WH...
BY THE TIME I DISCOVERED THIS SECRET...
...YOU'D ALREADY GONE MISSING IN THE WORLD OF THE LIVING.
WHAT?
BUT INSTINCTIVELY I KNEW...
...THAT KISUKE URAHARA WAS BEHIND IT.

READ THIS WAY

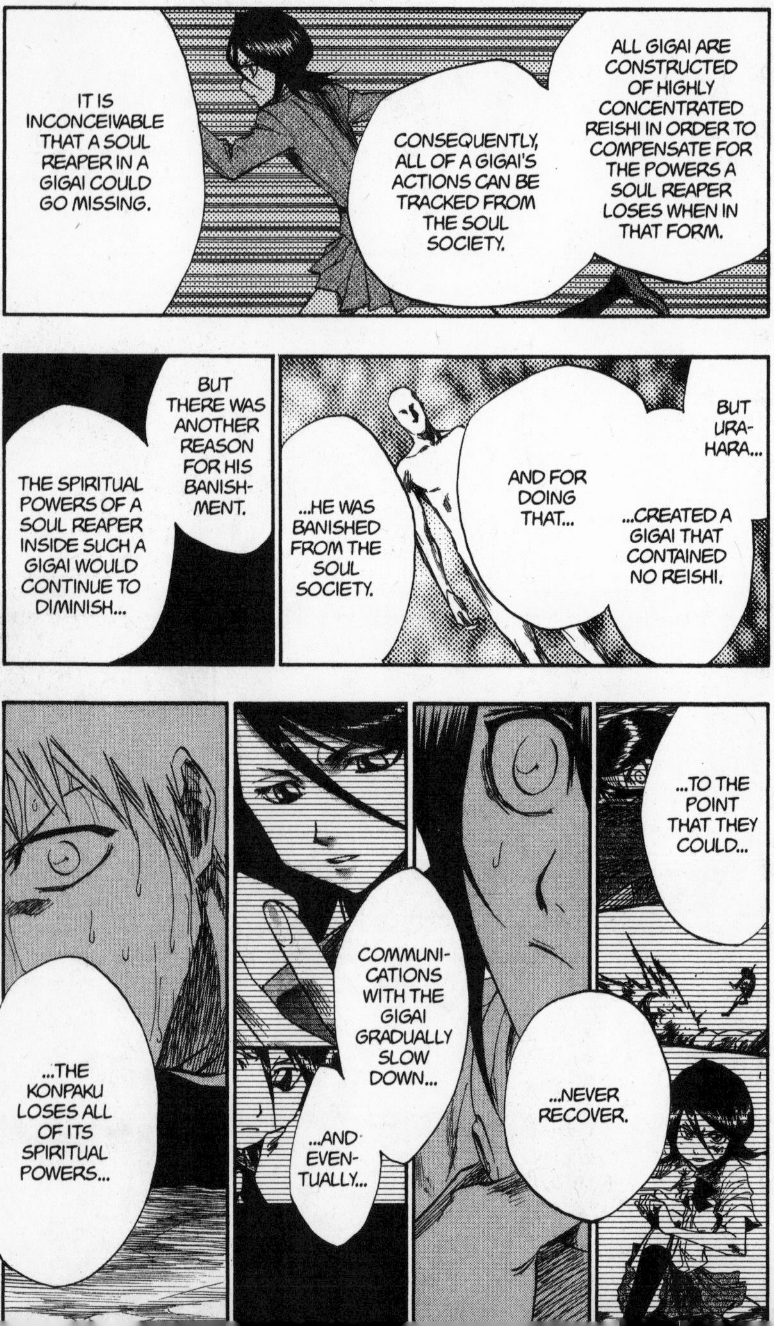

ALL GIGAI ARE CONSTRUCTED OF HIGHLY CONCENTRATED REISHI IN ORDER TO COMPENSATE FOR THE POWERS A SOUL REAPER LOSES WHEN IN THAT FORM.
CONSEQUENTLY, ALL OF A GIGAI'S ACTIONS CAN BE TRACKED FROM THE SOUL SOCIETY.
IT IS INCONCEIVABLE THAT A SOUL REAPER IN A GIGAI COULD GO MISSING.
BUT URA-HARA...
...CREATED A GIGAI THAT CONTAINED NO REISHI.
AND FOR DOING THAT...
...HE WAS BANISHED FROM THE SOUL SOCIETY.
BUT THERE WAS ANOTHER REASON FOR HIS BANISH-MENT.
THE SPIRITUAL POWERS OF A SOUL REAPER INSIDE SUCH A GIGAI WOULD CONTINUE TO DIMINISH...
...TO THE POINT THAT THEY COULD...
...NEVER RECOVER.
COMMUNI-CATIONS WITH THE GIGAI GRADUALLY SLOW DOWN...
...AND EVEN-TUALLY...
...THE KONPAKU LOSES ALL OF ITS SPIRITUAL POWERS...

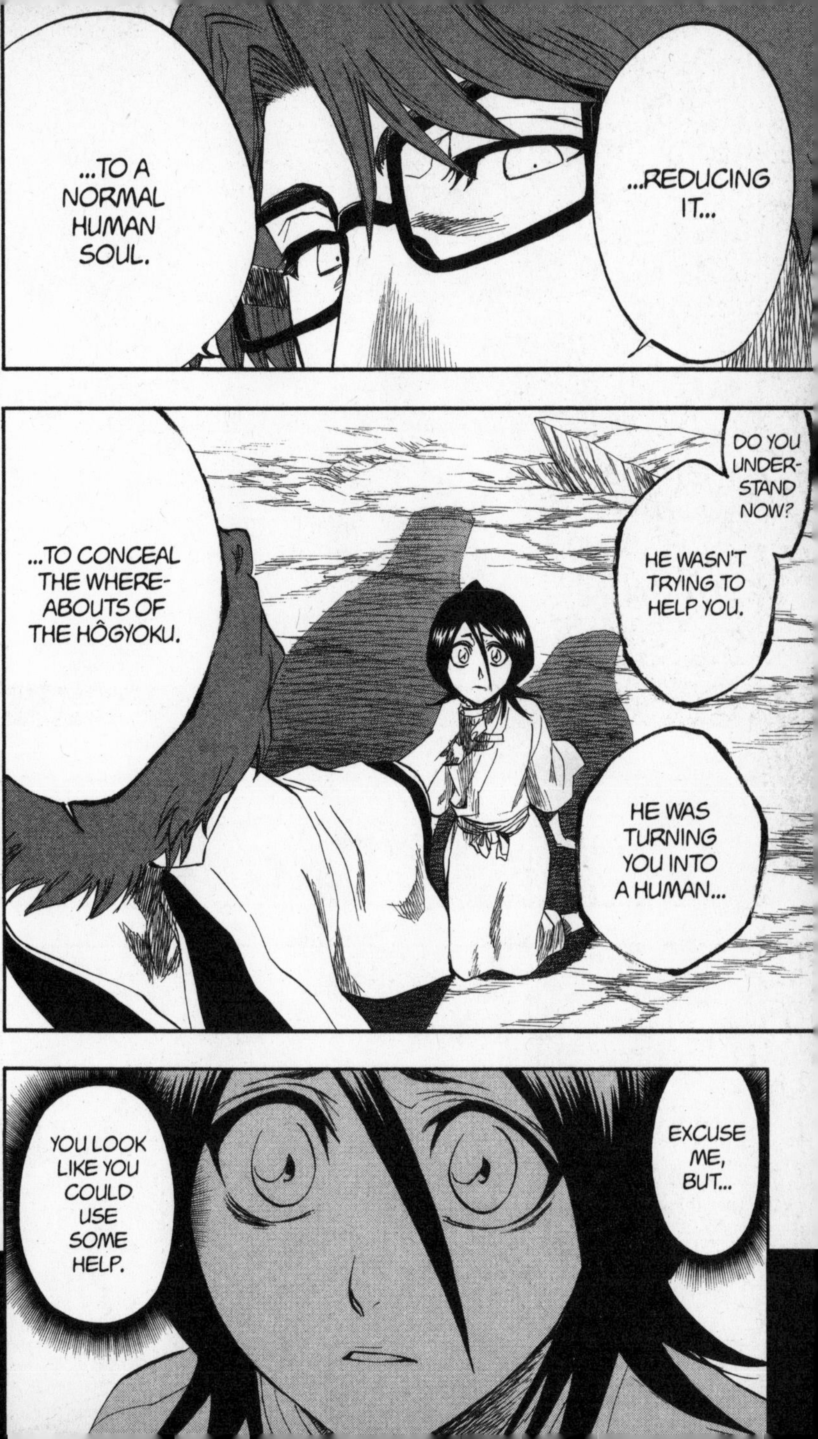
...REDUCING IT...
...TO A NORMAL HUMAN SOUL.
DO YOU UNDER-STAND NOW?
HE WASN'T TRYING TO HELP YOU.
HE WAS TURNING YOU INTO A HUMAN...
...TO CONCEAL THE WHERE-ABOUTS OF THE HÔGYOKU.
EXCUSE ME, BUT...
YOU LOOK LIKE YOU COULD USE SOME HELP.

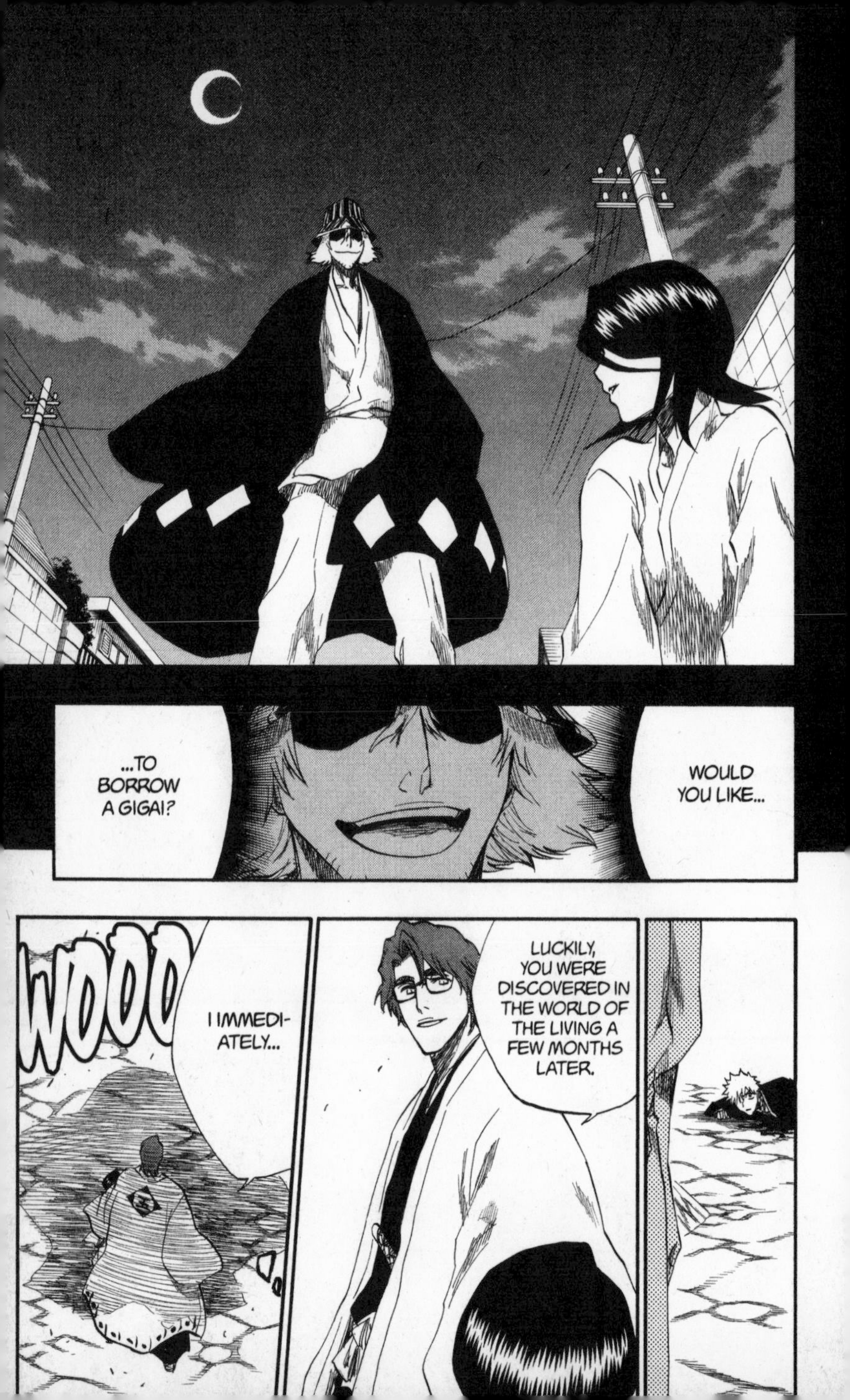
WOULD YOU LIKE...
...TO BORROW A GIGAI?
LUCKILY, YOU WERE DISCOVERED IN THE WORLD OF THE LIVING A FEW MONTHS LATER.
I IMMEDI-ATELY...
WOOO

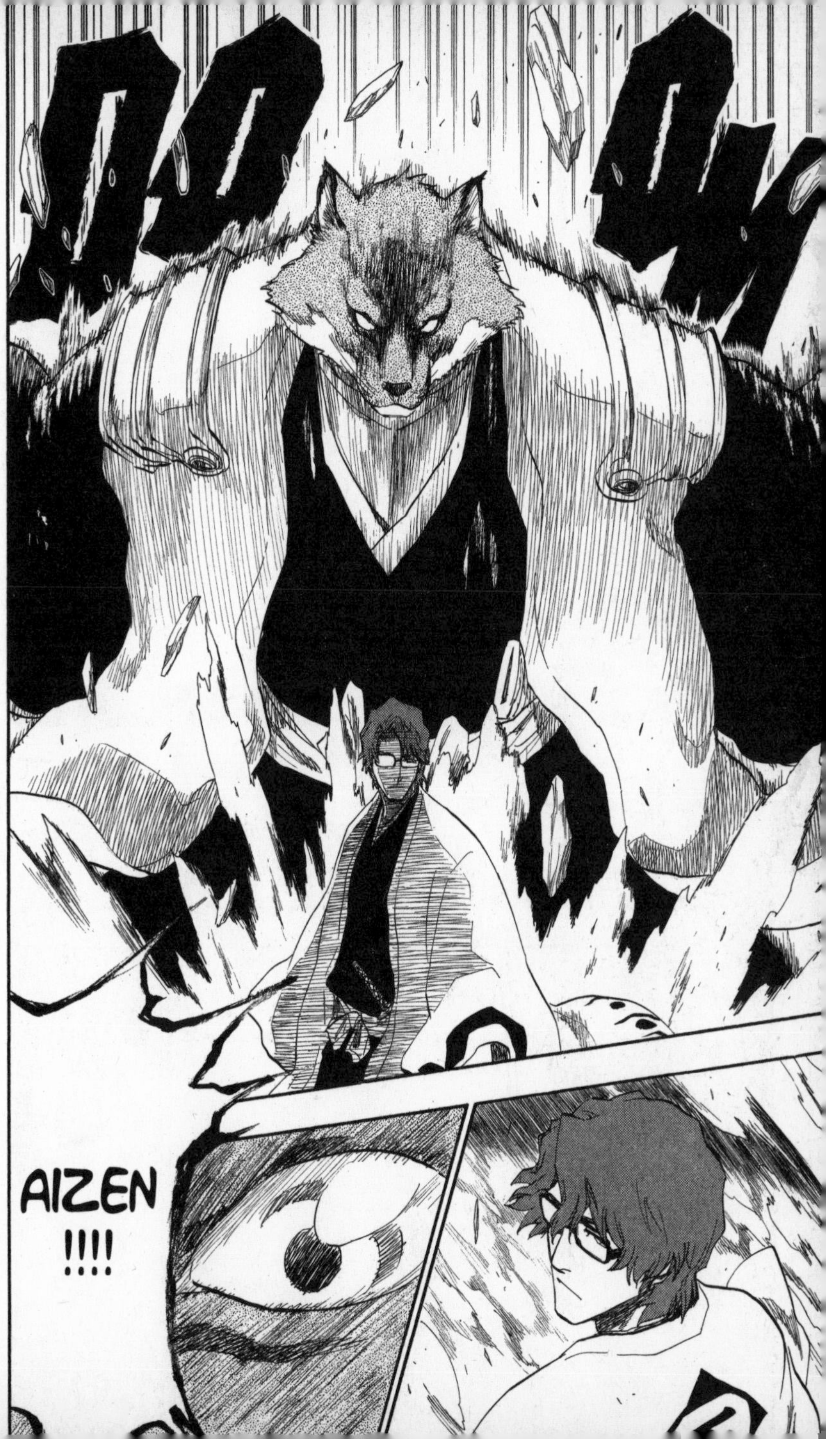
AIZEN
!!!!

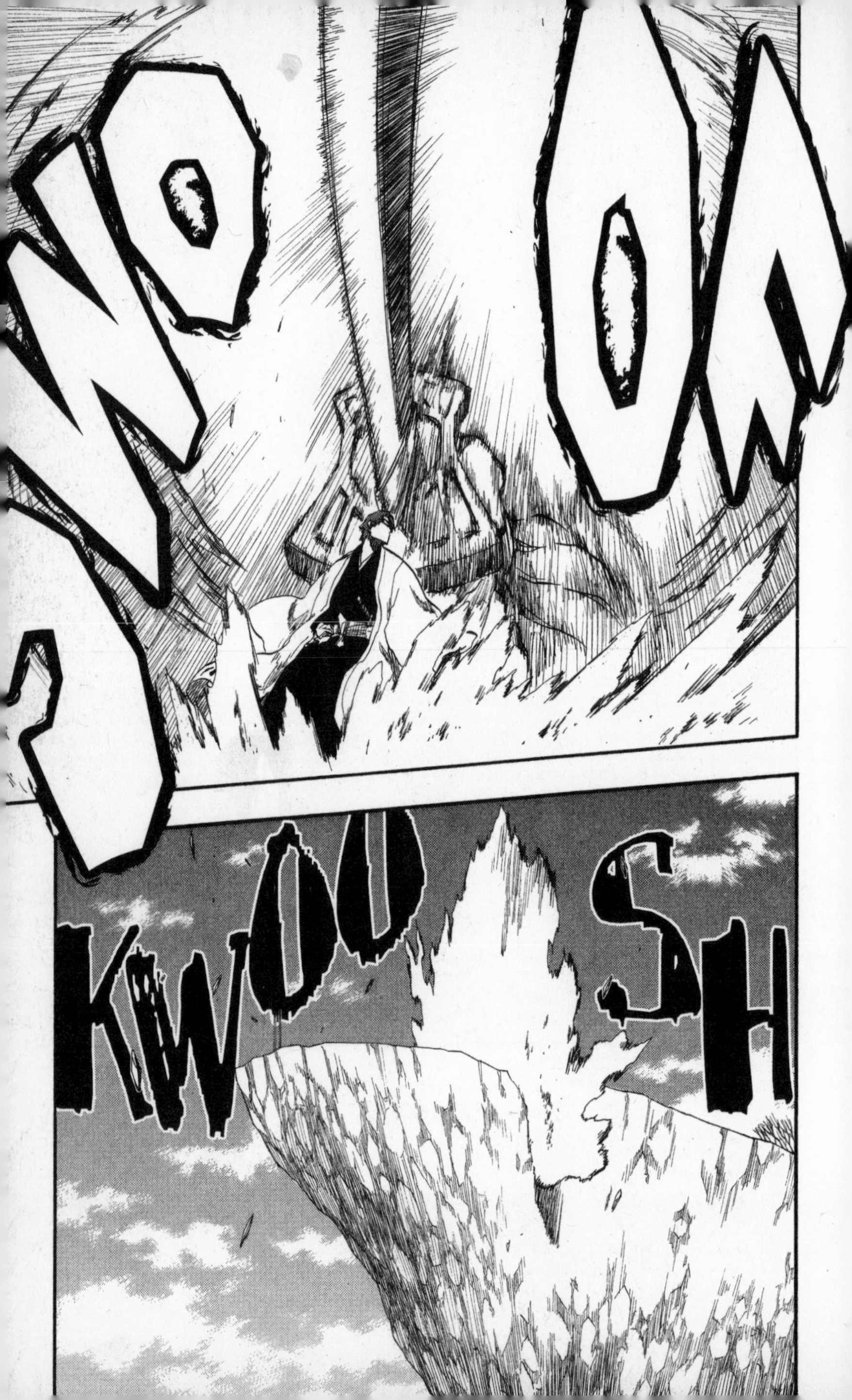
KWOOSH

BLEACH
ブリーチ

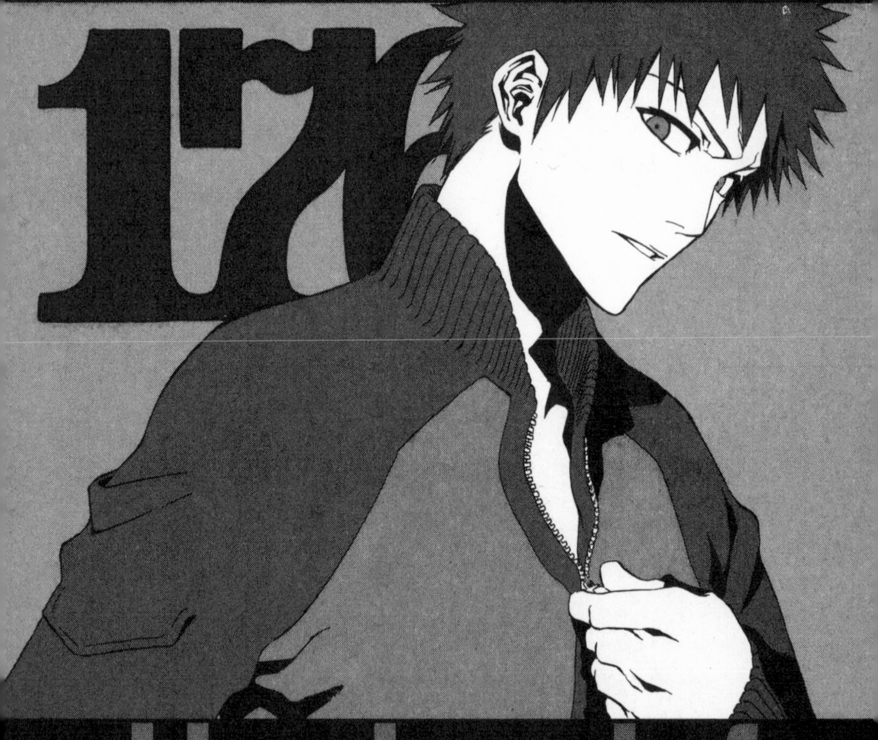

17

ブリーチ：エンド・オブ・ヒプノシス8
〔ザ・トランスフィクション〕

bleach:end of hypnosis eight (the Transfixion)

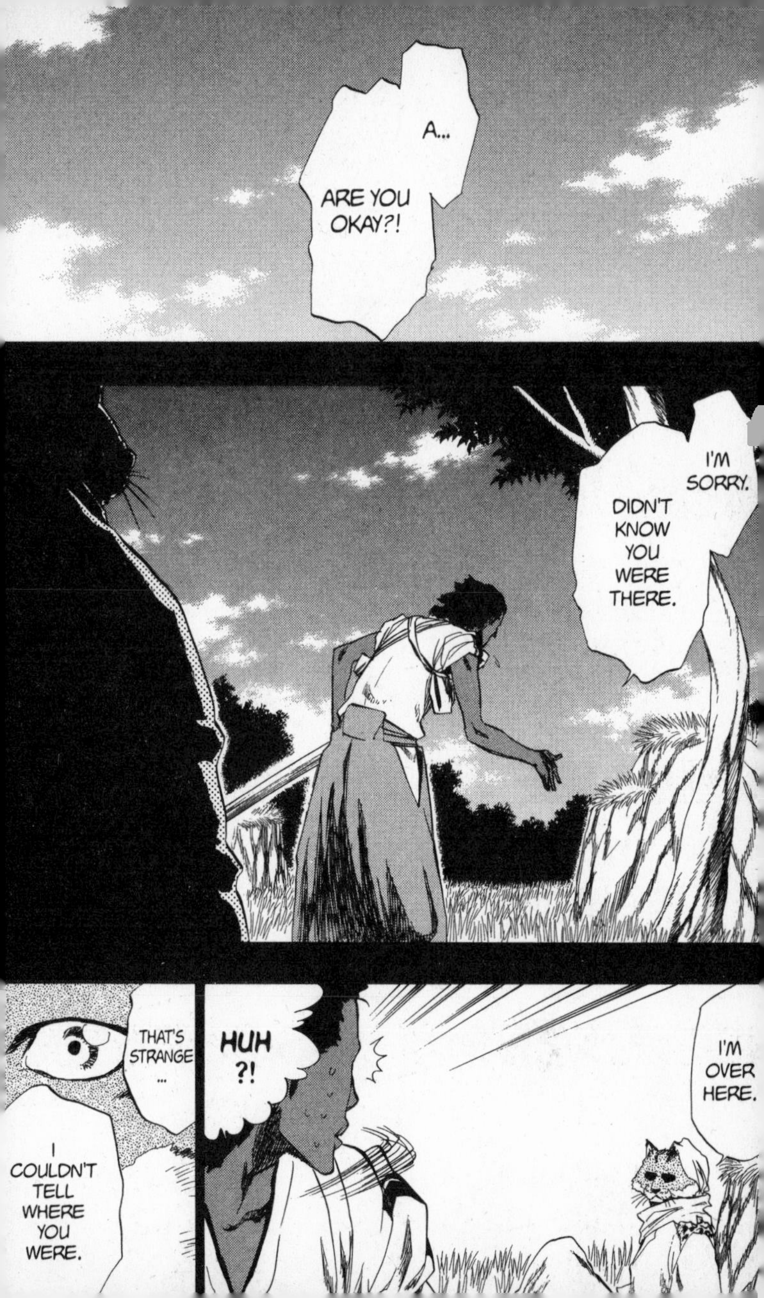
A...
ARE YOU OKAY?!
I'M SORRY.
DIDN'T KNOW YOU WERE THERE.
I'M OVER HERE.
HUH ?!
THAT'S STRANGE...
I COULDN'T TELL WHERE YOU WERE.

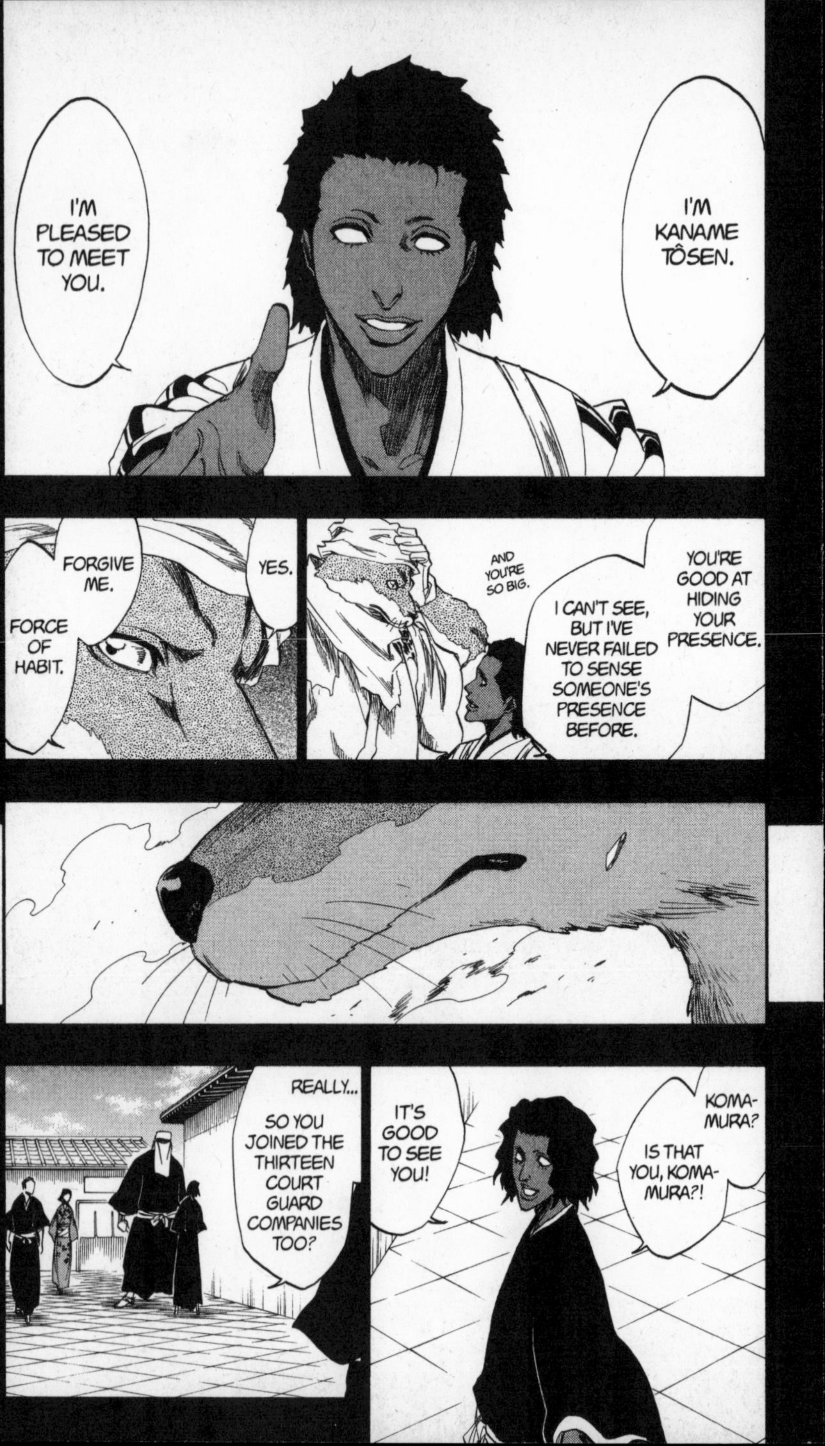
I'M KANAME TÔSEN.
I'M PLEASED TO MEET YOU.
YOU'RE GOOD AT HIDING YOUR PRESENCE.
I CAN'T SEE, BUT I'VE NEVER FAILED TO SENSE SOMEONE'S PRESENCE BEFORE.
AND YOU'RE SO BIG.
YES.
FORGIVE ME.
FORCE OF HABIT.
KOMA-MURA?
IS THAT YOU, KOMA-MURA?!
IT'S GOOD TO SEE YOU!
REALLY...
SO YOU JOINED THE THIRTEEN COURT GUARD COMPANIES TOO?

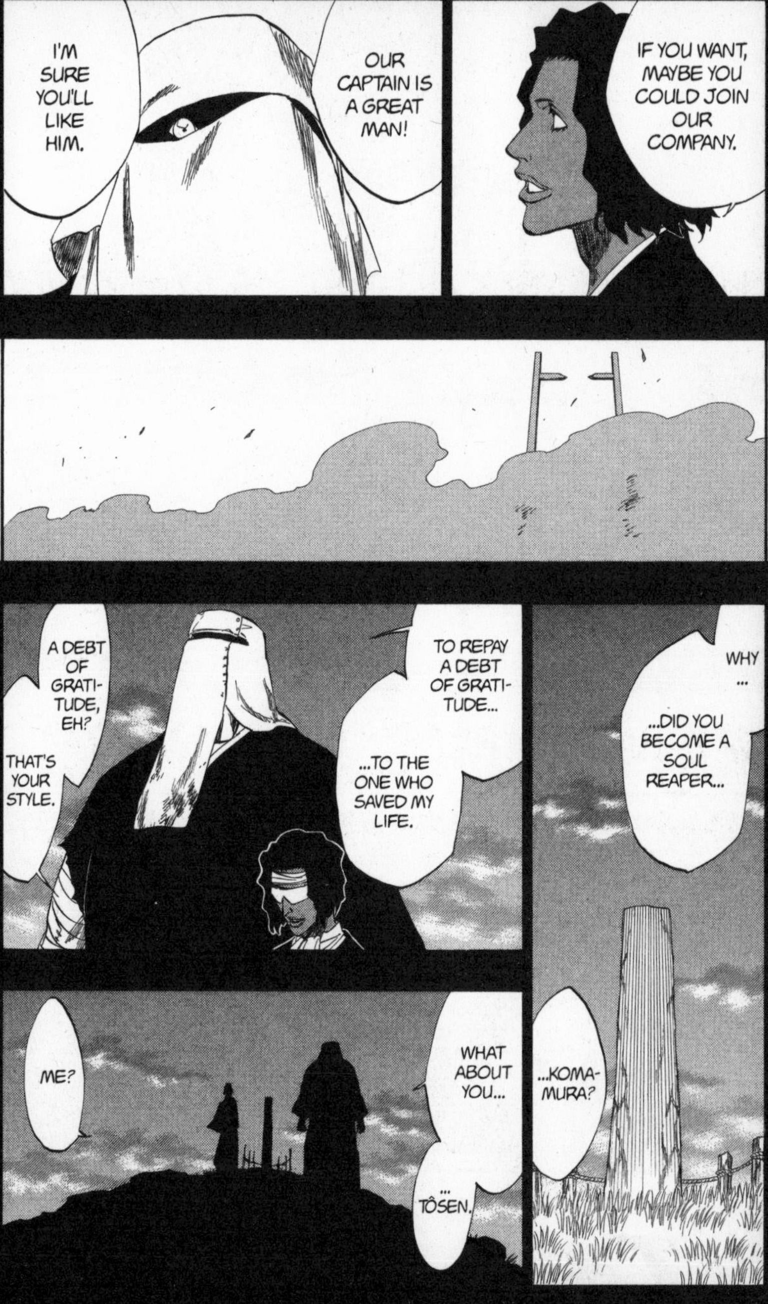
IF YOU WANT, MAYBE YOU COULD JOIN OUR COMPANY.
OUR CAPTAIN IS A GREAT MAN!
I'M SURE YOU'LL LIKE HIM.
WHY ...
...DID YOU BECOME A SOUL REAPER...
...KOMAMURA?
TO REPAY A DEBT OF GRATITUDE...
...TO THE ONE WHO SAVED MY LIFE.
A DEBT OF GRATITUDE, EH?
THAT'S YOUR STYLE.
WHAT ABOUT YOU...
... TÔSEN.
ME?

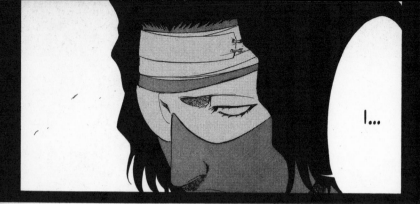

I...

RRMMMMMMMMMMMB

SO YOU'RE KOMAMURA.

TŌSEN TOLD ME ABOUT YOU.

TM... P

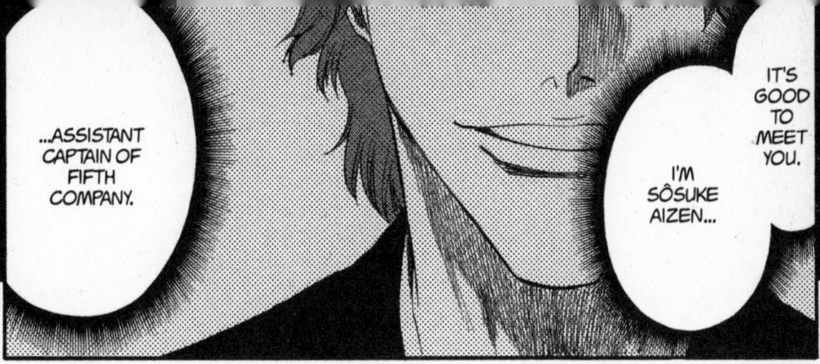
IT'S GOOD TO MEET YOU.
I'M SÔSUKE AIZEN...
...ASSISTANT CAPTAIN OF FIFTH COMPANY.

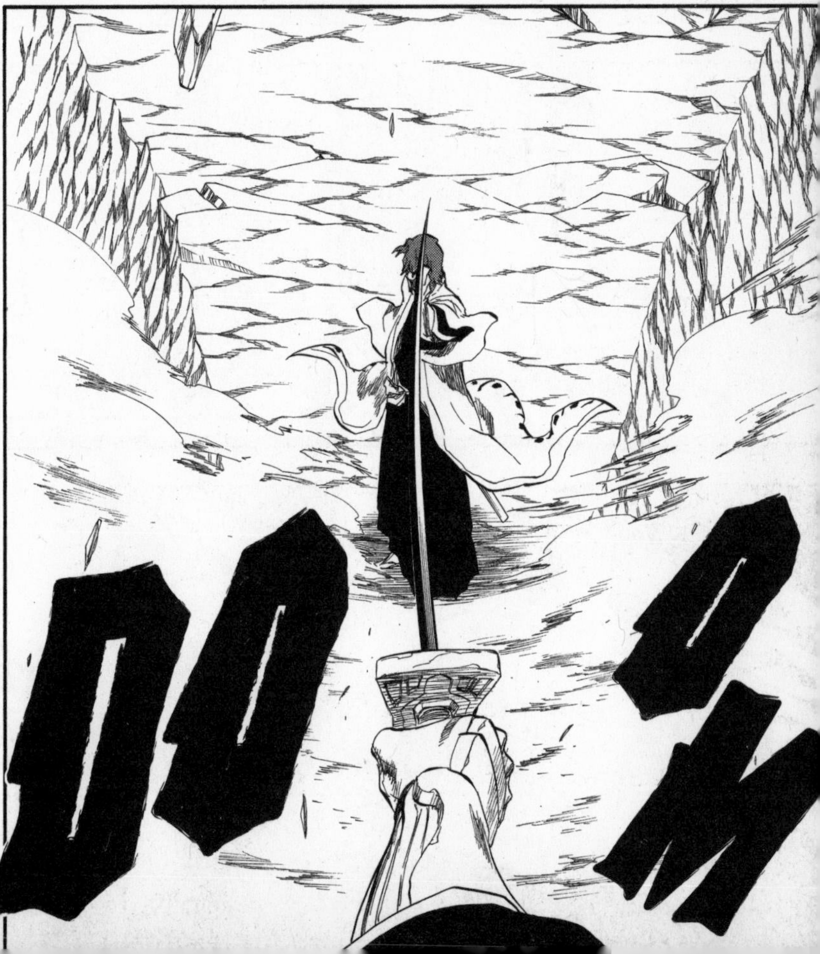
DOOM

READ THIS WAY

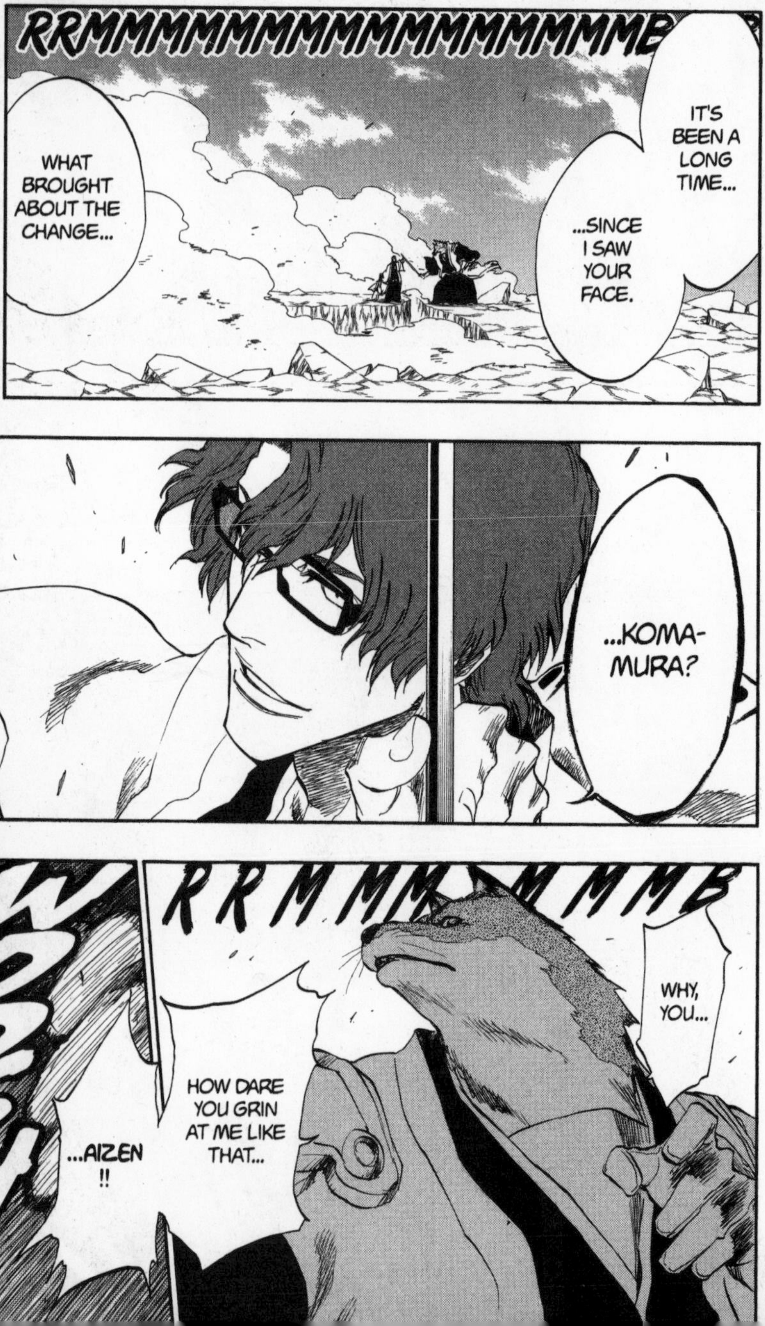
RRMMMMMMMMMMMMMMMMMB
IT'S BEEN A LONG TIME...
...SINCE I SAW YOUR FACE.
WHAT BROUGHT ABOUT THE CHANGE...
...KOMAMURA?
RRMMMMMMMB
WHY, YOU...
HOW DARE YOU GRIN AT ME LIKE THAT...
...AIZEN !!

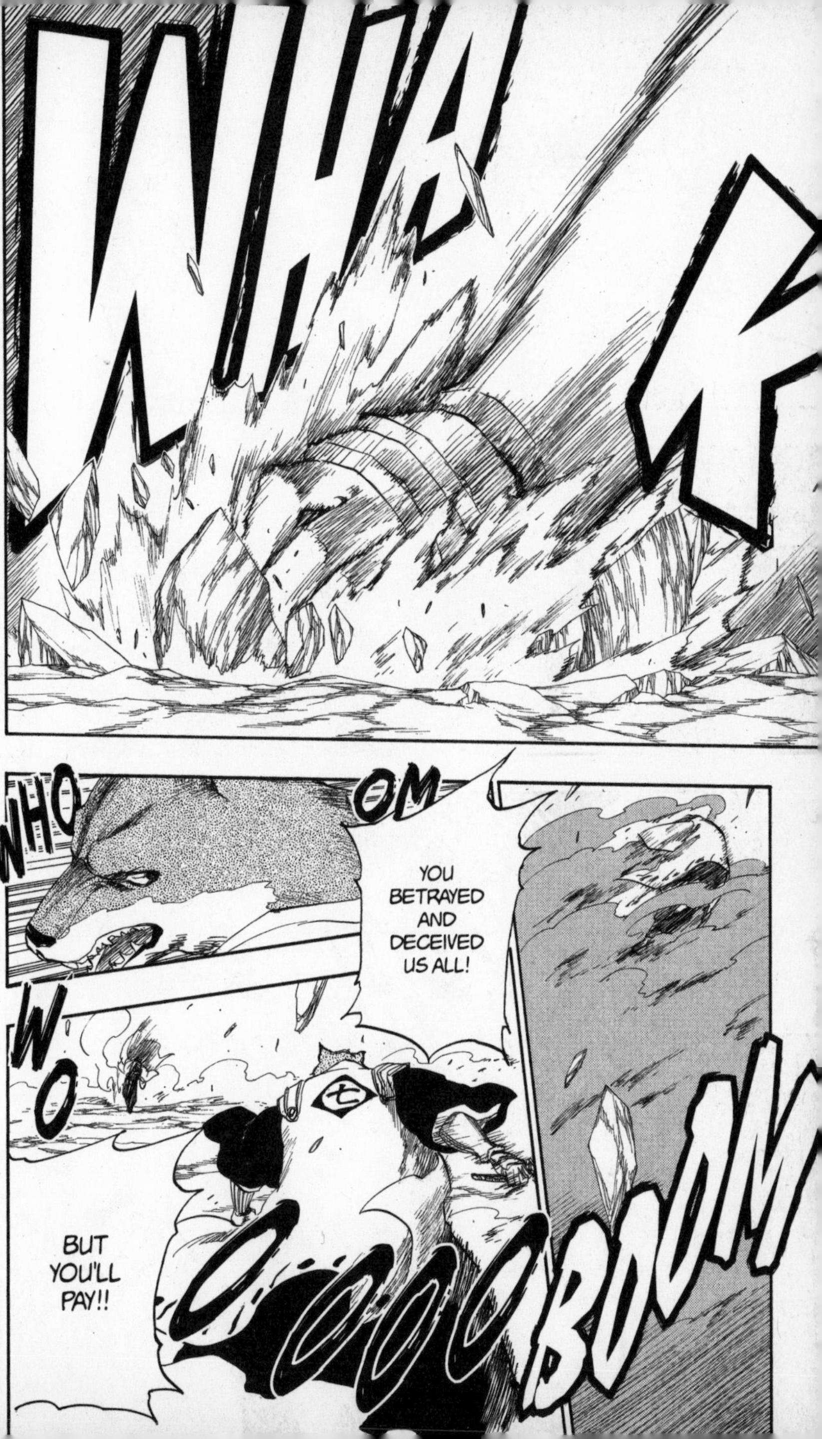
WHAK
WHOOM
YOU BETRAYED AND DECEIVED US ALL!
WOO
BUT YOU'LL PAY!!
OOOOBOOM

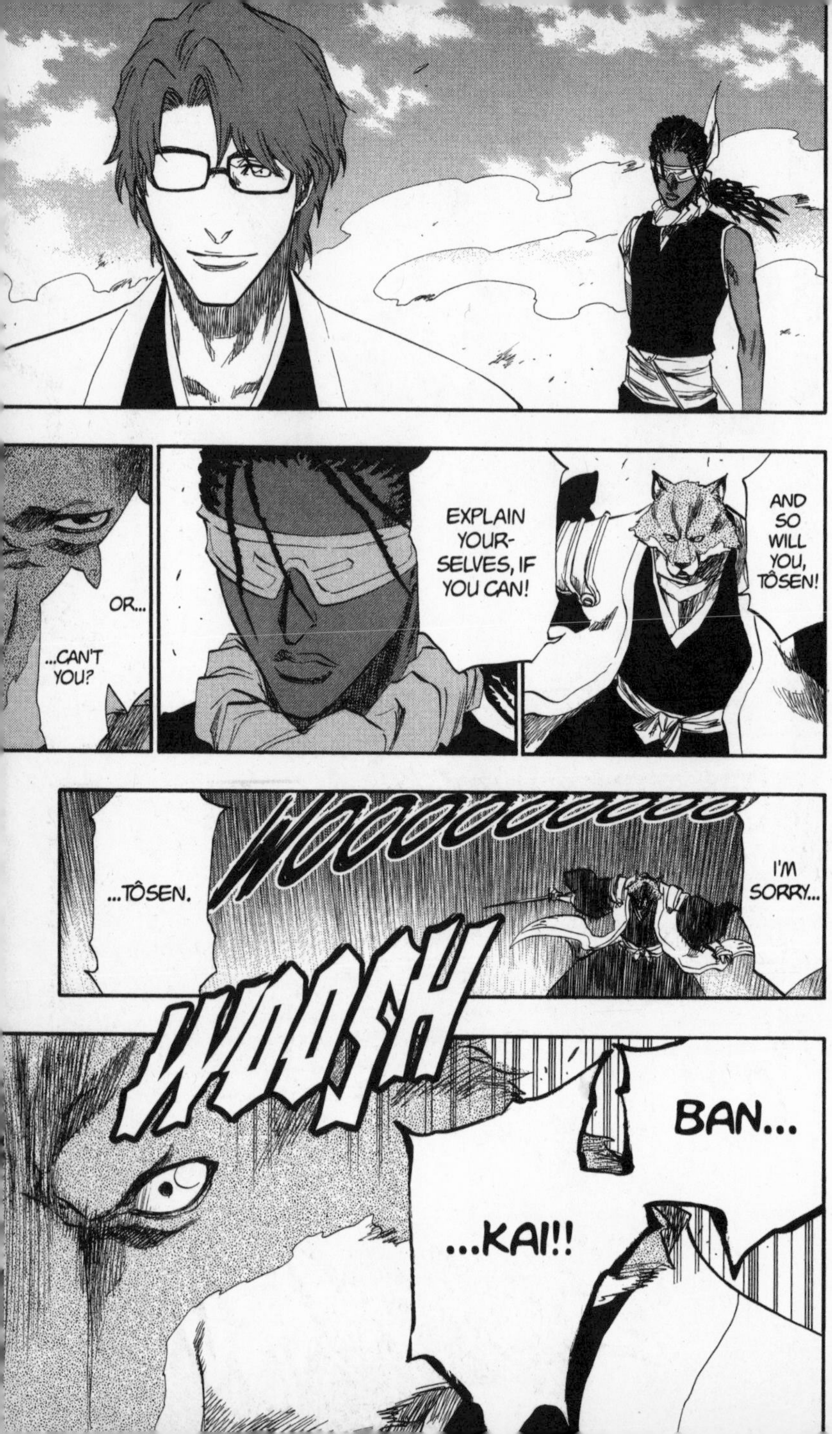

EXPLAIN YOURSELVES, IF YOU CAN!
AND SO WILL YOU, TÔSEN!
OR...
...CAN'T YOU?
I'M SORRY...
WOOOOOOOOOOO
...TÔSEN.
WOOSH
BAN...
...KAI!!

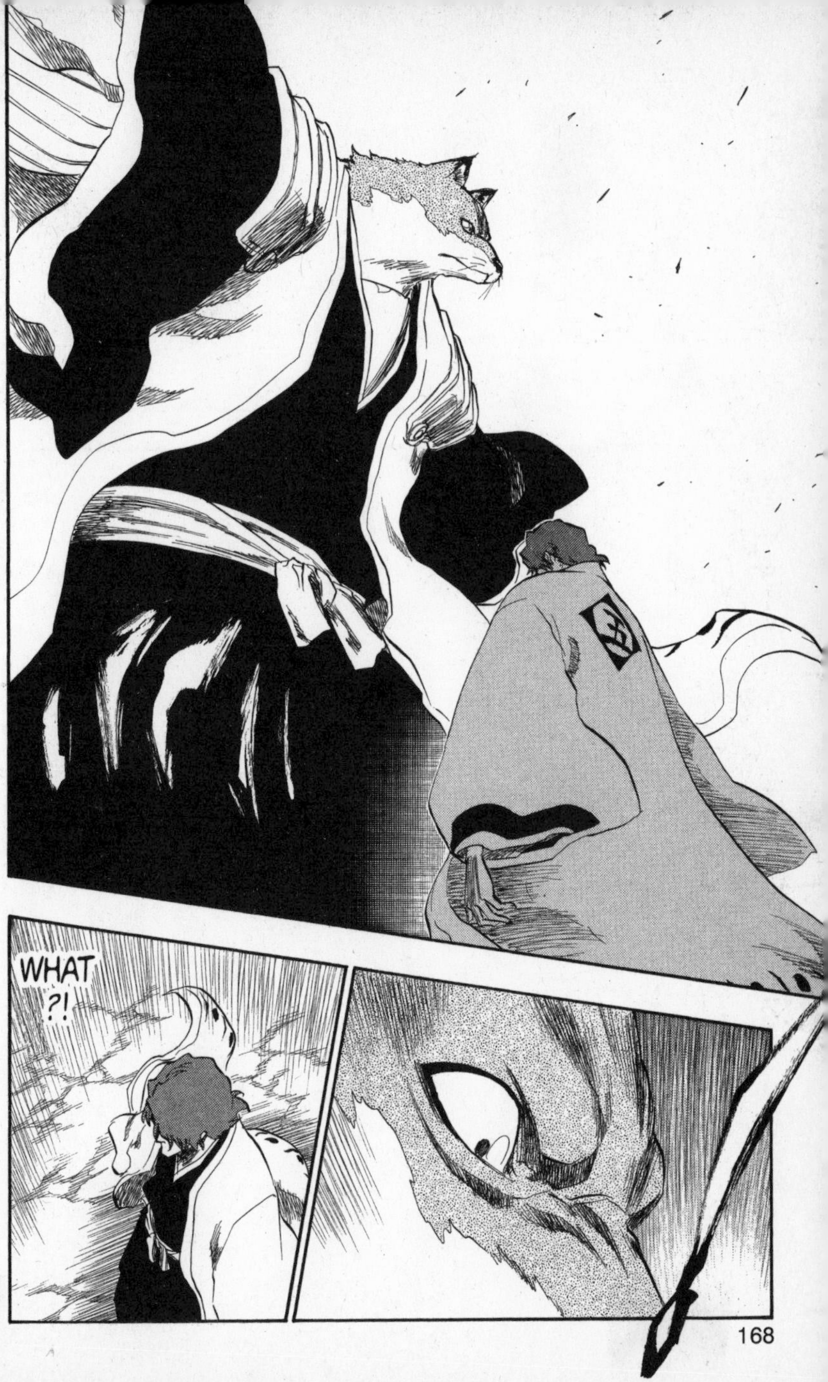
WHAT ?!

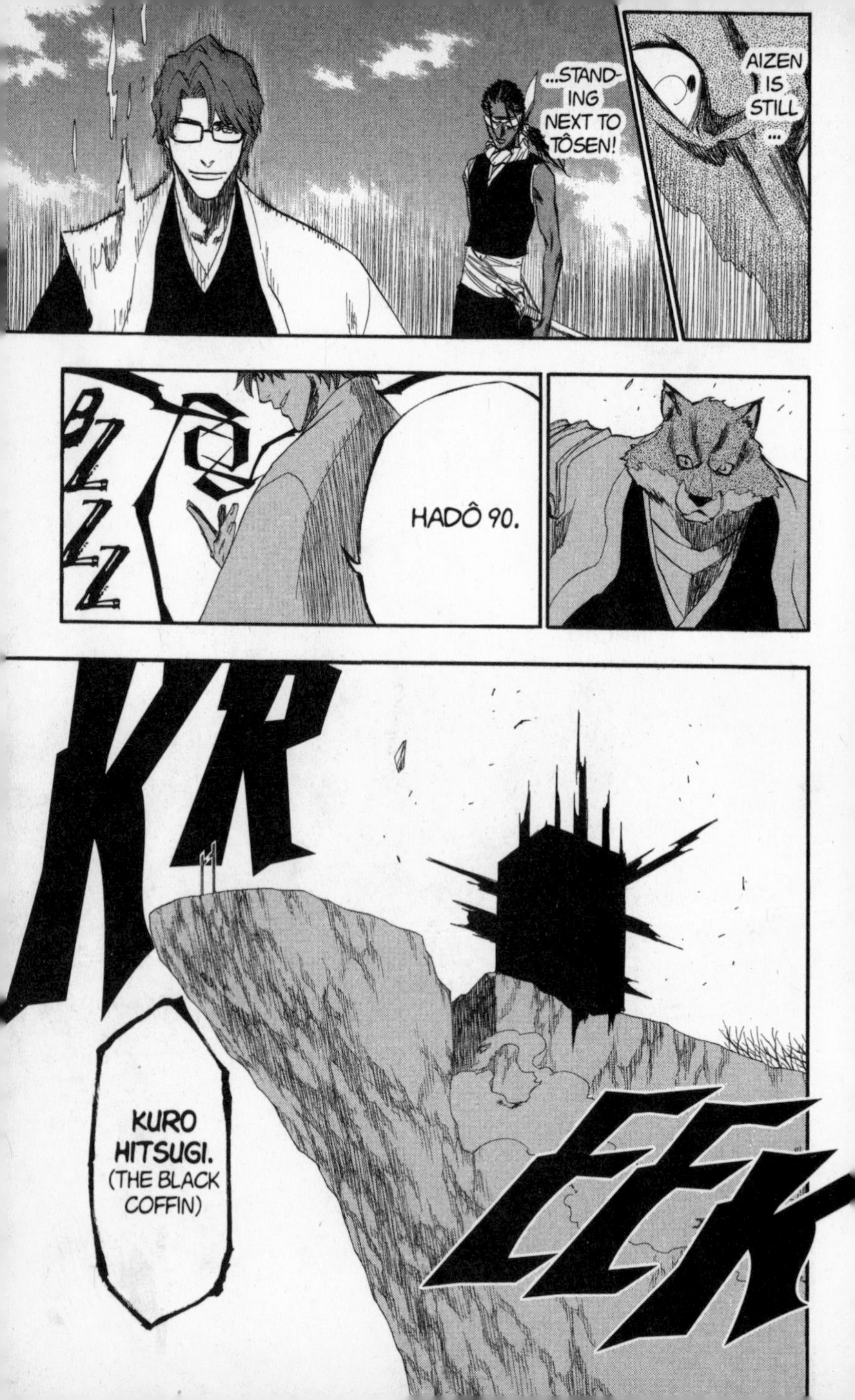
AIZEN IS STILL ...
...STANDING NEXT TO TÔSEN!
BZZZZ
HADÔ 90.
KREEK
KURO HITSUGI. (THE BLACK COFFIN)

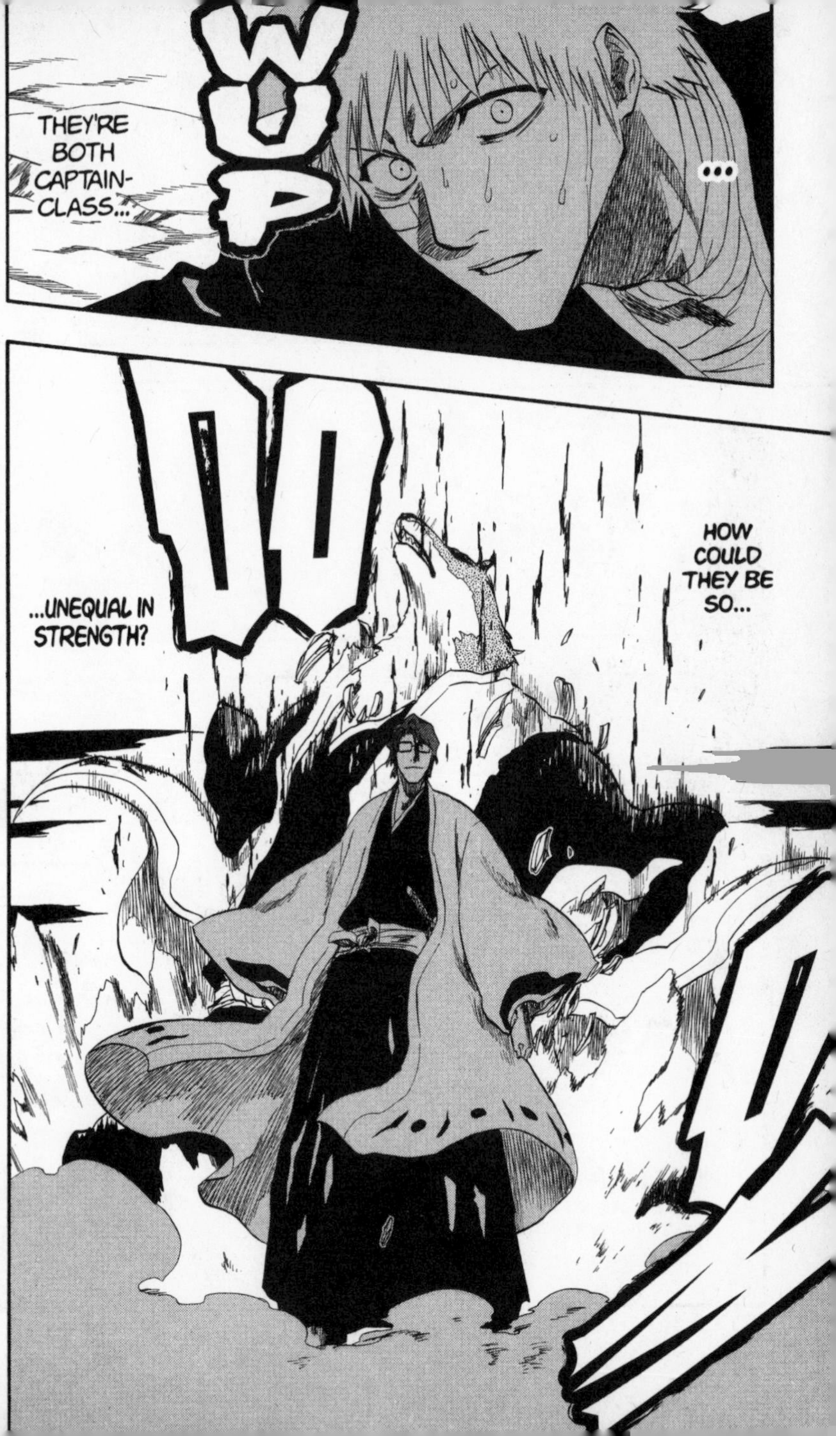
...
WUP
THEY'RE BOTH CAPTAIN-CLASS...
HOW COULD THEY BE SO...
...UNEQUAL IN STRENGTH?

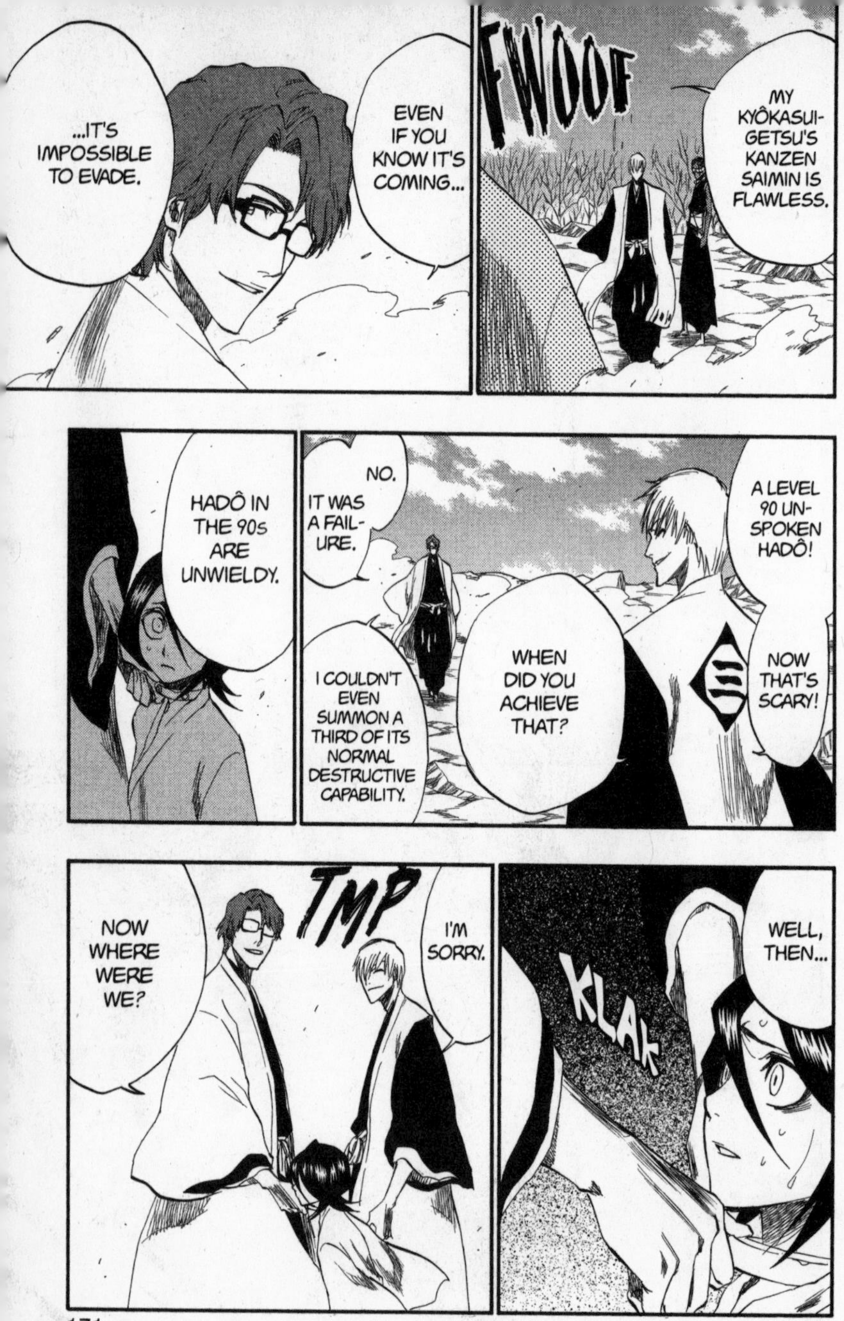
FWOOF
MY KYÔKASUIGETSU'S KANZEN SAIMIN IS FLAWLESS.
EVEN IF YOU KNOW IT'S COMING...
...IT'S IMPOSSIBLE TO EVADE.
A LEVEL 90 UNSPOKEN HADÔ!
NOW THAT'S SCARY!
WHEN DID YOU ACHIEVE THAT?
NO.
IT WAS A FAILURE.
I COULDN'T EVEN SUMMON A THIRD OF ITS NORMAL DESTRUCTIVE CAPABILITY.
HADÔ IN THE 90s ARE UNWIELDY.
WELL, THEN...
KLAK
TMP
I'M SORRY.
NOW WHERE WERE WE?

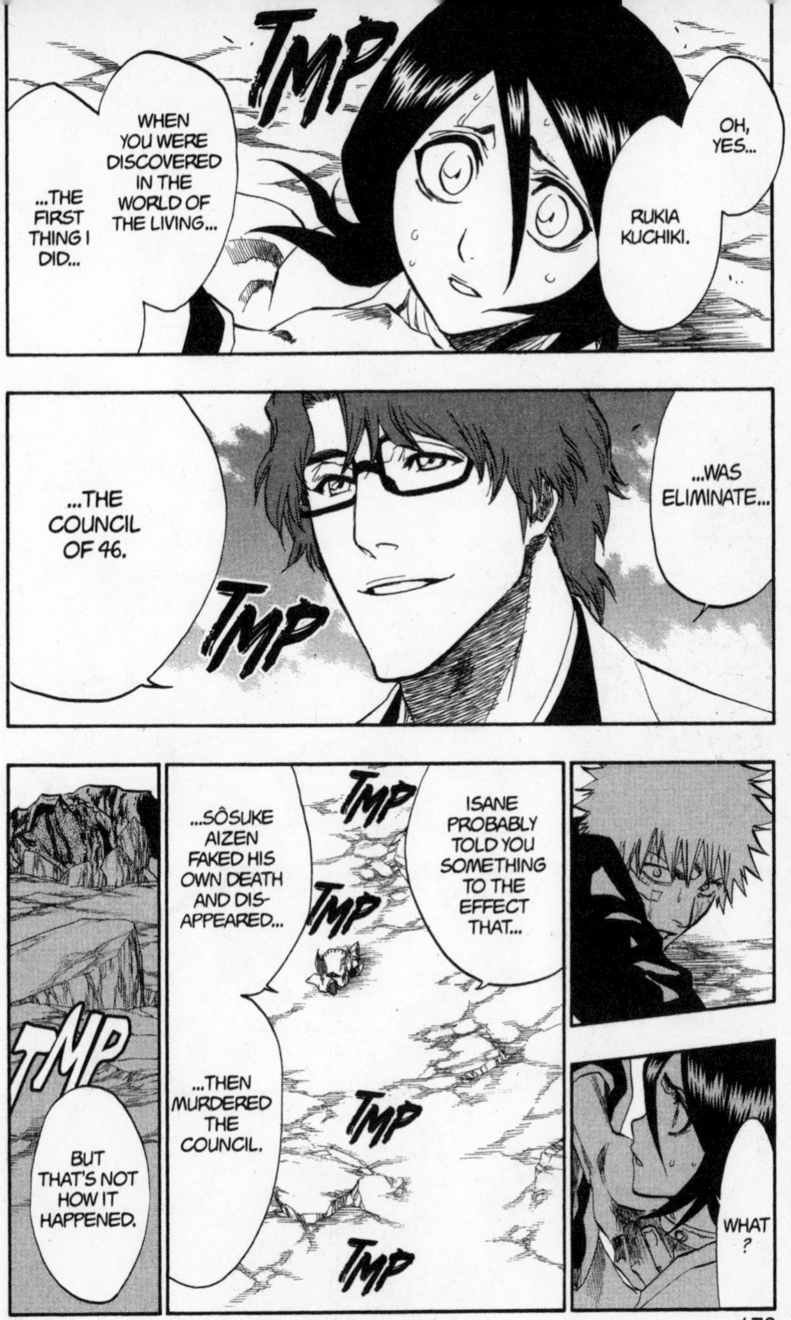
TMP
OH, YES...
RUKIA KUCHIKI.
WHEN YOU WERE DISCOVERED IN THE WORLD OF THE LIVING...
...THE FIRST THING I DID...
...WAS ELIMINATE...
TMP
...THE COUNCIL OF 46.
WHAT?
TMP
ISANE PROBABLY TOLD YOU SOMETHING TO THE EFFECT THAT...
TMP
...SÔSUKE AIZEN FAKED HIS OWN DEATH AND DIS-APPEARED...
...THEN MURDERED THE COUNCIL.
TMP
TMP
TMP
BUT THAT'S NOT HOW IT HAPPENED.

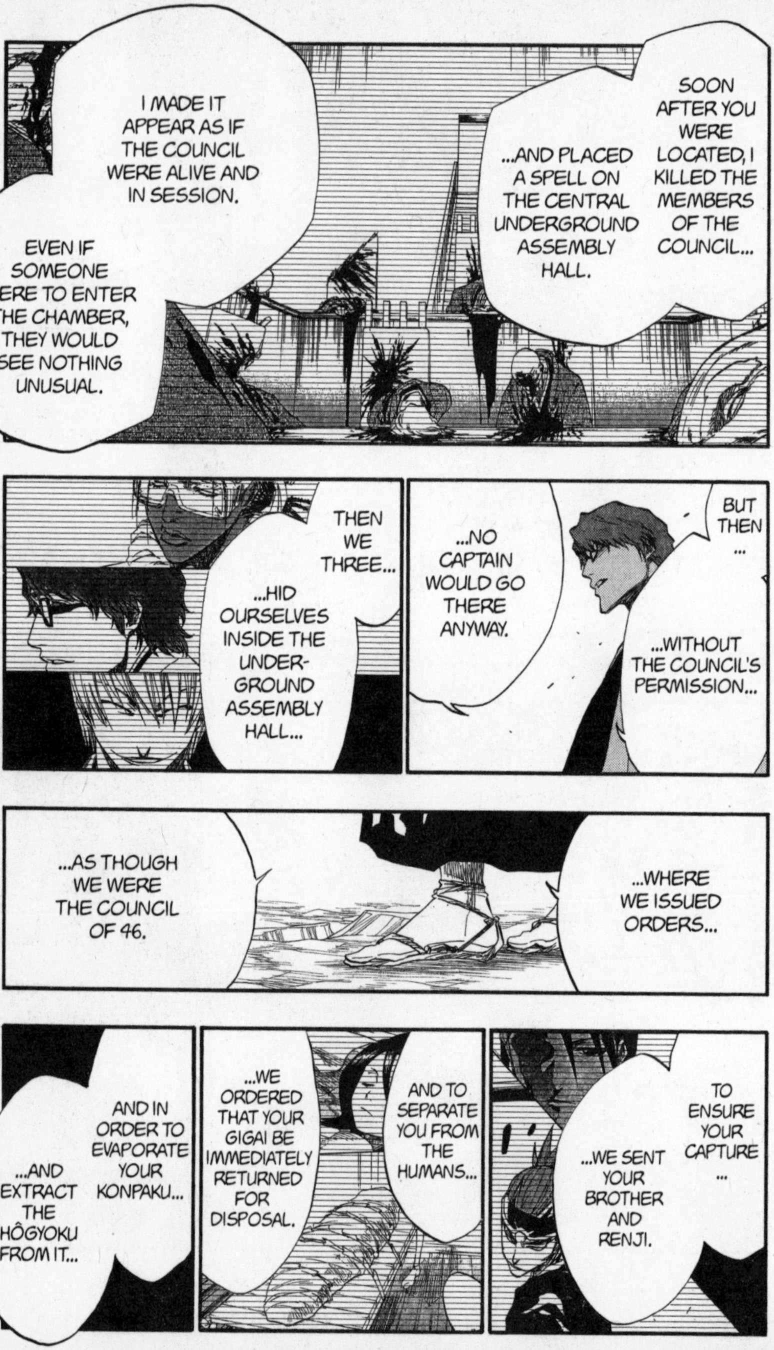
SOON AFTER YOU WERE LOCATED, I KILLED THE MEMBERS OF THE COUNCIL...
...AND PLACED A SPELL ON THE CENTRAL UNDERGROUND ASSEMBLY HALL.
I MADE IT APPEAR AS IF THE COUNCIL WERE ALIVE AND IN SESSION.
EVEN IF SOMEONE WERE TO ENTER THE CHAMBER, THEY WOULD SEE NOTHING UNUSUAL.
BUT THEN ...
...NO CAPTAIN WOULD GO THERE ANYWAY.
...WITHOUT THE COUNCIL'S PERMISSION...
THEN WE THREE...
...HID OURSELVES INSIDE THE UNDER-GROUND ASSEMBLY HALL...
...WHERE WE ISSUED ORDERS...
...AS THOUGH WE WERE THE COUNCIL OF 46.
TO ENSURE YOUR CAPTURE ...
...WE SENT YOUR BROTHER AND RENJI.
AND TO SEPARATE YOU FROM THE HUMANS...
...WE ORDERED THAT YOUR GIGAI BE IMMEDIATELY RETURNED FOR DISPOSAL.
AND IN ORDER TO EVAPORATE YOUR KONPAKU...
...AND EXTRACT THE HÔGYOKU FROM IT...

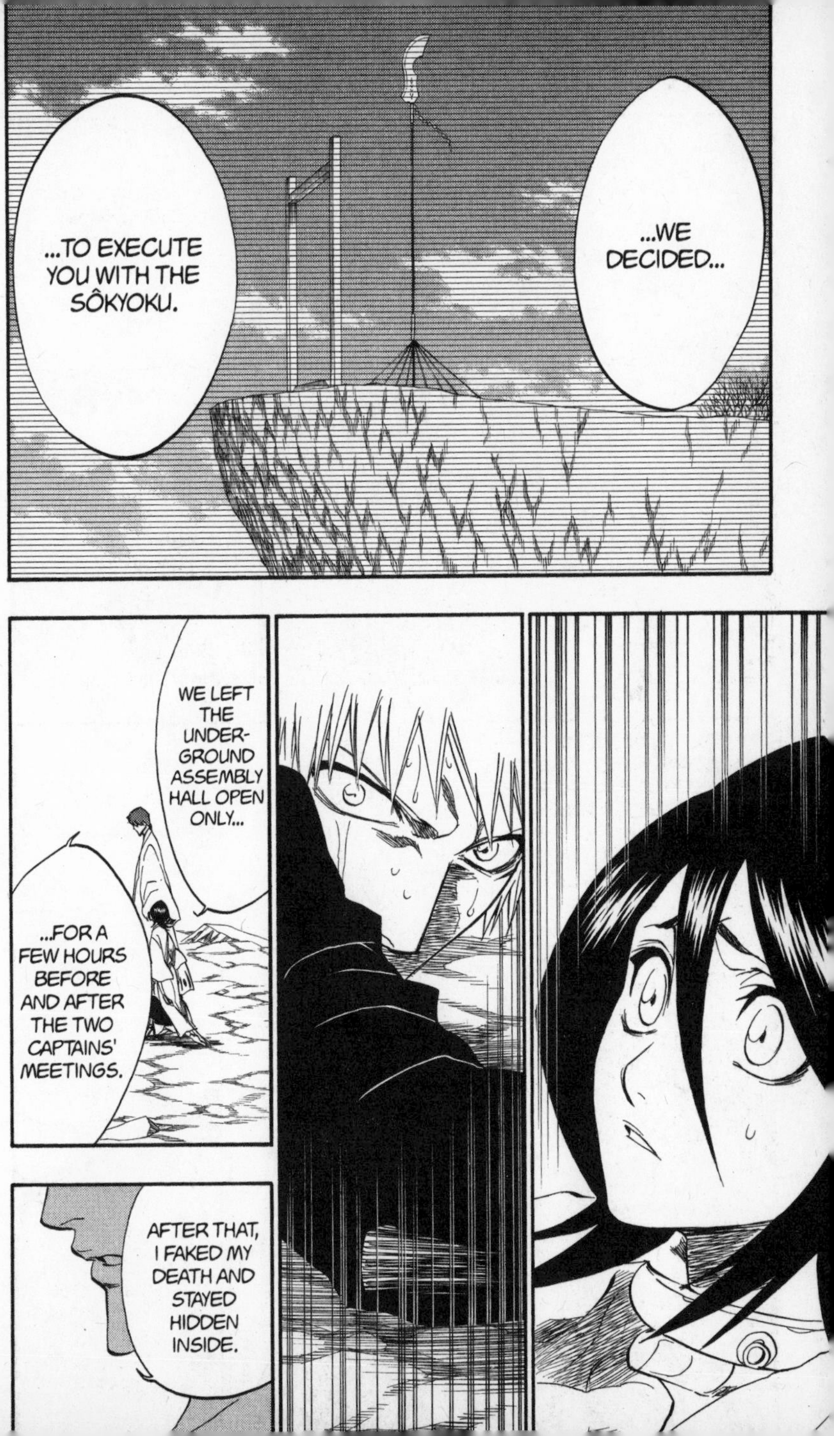
...WE DECIDED...
...TO EXECUTE YOU WITH THE SÔKYOKU.
WE LEFT THE UNDER-GROUND ASSEMBLY HALL OPEN ONLY...
...FOR A FEW HOURS BEFORE AND AFTER THE TWO CAPTAINS' MEETINGS.
AFTER THAT, I FAKED MY DEATH AND STAYED HIDDEN INSIDE.

READ THIS WAY

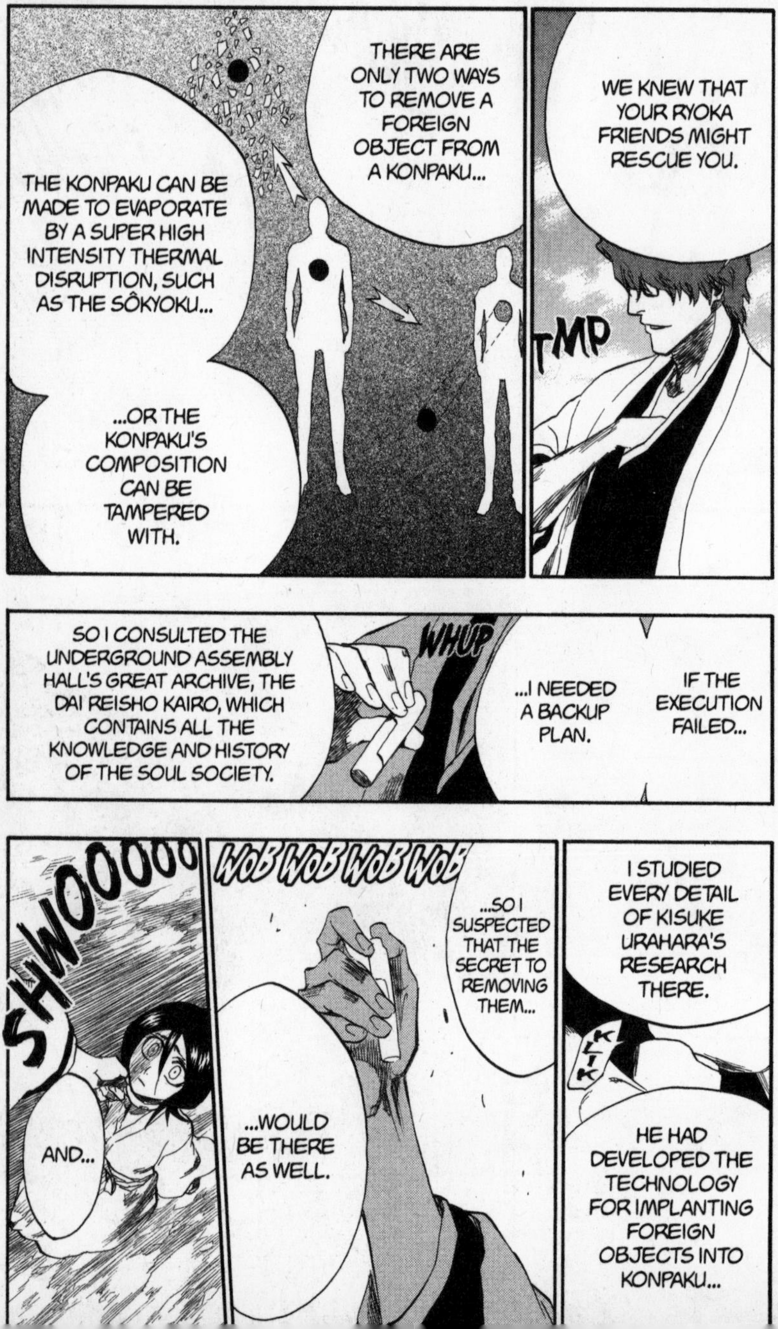
WE KNEW THAT YOUR RYOKA FRIENDS MIGHT RESCUE YOU.
TMP
THERE ARE ONLY TWO WAYS TO REMOVE A FOREIGN OBJECT FROM A KONPAKU...
THE KONPAKU CAN BE MADE TO EVAPORATE BY A SUPER HIGH INTENSITY THERMAL DISRUPTION, SUCH AS THE SÔKYOKU...
...OR THE KONPAKU'S COMPOSITION CAN BE TAMPERED WITH.
IF THE EXECUTION FAILED...
...I NEEDED A BACKUP PLAN.
WHUP
SO I CONSULTED THE UNDERGROUND ASSEMBLY HALL'S GREAT ARCHIVE, THE DAI REISHO KAIRO, WHICH CONTAINS ALL THE KNOWLEDGE AND HISTORY OF THE SOUL SOCIETY.
I STUDIED EVERY DETAIL OF KISUKE URAHARA'S RESEARCH THERE.
KLIK
HE HAD DEVELOPED THE TECHNOLOGY FOR IMPLANTING FOREIGN OBJECTS INTO KONPAKU...
WOB WOB WOB WOB
...SO I SUSPECTED THAT THE SECRET TO REMOVING THEM...
...WOULD BE THERE AS WELL.
SHWOOOOO
AND...

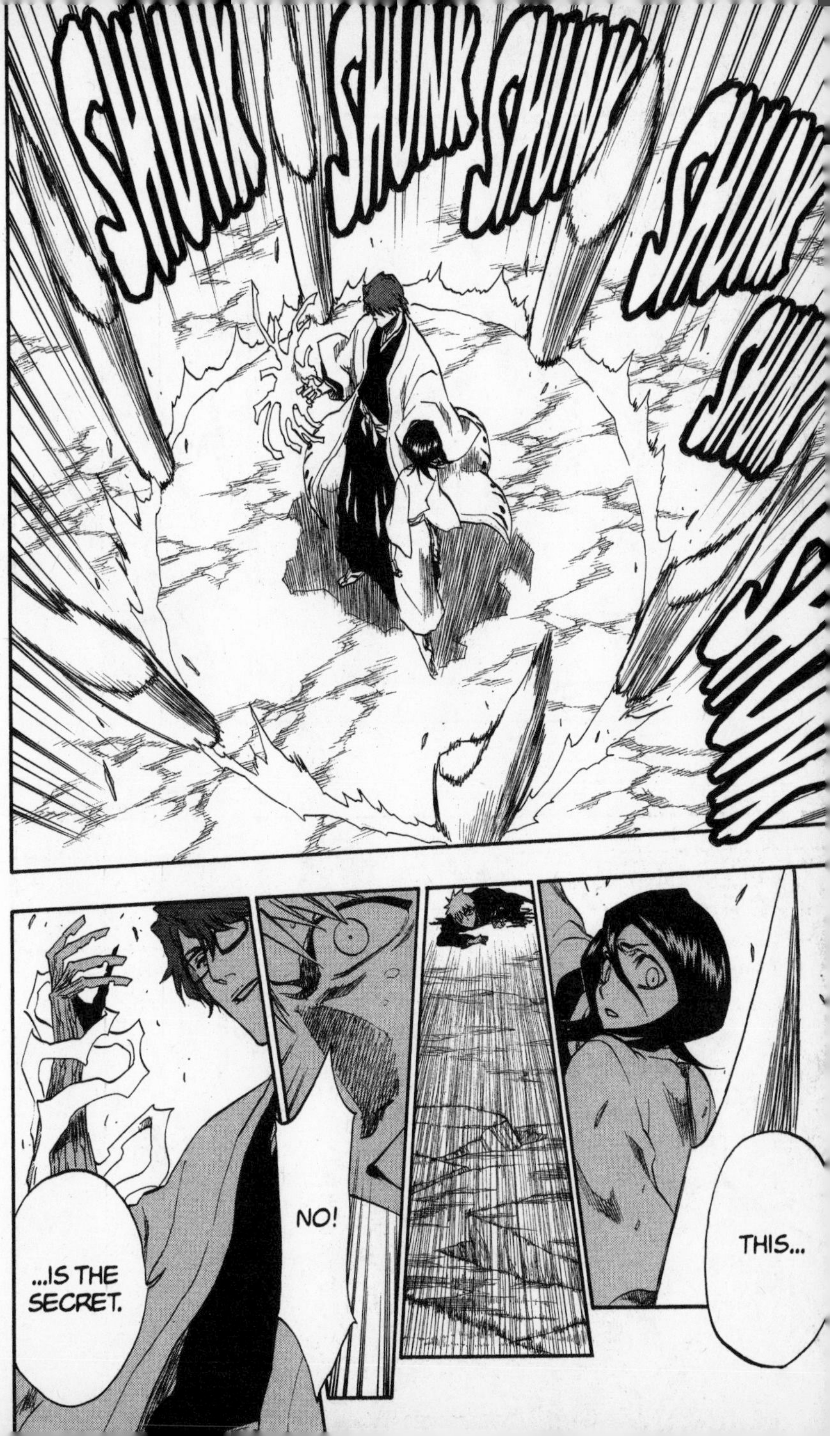

SHUNK
SHUNK
SHUNK
SHUNK
THIS...
NO!
...IS THE SECRET.

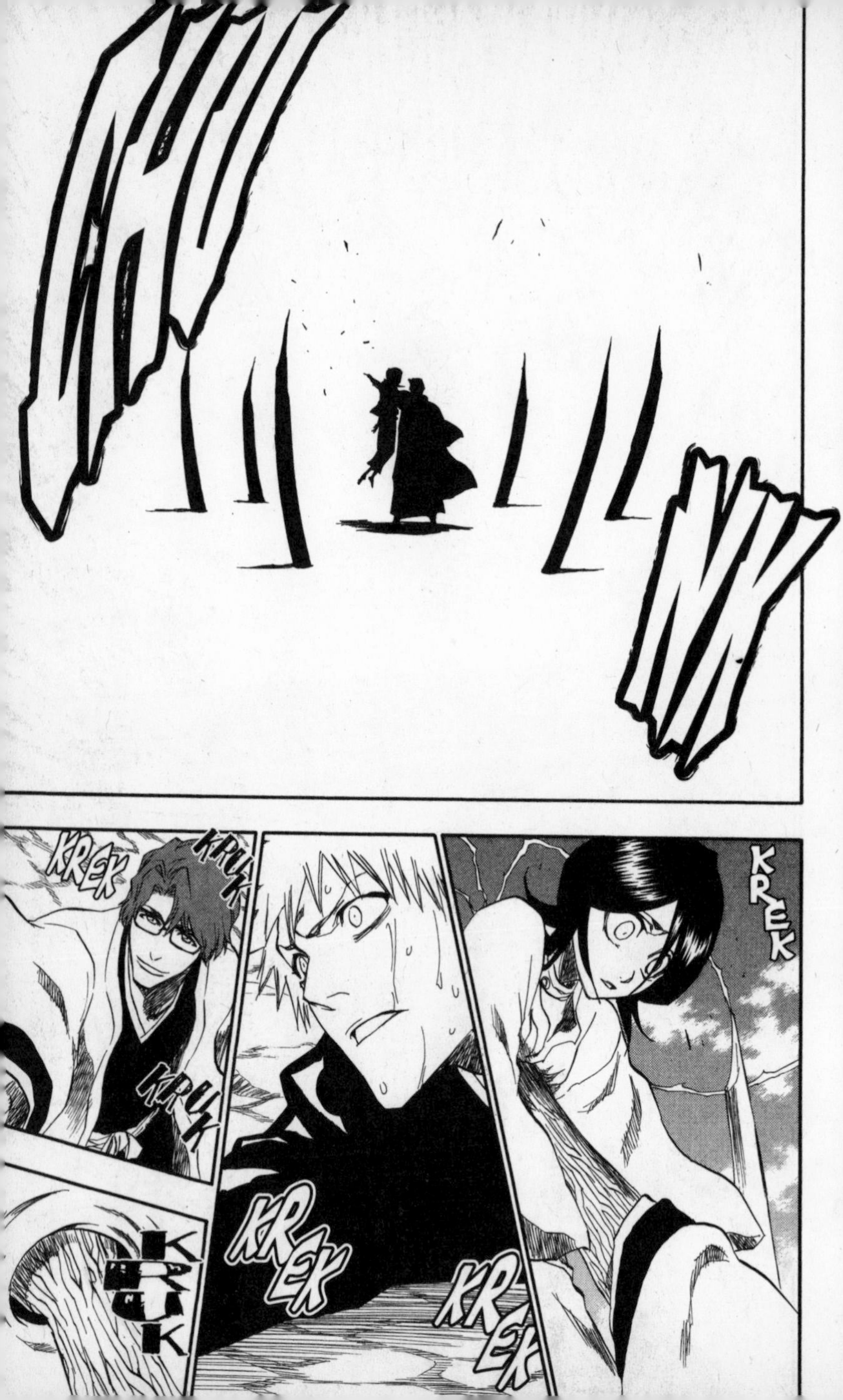
KREK
KREK
KR-EK
KREK
KRUK
KRUK

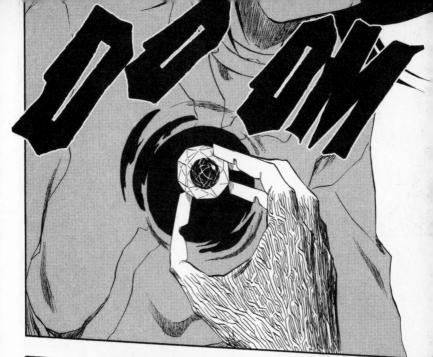

SOMETHING
SO SMALL...

AMAZ-
ING...

178

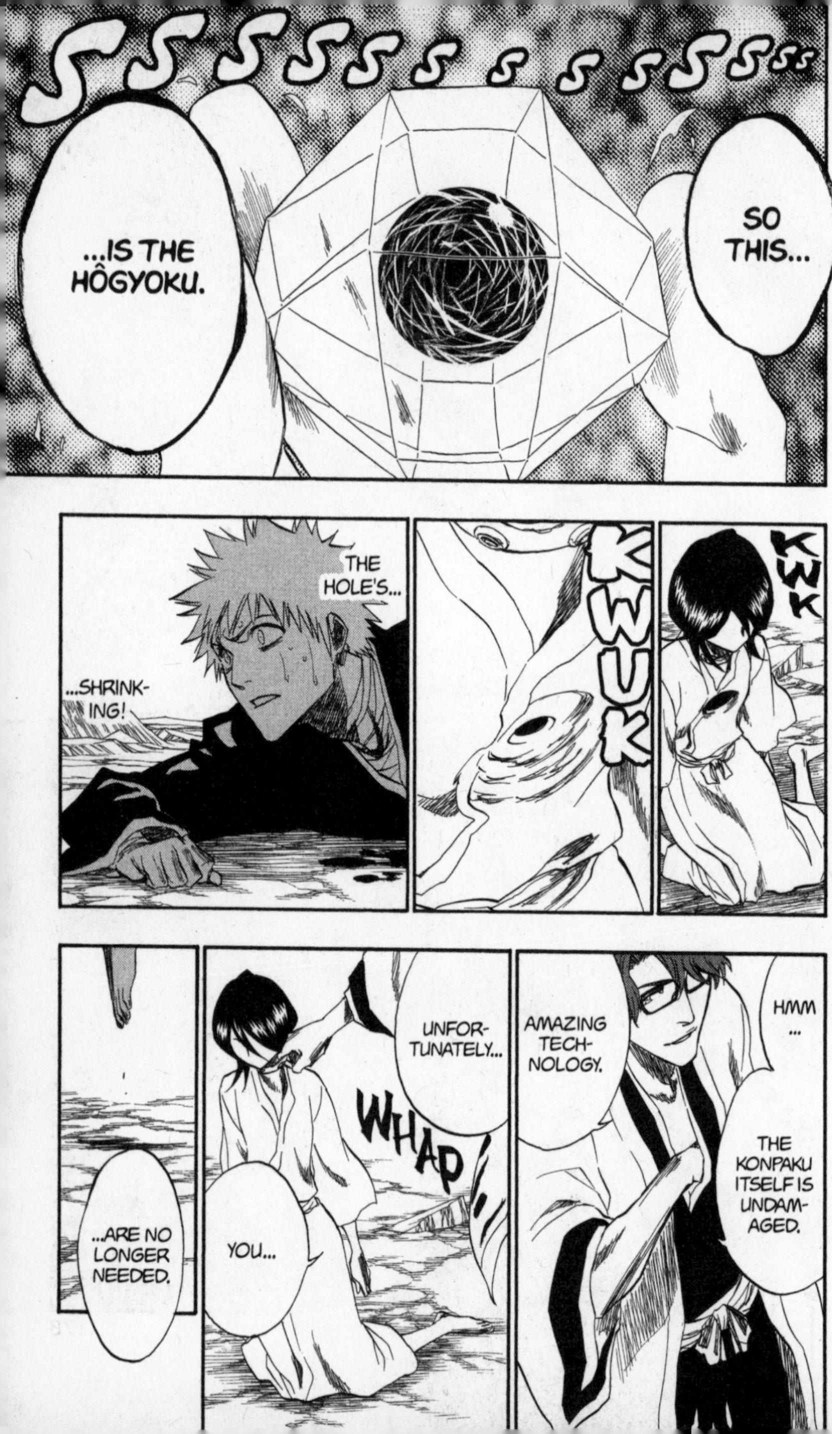
SSSSSSSSSSSSss
SO THIS...
...IS THE HÔGYOKU.
KWK
KWUK
THE HOLE'S...
...SHRINK-ING!
HMM...
THE KONPAKU ITSELF IS UNDAM-AGED.
AMAZING TECH-NOLOGY.
UNFOR-TUNATELY...
WHAP
YOU...
...ARE NO LONGER NEEDED.

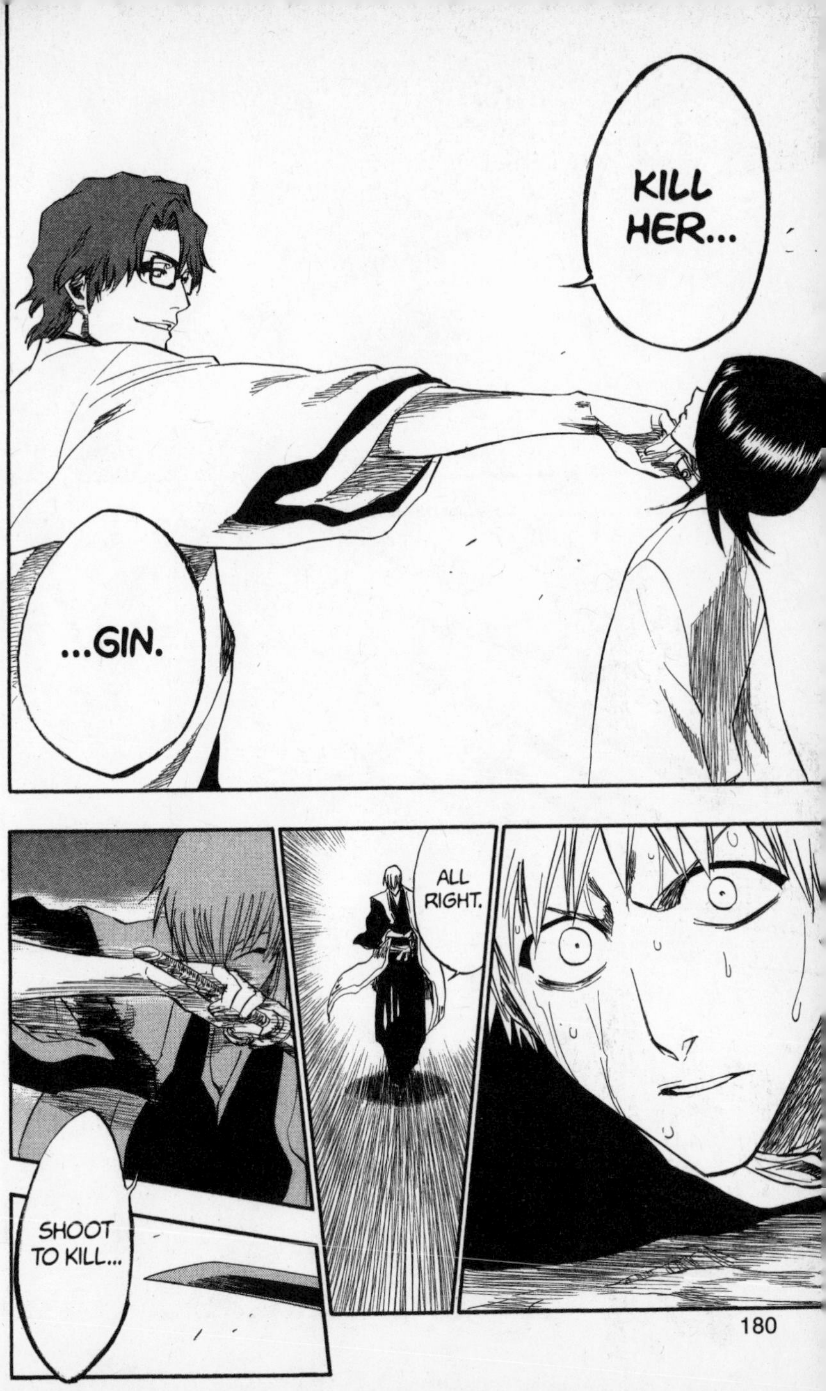
KILL HER...
...GIN.
ALL RIGHT.
SHOOT TO KILL...

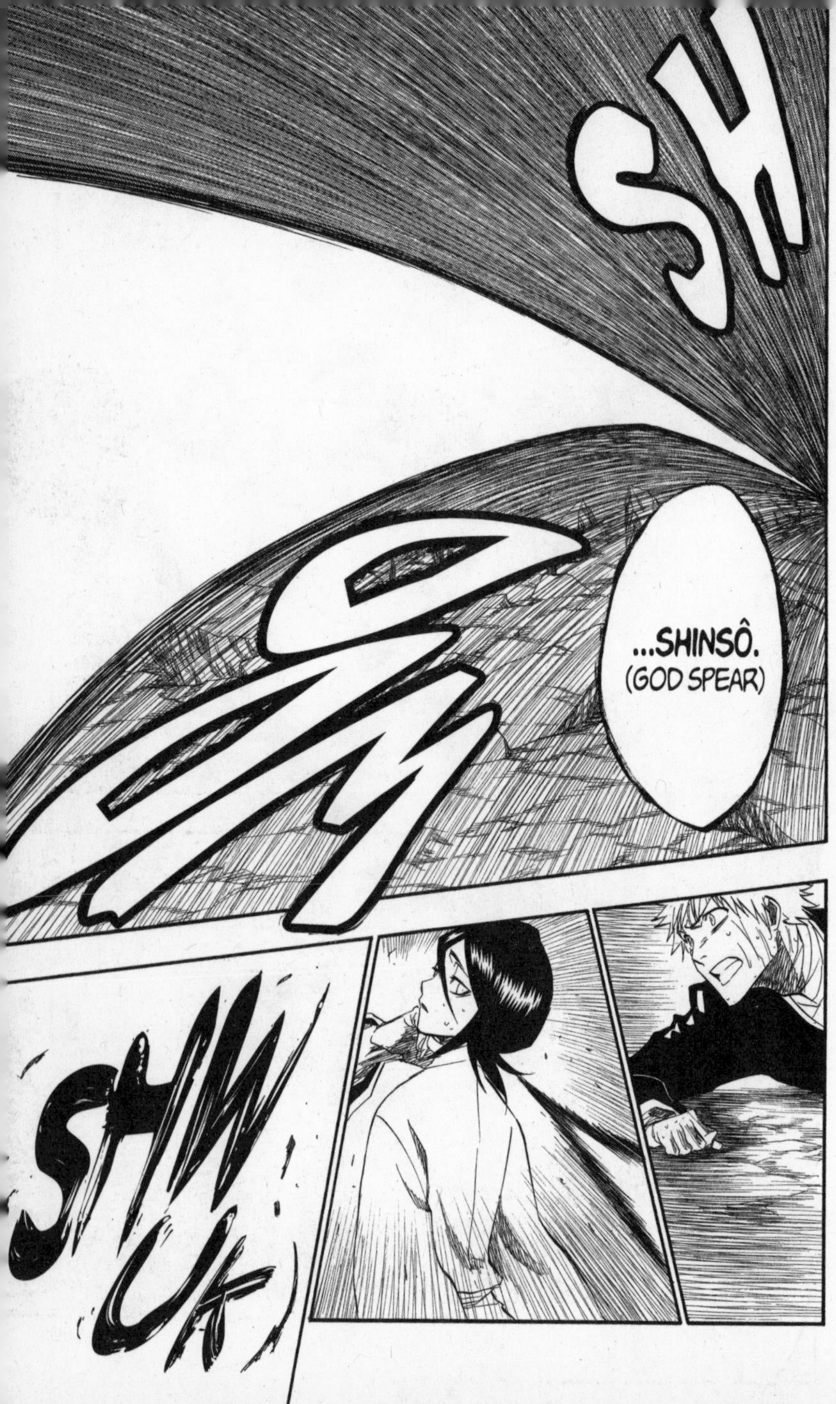
...SHINSÔ.
(GOD SPEAR)

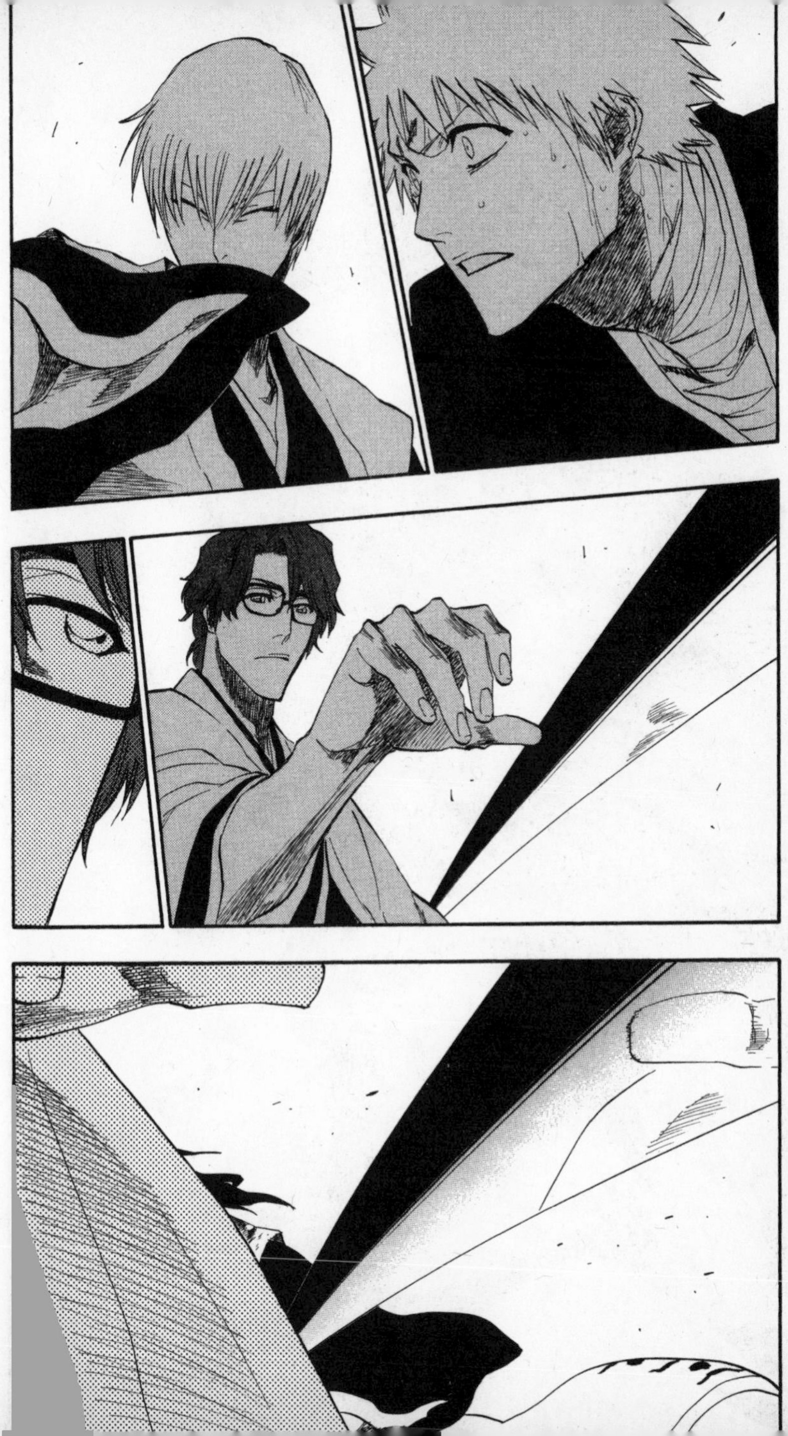

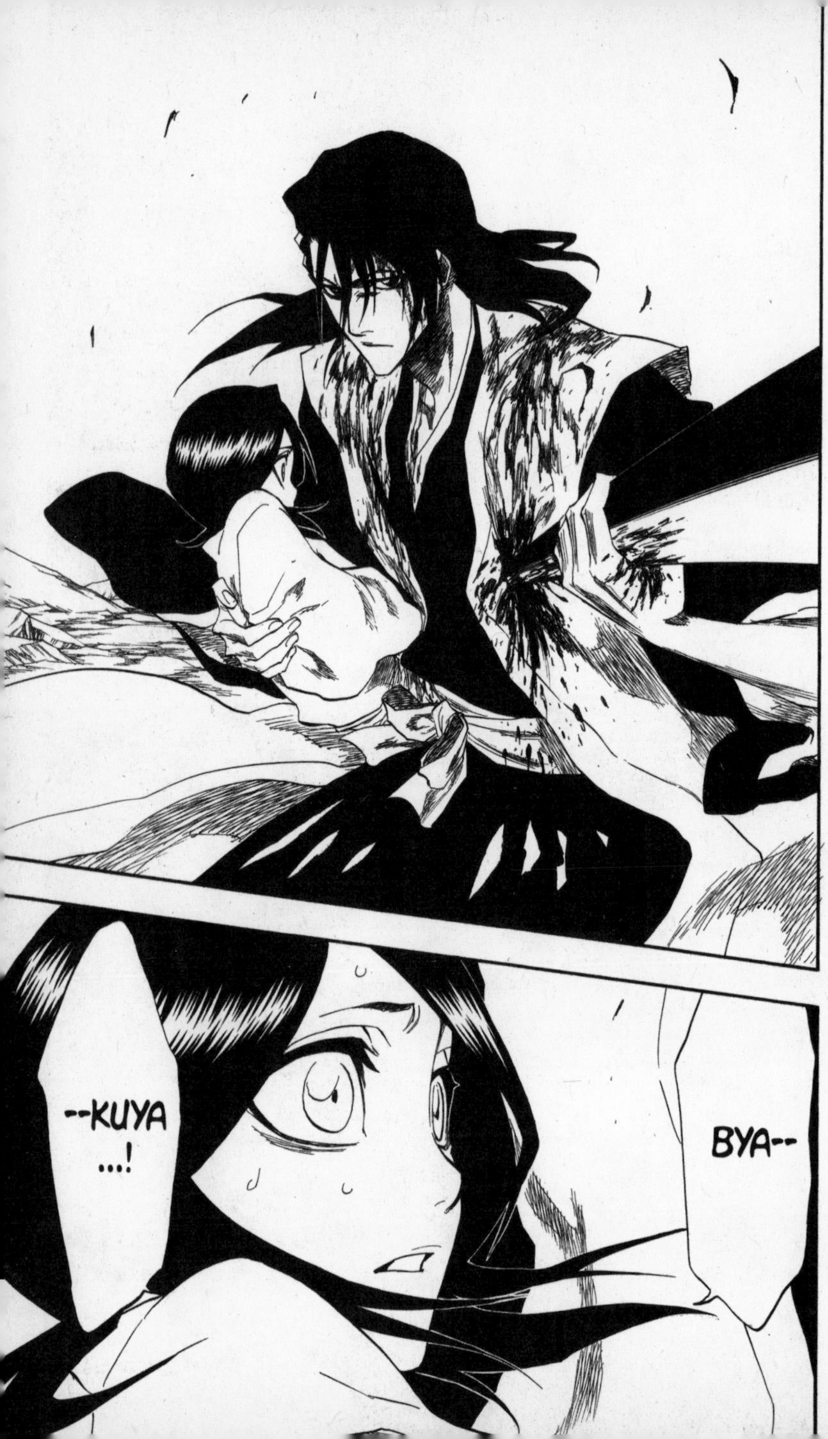
BYA--
--KUYA
...!

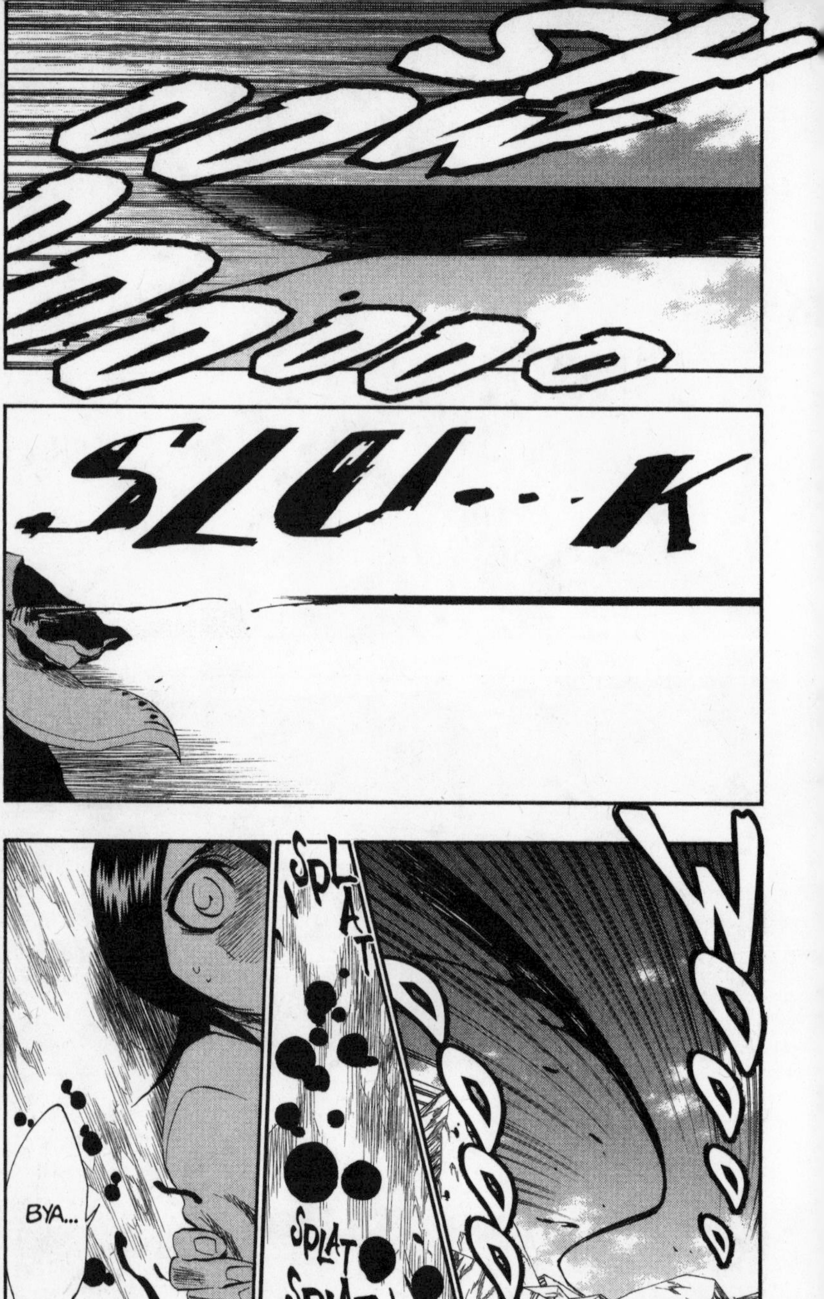
SLU--K
SPLAT
SPLAT
SPLAT
BYA...

177. end of hypnosis9
(Encompassed)

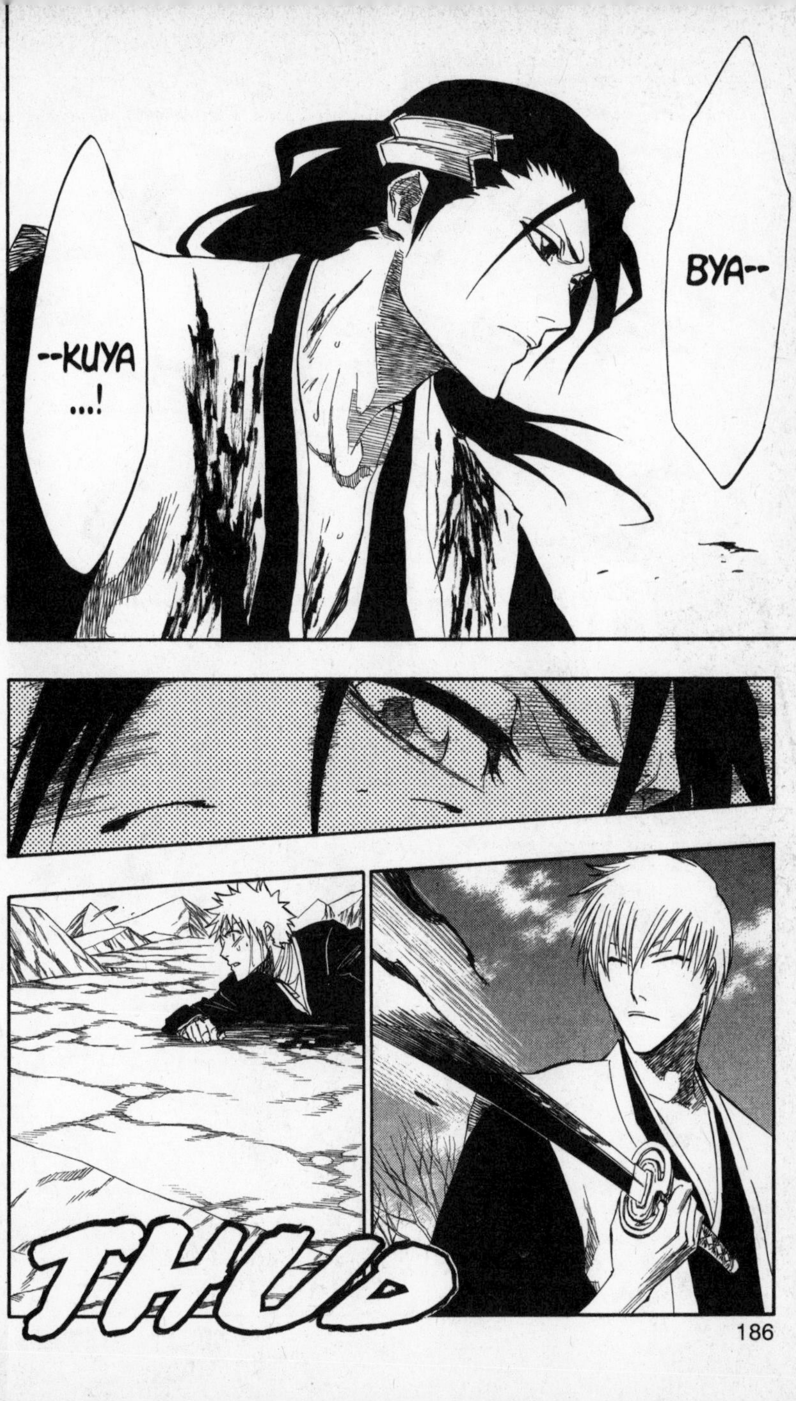
BYA--
--KUYA ...!
THUD

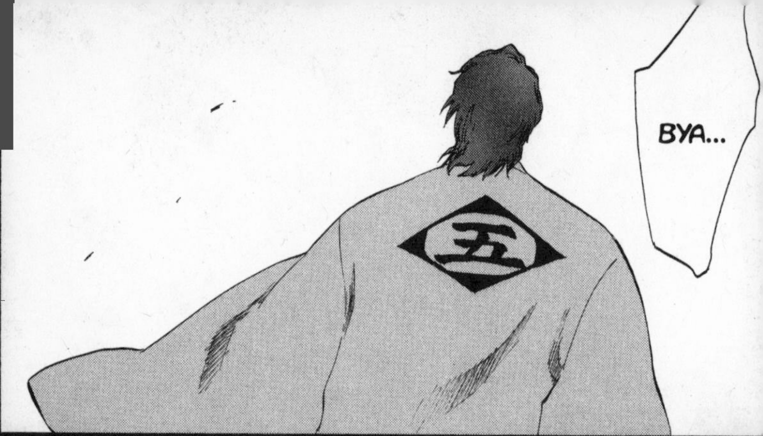
BYA...

BLEACH

−ブリーチ−

177. end of hypnosis9 (Encompassed)

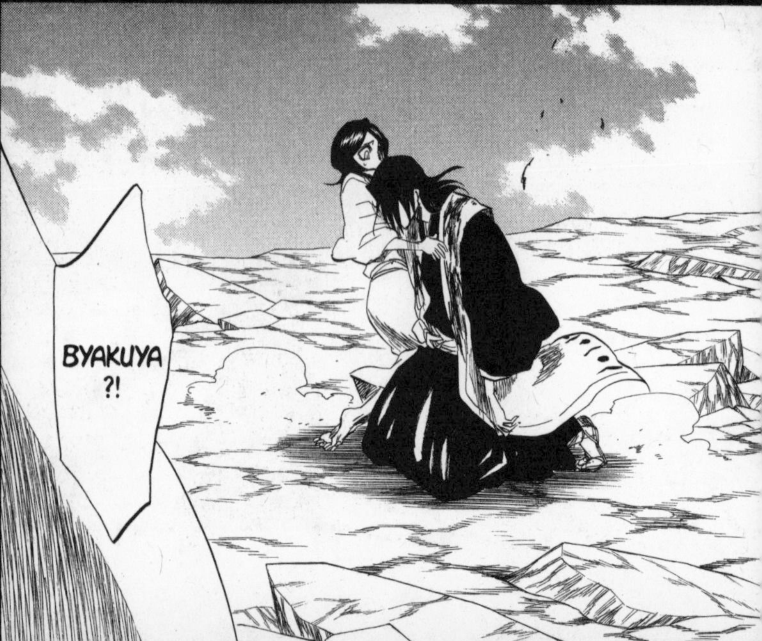
BYAKUYA ?!

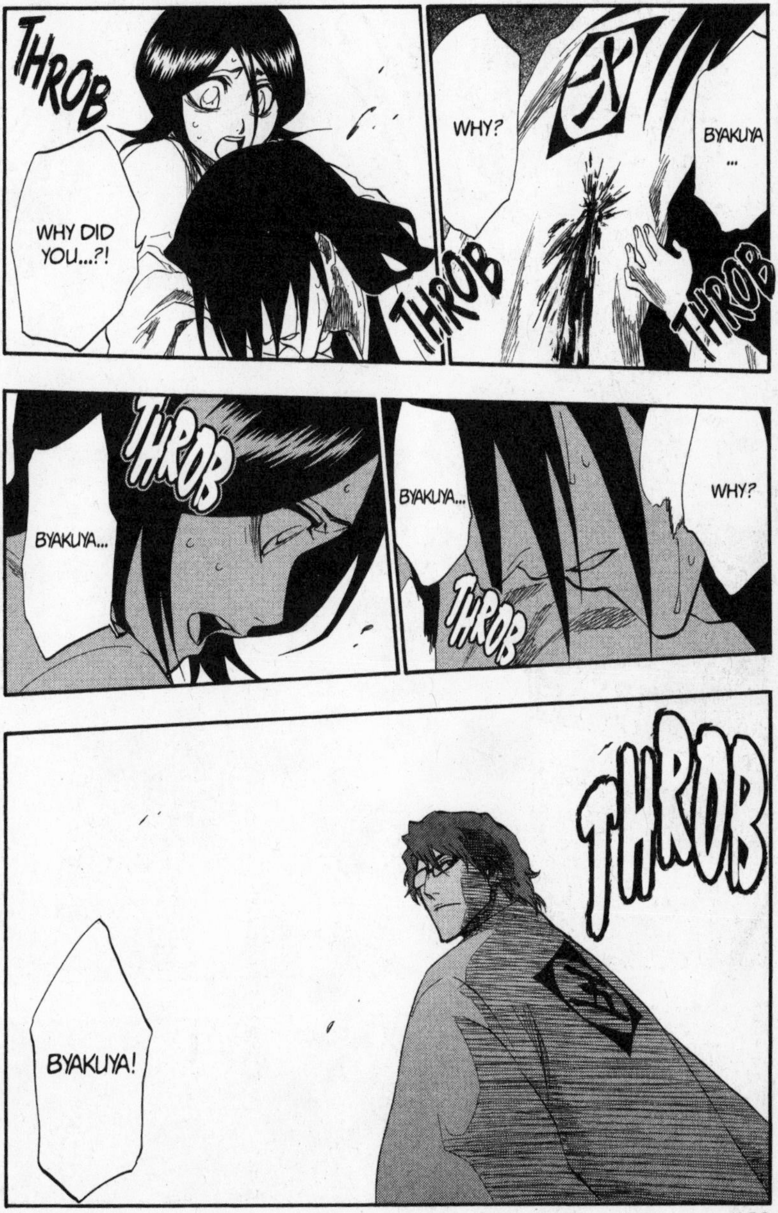
BYAKUYA ...
WHY?
THROB
THROB
THROB
WHY DID YOU...?!
WHY?
BYAKUYA...
THROB
THROB
BYAKUYA...
THROB
BYAKUYA!

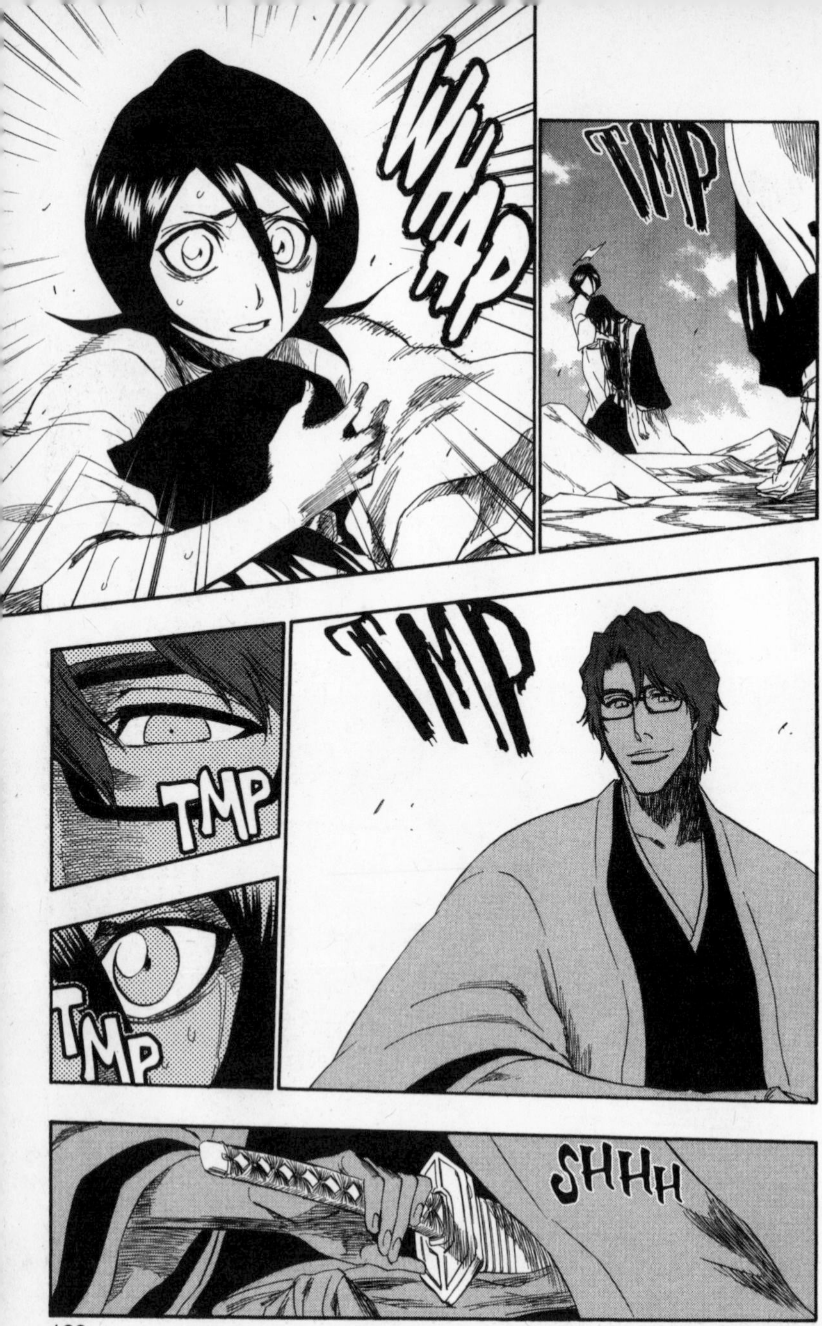
TMP
WHAP
TMP
TMP
TMP
SHHH

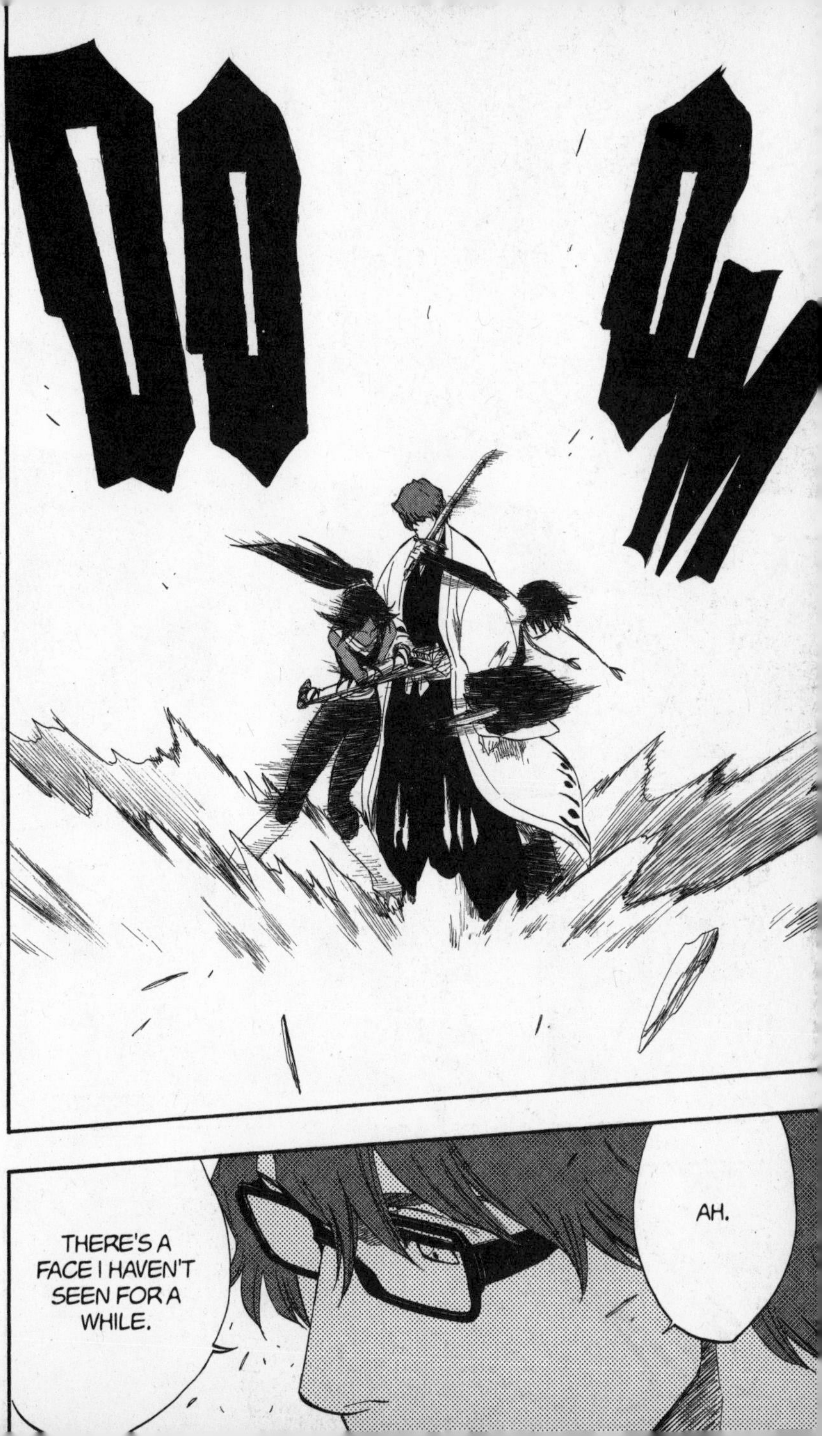
DOOM
AH.
THERE'S A FACE I HAVEN'T SEEN FOR A WHILE.

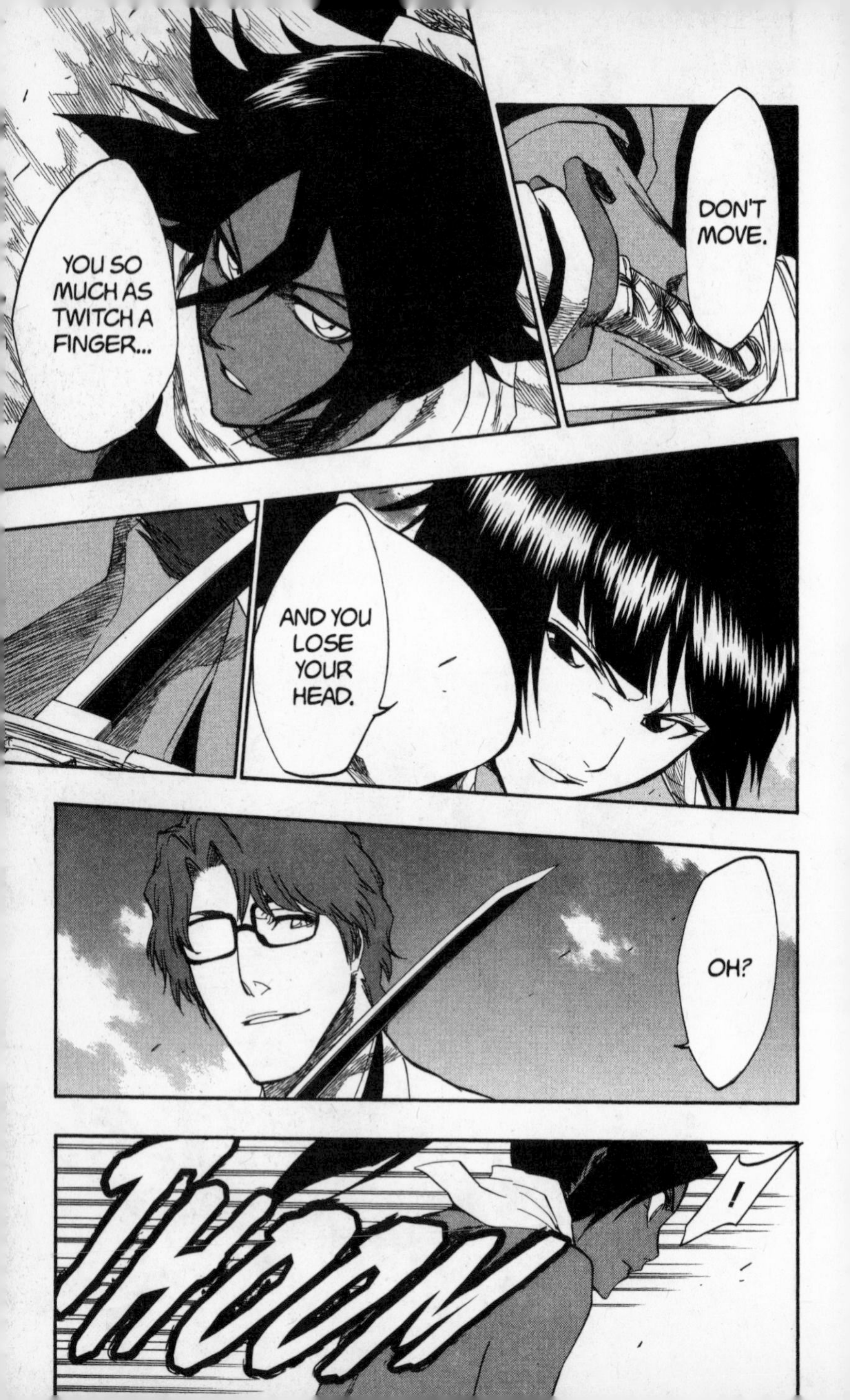
DON'T MOVE.
YOU SO MUCH AS TWITCH A FINGER...
AND YOU LOSE YOUR HEAD.
OH?
!

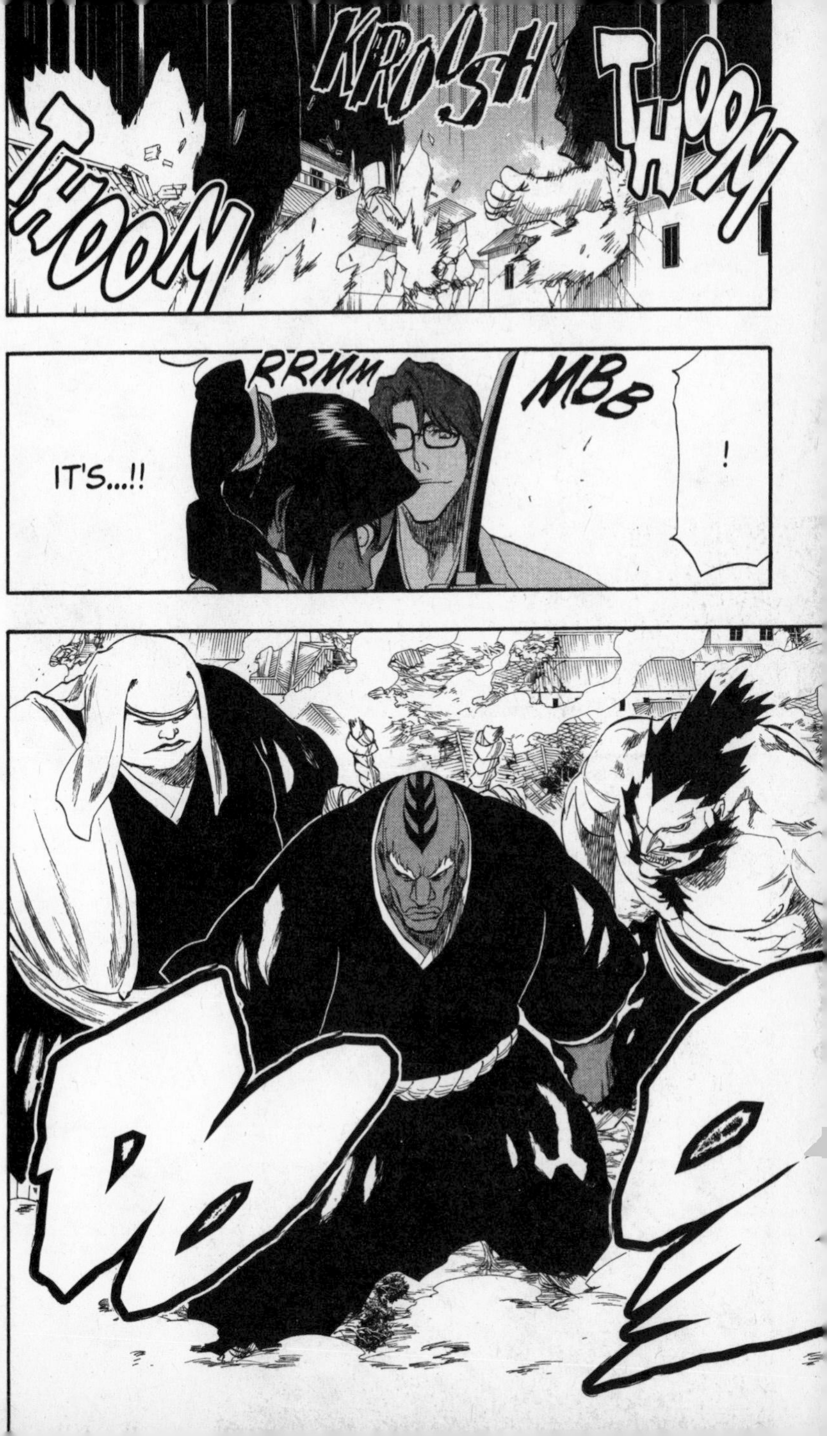
THOOM
KROOSH
THOOM
!
MBB
RRMM
IT'S...!!

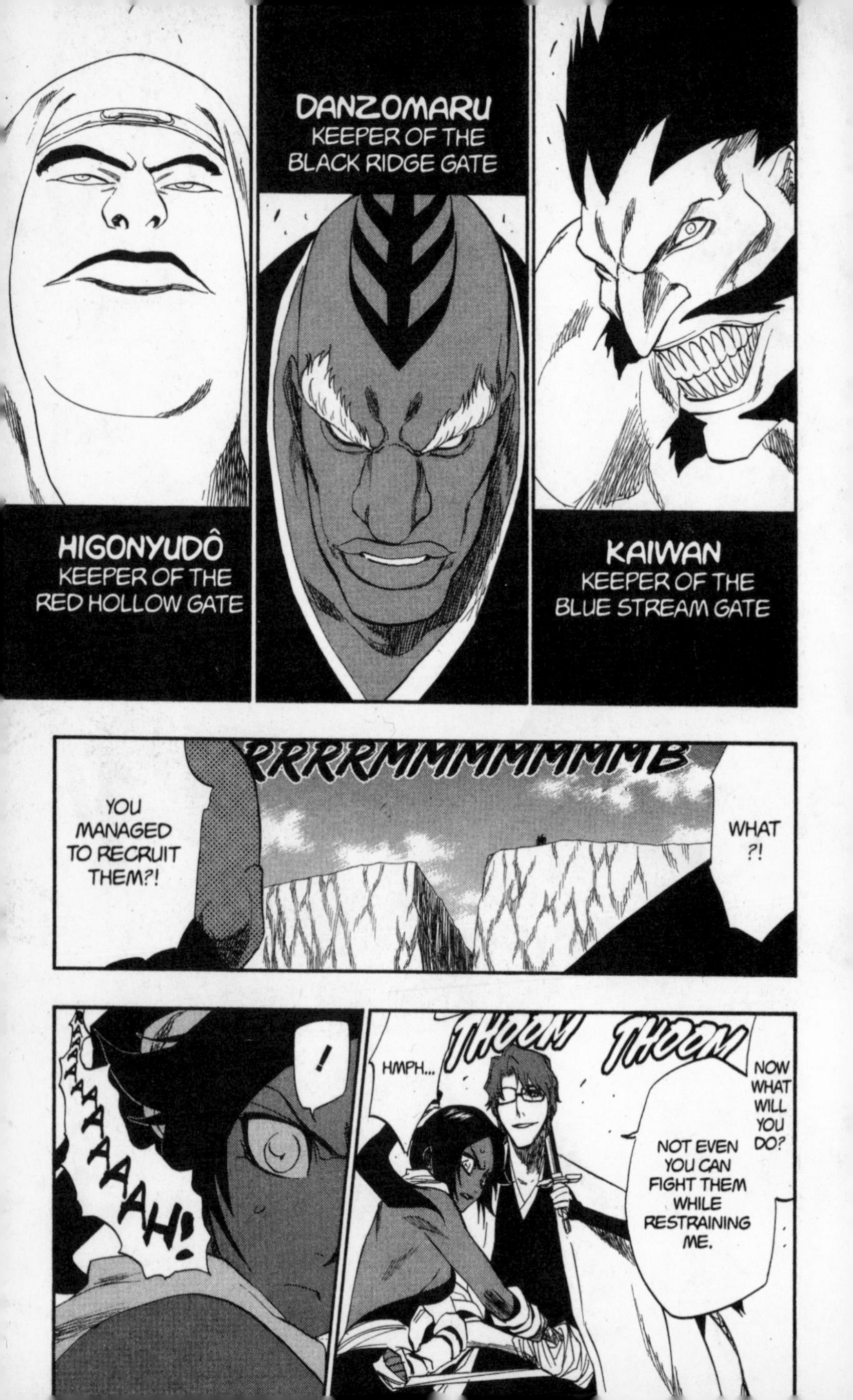
KAIWAN
KEEPER OF THE BLUE STREAM GATE
DANZOMARU
KEEPER OF THE BLACK RIDGE GATE
HIGONYUDÔ
KEEPER OF THE RED HOLLOW GATE
RRRRMMMMMMMMMB
WHAT ?!
YOU MANAGED TO RECRUIT THEM?!
THOOM THOOM
NOW WHAT WILL YOU DO?
NOT EVEN YOU CAN FIGHT THEM WHILE RESTRAINING ME.
HMPH...
!
AAAAAAAAAH!

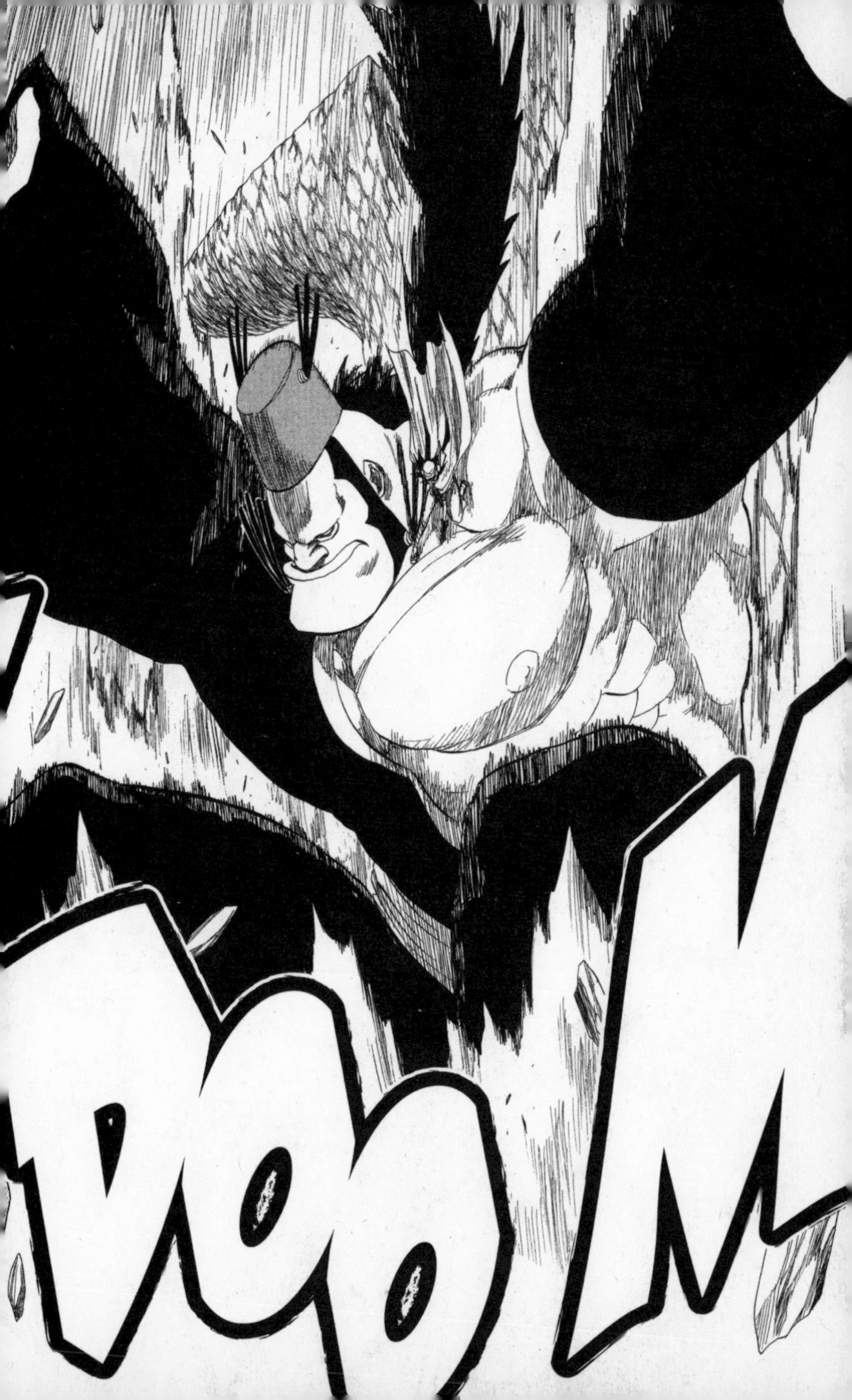
DOOM

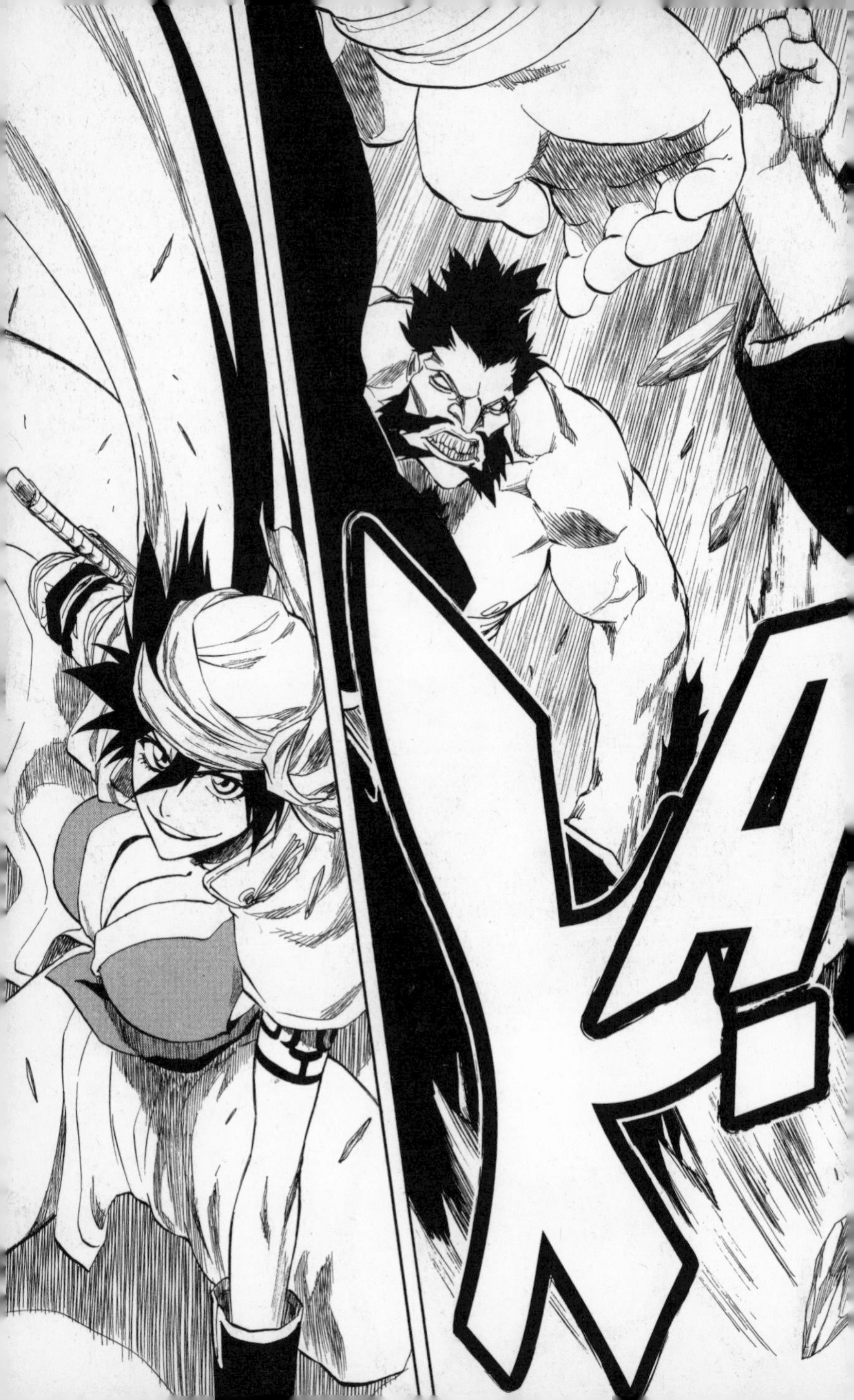

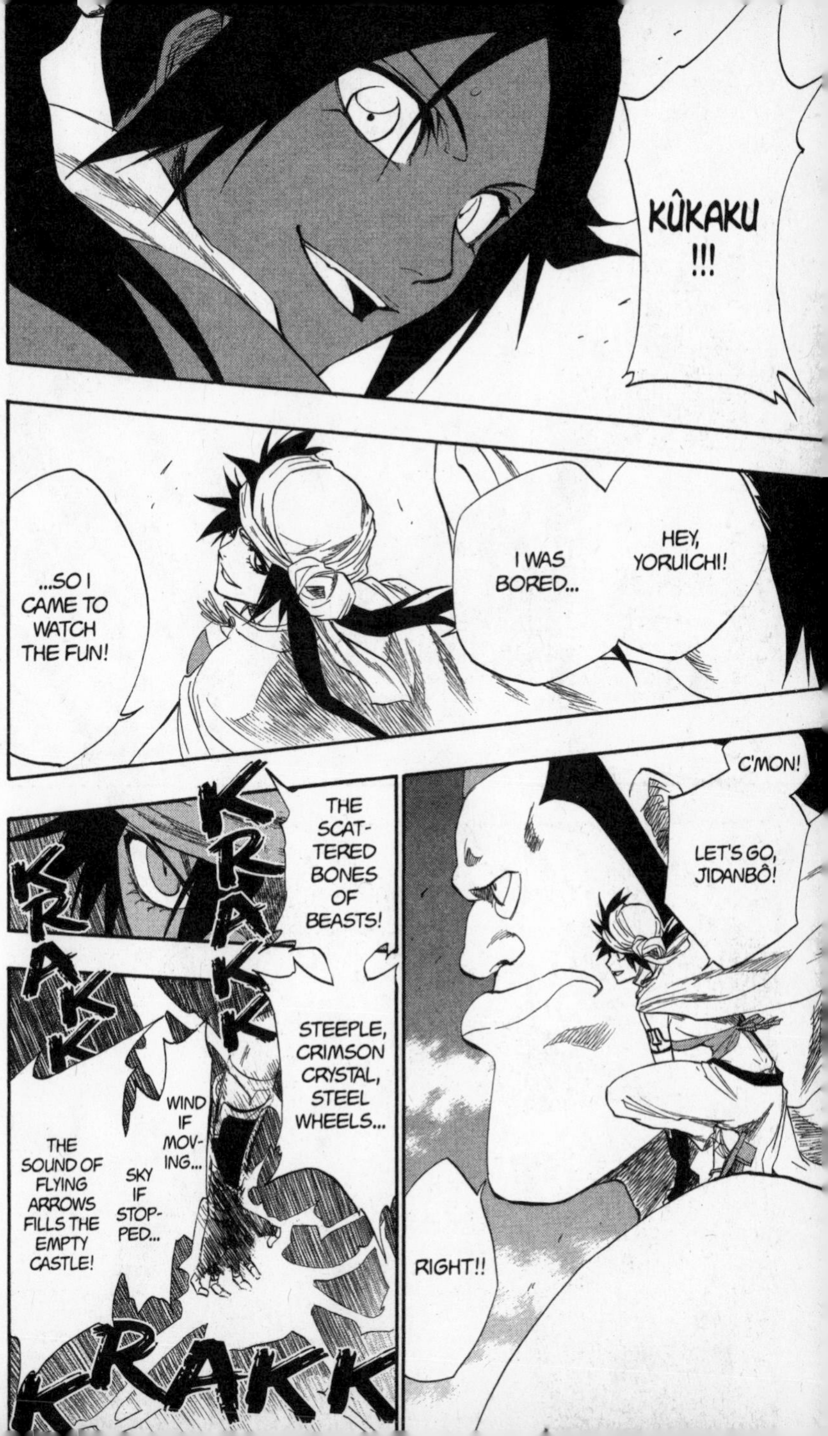
KÛKAKU !!!
HEY, YORUICHI!
I WAS BORED...
...SO I CAME TO WATCH THE FUN!
C'MON!
LET'S GO, JIDANBÔ!
RIGHT!!
KRAKK
KRAKK
THE SCATTERED BONES OF BEASTS!
STEEPLE, CRIMSON CRYSTAL, STEEL WHEELS...
WIND IF MOVING...
SKY IF STOPPED...
THE SOUND OF FLYING ARROWS FILLS THE EMPTY CASTLE!
KRAKK

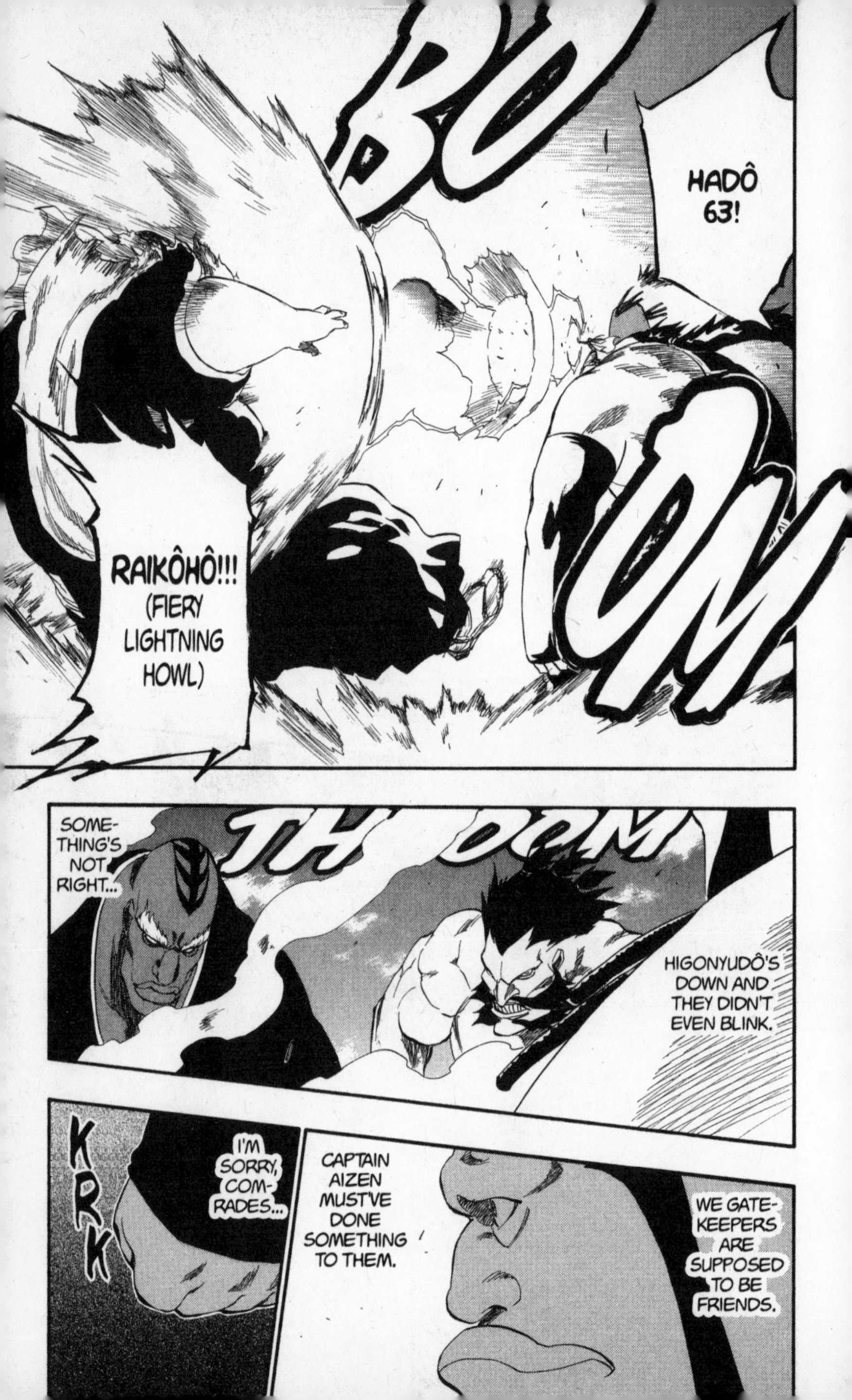
HADÔ 63!
BOOM
RAIKÔHÔ!!! (FIERY LIGHTNING HOWL)
HIGONYUDÔ'S DOWN AND THEY DIDN'T EVEN BLINK.
SOMETHING'S NOT RIGHT...
WE GATEKEEPERS ARE SUPPOSED TO BE FRIENDS.
CAPTAIN AIZEN MUST'VE DONE SOMETHING TO THEM.
KRK
I'M SORRY, COMRADES...

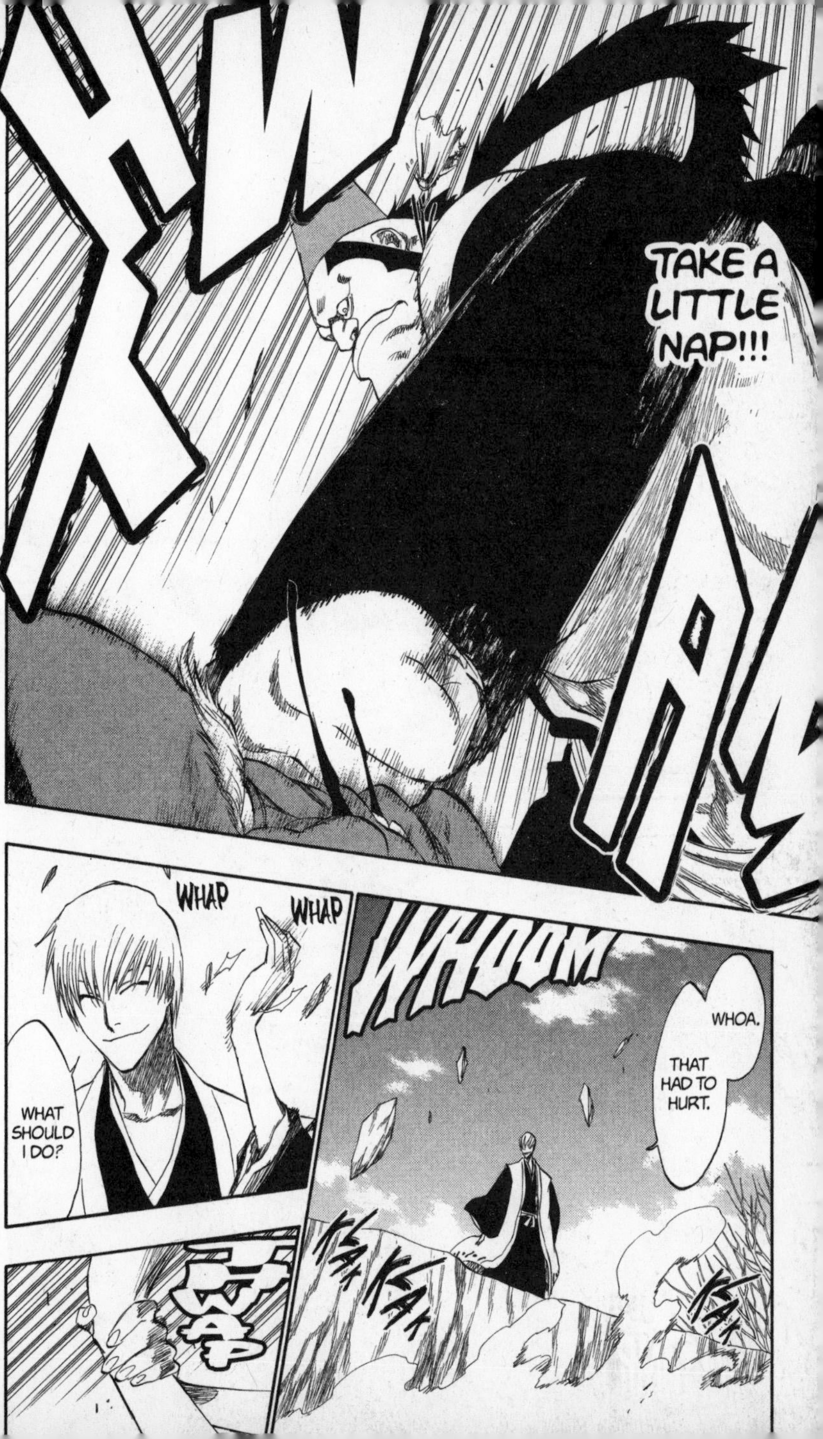
TAKE A LITTLE NAP!!!
WHOOM
WHOA.
THAT HAD TO HURT.
KAK KAK KAK
KAK
WHAP
WHAP
WHAT SHOULD I DO?

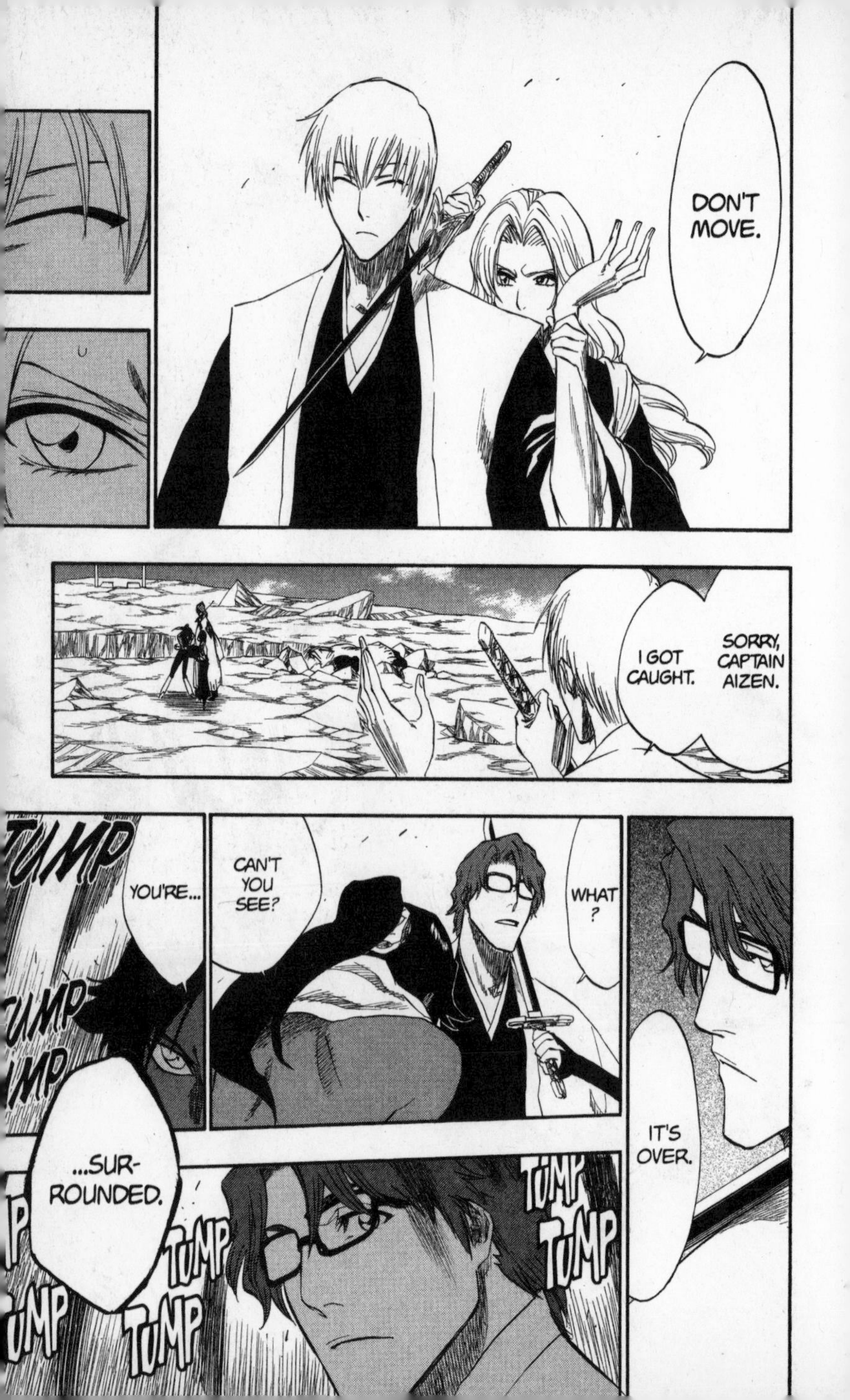
DON'T MOVE.
SORRY, CAPTAIN AIZEN.
I GOT CAUGHT.
IT'S OVER.
WHAT?
CAN'T YOU SEE?
YOU'RE...
TUMP
TUMP
TUMP
...SUR-ROUNDED.
TUMP
TUMP
TUMP
TUMP
TUMP
TUMP

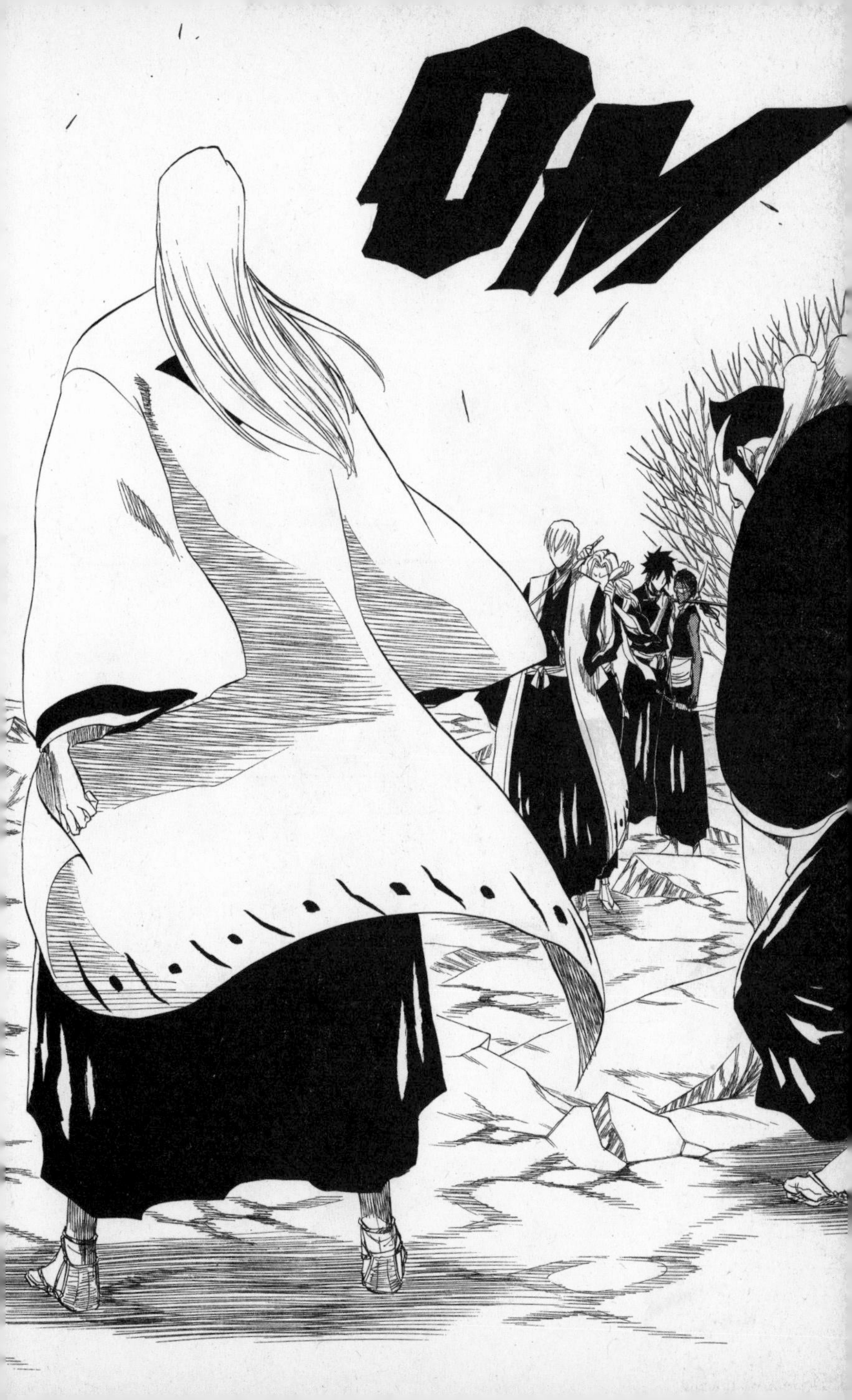
DM

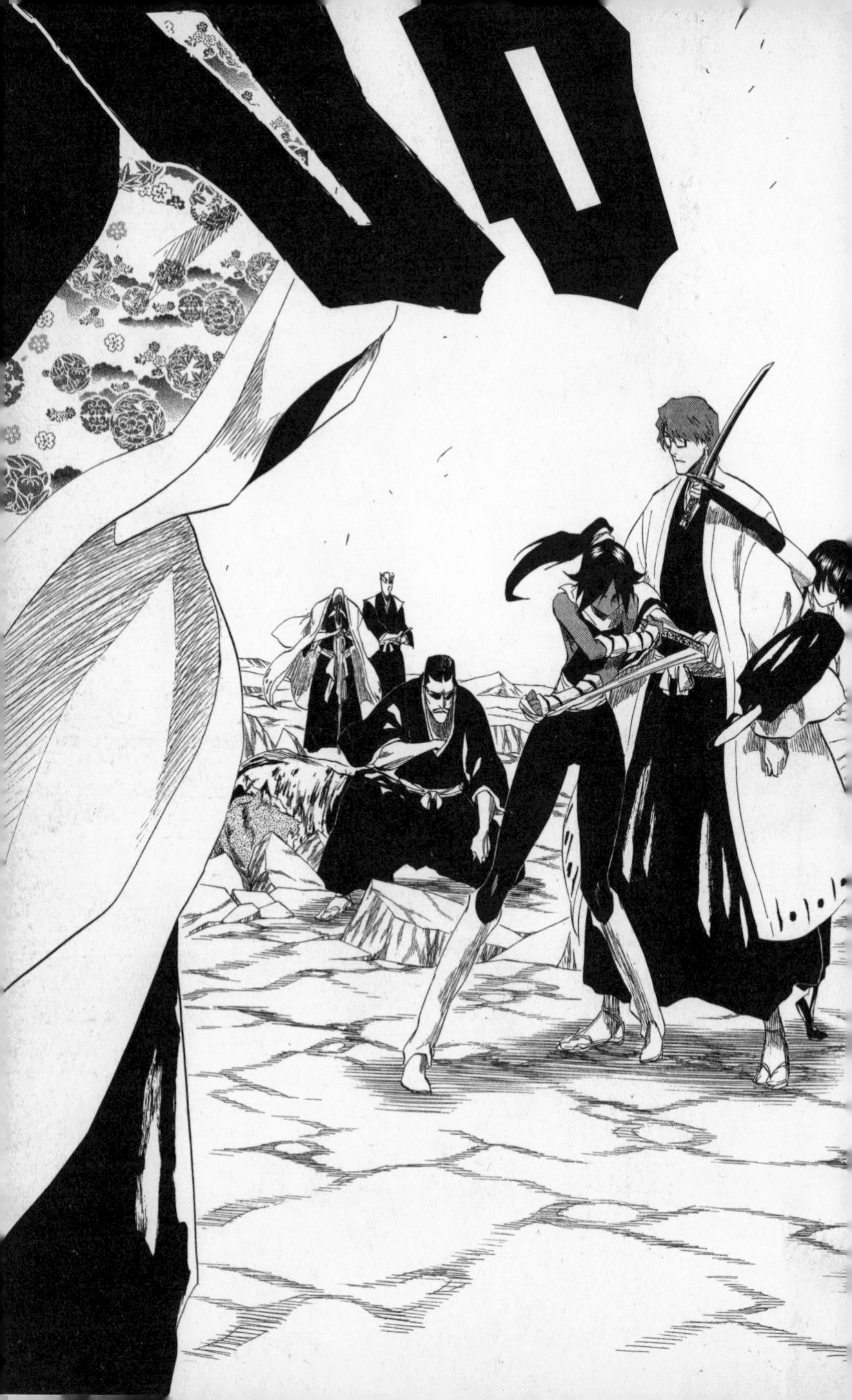

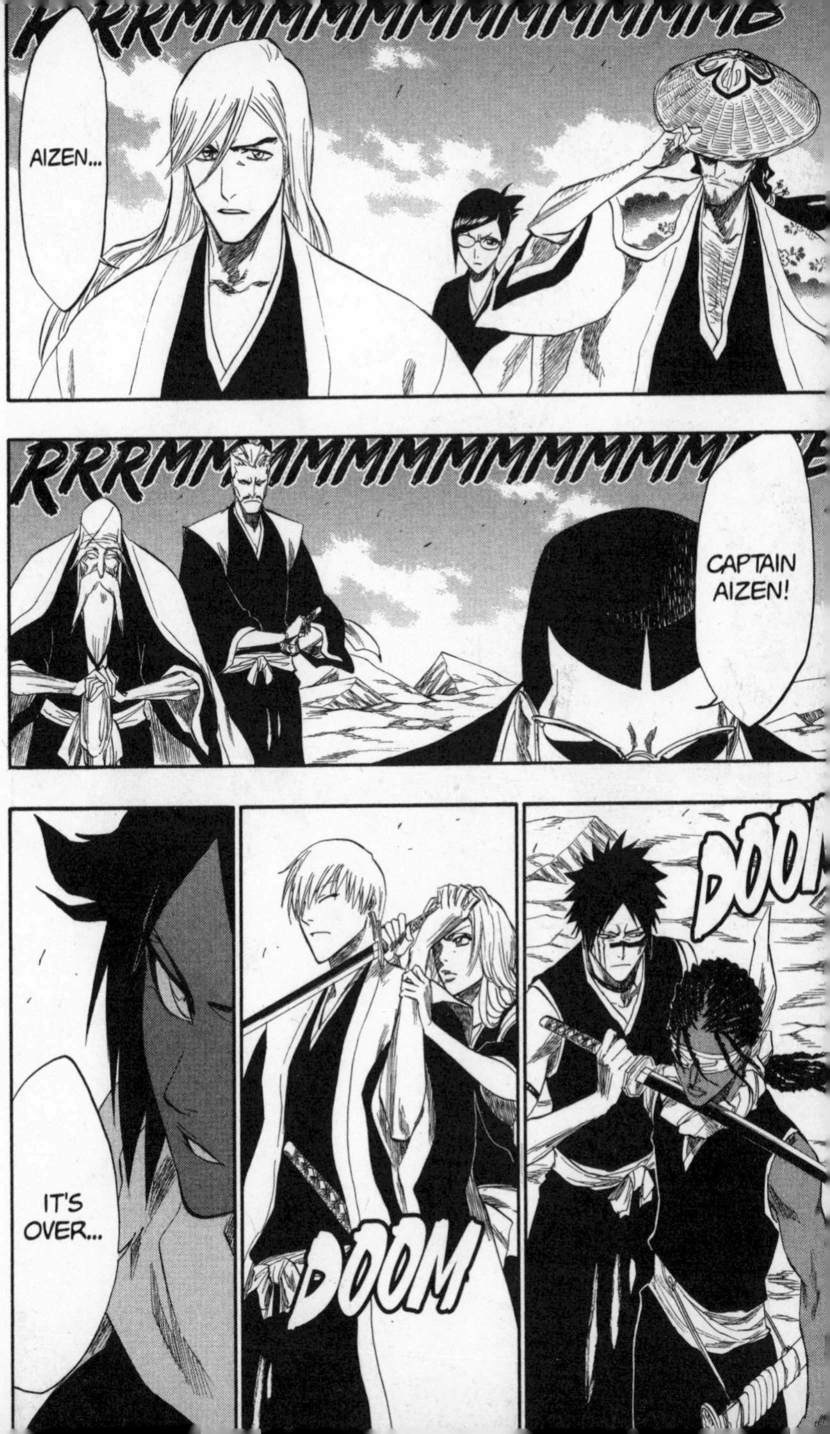
RRRMMMMMMMMMMMMMMMMMB
AIZEN...
CAPTAIN AIZEN!
RRRMMMMMMMMMMMMMMMMM
DOOM
DOOM
IT'S OVER...

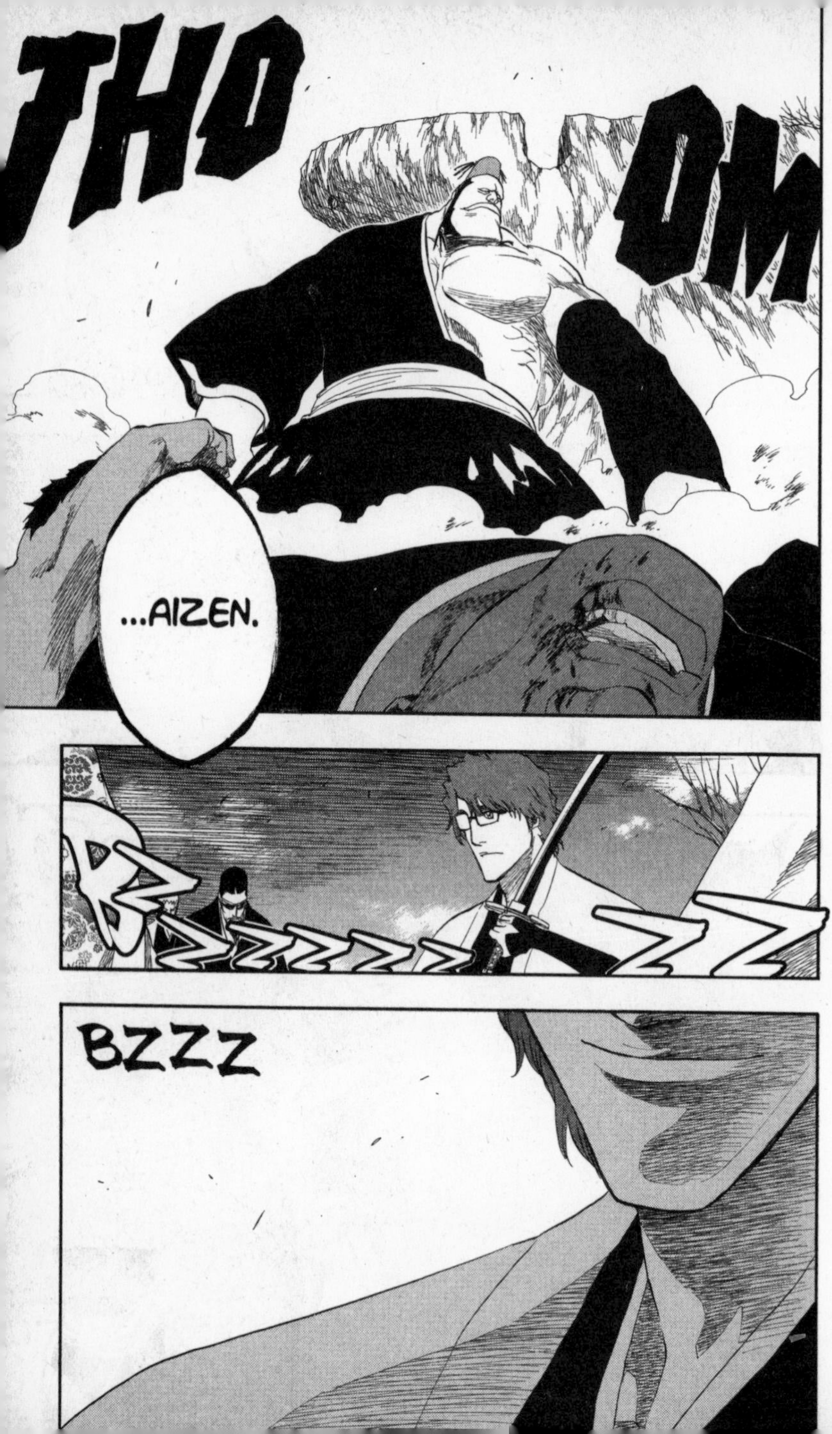
THOOM
...AIZEN.
ZZZZZZZZZZZZ
BZZZ

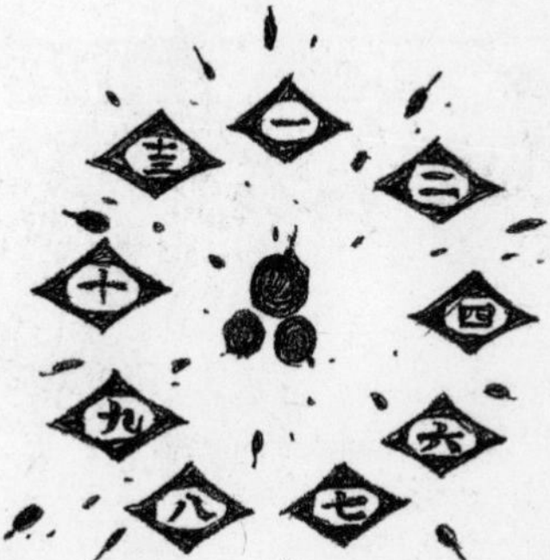
一
二
四
六
七
八
九
十

178. end of hypnosis10 (No One Stands On the Sky)

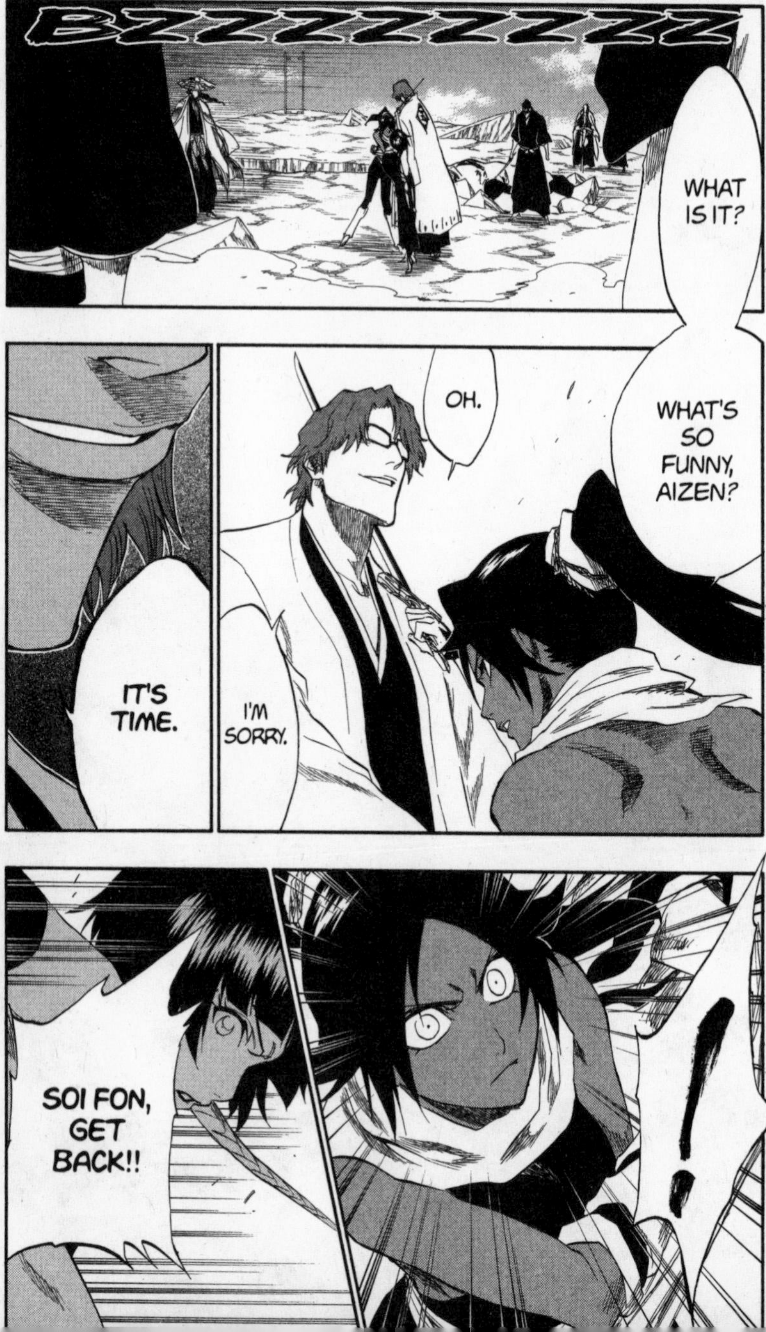
BZZZZZZZZZZ
WHAT IS IT?
WHAT'S SO FUNNY, AIZEN?
OH.
I'M SORRY.
IT'S TIME.
!
SOI FON, GET BACK!!

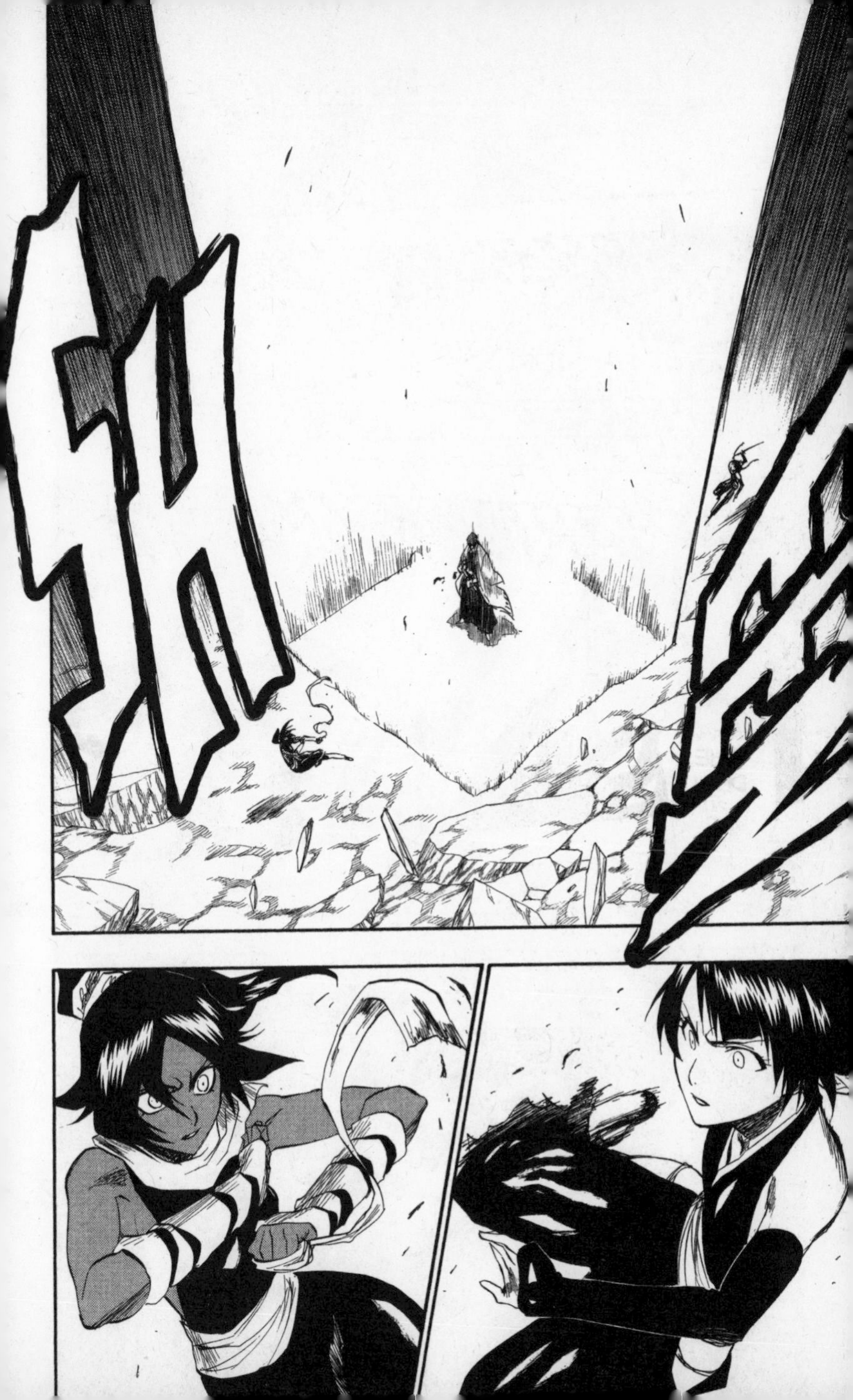

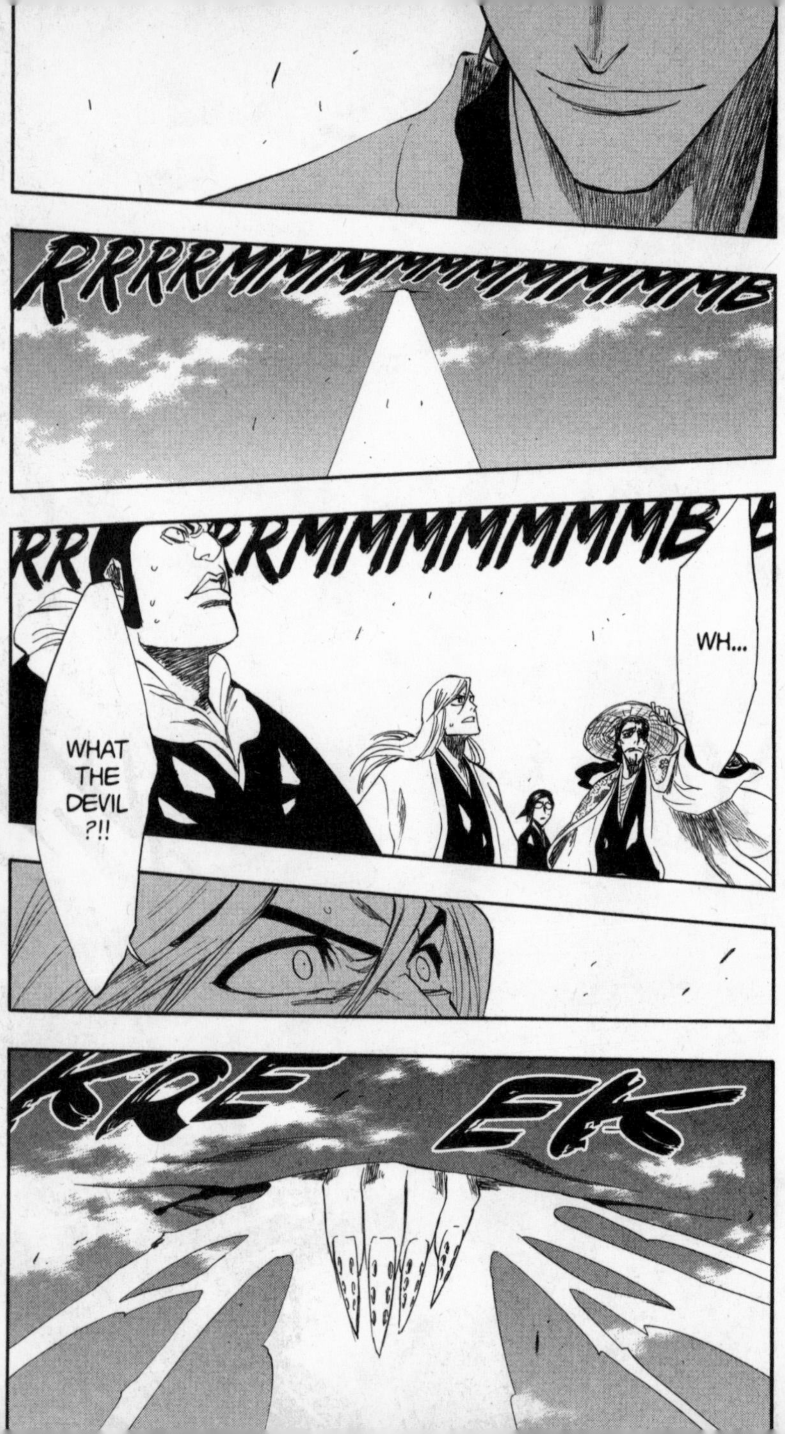
RRRRMMMMMMMMMMMMMB
RRRRMMMMMMMMMMMB
WH...
WHAT THE DEVIL ?!!
KREEK

178. end of hypnosis10 (No One Stands On the Sky)

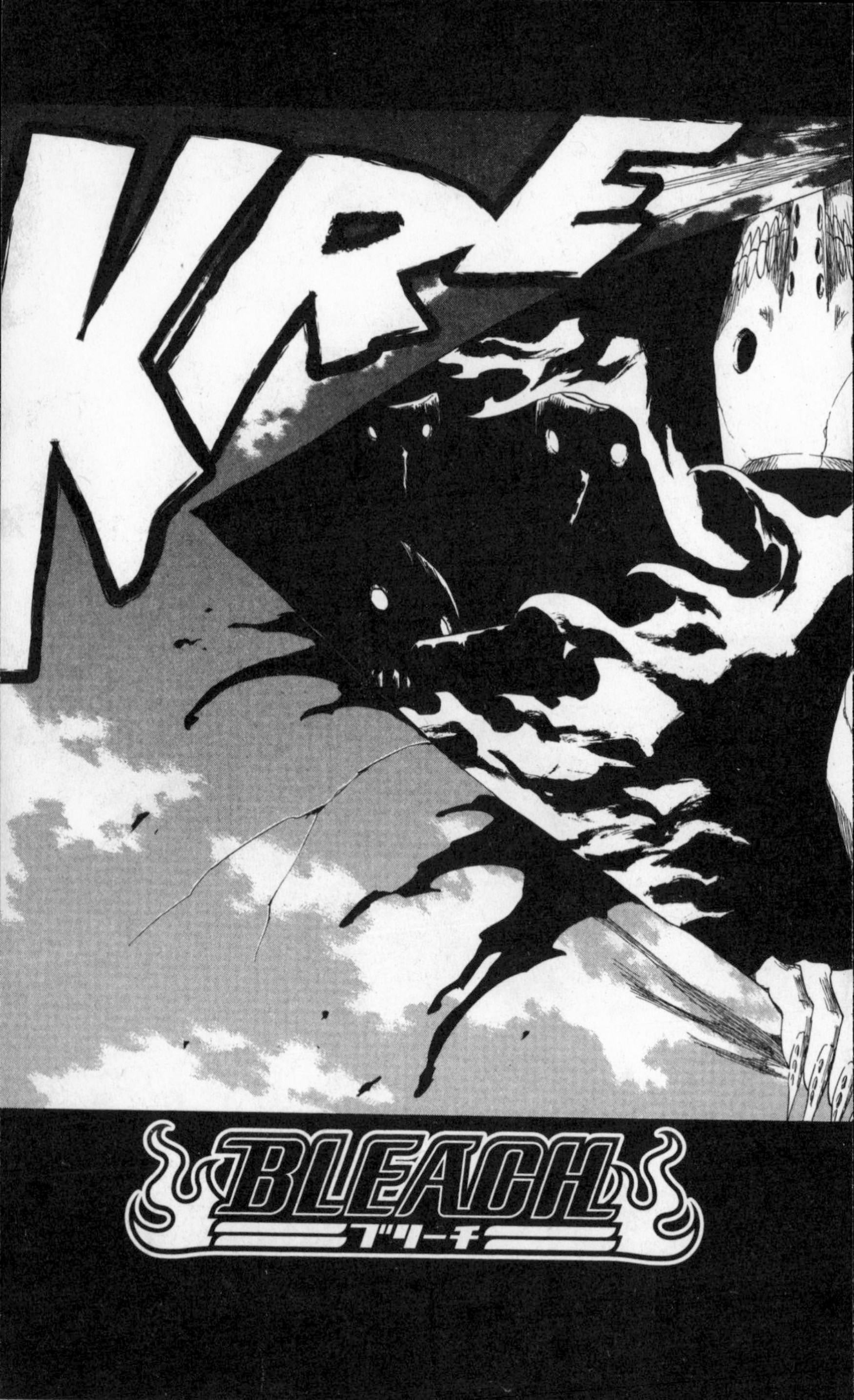

BLEACH
ブリーチ

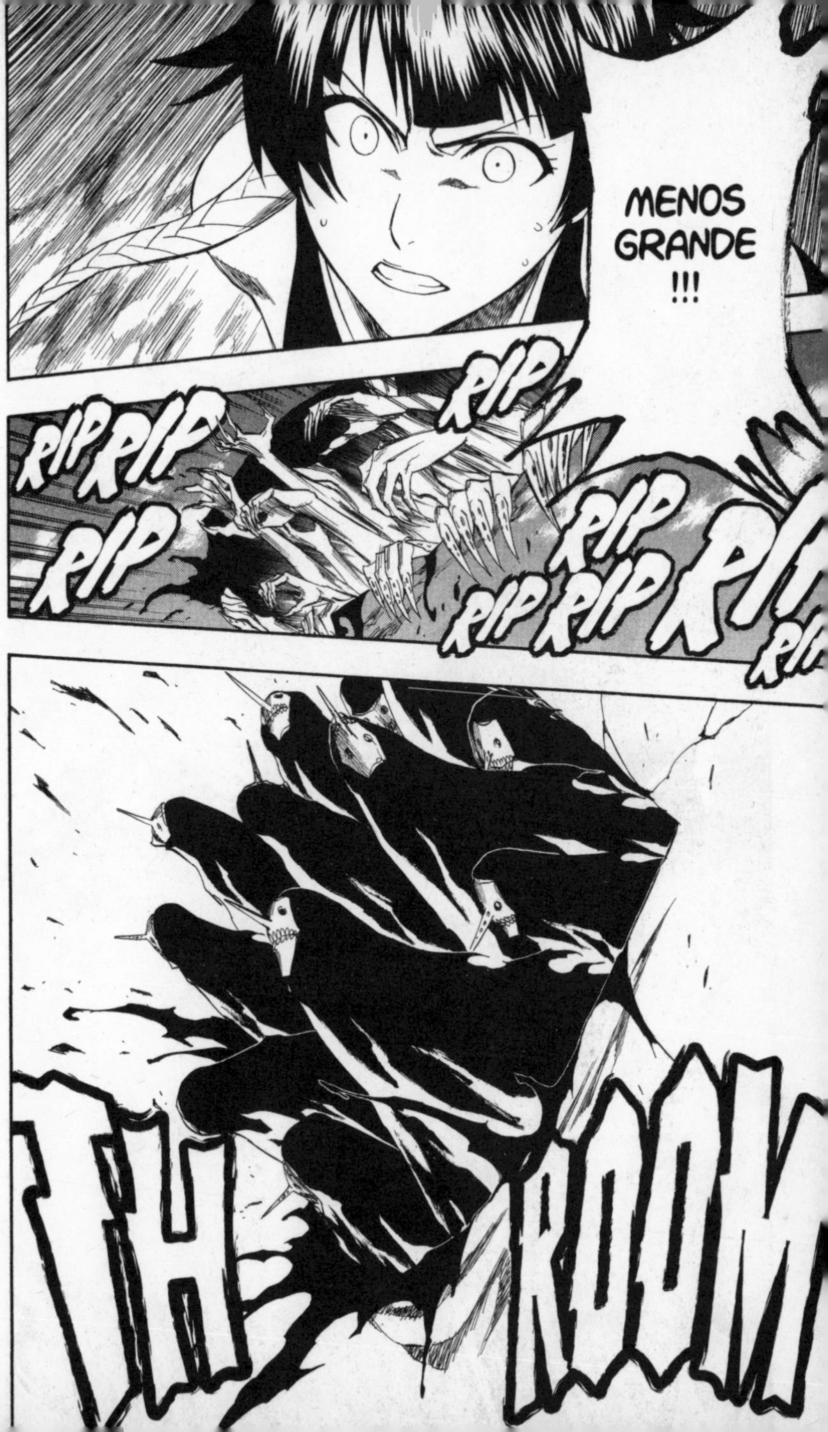
MENOS
GRANDE
!!!
RIP
RIP
RIP RIP
RIP RIP
RIP
THROOM

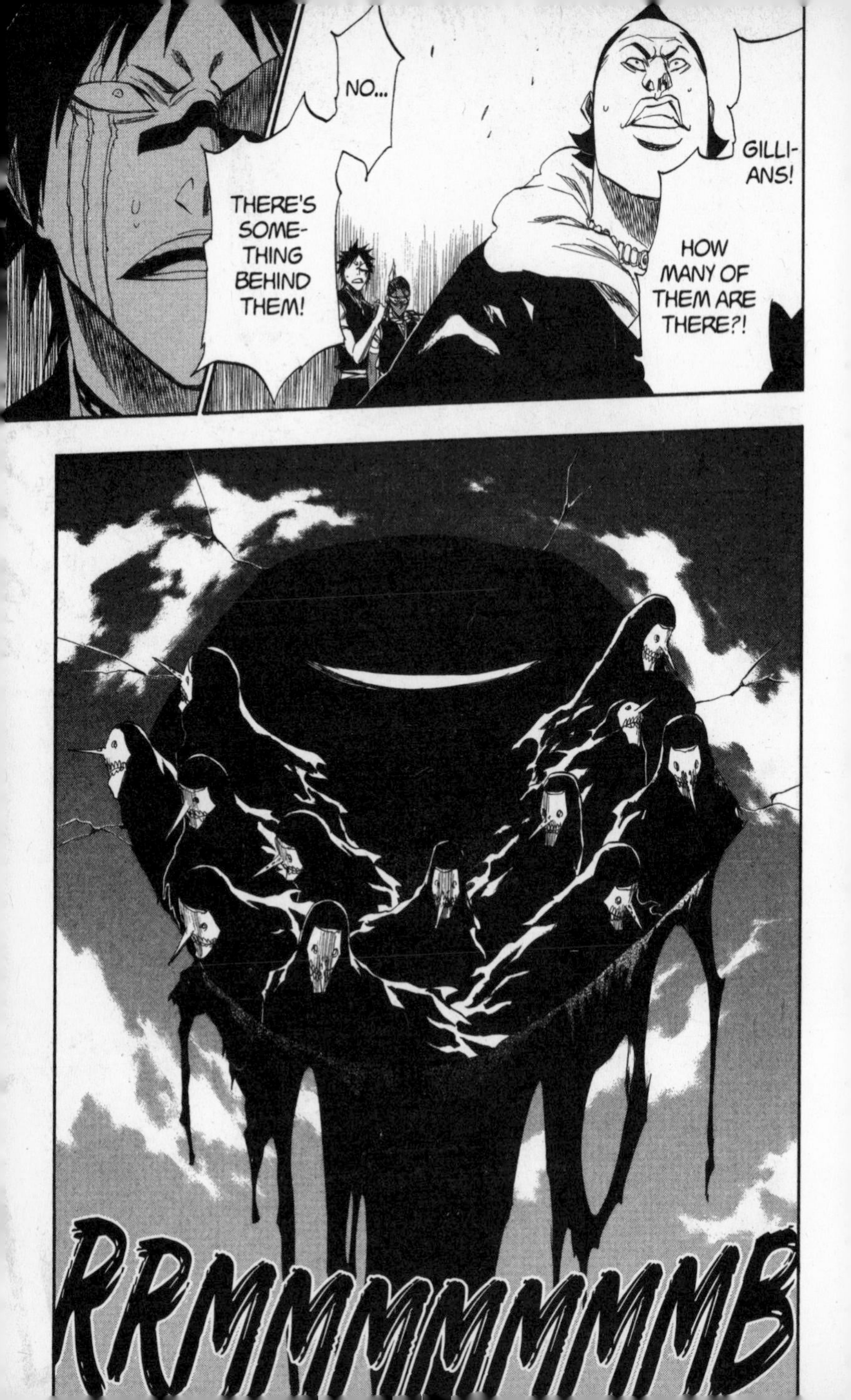
GILLI-ANS!
HOW MANY OF THEM ARE THERE?!
NO...
THERE'S SOME-THING BEHIND THEM!
RRMMMMMMMB

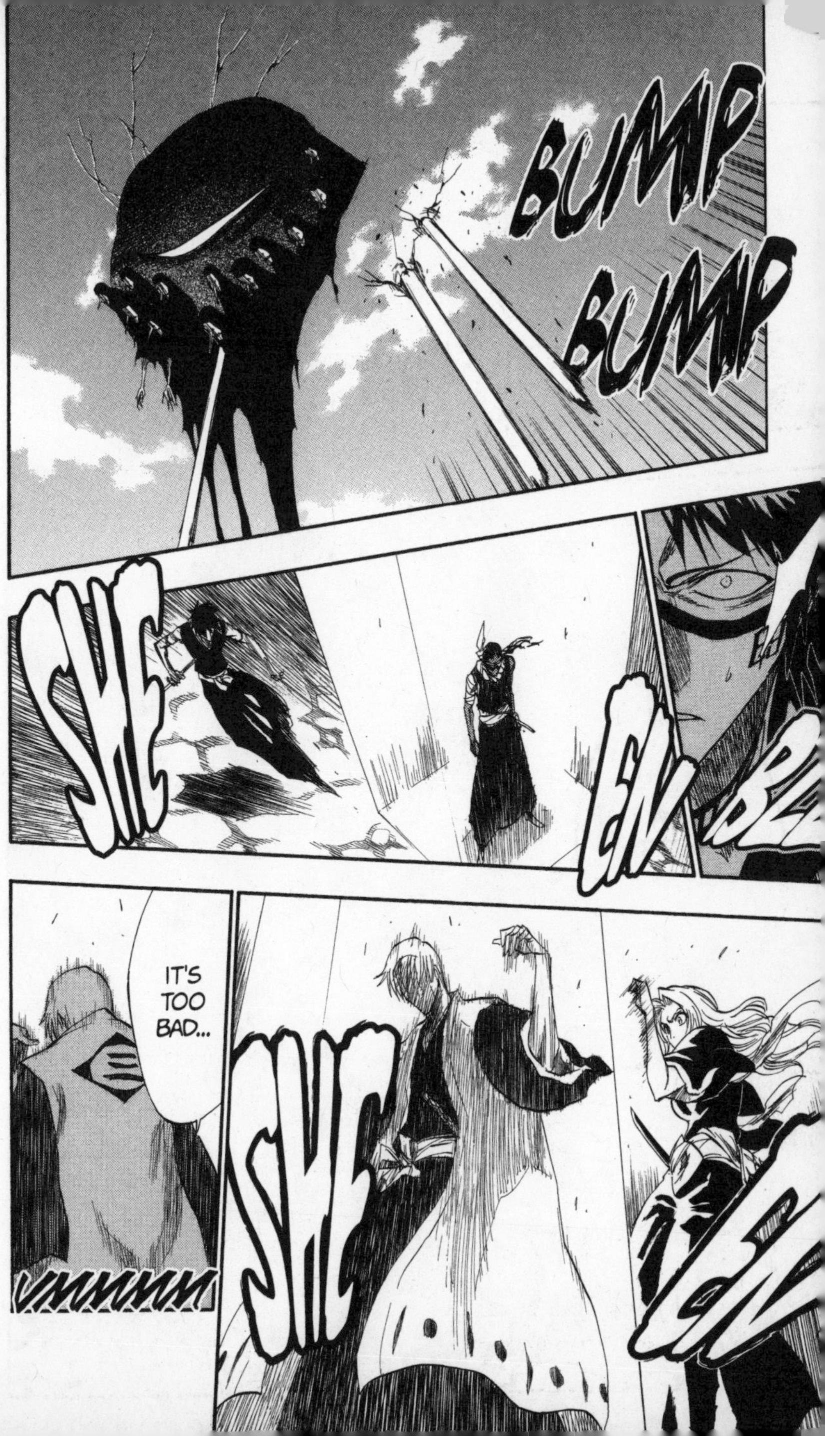
BUMP
BUMP
IT'S TOO BAD...

READ THIS WAY

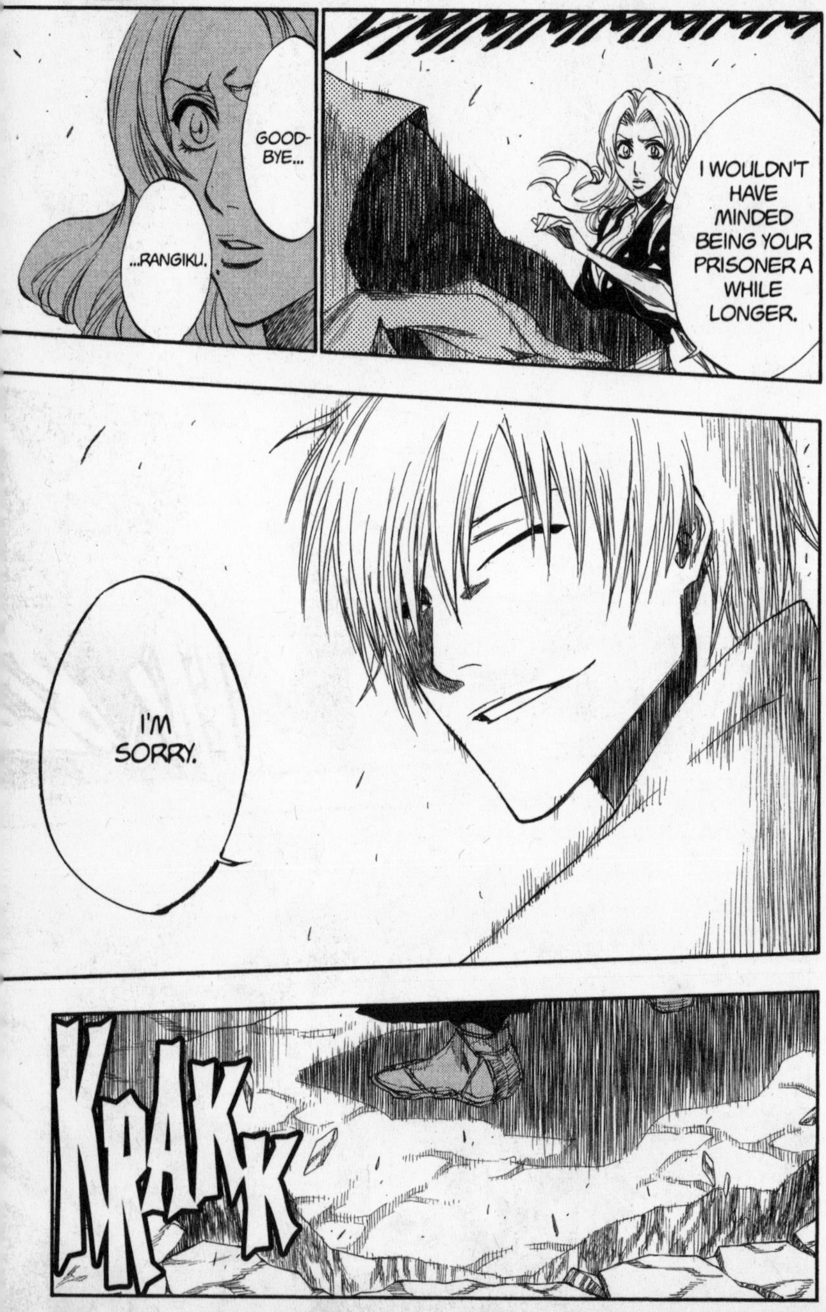
I WOULDN'T HAVE MINDED BEING YOUR PRISONER A WHILE LONGER.
GOOD-BYE...
...RANGIKU.
I'M SORRY.
KRAKK

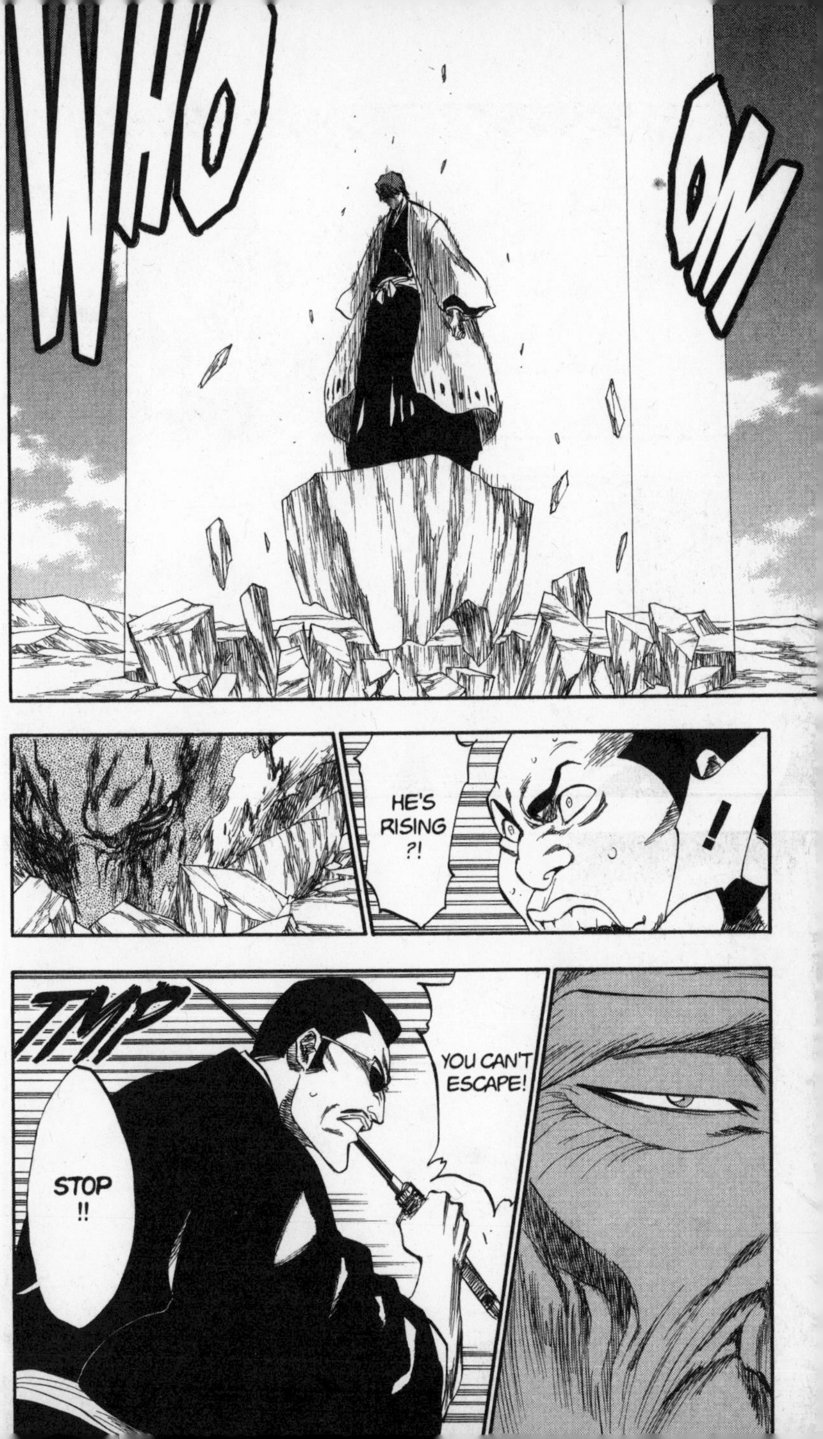
WHOOM
HE'S RISING?!
!
TMP
YOU CAN'T ESCAPE!
STOP!!

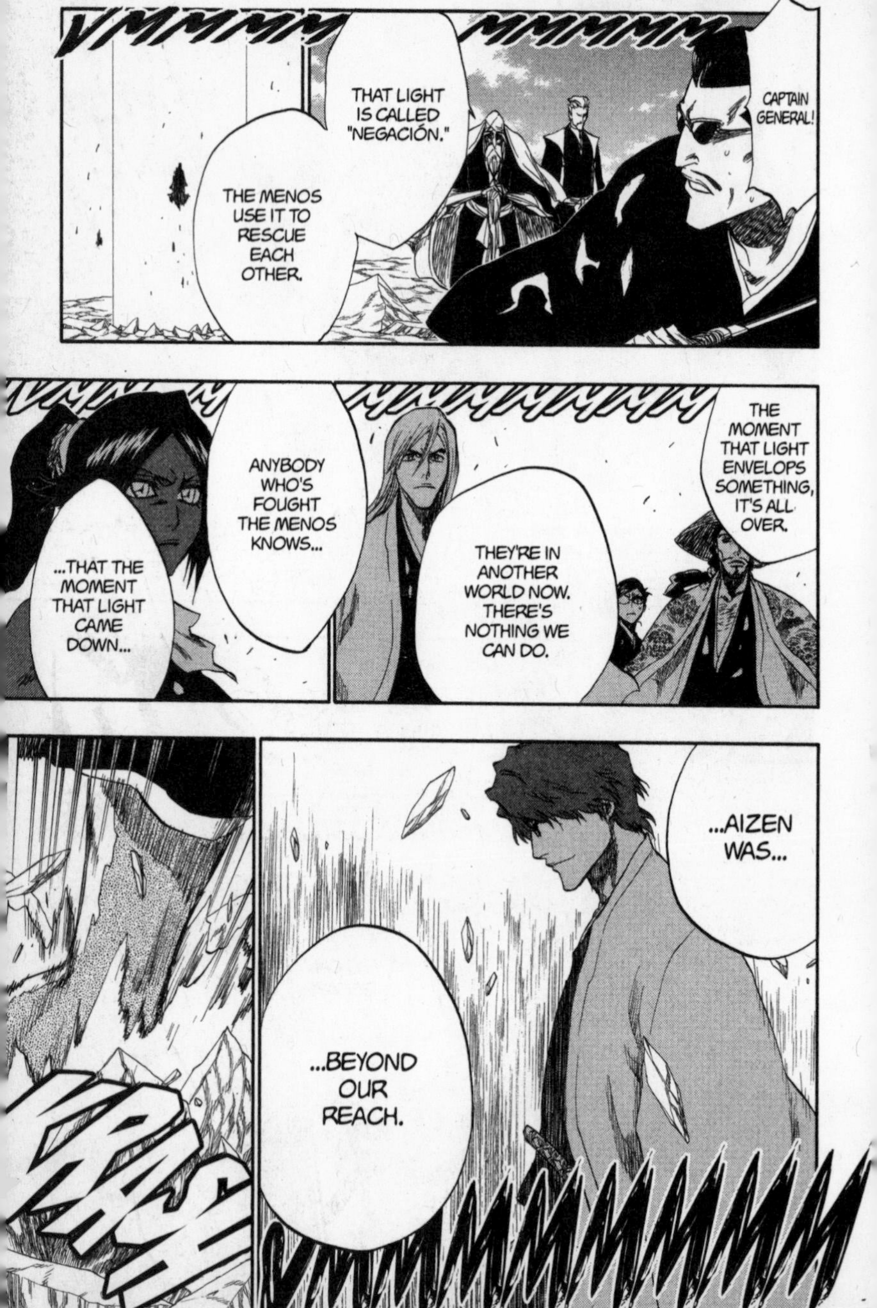
CAPTAIN GENERAL!
THAT LIGHT IS CALLED "NEGACIÓN."
THE MENOS USE IT TO RESCUE EACH OTHER.
THE MOMENT THAT LIGHT ENVELOPS SOMETHING, IT'S ALL OVER.
THEY'RE IN ANOTHER WORLD NOW. THERE'S NOTHING WE CAN DO.
ANYBODY WHO'S FOUGHT THE MENOS KNOWS...
...THAT THE MOMENT THAT LIGHT CAME DOWN...
...AIZEN WAS...
...BEYOND OUR REACH.

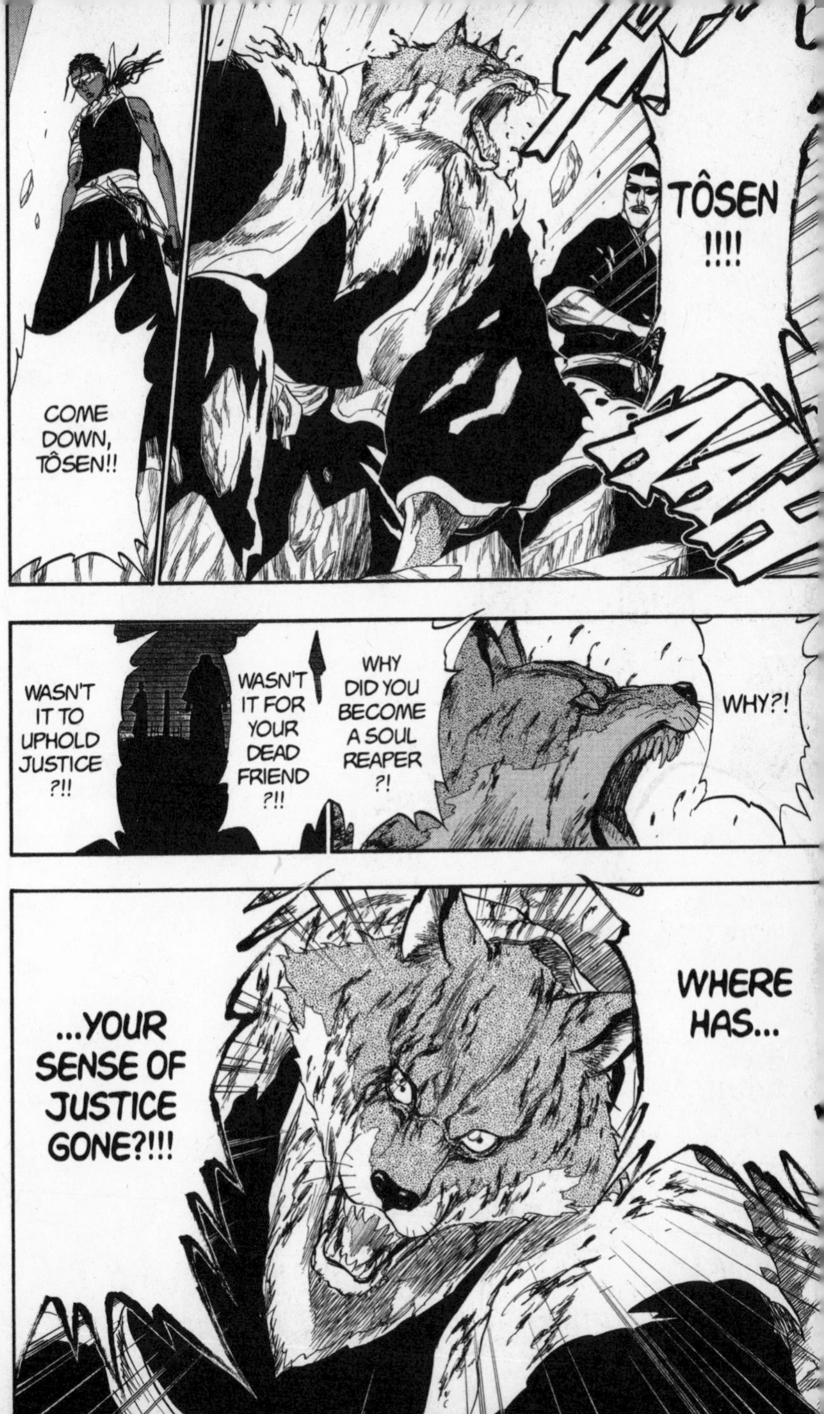
TÔSEN !!!!
COME DOWN, TÔSEN!!
WHY?!
WHY DID YOU BECOME A SOUL REAPER ?!
WASN'T IT FOR YOUR DEAD FRIEND ?!!
WASN'T IT TO UPHOLD JUSTICE ?!!
WHERE HAS...
...YOUR SENSE OF JUSTICE GONE?!!!

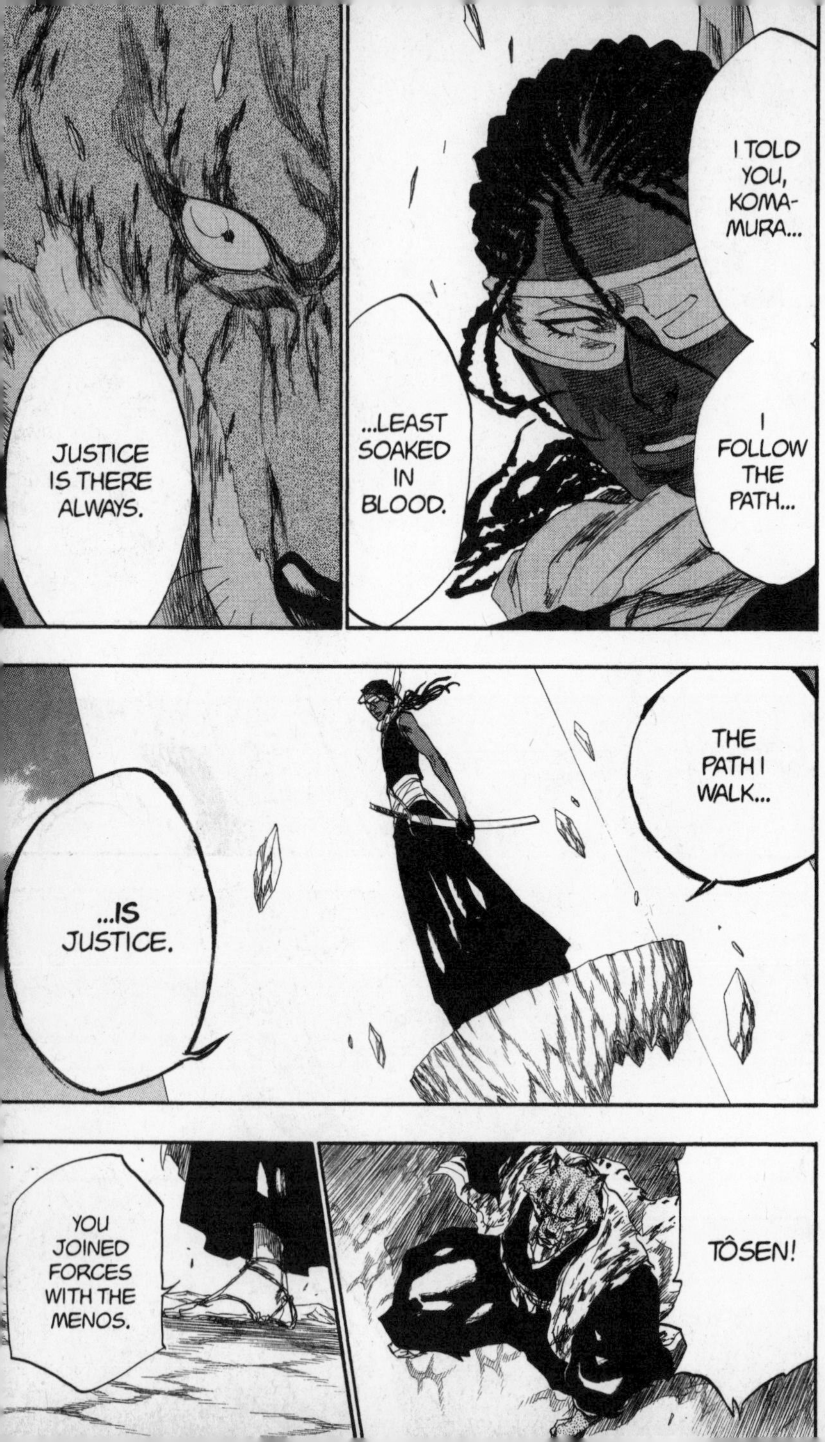
I TOLD YOU, KOMAMURA...
I FOLLOW THE PATH...
...LEAST SOAKED IN BLOOD.
JUSTICE IS THERE ALWAYS.
THE PATH I WALK...
...IS JUSTICE.
TÔSEN!
YOU JOINED FORCES WITH THE MENOS.

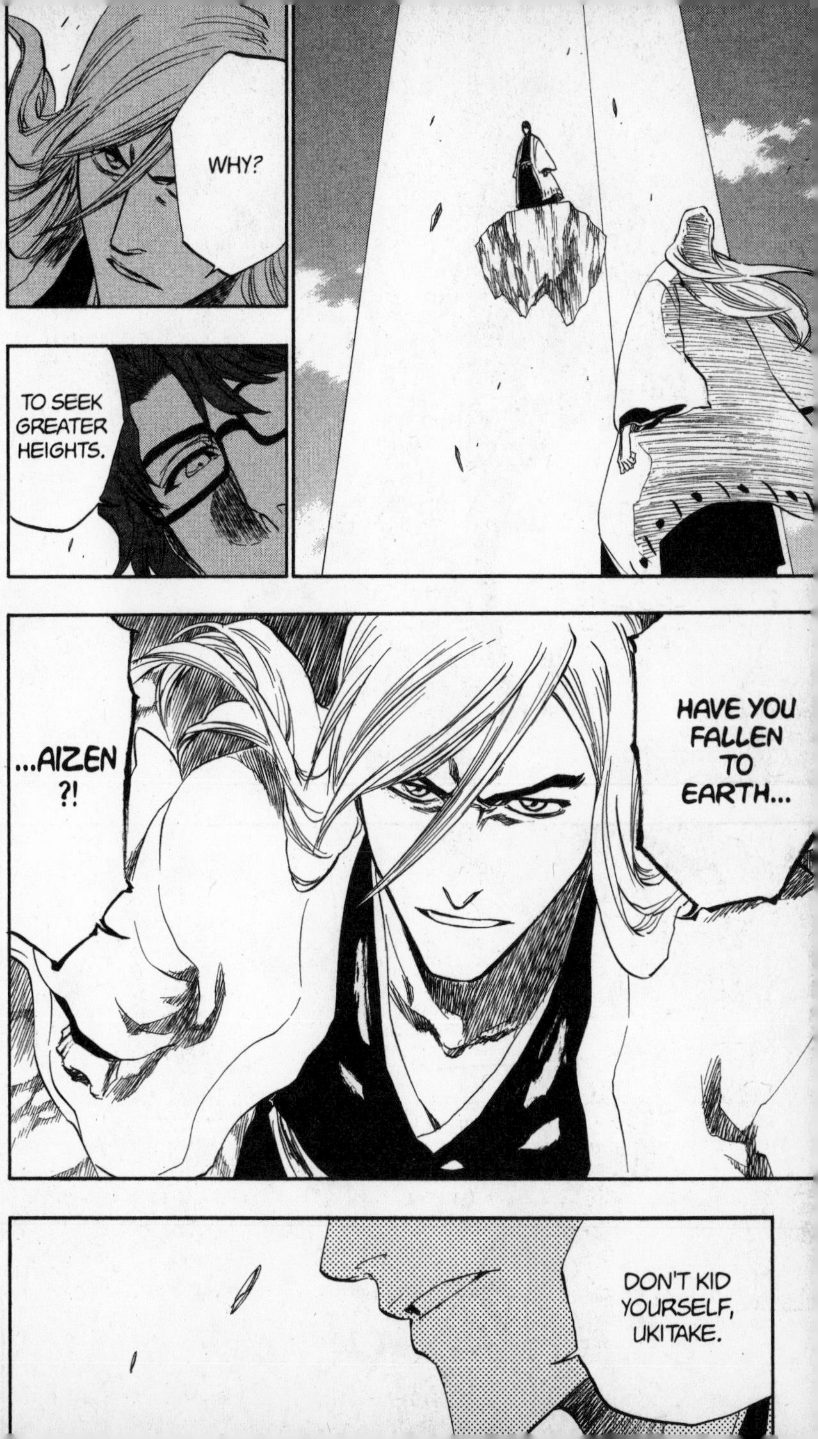
WHY?
TO SEEK GREATER HEIGHTS.
HAVE YOU FALLEN TO EARTH...
...AIZEN ?!
DON'T KID YOURSELF, UKITAKE.

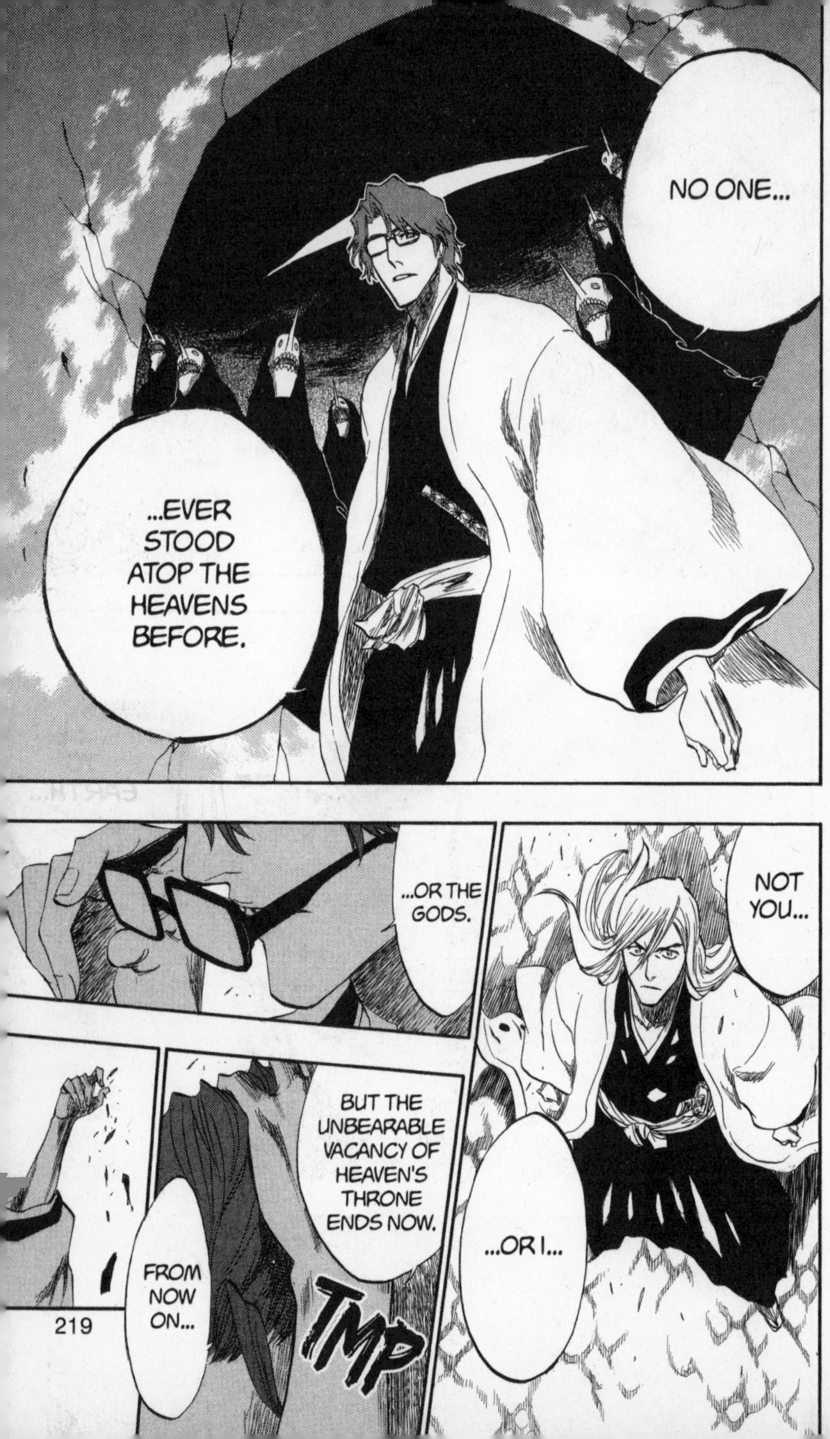
NO ONE...
...EVER STOOD ATOP THE HEAVENS BEFORE.
NOT YOU...
...OR I...
...OR THE GODS.
BUT THE UNBEARABLE VACANCY OF HEAVEN'S THRONE ENDS NOW.
FROM NOW ON...
TMP

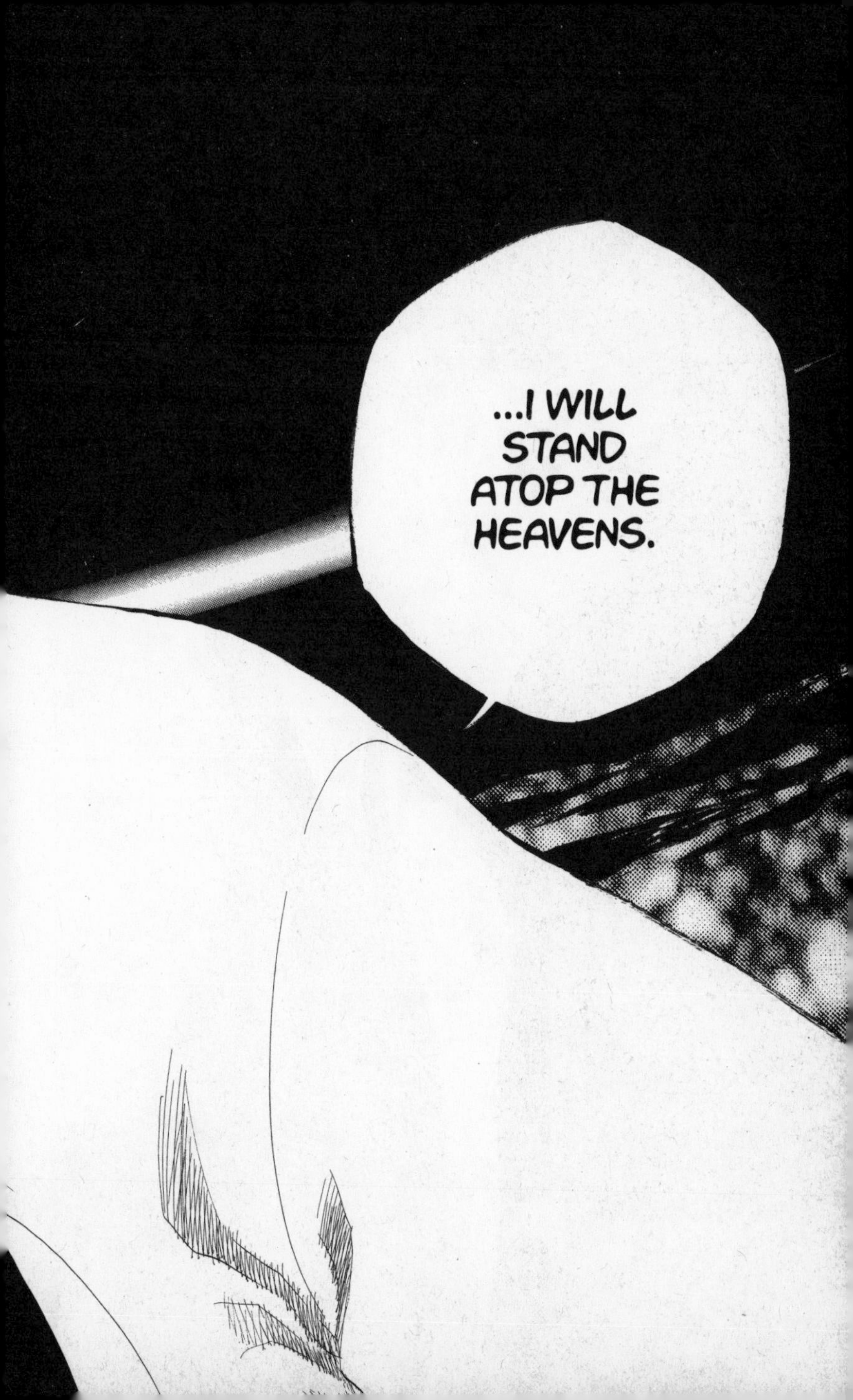
...I WILL STAND ATOP THE HEAVENS.

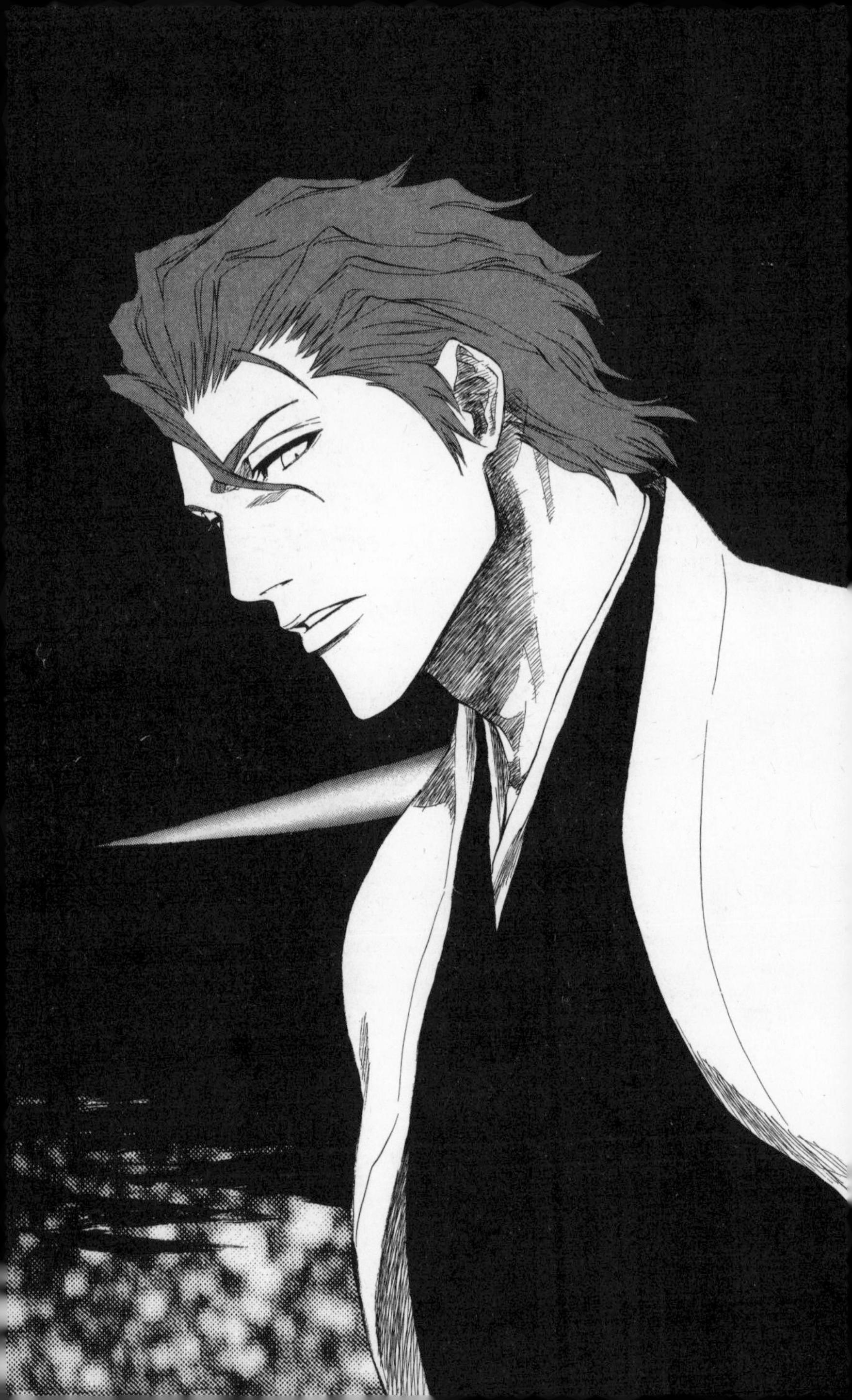

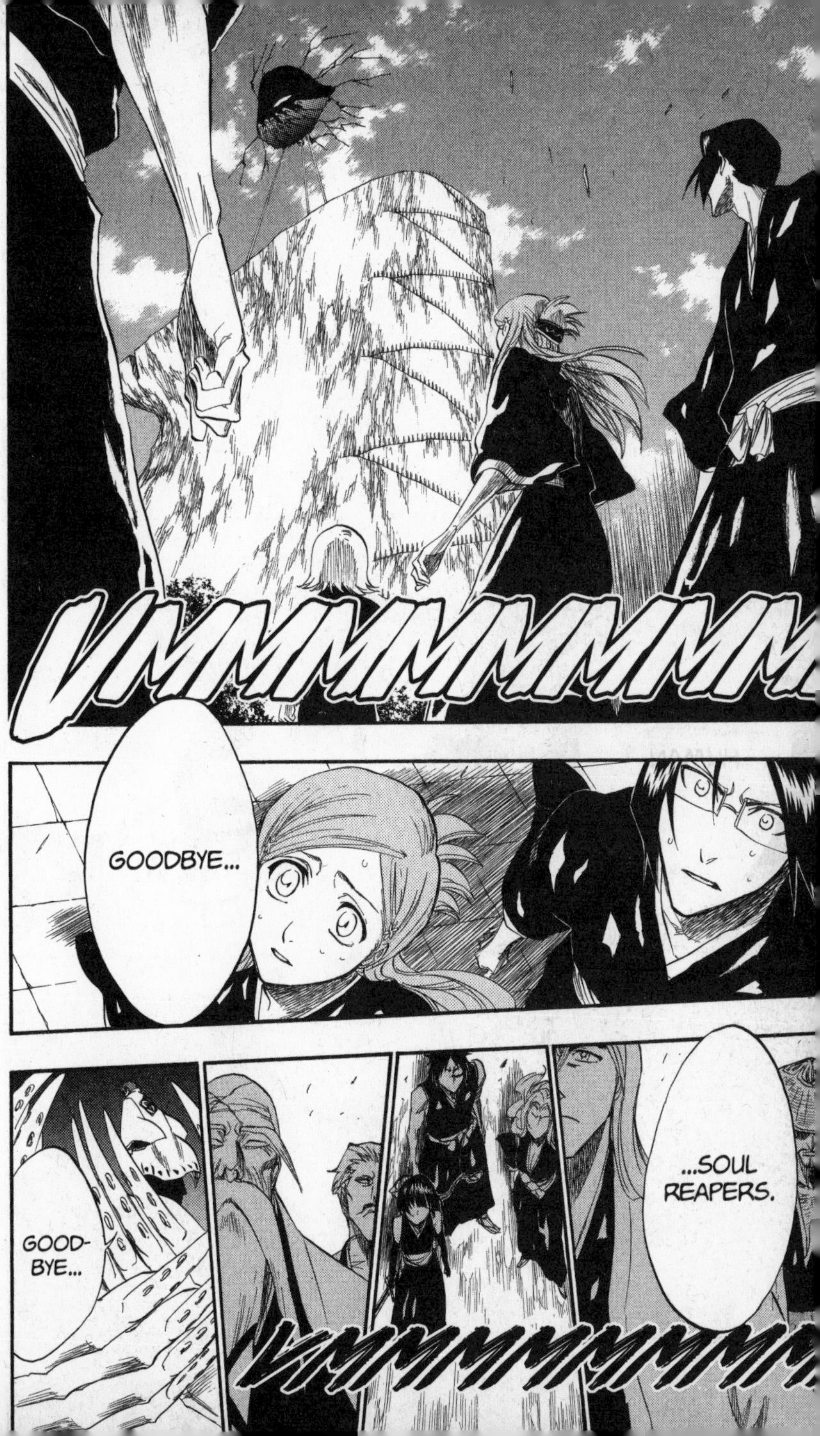
VMMMMMMMMMMM
GOODBYE...
...SOUL REAPERS.
GOOD-BYE...
VMMMMMMMMMMMM

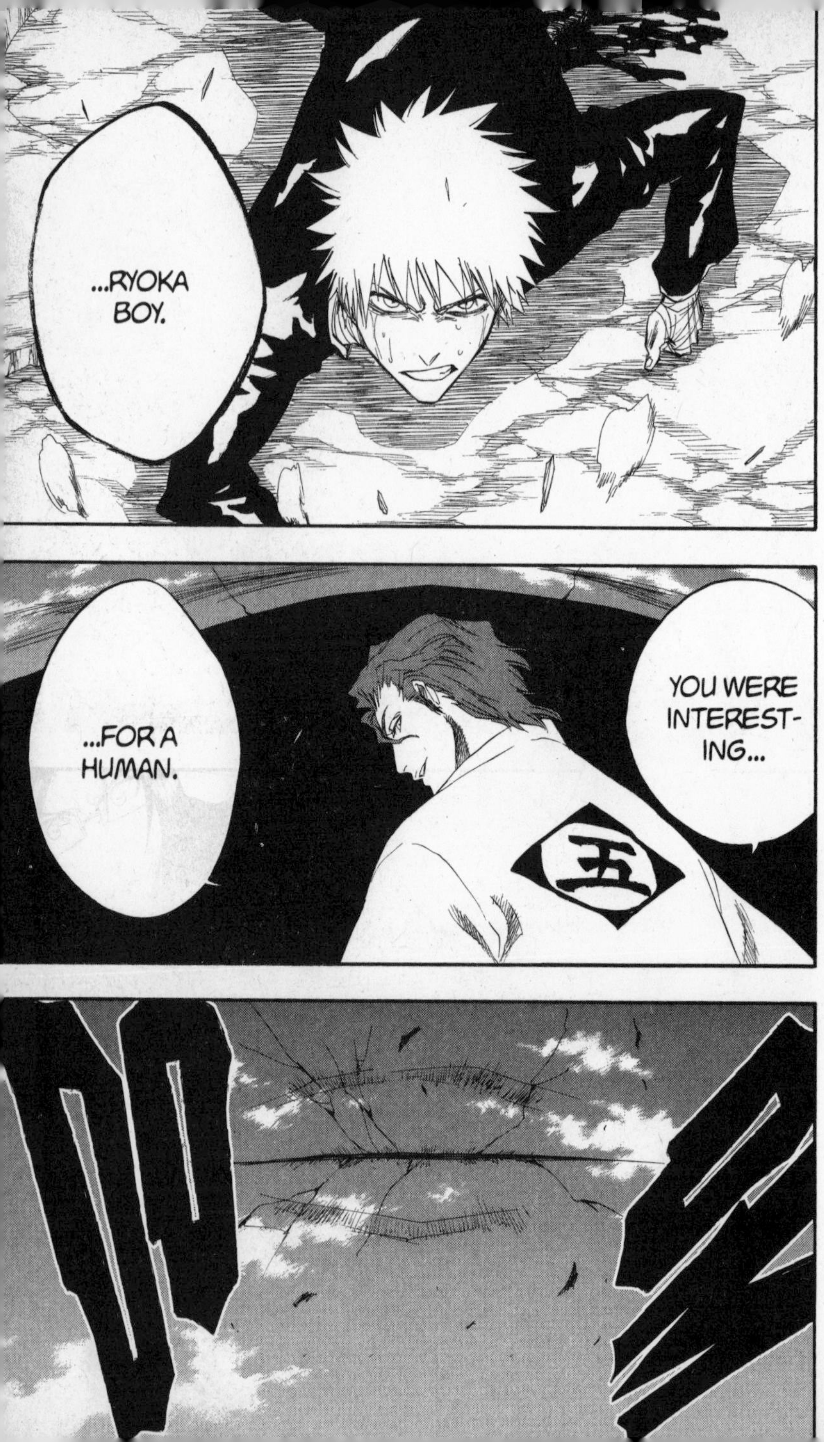
...RYOKA BOY.
YOU WERE INTERESTING...
...FOR A HUMAN.

Ichigo and his friends have returned to the world of the living and their daily routines, ready to put the Soul Society adventure behind them. But a mysterious new transfer student who wields a zanpaku-tô and wears a Hollow mask is about to make sure that they don't have time to get complacent!

Available in October 2007

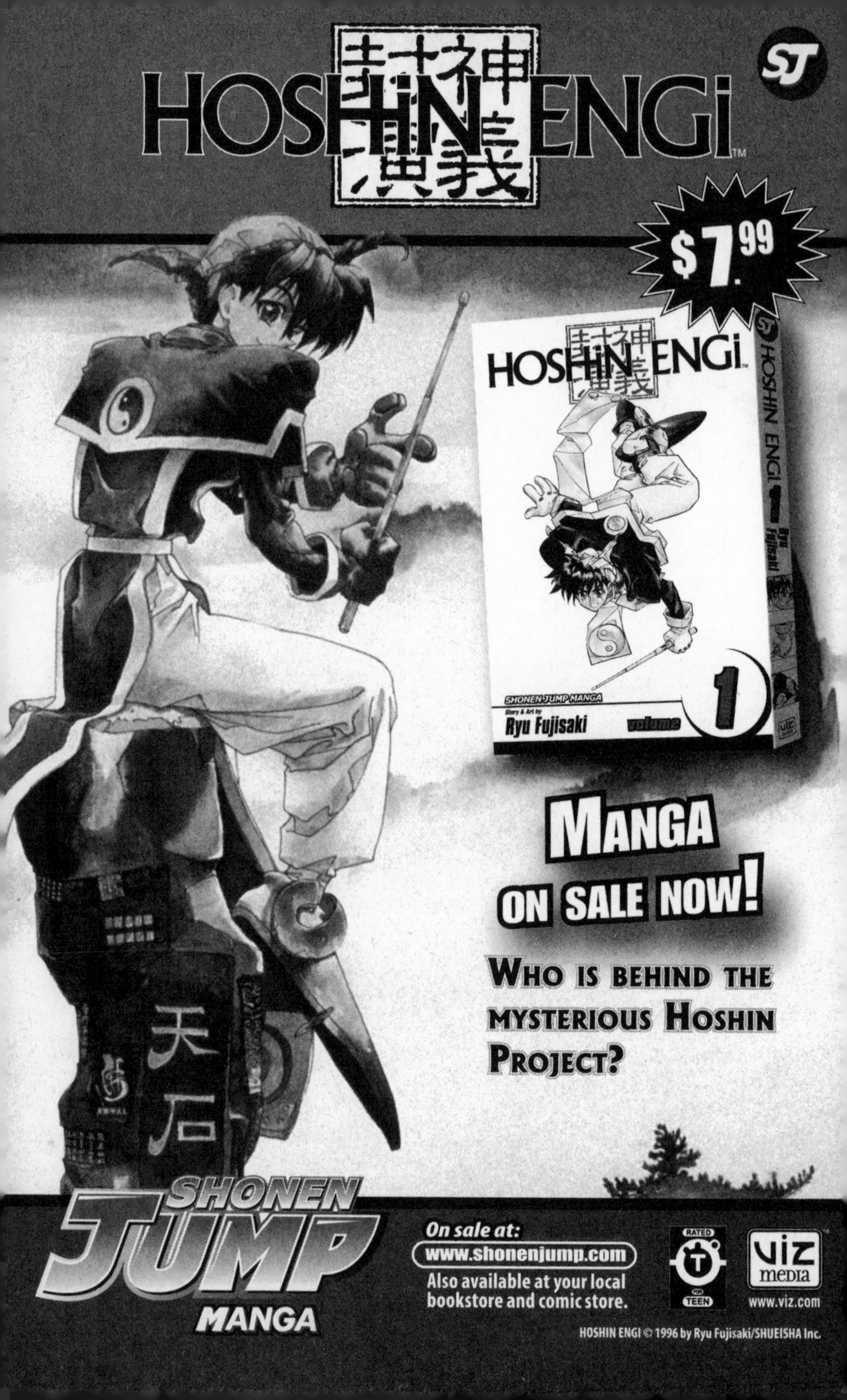

HOSHIN ENGI™
封神演義
SJ
$7.99
HOSHIN ENGI
SHONEN JUMP MANGA
Story & Art by
Ryu Fujisaki
volume 1
MANGA
ON SALE NOW!
WHO IS BEHIND THE MYSTERIOUS HOSHIN PROJECT?
SHONEN JUMP MANGA
On sale at:
www.shonenjump.com
Also available at your local bookstore and comic store.
RATED T FOR TEEN
VIZ media
www.viz.com
HOSHIN ENGI © 1996 by Ryu Fujisaki/SHUEISHA Inc.

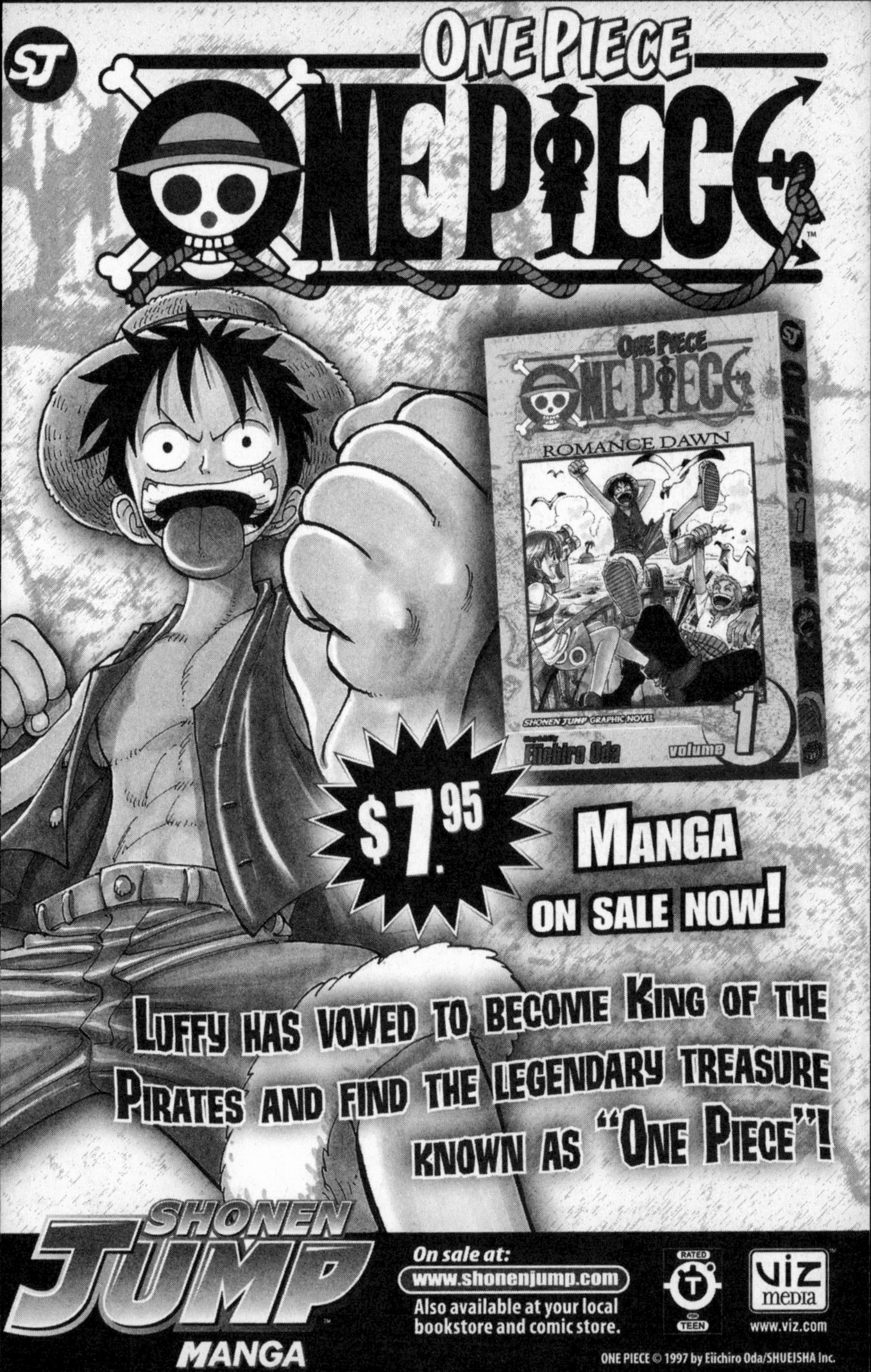

SJ
ONE PIECE
ONE PIECE™
ONE PIECE
ONE PIECE
ROMANCE DAWN
SHONEN JUMP GRAPHIC NOVEL
Eiichiro Oda
volume 1
$7.95
MANGA
ON SALE NOW!
LUFFY HAS VOWED TO BECOME KING OF THE PIRATES AND FIND THE LEGENDARY TREASURE KNOWN AS "ONE PIECE"!
SHONEN JUMP™ MANGA
On sale at:
www.shonenjump.com
Also available at your local bookstore and comic store.
RATED T FOR TEEN
viz media
www.viz.com
ONE PIECE © 1997 by Eiichiro Oda/SHUEISHA Inc.

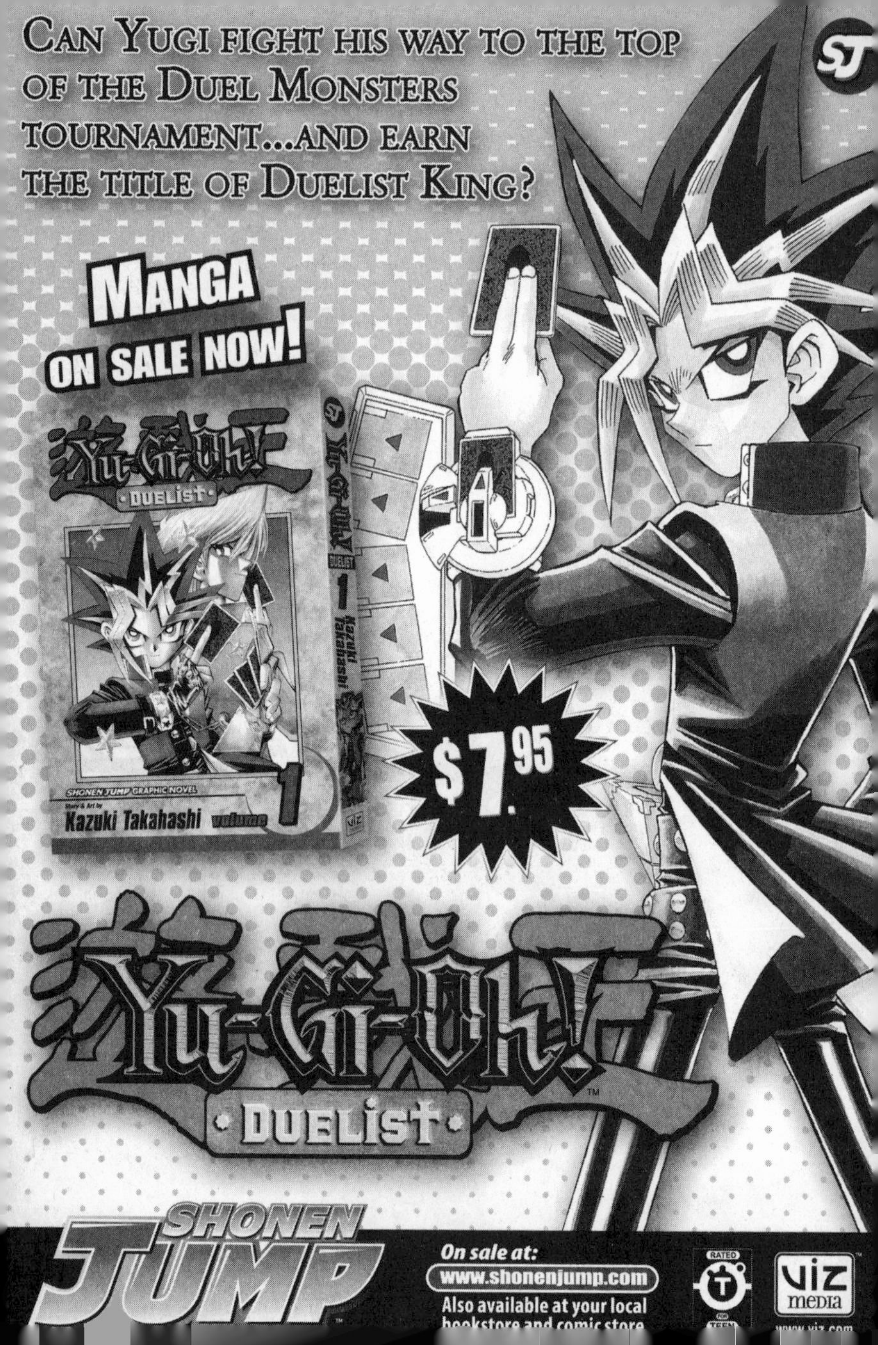

CAN YUGI FIGHT HIS WAY TO THE TOP OF THE DUEL MONSTERS TOURNAMENT...AND EARN THE TITLE OF DUELIST KING?
SJ
MANGA ON SALE NOW!
Yu-Gi-Oh! DUELIST
SHONEN JUMP GRAPHIC NOVEL
Story & Art by
Kazuki Takahashi volume 1
$7.95
Yu-Gi-Oh! DUELIST™
SHONEN JUMP
On sale at:
www.shonenjump.com
Also available at your local bookstore and comic store
RATED T FOR TEEN
viz media
www.viz.com

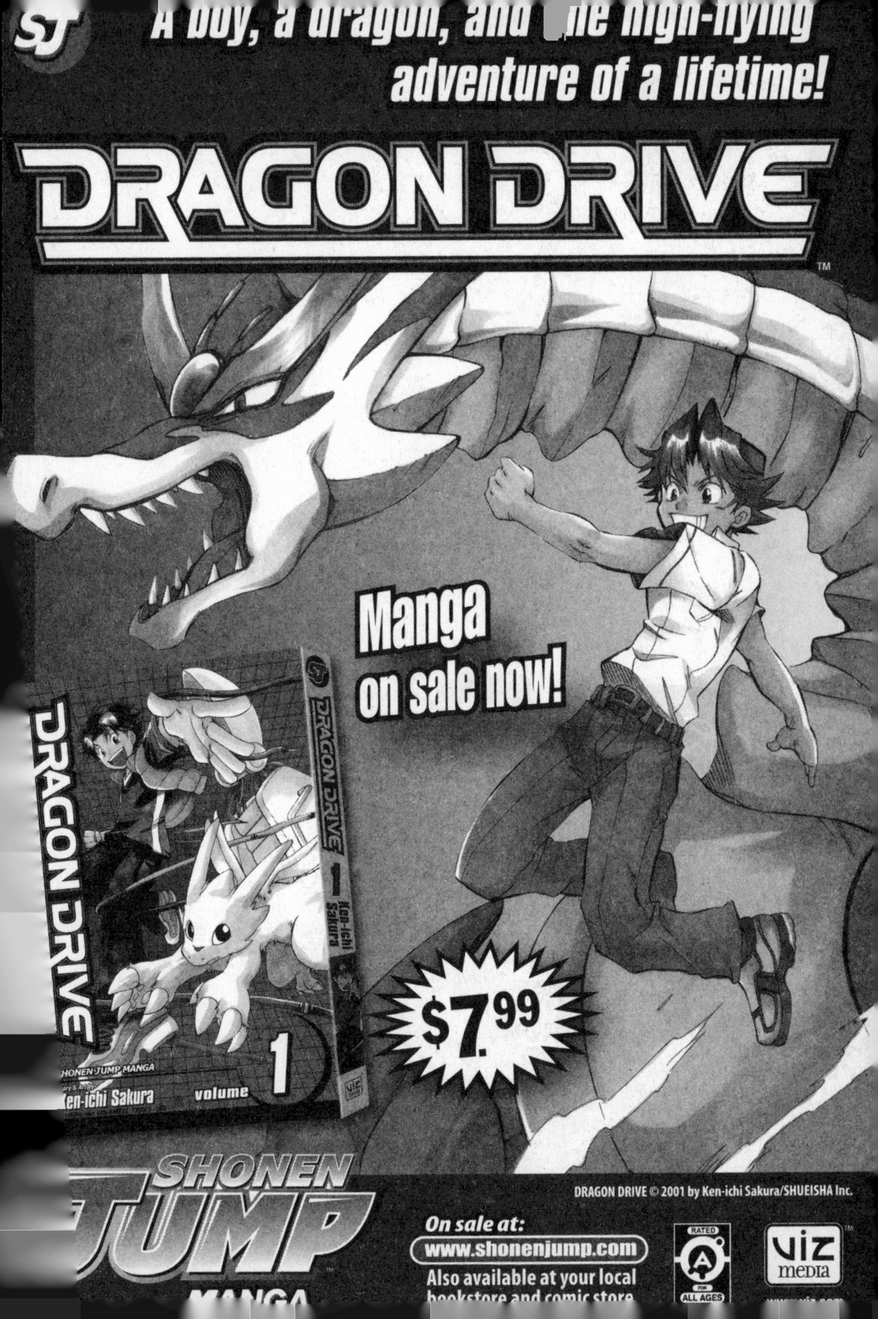
A boy, a dragon, and the high-flying
adventure of a lifetime!
DRAGON DRIVE
Manga
on sale now!
DRAGON DRIVE
SHONEN JUMP MANGA
Ken-ichi Sakura
volume 1
$7.99
SHONEN JUMP MANGA
DRAGON DRIVE © 2001 by Ken-ichi Sakura/SHUEISHA Inc.
On sale at:
www.shonenjump.com
Also available at your local
bookstore and comic store.
RATED A FOR ALL AGES
VIZ media

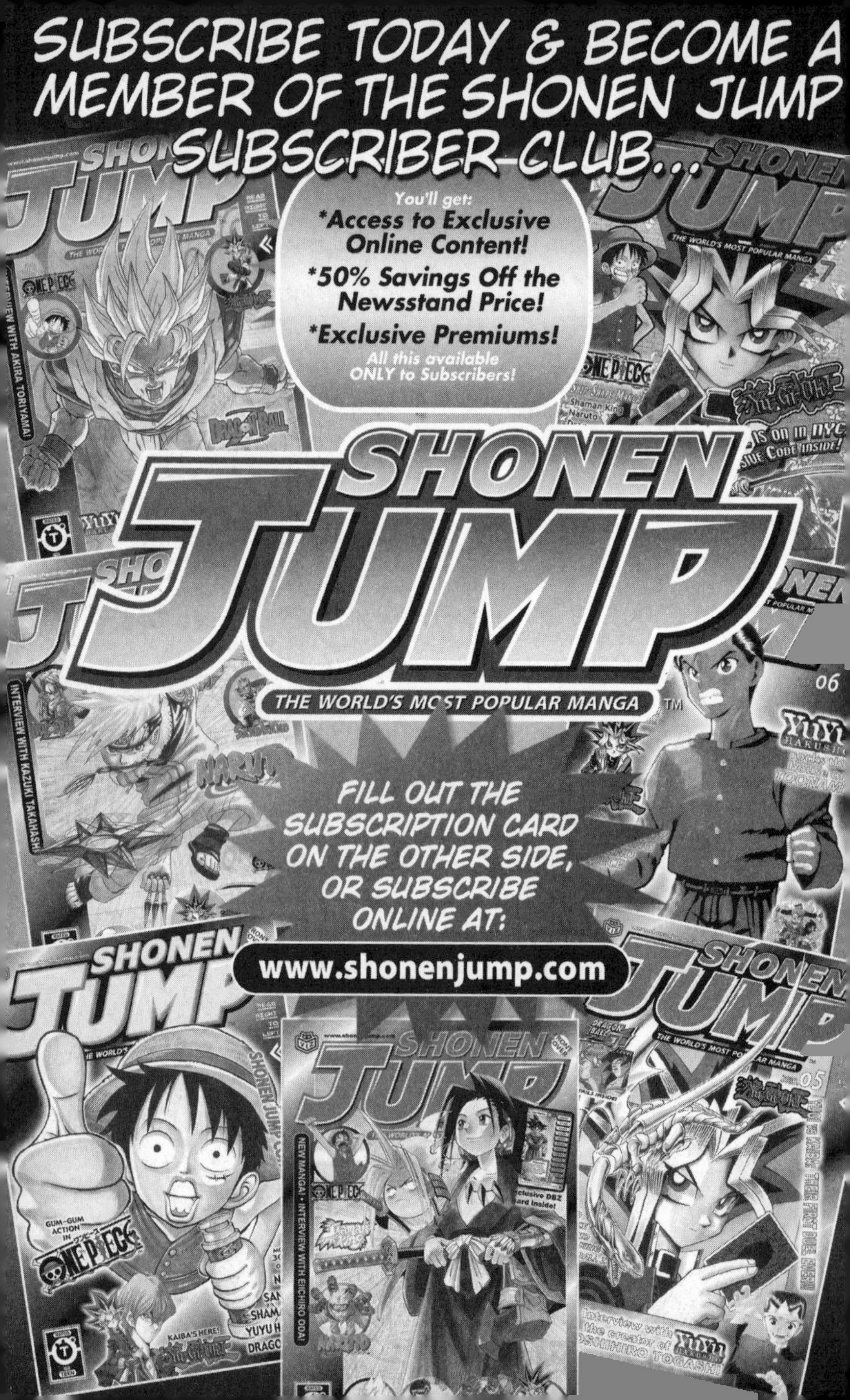

SUBSCRIBE TODAY & BECOME A MEMBER OF THE SHONEN JUMP SUBSCRIBER CLUB...
You'll get:
*Access to Exclusive Online Content!
*50% Savings Off the Newsstand Price!
*Exclusive Premiums!
All this available ONLY to Subscribers!
SHONEN JUMP
THE WORLD'S MOST POPULAR MANGA
FILL OUT THE SUBSCRIPTION CARD ON THE OTHER SIDE, OR SUBSCRIBE ONLINE AT:
www.shonenjump.com